Love for Family, Friends, and Books

Aleksandra Ziolkowska-Boehm

Translated by Agnieszka Maria Gernand

Hamilton Books

An Imprint of
Rowman & Littlefield
Lanham • Boulder • New York • Toronto • Plymouth, UK

Copyright © 2015 by Hamilton Books
4501 Forbes Boulevard, Suite 200, Lanham, Maryland 20706
Hamilton Books Acquisitions Department (301) 459-3366

Unit A, Whitacre Mews, 26-34 Stannary Street,
London SE11 4AB, United Kingdom

Library of Congress Control Number: 2015932030
ISBN: 978-0-7618-6568-1 (pbk : alk. paper)—ISBN: 978-0-7618-6569-8 (electronic)

Contents

Photographs

All photographs appear in a photospread following page 119.

Mother Antonina Ziółkowska
Father Henryk Ziółkowski
Aleksandra, her older brother Henryk, and her younger brother Krzysztof
Older brother Henryk Ziółkowski
Younger brother Krzysztof Ziółkowski
Aleksandra
Thomas and his dog
Thomas Tomczyk
Aleksandra and Thomas, Warsaw
Melchior Wańkowicz and Aleksandra, June 1972
Warsaw, 1985, Aleksandra and Canadian Senator Stanley Haidasz
Zbigniew Brzezinski, NN, Aleksandra, Warsaw
Roman Rodziewicz and Aleksandra, Warsaw
Aleksandra at Warsaw Kmicica apartment
Writer Ryszard Kapuściński and Thomas Tomczyk, Warsaw
Thomas Tomczyk, May 1993, graduation in Architecture, University of Arkansas
Aleksandra and Thomas, Wilmington, Delaware
Thomas
Aleksandra and Norman, 1990
Aleksandra and Norman, Mount St. Helens National Volcanic Monument, Washington State
Aleksandra in Rio de Janiero, Brazil, 1991
Aleksandra at home in Wilmington, Delaware
Barbara Wachowicz, Norman, and Aleksandra, Philadelphia, 2000
Aleksandra and Norman at Woodlands

Preface

I live in the United States with my American husband, who does not speak Polish. He brought me to another world, his own. Thomas, my son who filled a good part of my life for over twenty years, is now a grown man. The departure of our adult children when they leave home makes us realize the passing of time. We miss the childhood time when they knew how to show love and at the same time were receptive to handfuls of our love.

The life of every human being is unique and for each and everyone seems to be special. Goethe wrote that the highest happiness of man is just his individuality. When people talk of small things about others, it is called gossip. When they write about the same small things giving them literary form, it can be called literature. Time is a mystery, until it becomes a thing of the past that does not exist anymore. Valuing time requires a real or implicit distance. The distance causes sadness and constant thoughts. I wrestle with them, the memories, both the good and the bitter.

This book is written about the good, sad, moving and emotional recollections, which are gone, and easy to be idealized. I try to be cautious when I do not have the best experience and memories. Or maybe I belong to those who remember only the good and happy moments of life? I treat the reader like a good friend, whom I yearn to tell about myself. For good friends, I can say much, but not everything. For very close friends, it is a privilege to share my thoughts, or they can be kept private. In the U.S., where people easily talk about their very private matters, the exposure has not changed me. However, if someone reads this book and finds it too open, it was not my intention for it to be so. After reading the book manuscript, Norman remarked: "No Polish grass grew under your feet."

I have cited many names in my book. By doing so, I want to express my appreciation for their involvement. Also listing those individuals, I believe lends credence to my story. Many people help us go through life: the family, the friends, strangers and sometimes those from random meetings. Also important are the books we read, movies we see, stories heard. I am writing here about all of the foregoing influences and my fascination with them. Animals have played a significant role in my life, and I also devote extensive fragments to them.

This book is dedicated to a new generation, all the children who were born to my two brothers' families and to me: Thomas, Michał, Małgorzata, Paweł and Łukasz.

Chapter One

Family

I am thinking of the home of my childhood, my parents and grandparents. What we know from childhood consolidates with time inside us. I have a sepia-colored picture with Grandmom Genowefa and Granddad Józef, their daughters and the youngest son. I'd like to—if that was ever possible—to turn back time—to invite my grandparents to a dinner and to have a long talk. To also invite (it would be really very special—but an impossible—event) their parents, together with Marianna, my great-grandmother, and Paulina, my great-great-grandmother, about whom there were so many stories circulating in the family. To a separate meeting, I would invite all the women, my grandmothers and great-grandmothers, and great-great-ones as far back as I could. I would show them how I lived and what I thought, I'd tell them about myself. I would like to learn about their joys and dreams—particularly about the dreams, because they say so much about a person.

My childhood home was a modest one. The side walls were made of brick, the front and the back were wooden. A lush shrub of woodbine covered the right wall and peeked through the windows. In the autumn, the green leaves turned rusty and red. The house was built in 1935 by my maternal grandparents, Genowefa and Józef Laśkiewicz. During the Second World War, the Germans destined a part of Łódź to serve as a ghetto. The area was gradually enlarged, and finally it reached Franciszkańska Street, where my grandparents' house stood. Non-Jewish people resettled in other districts of the city. It was May 1940. The Laśkiewicz family moved to Piaseczna Street, and then to Sanocka Street in the district of Chojny. After the war, when my parents married, my grandparents gave them the recovered house on Franciszkańska Street. The house was damaged, but there was the large garden around it with lots of still beautiful trees each rendering its own quality to the home site.

Genowefa and Józef had four children: three daughters and a son—the youngest. My mother, Antonina, was the eldest. She was born on 11th December 1923. Then came: Anna, Daniela and Zdzisław, in that order.

In 1923, my grandparents founded a carpenter's shop and workshop, where incrusted period furniture was produced. They employed a few journeymen. After the war, Granddad Józef suffered from Buerger's disease. He had a leg amputated in 1948. Grandmother, who had a strong personality, took over all the management duties and work direction. She managed the shop and workshop, employing just two journeymen. The atmosphere was not in favour of any private initiative. Taxes increased, and life became more difficult. After Granddad died in 1953, Grandmother ran the business for eight more years. She sold it when she turned seventy. For a long time, she made plans of staying in the house with large garden, with her eldest daughter, Antonina—my mother. I remember the talks about expanding the house, plans to add a room. The plans remained unfulfilled. As Grandmom grew weaker, she was unable to make any great plans, being more concerned for her own failing health.

During one period with me, she devoted many hours to compile the genealogical tree of her family. That was after I'd read *The Forsyte Saga* by John Galsworthy. I then wanted to learn as much as possible about my own family. I remember a story Grandmom told me about her grandmother, Paulina Fliśnik nee Rychlewska (she then married a Stawiński), who "cut" a very colorful figure. She was the daughter of a pharmacy owner in Duże Garbary in Poznań, and herself a teacher by profession. One of her brothers was an engineer and the other an architect. Comely and attractive, she was quite popular with men. With her first husband, Jan Fliśnik, she had four children: Marianna, Adam, Stefania and Helena. After his death, she remarried and had another daughter, Konstancja. Konstancja's second son, Roman Strzelecki, lived in Warsaw and participated in the Warsaw Uprising in 1944. My Grandmother, Genowefa, born Szczypiorska, was Paulina's eldest granddaughter—Marianna's daughter. Genowefa married Józef Laśkiewicz, a handsome young man with great ambitions. They were married on 8th August 1920 in the old Our Lady's Church in Łódź. The Polish Laśkiewicz family came from Samogitia, Lithuania. Józef, like his brothers Felicjan, Aleksander and Teodor, went to school in Warsaw. My Granddad Józef had moved to Łódź, which for many years had been attracting young people who were drawn there as though a promised land, hoping to start their own businesses. At first he worked in the City Hall. After he married Genowefa and obtained the required master carpenter qualifications, he started his own period furniture workshop. For a Pole to manage a business in the ethnically diverse city of Łódź was a challenge, since most businesses were opened by German and Jewish entrepreneurs. But Granddad had a good head for business and liked his work. At one point, he employed twelve workers. For the furniture, he used oak, birch and pine wood. Other kinds of wood were refined with walnut, birch and mahogany veneer. He bought shellac from abroad for sealing the wood. The fragments of furniture which needed designs were given to a sculptor to make. Just next to the workshop was the shop where Granddad sold the furniture and accepted commissions. I remember coming with my mother to the shop on Przybyszewskiego Street (previously named Napiórkowskiego), and how it smelled with denatured alcohol and glaze. Grandmother was always very busy, and usually talking to someone. Each Friday, Grandmother gave us a generous serving of pork loin chops, and they were cooked for our Sunday brunch. My mother also brought our bed linen to Grandmom, who had a washerwoman come to her house once a week. Back in those times, laundering was a complex process and required much effort. Mother ensured that our bed and table linen was always snow-white. And such was the home I remembered.

My mother was sixteen when the war broke out, and she was unable to continue her secondary schooling. That the war interrupted her education possibilities was most distressing for her. She completed high school after the war. Granddad Józef—being Polish—couldn't run a craftsman's workshop during the Nazi occupation. He had to work as an employee in his own but German controlled carpenter's business. Henryk Ziółkowski also worked in the same business. If not gainfully employed, young men particularly would be shipped to Germany to work. He read a lot, and was a little secretive. Mother knew he was active in the resistance movement, but he said little of his activity so as not to endanger anyone. Henryk was also active in youth circles of the Camp of Great Poland,[1] then in the National Party,[2] where he spread Roman Dmowski's[3] ideas by holding lectures. Before the war, he was a rifleman in the 31st Rifles' Regiment of Kaniow.

My mother and father married shortly after the war, on 1st July 1945. They stayed in the house with the garden on Franciszkańska Street with hardly any furniture. After some years, with Grandmom's help, they acquired a set of bedroom furniture—the type was known as golden birch—and dark walnut furniture was acquired for the dining room.

On 5th May 1946 Henryk Andrzej, called Henio, Heniuś, my elder brother, was born. A year later, on 10th April, Andrzej Roman was born, called Jędruś. The story about him always moved our family to tears. Jędruś' baptism was postponed a few times. At first, Mother suggested that Aunt Dzidka be his godmother, but the aunt was pregnant and so she refused. The common belief was that she could not be both a mother to her own child and godmother to another one. Children of such an arrangement were thought to not grow up properly. Refusing to be a child's godmother was also thought to diminish his or her thriving. Eventually, Aunt Lola and Uncle Zdzisław were chosen as the godparents. Jędruś was then nine months old. The christening was set for Boxing Day, 26th December 1947. The day of the christening was exceptionally cold. The child was fretful and had a slight temperature. In the church, the boy cried a little, but later at home he was calm. Mother awakened at night, thinking she'd heard him cry. She went to his bed and leaned over it. The child had blood in the corner of his mouth. Mother uttered a terrible scream.

When the ambulance came, the attendants declared the baby dead. Jędruś was buried in the white garments that he had been christened in just two days before.

I remember very well the anniversaries of his death, on the second day of Christmas, when Mother would recall the tragedy with tears.

A year and four months after Jędruś died, on Good Friday, 15th April 1949, I was born at four in the morning. On 19th December 1950, my youngest brother, Krzysztof Bogusław, called Krzysio, Krzyś, was born.

According to family stories, my mother very much wanted to have a girl, and with my father chose my name even before I was born. She wanted a daughter who would learn well, graduate, have an interesting job and life, and who would learn about the world. Her daughter would "not be skilled in crocheting or sewing." Mother, who was expert in doing these things, wanted a different life for her daughter, a life that she never had a chance to live. As a young girl, my mother Antonina had a very fine singing voice. Years later, she remained a lover of music and admirer of beautiful voices. One day, she told me—her big secret—that as a girl, she dreamed of being an opera singer. Somehow she never liked me to remind her of the dream, as though she was almost embarrassed of it. Forever dedicated to singing and to the Catholic religion, my mother faithfully soloed with her alto voice and sang with the church choir for fifty years. Mother and Father regularly went to see operas. When we grew older, they took us with them.

When I consider my memories from the earliest part of my childhood, I realize that those years stayed in my mind only as short images of some experiences, some senses, and some impressions. I can't remember people's names, frequently I don't remember their faces, but I never forget their actions. Actions are the most telling and the most lasting.

I hardly remember Grandfather Józef. He died when I was four. I recall visiting him. After the amputation, he was chair bound. My mother was Granddad's beloved daughter and she was strongly attached to him. She was deeply affected by his death. I remember she grieved over his death for a long time. Among my earliest recollections, there is the scene at the funeral. The open coffin stood in a large and crowded room. Mother stood close to the coffin, and Father tried to stay back with us. It was a cold November day of 1953.

Grandmother Genowefa was not as emotional as my mother—she didn't coddle us, she didn't pay much attention to us. If she talked to us, it was to criticize our behaviour or appearance. Grandmom spent time with adults, and for her, children were from a different world. She had many problems running the business, and having to manage it alone, the problems became more complex and intertwined. She hired four workers, worried about their well being as well as many other things. After finally selling the business, she would come to visit us by taxi and usually caused a general commotion. Our dog liked her very much, because she brought him various treats. He always welcomed her with happy barking. During these visits, she started to notice us, and that we were growing from children to teenagers. She always expected something of us, and I believe I complied with such requirements rather unwillingly. I preferred to be left to myself and watch the adults from a distance. I think I was not quite but maybe a slightly recalcitrant child. I remember a comment she made about me when I was a small girl: "Haughty spirit in a meagre body..." Now it sounds funny, but back then the comment irritated me and made me even less willing to stay in Grandmom's company. I valued freedom, and the garden allowed me to withdraw to my own matters. Whenever I could, I escaped the confines of the house and hid in the garden.

Only years later I had better contact with my grandmother, as I grew up and became a better partner for conversation. During my years in high school improved relations with her developed. We grew to like each other, and I appreciated her kindness, which she showed me particularly at that time. Grandmother also showed particular favour to her second daughter, Anna, called Hania, and always engaged in some family politics with her. I remember that as a child I didn't want to have a sister, because I knew that sisters always competed with each other in various areas—their parents' favour, beauty, husbands and children. I was never close to Aunt Hania, although she was always friendly to me. She wanted to know a lot, and kept asking me about various family matters, which I didn't like to discuss with her. I wanted to be left alone and talk only about what was of interest to me. The enquiries of adults often seemed to me to violate my privacy, which I valued even as a child.

I remember very clearly one meeting at Grandmother's house. Aunt Hania and Uncle Jasiek were parents of a third son, Rysio. They already had two older boys: Włodek and Zdzisiek. I was three when Rysio was born. We all met at Grandmother's house. Rysio was in diapers and cried a lot. During the conversation, somehow, someone said it was a pity that Aunt Hania had another boy, and not a girl. She reacted with quite sharp words against girls and the problems they brought upon themselves and their parents. I learned then that "girls are constant trouble." I was deeply affected by the conversation, and I went to my Father and sat in his lap, seeking protection. Father cuddled me and laughed at Aunt Hania's remark.

Aunt Hania bought a big plot of land near Łódź, in Głowno, built a house and stayed there the whole summer. Often the whole family, with Grandmother and Aunt Danka, gathered there on Sundays. The adults chased us out of the house to "get some air." We ran about the huge garden, but I remember that the freshly planted fruit trees gave no shade, and the heat tired me out. I became better friends of my cousins, Aunt Hania's sons. I have some pictures from those visits to Głowno. In the pictures, I'm always in my father's arms. I can't remember my Uncle Zdzisław and his wife Hala's daughter Ewa from this period. However, I do remember her First Communion better, to which we were invited, and the pretty green dress that she later changed into. After graduating from the Academy of Fine Arts, Ewa wrote poems that were printed in newspapers in Łódź.

Mom was emotionally closest to her youngest sister, Daniela, called Danka—my "good auntie." Twice she took me home for the summer and often brought gifts for my brothers and me. Aunt Danka, a pharmacist by profession, was always an interesting figure for us to behold. There was always something happening around her, she would travel, and she lived far away. Once she took all of us kids for a walk, and as we were walking, she asked if we thought she was pretty and if we liked her dress.

Aunt Danka's only worry, the only one, she said repeatedly, was to be slimmer... in my view, she wasn't overweight. She always wore nice, colourful dresses. She often carried her handbag and shoes in a matching colour. I remember a red velour blouse which for me, a small girl, became the most beautiful blouse of my dreams. I touched it with awe. Later, when aunt got bored with it, and it shrank in the wash, though not losing its texture, it was given to me, and I enjoyed it for a long time. I vaguely remember a few visits of Aunt Danka with her little daughter Marysia, who was always sick and who was very much catered to by the whole family like a sick baby bird. Marysia was born in 1956; soon after, Aunt Danka left to Węgorzewo in Masuria. While I was at school Aunt twice invited me to spend some of my summer vacations with her. My godfather was Sylwester Pajdziński, father's friend from Tomaszów Mazowiecki. My godmother was Grandmother's youngest sister, Aunt Zosia, a well-to-do woman. Together with her husband, she ran a carpenter's workshop and a shop with furniture. She was always elegant and wore make-up. When my mother and I visited her in the shop on Południowa Street, she was nice to me, and showed interest in my affairs. But in truth, I never really managed to know her well. Many years later, I heard of her children's misfortunes, and her son's tragic death. By that time, I had already moved to Warsaw and would travel to Łódź to visit my parents and brothers.

I was christened on 13th November, the same year of my birth, in the Divine Providence Church in Marysin. I was given three names: Aleksandra Wiktoria Anna.

My Granddad, Józef Laśkiewicz, was Marshal Józef Piłsudski's adherent. Father said he'd married a "Piłsudski-ite's[4] daughter." My father supported

Roman Dmowski, whose books he had at home and whose political thoughts he valued all his life. Father came from the Poznańskie region and emphasised it proudly, saying that people from that region were very hard working and responsible. The Ziółkowski family had their own coat of arms: Korczak. Father was born on 23rd December 1916 in Kalisz, the oldest Polish city belonging to the Kingdom of Poland, and not to the Grand Duchy of Posen.[5] When he was nearing fifteen, his mother died. Her name was Wiktoria (hence my middle name), and she was only thirty-two years at her death.

Wiktoria's death was a tremendous blow to my father and his younger sister Zdzisława, called Dzidka. He sometimes said that if you grew up without a mother, you would have it hard later in life. All his life, he was a self-contained and very private man. His father, Józef, remarried and had two more children with his second wife, Weronika. Reportedly, my father didn't accept his stepmother for a long time, and it was only with time that they started to react well towards to one another. After his father's death, he had a friendly relationship with Weronika and her children. I reacted well to my father's stepsister and stepbrother. Wiesia is a little older than Henio, and Jurek is younger than me. Both graduated from the Łódź Polytechnic Institute and later married. Wiesia is living in the Hel peninsula near the Baltic Sea with her sailor husband. Jurek married Teresa and stayed in Łódź. Grandfather Józef Ziółkowski (his first name was the same as my mother's father), when he visited us in the house on Franciszkańska Street, always criticized his son, and our father, for various things that hadn't been done around the house. His remarks made my brothers and me extremely gleeful—there was someone who could allow himself to criticize Dad! Granddad did everything in his house in Studzienna Street by himself. I remember that once he went up on the roof of our house to repair it. He was nearing seventy then. A big event was the day when a cat fell into the well in Grandfather's garden. No one knew how that happened, but the cat had to be rescued. Granddad reinforced the chain and ordered us to lower him in the bucket to the bottom. The whole family surrounded him with loud protests, and he shouted back not to lose time for some useless predictions and "lower him down real slow-like." Reaching the bottom, he gathered the cat into his arms and was pulled back upwards with it.

I can hardly remember my great-grandmother—the mother of my Grandmother Wiktoria—who was always remembered fondly. We always talked well of the deceased and with affection. Great-grandmother liked visiting us at home. She said to Mom that her daughter would have surely been happy to know that her son had such a good and industrious wife. When Great-grandmother visited us, she slept with me in one bed, and I didn't like this sleeping arrangement. She woke early in the morning and whispered her prayers,

making it difficult for me to sleep. Children do not like very old people and
their habits.

A recurrent figure in family stories was father's cousin, Korczak-
Ziółkowski, a sculptor from South Dakota. His parents, Anna and Józef
Ziółkowski, immigrated to the States, and were killed in automobile an accident soon after his birth. He was raised by people who humiliated and de-
graded him, and made him work extremely hard. Korczak was sixteen when
he left the house of his adopters, and subsequently took up various jobs. He
came to the Boston shipyard, where he began to carve in wood for the first
time. The future sculptor met some people who took good care of him. In
1939, he showed his latest sculpture—the bust of an outstanding Polish coun-
tryman, Ignacy Paderewski—in the World's Fair exhibition in New York.
The bust was awarded the first prize. Almost immediately, he became a
famous sculptor. Soon he was invited by Gutzon Borglum to help him sculpt
the presidential heads on Mount Rushmore in the Black Hills of South Dakota. In 1948, he accepted the proposal of the Sioux Chief Henry Standing Bear
to sculpt the likeness of the Sioux chief Crazy Horse also on a Black Hills
site.

At that time, America was something very unreal, far-off, and didn't
affect any of us. Only later, when we started reading and attending moving
pictures, we learned about America from James F. Cooper's books or Wild
West films.

I greatly liked the attic at home, where I spent hours reading old, dusty
annual volumes of *Przekrój*[6] that my father had collected. He built wooden
shelves in part of the attic, and kept there his huge collection of books, which
continued to grow. Father was constantly reading books and this is how I
remember him best from my childhood: sitting at home or in the garden and
reading a book. He always had a notebook with him. Father's literary collection included valuable books that he took great pains to acquire, like Pobóg-
Malinowski's or Marian Kukiel's historical books, Dmowski's works, papers
on Katyń,[7] books on philosophy: Spinoza, Marcus Aurelius, the works of
Professor Tatarkiewicz, novels by Kossak-Szczucka, immigration editions of
Wańkowicz.[8] Father instilled his interest in history and literature in my
brothers and me. He had extensive historical knowledge himself. You could
refer to him without having to reach for a book. A great book-lover, he
passed this passion on to us. We learned that books were to be cared for, that
bookmarks and protective covers were used, that you had to wash your hands
before reading. Framed reproductions of historical paintings by Jan Matejko
and Artur Grottger (*the War* cycle), as well as images from mythology
adorned the walls of our home. Father told us about the Prussian Homage,[9]
Tadeusz Reytan,[10] about the uprisings, but also about the abduction (Rape)
of the Sabine Women and the apple of Helen of Troy. He admired Renais-
sance painting, and valued particularly Titian, the Flemish masters Van Dyck

and Brueghel, and Rubens. (Many years later I had the opportunity to see the original paintings in the Louvre in Paris, in the museum in Brussels and in an exhibition in the Kimbell Art Museum in Fort Worth, Texas.) In his collection, Father had among others a reproduction of a painting by the 19th century artist Thomas Cole titled *The Garden of Eden*. I used to gaze at it, with its extraordinary colors, and it had immense effect on my imagination. Years later, I saw the original in the Amon Carter Museum in Dallas, Texas. Father also had a collection of postcards with reproductions of paintings, folders with clippings and materials on the Warsaw Uprising or the Soviet war[11] (in Dad's language, Russians were either Soviets or Bolsheviks).

Father did not belong to the Communist Party. I remember that not belonging to the Party was talked about at home as something important. He said that there were no reasons which would justify belonging to the Party, because you could live more modestly, but also more independently. My parents often talked and worried "how will we survive with the kids." Father didn't go to the official Labour Day parades, and he didn't vote. I remember a few times some people came to our home, and thereafter Mother was worried. "We have children, what will happen to them?..." The remarks worried me greatly, although I didn't understand them.

Historic and literary heroes were our models, almost household members. We were given our names to honour some of them: Henryk—like Father's favourite writer, Henryk Sienkiewicz. The late Jędruś was Andrzej Kmicic. I—Aleksandra—was to be Sienkiewicz's Oleńka:[12] proud and deeply attached to her country. In Poland, I am often called as Oleńka, a common nickname for Aleksandra. Krzysztof was to honour the great discoverer of America.

Father was sensitive to the beauty of nature. He planted trees and took care of them until they reached mature growth. My father liked animals and was always surrounded with them. Whenever he saw a dog, he stopped to stroke it. He fed the birds, collecting bread crumbs at home for them. To us Father was strict, demanding, even overbearing. I was often afraid of his severe judgement. He would speak to us in adages, for instance: "Do as you would be done by," or "An intelligent man knows what to say, a clever one knows when to say it." He particularly worked to develop a sense of responsibility in us. My Father was a righteous, honest man, stubborn and devoted to the cause. He was introverted, and couldn't show his feelings. Mother was the opposite. I remember my surprise when after many years I found among family papers Dad's postcards written to Mom when we were little. They showed his emotional side, one that I didn't know. He wrote:

Iwonicz Zdrój, 23rd June 1954
To my Dearest Tosieńka[13] —Loveliest Wife, Heniuś, Oleńka and Krzyś heartfelt hug and love from your husband and father. I am in Iwonicz and despite

the beauty of the region I am missing you so much; I would love to be here with you and our children. Yours always, Heniek.

He sent a separate card to Mom on the same day with wishes on her name's day:

> ...On your name's day, Dearest Wife, I wish you all your desires may come fully and completely true. Here's wishing you faith in love that is patient, trusting, "not seeking the winner," ardent like in its first days, the love of a husband faithfully and utterly devoted to you, with his heart and soul... wishing you to see one day your Hopes fulfilled in our children—Henio, Oleńka and Krzyś. Heniek.

A few days later he sent another postcard, this time cautioning us, "...Dear children, listen to your Mama and do not eat the gooseberries, as this may make you ill..."

He also wrote other directions to us:

> Warsaw 5 XI 1954. Dearest Tosieńka, Dearest Children. Sending best wishes from Warsaw, I would like to remind you, kids, how necessary it is to help each other, live together in good relations, and provide help to your Mama whenever possible. They, who help their Mama more, love her really.

Yet Father could show his very emotional side only in letters. When I left to Canada with my son, he sent us moving letters, even poems with wise advice and much love.

I remember my first mature thought very clearly. I was standing on tiptoes and, barely touching the top of the kitchen table, blindly seeking with my hands something to play with. I found nothing and was disappointed. I remember comforting myself: It will pass, I will soon grow up and everything that's up there will be available...

Growing to the height of various furniture pieces became growing stages for me. As a small girl, I would sit in my father's lap and everyone around me said I was "Daddy's girl." Once Krzysio, my younger brother, was taken very ill. Much later I learned he was ailing from gastroenteritis. Mother cried over him and said to Father: "Henio, I so hope he doesn't die on us, like Jędruś..." I remember being terrified by hearing that. I came up to the bed and bent over it with a toy. Krzyś wasn't even looking at me, just lying there so very pale. When he recovered, he was still so weak that he had no strength to walk, and Mother carried him, wrapped in a blanket. He was still protected by everyone for a long time, being the youngest.

Once we all came down with diphtheria. Henio, a second-grade pupil then, was the first to fall ill, and our parents tried to isolate him from us.

However, soon Krzysio and I also had "sore throats." Even Mother did. Aunt Danka, the pharmacist, brought us serum and penicillin. A nun came to make the injections. I remember Mom telling Dad that "the crisis has passed."

I liked being sick, because after first receiving my share of blame (that I hadn't dressed warmly enough when going out in the garden and so had caught the cold), being sick meant lying in bed all day long without any sense of guilt. Usually Mother didn't allow us to loll about in bed, saying that "you get silly ideas from lying around" and Father said: "The early bird gets the worm." When I was sick, I was the centre of everyone's attention, and everyone was good to me. Mom gave me a delicious egg concoction called *kogel-mogel* to drink, tea with lemon juice, sweetened with honey; she usually cooked chicken broth and gave it to me in a cup. When I'd learned to read, Father brought me books which I could then enjoy all day. I even found it pleasant to go to sleep after being in bed all day. The softness of the bedding gave me a sense of security. I was very unhappy when I was given a separate bedroom. I was six then. I would listen to the ticking of the cuckoo clock. The cuckoo jumped out at each hour to announce the time. I couldn't stand being alone in the room, and most of all, I was afraid of the dark. I was afraid of ghosts, I was afraid of monsters and bad people. I was always afraid of the dark; I still don't feel comfortable when it is dark. I remember a dream from my childhood: I was attacked by a large, heron-like bird with long, thin legs. I fought it and grabbed one of the legs, and it... broke. The snap of the breaking bones was so awful that I woke up and shook. The dream was the most disturbing one I remember, and I still shudder when I recall it. Once I dreamed of my own death. I saw myself lying on the bed. I peeked at myself through a window, terrified with the situation, and embarrassed that someone may notice I was there in two persons—alive and dead. I somehow turned to a mirror, looked at myself and was astonished... with my own beauty.

Life centred mainly around the spacious kitchen. The house was heated with stoves. The kitchen stove was always warm, and all important things took place in the kitchen. We slept in cool rooms, hurriedly slipping under the feather quilts at night. On particularly cold nights, our parents put hot-water bottles under the quilts to warm the beds. In the rooms, there were big tile stoves. It was nice sitting next to them in a chair—they warmed my back and gave a cosy sense of security.

We were a family of modest means. We didn't have an affluent life, but as kids we didn't know if we were poor or not. My dream was to own a bicycle, but I wasn't given one until my studies began. Mother took very good care of the house, cooked well, and made our clothes herself. She used the large garden that we had. She bought chickens and ducklings and kept them in the garden so as to have fresh eggs for us, and broth each Sunday. In the summer, we sometimes had duck blood soup. I hated it, and my mother gave me duck broth before she added the blood with flour. We always ate homemade pasta by Mother, and for a long time I didn't know the taste of the "shop" pasta. We had to value food, and we were required to eat up everything on our plate. If a slice of bread fell to the floor, we picked it up, and kissed it before eating. Prior to starting to cut a new loaf of bread, it was blessed by making a sign of the cross on it with a knife.

I remember that in the mornings, Mother seated Krzysio and me on chairs in the kitchen (Henio ate by himself by that time) and with a small spoon fed us each two soft-boiled eggs, along with buttered bread and a cup of hot milk. In the evenings, in turn, Father had the three of us stand in a row and gave each of us a tablespoon of fish oil to drink. A piece of bread was also given to us to kill the fish oil taste. I couldn't stand fish oil and often felt nauseated. When I was little, our parents complained about my "picky" eating. For instance, I hated drinking cocoa, although later I matured and liked it very much.

Once, Father took me to a restaurant. I don't know what the occasion was. We ordered a full course dinner. The waiters brought us red borsch with patties, some meat with potatoes and green peas. Father wanted to please me, but after the borsch I felt full, and sat there with my mouth full, refusing to take more. The waiter would glance at us, take the untouched food away and bring new plates. I felt dreadfully guilty.

Mother spent a lot of time with us, even though she was always busy. I liked looking at her. She had long hair which she did in a crown of braids, and in the later years, she changed her hair style to a bun. I remember how much I liked some of her clothes. For winter, she wore a coat that was lined with fur, and I loved snuggling my cheeks into it. I liked her light, green spring coat. I hated the grey skirt suit. To me, grey seemed a dreadful color. Mother made my dresses. I remember a few of them, because they were colorful and really nice. She often consulted about her sewing with her friend from the Salesian Sisters, Jadwiga, called Dziunia, who worked in the Łódź Fashion House *Telimena*. [14] My dresses were usually in what were considered practical colors. A friend of mine had a white coat, and I always had a dark-blue one. The white coat, the "impractical" one, came back to me in my dreams. I also remember running out into the garden, which was still wet after a rain, in white stockings and a new dress (it was Easter). I came back dirty, and Mother was very annoyed with me for my lack of responsibility. She also complained when I went to church in my Sunday best with ribbons in my hair, but my bruised knees were a constant reminder of my stunts. I was afraid of my mother, but I was more afraid of Father. Mom sometimes threatened that if we weren't obedient, she would leave us and go "off into the whole world." I didn't understand the words, but they sounded so awful that I sometimes woke up at night as if I'd had a nightmare.

She knew how to make a lot of useful and beautiful things. She complained that due to her industriousness, she had no free time. She crocheted tablecloths and net curtains, she embroidered bed linen with white thread. She knew *broderie anglaise*, drawn thread work, appliqués. She sewed clothes for us and for herself. Only coats and suits were made by a tailor. She brought bread from a private distant bakery. The bread from Romanowskis' bakery on Inflancka Street, delicious, with a crispy crust, continued to be eaten in my parent's home, even though many new bakeries have appeared in closer vicinity. Mother was also a great cook. I remember her hand-made and so deliciously yellow pasta and dumplings, which I've already mentioned here, her Sunday chicken broth, tripe, roulades, cakes, delicious doughnuts, bilberry buns, dumplings with strawberries, home-brew[15] to drink on hot days. Of Mother's many cakes, I always liked the cheesecake and poppy-seed the most. When the dough was kneaded, I loved to scrape the brim of the bowl clean with a finger. Baking cakes involved a whole ritual. She never used mixers or any other aids. She did everything by hand, keeping adequate proportions and sequence of activities, and thus baking took all afternoon.

Thanks to my parents, I grew up loving and enjoying opera and operetta, and I knew all the popular arias that Mom hummed at home. Opera music has shaped my emotional side to a large extent. Many composers I didn't like— for instance, I've never had a liking for Wagner. In Warsaw, I have a collection of recordings of famous opera and operetta arias—a gift from Father. Arias from Paul Ábrahám's *Ball in Savoy*, *Rose Marie* and *Madame Dubarry* were sung by Krystyna Nyc-Wronko, Romuald Spychalski, Bohdan Paprocki. Father had recordings of arias from Giuseppe Verdi's *Rigoletto*, Giacomo Puccini's *Tosca*, or *La Boheme*. Papageno's aria from Mozart's *The Magic Flute* and Troubadour's from Verdi were sung in a beautiful baritone by Andrzej Hiolski. Wanda Wermińska's soprano performed Puccini's *Madame Butterfly* and Liza's aria from Piotr Tchaikovsky's *The Queen of Spades*. Father also admired the voice of the legendary singer from Naples, the singer of his childhood, Enrico Caruso, as well as that of Beniamino Gigli. I remember him also listening, enraptured, to the voice of Yma Súmac.

Years later, our parents would impatiently wait for the television programs of Bogusław Kaczyński,[16] who presented much of great opera and great singers to all Poles. I believe you could hardly find more appreciative recipients of his programs than my mother and father. For me, opera was my childhood, almost like home, and I am always moved by certain arias.

Another collection of recordings—another present from Father—are soldiers' songs, folk songs by *Mazowsze* and *Śląsk,*[17] and Christmas carols. At home, we often listened to soldiers' songs. Father liked them in particular, and in those moments, he was somehow solemn and lost in thought. *O mój rozmarynie* (*Oh, My Rosemary*), *Czerwone maki na Monte Cassino* (*Red Poppies in Monte Cassino*), *Idzie żołnierz borem, lasem* (*The Soldier Goes Through Woods and Forests*), *Oto dziś dzień krwi i chwały* (*Lo, the Day of*

Blood and Glory), *Warszawskie dzieci* (*Warsaw children, going into the battle, each of your smiles, oh, Capital, they will buy with blood...*)[18] ... I still remember them all well. Father also put on recordings of recited poetry in a Polish Poetry Masterpieces cycle. We attentively listened to Adam Mickiewicz's poems: *Reduta Ordona* (*Ordon's Redoubt*), *Sonety krymskie* (*Crimean Sonnets*), *Stepy akermańskie* (*The Akkerman Steppe*), *Burza* (*The Storm*), *Ajudah* (*Ayu-Dag*). I still hear the voice of Jan Kreczmar reciting *Reduta Ordona.* I didn't quite understand the poem's content, but I was very impressed by it. Marian Wyrzykowski recited Mickiewicz's *Oda do młodości* (*Ode to Youth*), *Pieśń Wajdeloty* (*Wajdelota's Song*) and the moving *Powrót Taty* (*Father's Return*).

When Father bought our first radio, a Pioneer, we knew this was an important moment. We used the radio extensively. In particular, we liked radio dramas. We checked in the paper at what time they would be on, and waited for them. Father regularly listened to Radio Free Europe programs. The station financed from abroad was sponsored by the USA, and it gave a free and non-censored version of the news and comments.[19] I remember Jan Nowak-Jeziorański's talks *Poznajmy się bliżej* (*Let's Get to Know Each Other Better*) as well as his later political comments when something important was happening in Poland. I remember Marian Hemar's cabaret, the Lviv songs sung by Renata Bogdańska and Włada Majewska. Many years later, when I visited Zbigniew and Stanisława Racięskis in London for supper, I said both to Włada Majewska and to Irena Delmar (who'd sung Hemar's songs) that I grew up in a home frequently visited by Ref-Ren[20] and Hemar in their programs.

Chapter Two

Church

Church is present in all my childhood memories. Already when I was three, Mother made a bow of white ribbon for my hair, dressed me in a white dress with frills, and hung the basket with dried flower petals on my neck: I "scattered flowers."[1] She always freshened up the dress, washed and ironed it. She gathered flower petals and dried them on a paper lying on the window sill in the sun. During the Corpus Christi procession, which always seemed too long to me, I was often thirsty. Mom usually walked by my side, carrying some compote which she then gave me in a cup to drink. During the Easter morning mass, the Resurrection Mass, I was usually still half-asleep and cold. I remember Mother conversing with Mrs. Bienias, the mother of Ala, a girl who also scattered the flowers. My mother and Mrs. Bienias exchanged opinions on our dresses and the details of them. Sometimes, Mrs. Bienias came to our house, and Father would show her the book about the Katyń Massacre. They both bent over the list of names of the Polish officers killed in 1940 by the Soviets' NKVD. Mrs. Bienias' brother, Henryk Skowroński, was listed there.

Mother had connections with the Salesian Sisters since her childhood. Years later I read that the Salesian order was founded in Italy in 1856 by St. John Bosco, and named for St. Francis de Sales. The main aim of the Salesians was to provide care for children. Currently, there are forty thousand fathers, sisters and brothers of the order in the world, working in over a hundred countries who thus continue the work of their patron saint. They work in schools, orphanages, nursing homes and hospitals. Like many Americans, Norman—my husband—like his father—regularly supports their work, and as thanks, the New York Salesians send him their publications. Before the war, the order ran extensive vocational schooling in Poland, and currently it is involved in chaplaincy and foreign missions. The Salesian brothers founded oratories, built craft and agricultural schools, created dormitories and colleges, initiated summer camps, and developed a childcare system. To education, they introduced theatre, music, sport, and trips.

The convent of the Salesian Sisters, located in a modest tenement behind a fence, was relatively close to our home on Franciszkańska Street. The Sisters taught religion to children in the Good Shepherd parish, which we belonged to. We all: Henio, Krzysio and I were taught religion by a young, pretty sister named Halina Najmowicz. She prepared me for the First Holy Communion. She required us to report what "good deeds" we had done at home. I listed washing dishes, helping in unpacking the shopping, but I didn't have many of those good deeds to list. I do not think I was very helpful in the household. Mother, always busy, often overworked, and did all the housework by herself. Sister Halina smiled easily, but she was very demanding, and I was a little afraid of her. She had an exceptionally melodious voice. She taught us a prayer I remember—all kids likely remember it: Angel of God, my guardian dear...

My mother was friends with some of the sisters: Jadwiga Kondratowicz, Wanda Michalska, Sister Genowefa and Sister Aniela Olczyk. Sister Aniela, an educated and well-read person, was transferred to Lublin to the Lublin Catholic University,[2] where she ran the library. She sometimes visited Łódź and met with her friends there.

A great event of my childhood was the day of my First Communion, which took place in our parish, the Good Shepherd parish. It was a very warm day, 17th May 1959. Aunt Zosia, my godmother, gave me a golden chain with a pendant with the Virgin Mary. My parents gave me my very first wrist watch. It was a small golden Swiss watch, that I was very proud and fond of, and which I later used for many years. I often put it somewhere and then couldn't find it. Once I looked for it for a week, praying to find it. It turned out that Father had hid it, trying to teach me to "put things back in their place." Father really wanted us to be neat and organised. He hated untidiness and disorder.

After the church celebrations, my godmother came to us with three musicians, and they played for the guests in the garden for several hours. We all danced and had great fun. Almost all of our family was there, from Mother's side and from Father's side. Aunt Zosia said it was a good sign for my future, that warm, joyful, happy day. I wore a long white dress, called a liturgical robe. The embroidery and the golden string had been made by the Salesian Sisters, and the lily and pearl rosary my mother bought from the Carmelite nuns. On my head, I wore a myrtle wreath.

The day after the First Communion, Mother took me to visit the Carmelite nuns. They asked me questions, and asked me to sing something. In a tiny, shaking voice, I sang a hymn about Jesus. I sang quietly and then more quietly, quite out of breath. The nuns began to raise their veils and show their faces. They were clearly amused.

"Am I pretty?" asked one of them.

"Yes," I said, frightened, even though I didn't think she was.

The nun was clearly happy. Another one asked:

"Would you like to be a nun, too?"

"Yes," I replied, even more terrified.

"Then we will pray for you..."

I was affected with the visit for a long time thereafter.

"I don't want to; I don't want to be a nun. I'd have to wear one dress all the time," I said to Mom several times.

"I don't want you to be a nun, either. I want you to a have a happy life," Mother comforted me.

Church holidays defined the rhythm of life. A few weeks earlier, there was a big cleaning: windows were washed, fresh, starched curtains were hung, white paper was put on the bottom of each shelf in the cupboard, and in the wardrobes. On the last day, floors were waxed. The smell still makes me think of holidays, Easter, Christmas. I think Christmas was the loveliest. The garden was usually covered with deep snow. Several weeks before Christmas, under Mother's directions, we made stars for the tree out of white paper strips. Each year, we bought some new Christmas baubles. A few days before the holiday, Father brought a big tree, which he kept in the cubbyhole in a bucket filled with water. We decorated the tree the day before Christmas Eve. It stood in the room I slept in; we called it the dining room. The intensive scent of the tree dazed me, and I had trouble waking up in the morning.

Before Christmas—first with Mother's help, then by myself—for a few years I wrote a letter to Santa. I asked for toys, and always for a little live bear that I'd dreamed of for all my early childhood. I put the letter into the mail box, and on the next day it was always gone. Mother said that Santa took it at night. A few weeks before Christmas, our parents bought pork, ham, some cured pork, and then pickled them, keeping them in saltpetre, salt and herbs. Father wrapped the meat neatly with a string and smoked it. In the garden, a special smoking barrel was installed. Earlier he brought juniper branches from the forest "for the scent." The smoked hams and cured pork cuts were hung in the cubbyhole by the house. We thus had cold meat from Christmas to Easter. For Easter, all the smoking activities were repeated and we had a new supply for the next several weeks. In the summer, we ate mainly eggs, fruit and vegetables. One day before Christmas Eve, Father brought live carp and a frozen pikeperch. We stood together over the tub where the carp were swimming. At night some of them died, and others Mother had to kill on the next day. These were not little dramas for us, and as such they always occurred at Christmas. The preparations for Christmas Eve supper lasted several hours. All activities and customs were traditional and symbolic, almost sacred. Strict rules had to be followed from early morning onward. Mother said: "Christmas Eve shows what the year will be." We arose early, because this indicated that for the whole year we'd continue to get up. On that day, you had to eliminate whatever might prophesize a bad year, so all work had to be done with particular care. Since morning, I impatiently watched my mother preparing the supper. For the whole day we observed fasting, and Mother reminded us not to eat ourselves full before the supper, because we ought to start it "slightly hungry." In the afternoon, she told me to look up at the sky to spot the first star. Reportedly, this would be the star that had led the Three Magi from the East to the Bethlehem stable. Father came back home earlier than usual. For the supper, I wore my prettiest dress. The table was covered with a white, starched tablecloth, in the middle lay the Christmas wafer[3] on the plate, and next to it was some hay (to commemorate Christ being born in a stable). Before the supper we shared the wafer. This was the very thing that gave some unreal, universal dimension to Christmas Eve. Each of us came up to the others, separately, and said their wishes; that took quite some time. I shall never forget the emotions and the effort to make the wishes personal and special for each one. Then Mother served delicious soup made of dried mushrooms—the best one was made of boletus—with small square noodles. We ate a bit of everything that came on the table—millet groats, dried mushrooms from the soup, fried in butter and coated in egg and breadcrumbs, fish in various forms and shapes: fried carp and pikeperch, carp in sweet sauce, herring coated in flour and fried in hemp oil, herring in oil, in cream, rollmops. There was also a special Christmas dish *makiełki* (it was a roll dipped in milk and topped with a filling of poppy seed, nuts and raisins). Our parents told us that *makiełki* would give us colourful dreams. For dessert, we had cakes: *babka* and my favourite poppy-seed cakes. There was also compote made of dried plums, apples, pears. There had to be eleven or thirteen dishes, always an odd number and all of them had to be those for fasting. As I've written, you had to take a little of each of the dishes during the supper, because that meant that there would be no hunger in the coming year, and the abundance of various dishes indicated the good things in the year. Only after the supper, were we given our presents. I always received a book and some toys. As a present for Henio and Krzysio, Father once made a large wooden airplane all by himself. The plane had movable wheels and propeller. After some years, the paint started to peel off, and Father sometimes repainted it. The plane was so durable that my son Tomek still played with it for quite a long time when he was little. I particularly remember the furniture for my dollhouse, which I put in the corner of the bedroom. I had several dolls, but my most impressive one was a really large and beautiful sleeping doll, dressed in a traditional folk costume. I still have it. When I went to school, I usually got books "suitable to my age" and pens as presents.

Playing and listening to carols, we waited almost until midnight, and we all went on foot for the Shepherd's Mass[4] to the chapel of the Salesian Sisters. The chapel was closer than our parish church of the Good Shepherd and seats were always available. The first carol to be sung during the midnight Mass was a most beautiful carol, one of the oldest, with lyrics written in the 18th century by Franciszek Karpiński.[5] *Bóg się rodzi* (*God is Born*). The only carols which match its popularity are the anonymous carol *Anioł pasterzom mówił* (*Angels to the Shepherds Came*), older by some three hundred years, and the polonaise one *W żłobie leży, któż pobieży kolędować małemu* (*In a Manger He Lies, Who Shall Come Carol the Little Jesus*).[6] To me as a small girl, the flavour of Polish carols made it seem that Jesus was born somewhere in Poland, in a little stable in the country.[7] The shepherds awakened by angels and hurrying to the stable seemed to be Polish farmhands. And Christmas was for me the most Polish of all holidays, with December's freezing temperatures, sheep skins, boots and warm caps. I was disappointed to learn that Jesus was born in faraway Bethlehem, the smallest of Judah's towns. When I saw the town as an adult, I found it extraordinary: built of white and pink stone, spread over two slopes covered with vineyards, fig and almond groves, pomegranate and olive trees. I was deeply affected when visiting the Nativity Church leading to the Grotto. But I was truly moved when I found Polish accents in Palestine, such as: the 3rd and 4th Stations of the Cross in Jerusalem, a monument with low reliefs showing Our Lady of Częstochowa in Tiberias, in the yard of St. Peter's church, built in 1945 by soldiers of the 2nd Polish Corps, the image of a Polish Madonna with Mieszko I and Dąbrówka[8] in the Church of Annunciation in Nazareth.

The little chapel of the Salesian Sisters was filled with strong voices, and among them my Mother's melodic voice particularly distinguished itself. I came back sleepy and quickly went to bed with a resolution to remember what I'd dreamed about, because this was a prediction for the coming January. Dreams from Christmas Eve to Epiphany gave predictions for the whole year. Mother also used to say that that if we weren't obedient on Christmas Eve, we would remain like that the whole coming year. I did my best on that day, but there was always something that made me irritable. Maybe it was because the day held so many impressions and emotions.

We spent New Year's Eve at home, without waiting for midnight. On New Year's Day, we went to church to be blessed "for the whole year."

Later we waited for the priest to come with the traditional New Year's visit. He prayed with us and left us colorful images of Jesus or the saints. I put those images into my prayer books, and I think I still have them all.

After the New Year, we went to Nativity plays, organized in the Good Shepherd's Church and, very diligently, in the Salesian Fathers' Church on

Wodna Street. The figures of the Virgin Mary, St. Joseph, Archangel Gabriel, Herod, the Devil, filled my imagination for long winter evenings.

I liked winter holidays, because they seemed to grow longer and longer.
After Christmas, there came Epiphany, when Christ showed himself to the
world for the first time. The church procession went three times around,
because the Magi took a different way back. In the Christian tradition, they
were called Kings, Wise Men, or Magi. Although we do not know exactly
who they were, we can guess they were scholars—they likely concerned
themselves with astrology and the occult. The star they saw was the star of a
new ruler—according to the then belief that each person had their own star.
They set off for a long and dangerous journey to pay homage to the newly
born King, a tribute due only to monarchs. A star of extraordinary brightness
led them to Bethlehem, to a shepherds' shed, where they offered their gifts to
Jesus. The gifts were symbolic: gold as an attribute of power and rule, frank-
incense as a symbol of priesthood, and myrrh prophesied Christ's passion
and death on the cross. Myrrh is the aromatic resin used by peoples in the
Middle East as embalming ointment. The Three Magi were named: Caspar,
Melchior and Balthazar. On return from Mass that day, Mother wrote with
blessed chalk the initials of the three names together with the current year on
the front door. The belief was that doing so would protect the house from any
misfortunes.

During the winter we played inside the house. I liked the kitchen, but I
didn't like the big dining room, because on the china hutch, crystal glassware
was displayed. Mother was very proud of it, and Father kept adding to the
collection. She handled the glass in kid gloves and told us to be careful and
"God forbid, to not break any." However, we brushed against some crystal
every now and then and chipped many of them. Then I discovered that we are
judged by our bad deeds, that the wrong is stronger than the right, it is
heavier, in a way, and outweighs the good. That belief born in my childhood
is still in me. One person with a negative attitude towards others, aggressive
and spiteful, can impose an unpleasant atmosphere on a whole group of
otherwise cheerful and kind people. They somehow fade, and only the aggressive one is disclosed. The right is not as pushy as the wrong, and it is not
so that the right "shines in the darkness." We are also judged by our wrong-
doings. You may live all your life in harmony with yourself and others, and
only once do something that does not fit within the right, do something
wrong, and then that wrong act hangs onto you all your life. People don't say
that we were good citizens for so many years, but—for instance—if we stole
something, or cheated someone, or hurt someone, we became a bad citizen.
Even if a wrong act happened only once, it follows a person and sometimes
dies only with them. Even if the person was noble, after his death, the wrong
act grows even greater and clings to the soul of the deceased like a vine.

After Christmas and Epiphany, we took down the tree, the winter slowly started to withdraw, and new holidays were coming. According to Christian tradition, Christ went out into the desert and fasted for forty days, mortifying himself before his death that he knew would come soon. The Church has given particular significance and setting to Lent. I remember the Holy Week. Ash Wednesday and Good Friday were strict fasting days—no meat, and three meals a day with only one of them a filling one. In the Holy Week, we went to various church services: meditational and lyrical contemplation of the Lord's Passion, preparation for confessions, accompanied by retreat—separate for children, for young people, for women. We sang, "Come, oh bitter sorrow..."[9]

Easter was associated with the coming of spring. On Good Saturday, a priest came to our house on Franciszkańska Street. Mother and I decorated the table with green huckleberries and boughs of ground pines, which Mom bought in the marketplace (ground pines were under protection and the boughs were bought in secret). On the table, Mother put a lamb, called *agnuszek*, decorated with a small cross-emblazoned flag, some boxwood leaves and a red ribbon; a cut glass dish with holy water and an aspergillum brush; a loaf of bread; a ham piece with the bone sticking out some; cured pork; rings of white sausage; beef loin; fried pork loin; veal; painted eggs (the easiest way to obtain a color was to cook them in outer onion peels—it made them reddish); Easter cakes, gingerbread, cheese cakes. The table was laid with food, and the neighbours brought their baskets, as well since not every family refrained such hospitality. The priest blessed the whole house and the table of food. In the afternoon, we went to visit the holy graves in churches.[10] We visited at least three churches. Next day—Easter Sunday—at six in the morning, we dutifully went to the Resurrection Mass. The bells rang in all churches, people were shooting guns and cap guns. "A good day has come for us, one awaited by each man, on this Day Christ has arisen, Alleluia..." The words were first heard during the morning Resurrection Mass. They announced to the world the joyous news that Jesus Christ had risen from the dead. That event is the essence of the faith of all Christians and is the basis for our religion. The Resurrection is the foundation for the whole of Christianity. I loved the joyous *Te Deum*. I still do.

On the first day of Easter, we shared the blessed egg during the festive breakfast. The second day was *Dyngus Day*, or *Wet Monday*,[11] which had us all excited. Usually Father got up first and gave us a good sprinkling, although we always promised to be first.

When spring started, life moved into the garden. Everyone likes spring, without any reservations. Just its first signs are enough to invariably evoke joy. The shift from winter to spring is like an annual hope for the better. The house was also prepared for spring by cleaning after the winter. The coming of spring brings relief after winter. It is also a moment of dreams, because a miracle is happening in nature. Spring is the longing for the unknown, for what has never come true in life, for something we don't know well yet, but which we want very much and which we will likely never obtain, or we won't obtain it in our individual lives. There is something particular about the scent of spring, and the fresh anxiety of awaiting new events. All the values of spring seem actually so trite: the rebirth of life, hope and love. The scent in the air brings hope, not apprehension. You are certain that flowers will bloom, and that birds will build nests. In the spring, people love each other and are gentler.

On the 1st of April, our parents outrivaled us in lies, which were usually exorbitant. "April fools," they laughed when we believed their stories. In mid-April I had my birthday. Mom always remembered the date and tried to make that day particularly nice for me. However, in April we mostly focused on expecting May. In May, the wind was scented with blooming herbs. You could smell mint, absinthe, stonecrops. There were spring scents, humours, feelings and thoughts—the time of spring transformation.

The month of May has a special significance in Polish traditions. At our house, it was mainly the anniversary of the Constitution,[12] about the significance of which I'd heard since I was little. "The memory of the Constitution," Father said, "has for years united Poles when the three occupiers wiped the Polish state off the world map.[13] In this time, we must also find support in the holiday..." On the third of May, he hung out the Polish flag, and in those times such action proved particular courage, or even daring. I heard that Father very much wanted Henio to be born on the third, and at first he was somewhat disappointed that the boy was born two days later. May also holds happy and joyful church traditions—it is devoted to the cult of the Virgin Mary. As a little girl, I went with Mother to May services every day. We sang the traditional Marian songs—"Praise, you meadows draped in greenery, Verdant hills and valley scenery, Shady groves though which we wander, Praise, you springs, the brook's meander... Praise with us the Queen of Nations, weave Her garland, you God's creations"[14] and "Mary, Queen of Poland."

Father didn't go to church as often as Mother did, but he always went to Mass on important holidays. Mom didn't mind—he stayed home monitoring the cooking of the chicken broth.

Pentecost, the descent of the Holy Spirit, also called the Green Holiday, is celebrated forty-nine days (seven weeks) after the Resurrection. In Christian liturgy, this spring holiday is celebrated very festively. Houses and churches are decorated with greenery. We all went to church with birch twigs picked from the tree that grew by the windows. On return, we placed the twigs in a vase filled with water, and soon they sprouted leaves.

June—the longest days and short nights. Summer bloomed with the scent of warm evenings, the tartness of blueberries, which Mother bought in the market in the Bałuty district and later used for blueberry buns. Frogs croaked in ponds and pools.—*Oh, the nights, the June nights...* sung Hanka Ordonówna,[15] Father's favourite singer. On the eve of St. John the Baptist's day, when the June solstice or Midsummer arrived, Mom told us of throwing flower crowns into the water,[16] a custom common in other areas of Poland.

Corpus Christi brought summer, and summer brought vacation. That meant garden, freedom and liberty; skipping on the jumping rope and playing hide-and-seek; May beetles, chafers and butterflies. I greatly admired butterflies and waited for them to sit down so that I could catch them in my hand. I watched them as I held them by their wings with my fingers, and when I'd watched to my heart's delight, I let them go. However, poor butterflies could not fly, could not go up. They struggled and flapped with the wings, and sat back on my hand, exhausted. I looked down on my palms and the pollen left there by butterfly wings, and I felt really ashamed. I learned that you can admire butterflies from afar, that when you catch them and hold them in your hand, you take away some of their strength and cripple them forever. Later I often thought that there are things to be admired, analyzed, or loved only from a distance. When you put them under the microscope, in a way, turn them every other way to examine, they lose their color, charm, and their ability to "fly high."

The scorching August days soon came. I was able to measure how long the heat lasted during the day by watching how long the cat slept. Cats always slept on hot days. Then came September, and autumn slowly approached. Autumn in Poland...it is felt as some threat. No one is waiting for autumn. And it comes unnoticed. There is no longing, no expectation of something better to accompany the change of the weather. You just know that it will be worse and worse, and All Souls' Day will come amidst rotting leaves and the first snow. You see fog-enveloped fields, dried plants and barren trees. Some dread looms in the air. Autumn should evoke some trust, some hope that you will find shelter in the house from the approaching chill, but no, strange unrest was actually waking. People said that all wars started in autumn. Memories of the last war were still very vivid. Mother recalled the warm September of 1939.[17]

I never liked November. On All Saints' Day, we traveled by tram to the distant cemeteries. First to the Doły district to visit Jędruś, then to the other end of Łódź, to the cemetery in the Chojny district, where Grandfather Józef and Grandmother Wiktoria were buried. We ignited the lights on the graves, we met Grandmother Genowefa, Aunt Hania and Uncle Jasiek, cousins and further family. Despite great fatigue, I also remember the warmth of the lights and the sight of the cemetery ablaze with them. Today, such images seem like some different reality.

November was always cold and somehow soaked with a sense of death. Only the December promise of Christmas changed the mood. Snow appeared for good and covered the garden with its white quilt.

Chapter Three

Garden

We saw all seasons in the garden. The large garden was our greatest playground and our freedom. It had nearly 800 square meters (about 960 square yards) and seemed really large to us kids. I named the very end of the garden the "far away." My whole childhood, youth, and then the early childhood of my son have passed in this garden. In the winter, we longed for the first signs of spring, which would allow us to go out into the garden and then spend all the warm days there. In the spring, trees were covered with white blossom. Cherry and apple trees bloomed, gooseberry, currant, elder-tree, jasmine bushes sprouted leaves. In the garden, there were several cherry trees and tall poplars, planted by Father, which have grown so tall that you could see them from afar. Once Henio climbed one of them and attached a flag on the top. Surprised, our neighbours commented much on his bravado and recklessness. Out of three siblings, Henio had the least predictable ideas. He had a tendency to break things. Once he was given a shooting bow. Together with some friends, he journeyed out in the fields on the same day and brought back a broken bow. Only the arrows remained.

Around our garden there were three neighbouring ones, equally large. In the garden of the Dyjaczyńskis, there were apple and pear trees. We also had an apple tree, but their apples were sweeter, or so it seemed to us. Henio sneaked there by crawling through the Skoniecznys' garden, climbed a tree, picked a few apples and returned with the booty. I watched his proceedings with Krzysio, both hidden and exceedingly nervous. Once when he was up in the tree, picking apples, he froze in fear because the older Mr. Dyjaczyński came out into the garden to rest in a chair. Immobile, Henio remained in the tree for a long time, until dusk came and the neighbour went back into the house.

We usually formed pairs—it was either Krzysio and I against Henio, Henio and I against Krzysio, or both of them against me. We liked playing battleships, which allowed all three of us to participate at the same time. When our parents were absent, all three of us snooped through their things. We opened Mother's big china hutch and perused it thoroughly, or rummaged through the cupboard in Father's library, which was even better. He kept colorful postcards in envelopes, fountain pens in boxes, pins with the crowned eagle,[1] a collection of coins. Bent over the collections, we browsed through them carefully and passed each from one to another, so that each of us could look their fill. Once we discovered a real bayonet. It was well-oiled and left dirty marks on the hands. Father kept it carefully hidden. We looked it over with respect. We knew this was one of the reasons why the cupboard in the library was locked with a key. The key was kept in the box in a drawer of Mother's hutch. We quickly discovered such things. That ferreting was our secret. We could quarrel, fight and take offense. We would also tell on one another to our parents, although usually all three of us were punished together. Father didn't investigate who was right, and I think that with time this made us avoid complaints. There also appeared a sense of loyalty. Krzysio, being the youngest and the weakest, was usually well-behaved and obedient, but there came a time for change. I remember our first fight which he won—he'd grown strong. I avoided confrontation since then. Still, I've always had this specific, protective attitude towards Krzysio.

A generously branched giant birch grew in front of the house. The tree grew on the line between our garden and that of our neighbours, so both families used it when plucking branches for Pentecost. We used a tall ladder for that. There were so many cherry trees, and they bore so much fruit, we didn't value them much, and the fruit often dried up on the trees. We picked the cherries in enthusiastically: only children and birds will truly tell you the taste of cherries. In later years, Henio picked the cherries and sold them in buckets. I remember the blooming lilac and jasmine bushes. Mother picked the blooming branches and decorated the rooms. The scent was so intoxicating that I still remember it. I snuggled my face into them and my nose got yellow from the pollen. We had lots of gooseberry bushes. We couldn't wait for the fruit to ripen and picked it when it was still green. In the middle of the garden, a well-branched apple tree grew. The tree bore fruit every other autumn, and I mostly remember it because it was my favourite tree. I climbed it and even had quite a comfortable seat among its boughs. I escaped mainly to the garden, and up on that tree I felt happy. Once when Mother was looking for me, she found me up there and said loudly, and in the presence of some other people, too, that it was time for that tree-climbing of mine to stop, that it was high time for me to behave "like a proper girl should." Her remarks were greatly unpleasant for me, and embarrassing. I felt similarly when Father put up a tent in the garden, and the boys decided to sleep there.

At night they got cold, and Mother brought them a quilt. I was not allowed to sleep out in the tent, because I was a "girl," and for me this also felt like an undeserved vexation. When Father took Henio and Krzysio for a trip to Biskupin, Kórnik and vicinity, deciding it would be "safer" to leave me at home, I started to see my otherness as something that prevented me from playing together with them. Earlier I fought with my brothers, we played hide-and-seek in the garden, I waded barefoot in puddles after a rain, and I felt wonderful. I liked being seven, eight, nine, and wouldn't have minded at all if time were to stand still. That was a time when I had a sense of joy within me, a specific certainty as to where I was in the world. "You have beautiful eyelashes, boys will like you," said one of Mother's friends. I remembered it like all little girls remember compliments. When I was little, I dreamed of my own little bear cub. My parents promised to go to the zoo and buy me one. I believed that for a very long time, and sometimes couldn't sleep at night, thinking of a small, fluffy animal, just like in the pictures in a book. After that wonderful period, however, there came a new time: I was treated differently, and courteous conduct of a "well-bred young lady" was required of me. Everything I'd done before, all the freedom was somehow questioned, while it was all left unlimited to Krzysio and Henio. I was treated differently as a girl, and—to my dismay—I was viewed almost as an adult. When I said I wanted to travel the world and discover new lands, in response I heard serious remarks that first I needed to learn a lot, and learn foreign languages, and not even that could guarantee my dreams would come true. My parents became more serious with me, and there was no more hugging and smiling and accepting whatever I was planning for my future. They stopped promising to buy me the bear cub. They said it was impossible, and that I should start thinking in real terms. They started to talk to me like to a maturing person, not a child, and I didn't like that new time at all. I had no one to discuss it with, and was unable to analyse it by myself. I only knew that something had changed and that I was losing something, and I didn't know what I might be gaining. I felt very lonely then and withdrew to my books and dreams. I was missing something that was to come in the future. I stopped sharing my thoughts and troubles. I had no friends. I wasn't that close to the girls in the neighbourhood, Renatka Petrykowska and Tereska Dyjaczyńska with the long braids. I think I didn't feel the need of friends at that time. I had a place in the garden, hidden under a gooseberry bush, where I collected colorful glass pieces and arranged them into a mosaic. The glass glistened in the sun. I named the place "kino[2] -lino." It was my secret place. My secret place allowed me to be as aloof as I preferred.

The dreams of my childhood...usually they blossomed out of impressions from the books I'd read, or stories I'd heard. I wholeheartedly grieved for the little fawn's mother and considered how I would have taken the most tender care of it. I dreamed of animals, of that magical contact with them that you find in fairy tales, when they speak in human voices and have various adventures. I didn't watch films then, we had no TV, and I based my dreams on pure imagination. I had Kipling's *The Jungle Book* to help me, and earlier on, fairy-tales. I really liked the book *Ring of Bright Water*. Father read some books to us, for instance our favourite adventures of monkey Fiki-Miki and Koziołek Matołek (*Silly-Billy-Goat*). Years later, when I lived in Warsaw, Melchior Wańkowicz read to my little son Tomek fragments of the same book: *Przygody Koziołka Matołka* (*The Adventures of Silly-Billy-Goat*).

Chapter Four

Pets

Animals of my childhood...I was a friend to all living creatures. I remember there were always cats and dogs. I cuddled cats in my arms. I was called a "cat mama" for my love of them. I remember Filut well—our large cat in black and white spots. He brought home the mice he'd caught, proud and willing to boast, and that scared us all. Our neighbour called him mean and used to tell a story about once leaving some meat on the kitchen table. Leaving for a moment, on return she found the cat holding the meat in his teeth and trying to get out. Unable to save the meat, she still managed to hit the cat with a dishtowel. A few days later, she found cat "poop" in her bedroom, right in the middle of the bedspread. Filut had obviously taken his revenge for the punishment dished out to him. He always fought with other cats and bore the various marks of his fights: he always got new cuts and scrapes. He was independent and didn't seek our caresses. A tragic story is connected with him, and I recall it still with much distress. One day Mother brought a cat with kittens to keep while the owner was away. The cat's owner left for two weeks and had asked us to take care of them. Her cat was a Siamese, with beautiful, beige-brown fur. The kittens were adorable, even though we couldn't play with them much because their mother didn't allow it. She felt insecure in our house—she hadn't been there before and what was more, she knew that another cat was living there. Whenever Filut came back home, she always greeted him with angry hissing. He was clearly afraid of her and tried to get back home late in the evening. A few times the she-cat attacked him and Filut barely escaped. One night he didn't back down and started to fight. He was desperate and furious. They went at each other with claws, then clung to each other with the teeth, trying to get the other's neck in a deadly grip. We were all surprised with the rapid course of events and looked upon the fight with horror. Father grabbed a broom and tried to separate the fighting cats. He intervened for what seemed a long time before they finally jumped apart. Filut escaped outside and was gone for several days. The female returned to her kittens, clearly weakened. In the morning, we found her dead. There was a terrible atmosphere in the house. We had to feed the motherless kittens as we anxiously expected their owner to return. When she came, she took the news calmly. She left us the smallest kitten and took the other two with her. We then had two cats in the house. Filut treated the little kitten indulgently and carefully, and I was affected by the whole experience for a long time. I kept cuddling the kitten in my arms and in my family album I have pictures of me in the garden, holding her. We called her Basia. Being a Siamese cat, she required special food. We bought fish for her, and she also liked raw eggs. She drank water, she didn't like milk. Basia quickly grew and became a real beauty. In the morning, she usually awakened everyone with her loud meowing, quite unpleasant to the ear, calling us to give her breakfast. One day she came home sick. She didn't want to eat anything and died after several hours. In our opinion, she had likely been poisoned by a neighbour. We had a neighbour nearby, living in a small, two-room house, and pigeons were his whole world. The cats from the neighbourhood pounced on the pigeons, and the neighbour didn't like cats. For me, the neighbour was like a villain from a fairy tale. Once he told us how he put our adult Filut in a briefcase and took him to the other end of Łódź in a tram. When he returned home after a few hours, he found Filut in his yard, lying in wait for the pigeons. The cat had gone through the whole city to get back home. We tried to protect Filut from that neighbour's anger, but it was difficult to constantly watch him. Filut followed his own paths, he was independent.

There were many instances of cruelty towards animals, and we often saw it as children. I remember one scene well. I was quite little and I was coming back home with Mom. On the street I saw a horse that pulled a huge cart filled with coal. The horse walked slowly, and finally stopped. A big, strong man started to hit it with a whip, and he yelled and cursed at the animal. The animal tried to pull, but lacked the strength. The man whipped it with growing fury. I started to scream terribly and I remember nothing more. The next thing I remember, I was at home, Mom was hovering over me, telling others that I was distressed on seeing a beaten horse.

Eventually Filut was poisoned like Basia. He was cunning and careful, but the person who poisoned him must have been more cunning. Seeing animals die, I asked Mom about the phenomenon of death. With dread, I learned that people died, too. "And you will die? And Daddy, too?" I asked in bewilderment. Sometimes on the street we saw a black hearse, occasionally used for funerals at that time. Large angels supported the glass doors of the dreary, black coach. That hearse would scare little kids with just its appearance.

Violent animal deaths were not uncommon and were tragic experiences of my childhood. On one occasion, my mother brought home a little tiger-striped kitten. The kitten was delicate and trusting. I didn't let it out of my sight, but time passed and the cat felt more and more at home both in the house and in the garden. One day, it approached the bowl of our large yellow dog, Aza, and started to eat something out of it. Aza looked at it watchfully. The cat left the bowl and came up to the dog. At some point, the dog grabbed the kitten in its muzzle and started to shake it. I started to scream in terror, but the dog wouldn't let go. I ran into the house, crying: "It's not true, it's not true!" I ran out again—the dog was still shaking the kitten. I started screaming, everyone came running, Mother pulled the kitten out of the dog's muzzle. The kitten was wet and terrified, but it seemed that it would recover with some rest. However, it died after a few hours. The sense of guilt remained inside me for many years. I believed that if I had screamed for help immediately, and not run into the house in terror, losing valuable minutes, I would have saved the cat. I am still ashamed of that ostrich-like behaviour. An ostrich hides its head in the sand not to see what is happening. Nothing is achieved that way, and nothing is avoided.

We had cats and dogs, but also a lame starling, and a hedgehog. We brought it home from the garden, and afterwards the hedgehog lived in the house. It drank the milk we left, and at night we were awakened by its noises—it made funny rapping sounds as it walked about the kitchen. But it escaped at the first opportunity. Other cats from the neighbourhood appeared in our garden, attracted by the presence of small chickens. Mother kept them in the garden and bought some small ducklings, sometimes turkeys, breeding the poultry for Sunday dinners and to have eggs daily. I also remember getting attached to some of the hens. They got quite tame and friendly. From time to time, my favourite hen would end up in the pot, and then I would not touch dinner, dissolving into tears. Perhaps this was the beginning of my aversion to eating chicken meat. Much later, far away from Poland, my aversion disappeared.

Henio shot his sling at a neighbour's chickens and once hit and killed one of them. We quickly brought a spade and instead of confessing, we "chickened out" and buried it. The neighbour couldn't even make dinner from it. Some time later, the same thing happened. We brought a spade, dug out a hole, and wanted to bury the chicken, but then it came to and escaped, screaming. Our hens were watched by uncommonly fine and large roosters. I believe my earliest recollections are about a huge "chicken" that attacked kids. Once it attacked Henio, who fell and was lying on the ground, yelling, and the furious rooster was pecking at him. Terrified, I ran for Mom, who chased the rooster away while laughing aloud at the whole event, which seemed highly inappropriate to me at that time.

There was a short time when Mother bought small chickens in the hatchery. The chicks had to be watched and protected from the cats in the neighbourhood as long as they were little. That was my job, and one that I didn't like, because almost every day a chicken would be lost. The cat always got the intended chicken and ate it up almost before my very eyes. Also, a few times a hen would try to hatch the eggs. I remember covering the eggs with a pillow and taking the hen "off the eggs" for a short time to allow it to eat something and stand for a few moments. Sometime later, we spent hours watching the hatching. We often brought the basket with the hen and the hatching chickens to the kitchen. The tiny baby chicks, fluffy and peeping, were an extraordinary attraction for me. I watched them with much pleasure.

Yet the most important in animal hierarchy were dogs. We had a watchdog and a home dog. I remember two watchdogs: a German Shepherd named Bari and a huge yellow dog named Aza, the one I'd mentioned earlier in the tragic incident with the kitten. Bari died at quite an old age, and I remember that Father had tears in his eyes when he buried the dog in the garden. The next day Henio, Krzysio and I made a sort of a mound for it. I even put a jar with flowers there. On seeing our work, Mother got very upset and wrecked it all, yelling that you shouldn't play like that because you could cause bad luck. But for us, this was not play.

After Bari, we had no watchdog for a long time. Bari was gentle, anyway, and only barked to scare away potential intruders. He was quite an old dog, and that's how I remember him. I was too young to remember Bari as a younger dog. Aza, in turn, was the dog that I recall as the watchdog of my childhood. The home dog was named Psotka. Aza was a stray dog. The large, yellow dog just appeared one day in our neighbourhood. All neighbours fed it, and it slept in our garden, in the doghouse that Bari once had. He not only slept there, but guarded the house, and whoever came to us was greeted with its barking and bared white fangs. Finally my father decided that since the dog slept in our garden, we fed it and it protected us, we ought to adopt it and keep it for good. So he put the dog on a chain, like Bari had been. We called the yellow dog Aza. Aza quickly accepted all norms and requirements. Our doghouse was not the usual outside doghouse. The dog's abode was located inside a large extension and had access to the house, where we gave the dog food in winter. The doghouse was well covered, and it protected the dog from the cold. In the summer, the dog had a summer lodge and the chain was tied on a long wire, so the dog was free to run about. During the night from Saturday to Sunday, we let the dog loose. He came back on Sunday morning, very tired, drank almost a bucketful of water and rested for half a day. We didn't know where Aza ran off to, but he made no problems for anyone, and always returned in the morning. We didn't know how the dog counted the days of the week, either, but each Saturday evening it was excited and impatient to be freed. Aza was very close to us and devoted to the family. Aza accepted Psotka, but maybe this was easier, as Psotka came to the house as a two-month-old puppy. One day Mother brought a small black fluffy puppy from who knows where and gave it to me. This was my own first dog. I brushed it, bathed it, kept it always in my lap. The dog literally "dogged" me, never left my side, never went away alone, and was very friendly. I transferred all my caresses to him that were unwanted by the earlier dogs and unsought for by Filut the cat. Psotka was our first home dog. The dogs we'd kept before were all watchdogs. We always had cats in the house, but all of them chose their own paths and didn't return feelings in the way that only a dog can. Later in life, I learned about a very special cat. Her name was Suzy.

Chapter Five

School

The first opera I saw with my parents was Stanisław Moniuszko's[1] *Halka*. I drank in the action, music, scenery. I was also affected by the reactions of my mother, who knew the opera and nudged me in excitement, saying: "Listen carefully now, there's Jontek's aria..." Thanks to my parents, as a young girl I'd seen most operas staged in the Grand Theatre in Łódź. I knew opera arias from *Carmen, Madame Butterfly,* Moniuszko's *Straszny dwór* (*The Haunted Manor*), or *Traviata.* I knew arias from Giacomo Puccini and Franz Lehár— my Mom hummed them at home, and we had recordings of many of them.

The operetta arias from *Die Lustige Witwe* (*The Merry Widow*), *Der Vogelhändler (The Bird Seller), Eine Nacht in Venedig* (*A Night in Venice*), *Das Dreimäderlhaus* (*Blossom Time*), *Die Försterchristl* (*The Forester's Daughter*), *Gräfin Mariza* (*Countess Mariza*) were also sung by... our primary school physics teacher. I can't even remember his name. He adored operettas and was happy to tell us about the newest spectacles staged in the Łódź Musical Theatre that he'd just seen. "Such beautiful arias," he'd sigh. "I remember them so well, I can still hear them in my mind..."

Seeing interest in our faces, he added: "I can sing them to you, but please promise to do some work at home..." We promised, and the physics teacher sang in class with a nice, full voice: "...Do you remember that Viennese waltz..." or: "In the spring stillness a gypsy sings afar..." I suppose he noticed the operetta lover in me, because often he turned to me when he sang. It might have also been because I sat in the first row. The "physics teacher" liked me well enough not to penalize me with a C grade, although the good grade I received had little to do with my level of knowledge. I didn't have much luck with teachers of physics even later, in upper grades. They were busy with some business of their own and didn't work very hard to pass onto us an interest in this beautiful branch of science.

In general, I didn't like school. I might have liked some lessons, and a few teachers. There were no admirable figures among my teachers—no outstanding individuals with distinct personalities, no eminent figures and no monsters. Some were better, some were worse. I prefer to remember the better ones. The first day of school...a large group of boisterous children and no one knew the other. I noticed a boy in blue shorts, who sat in the last row. His name was Wojtek Pawlak. I told my mother about him—she walked me to school those first few days. As our teacher of Polish, I was glad to have a young class tutor. We always wanted to have a young teacher. A range of such things were important to us at that age. For instance, we didn't want to be placed in first grade group B or C, only group A. As if that group A were better for being marked with the first letter of the alphabet. Only in later grades this ceased to be important, as did the age of our teachers. We grew up and it became important how attractively and accessibly a topic was introduced. If the teacher could awaken our interest in the lesson, we valued and respected him or her. I think that to a large extent, I owe my passion for certain subjects to having the right teachers. From primary school, I remember Ms. Bronisława Salska. She was a calm lady of great personal charm, who was very demanding as a teacher and knew her subject—Polish language and literature very well. I owe her a lot, and always remember her gratefully. I never found the chance to meet her again after completing school, to tell her a few words of thanks. I have good memories from geography classes, conducted by Ms. Adrianna Gałązka, who could talk about corals in such an interesting manner that at home I secretly sawed off a piece of Mother's red coral beads with a file and looked it over and over in awe. Many years later, when I was in Venice, I bought a string of white corals with a pink tinge. The corals were still particularly beautiful to me. In nature classes, in autumn, we gathered tree leaves and chestnuts. Biology lessons, where we learned the Latin names for animals and their anatomy, were never boring. We took animals and birds from the biology classroom to keep at home during the summer and winter breaks. I kept a guinea pig and parrots, which drove my dog nearly mad. Psotka would stare at the guests for hours. She didn't want to eat or play, as if surprised with the tamed little creatures. At that time, I wanted to become a veterinarian and dedicate my life to animal care. In art classes, we made little creatures of acorns and matches, drew real and imaginary homes, with Mom's figure reigning in the front.

At the end of the school year, I was awarded books. In the first grade (1957/58), I received *Baśń o ziemnych ludkach* (*Tale of Earth Dwarfs*) by J. Ejsmond, with a round-lettered dedication from my class tutor, Zofia Ptak, and the headmaster, Wacław Słomkowski. I read it again and again during summer, and learned some fragments by heart:

Deep down among tree roots
Earth dwarfs found habitation…
They're nice, cheerful—and powerful
Although a tiny nation…

I was awarded books for winning literary contests, although I didn't like public appearances. I preferred listening to others. The first years of primary school were all about the pleasure of learning new things again and again. The world broadened in some orderly way. Only later there came the fear of bad marks, and we started to be more critical towards our teachers, judging their knowledge and how they treated us. A very important thing was fairness, which teachers didn't always extend to their pupils. Those were our first encounters with the principles of community life, friendship, loyalty, rivalry.

I had no close friends. I remembered the fair-haired Ania, whom I visited when she was sick. Once she showed me some pictures in great secrecy. She'd found them in her father's jacket. They showed a pair—a middle-aged man and woman—making love. I didn't like them, because they presented no great beauty, and their nakedness wasn't appealing. I listened to the excited explanations of Ania, and while I was surprised with them, they didn't disturb my sleep or cause any shock. *Sexus*, as Wańkowicz would call it, was still far ahead.

I returned from school together with Krysia Małowiejska, a girl with a nice, round, freckled face, who was very talkative. I realize now how much girls talked back then, confided in one another, in breaks or during classes. Chatterboxes we were. Krysia told me about programs in television, which her parents already had. There was no TV set in my home (we didn't have one for many years). Krysia bought "pumps" (heeled shoes) and told me how boys reacted to them (or to her). She said they'd whistled with admiration. I had the same kind of "pumps," but no one whistled at me. I was popular neither among girls nor among boys. Maybe it was because I was shy, I preferred to spend my time alone over a book, and it was difficult to impress me. Girls at that time did everything to be noticed with awe, and constantly sought new "victims." I didn't talk much about myself. I believed that the most interesting things happened in books or in films. I had no confidant, as I had nothing to confide. I read my books alone and had no one to talk with about them. Most girls I knew read nothing except obligatory school reading. From school reading of that time, I best remember *Anielka* by Prus[2] and the story in it of how Karuś the dog got lost. I shed heartfelt tears each of the many times I read the scene where mortally exhausted Karuś returns to Anielka.

I dreamed of true friendship, a true friend, such as, for instance, Diana was for Anne of Avonlea. For a time, I was even bothered by not having a "real friend," and I confided this to my parents. They told me that you usually found friends later in life, that during primary school you only had classmates. Thus, I continued my aloofness.

I started to learn to write by myself, copying letters or whole words on the margins of newspapers. My parents told me what the particular letters were, and I slowly learned them. I heard I was a good learner from my father, who once came back from a meeting with one of my teachers who praised me. I got A's from all subjects, but that didn't last. In mathematics, I was moved from the third row to almost the rear of the classroom. Consequently, the most "chatty" person was moved to the front. I remember Mother always asking me in which row I was sitting, and it was good to answer that I sat somewhere in the front. The last rows were reserved for "lazybones" or for the boys. From the rear, it was usually difficult to hear much of a lecture. The teachers often spoke quietly, and they usually spoke to the diligent girls from the front rows, leaving the other students to themselves. In the last rows, you played battleship, read books, talked to your neighbours. I quickly noticed that I wasn't as good at school as I once was. I never thought to ask to be moved back closer to the front. For a good few classes, I didn't pay much attention, busy with some other things—"important" to me at that moment—and any love for mathematics died once and for all.

In primary school, I wore what we called an alpaca pinafore, and underneath usually a white blouse and dark blue skirt. Dark blue was the mandatory color throughout school. We mostly wore beige cotton stockings. Once I put on my mother's silk ones, and Ms. Salska gave me a severe look. To me it seemed that I looked beautiful in them and that they drew everyone's attention.

I remember walking on foot to school and back home. It took about half an hour. Sometimes it was so cold and snowy in winter that my fingers grew numb in the soaked gloves. They were soaked, because I usually made snowballs from the fluffy snow. I remember my struggles with the cold. I remember snow falling in my face, clinging to my eyelashes, covering my cap, my coat—and I remember returning home slowly, covered in white.

In primary school, I waited for summer holidays, for the freedom, for all-day-long reading. When I was thirteen, Father took me for a trip to Zakopane. He remembered that once he'd taken the boys for a trip to Biskupin and Kórnik, so now he took his daughter for an organised trip to the mountains. I very much enjoyed visiting Zakopane, Morskie Oko, Gubałówka, Kasprowy,[3] but I must admit with a grade of embarrassment that I was more interested in the company and the pleasure of being with other people than in the beauty of nature. I was in a way accustomed to nature. The garden was my whole world and satisfied all my needs at that time. Delight in nature came later.

Pictures from school years are funny—the little portraits needed for identity cards. When I was in the first grade, a photographer was brought to school, and beside the collective class picture he took a picture of each of us separately. In that small portrait, I have short hair that barely covered my ears, and a large lock pinned up on the top of my head. I remember trying hard not to blink, because the photographer cautioned us against that. Collective class pictures were taken for some more years, but finally the tradition was abandoned. I usually stood in one of the last rows. Usually, the shorter kids were placed in the front, and as then I was rather tall. In the first row, with her laughing face, little Helenka Gajewska sat. I remember a rainy day when Father took me, Henio and Krzysio in a tram to a photographer in the Plac Wolności square. I was in the third grade then. In the picture, I have shoulder-length braids, in which Mom used to put dark blue bows. (Twenty years later, my then ten-year-old son sought out this picture and put it in a leather frame on a shelf in his room. I was his age in that picture.) In the picture from my last primary school grade, you can see a serious, fair face with two long locks falling on my shoulders. In a later picture, I have a slight smile, and my hair is pinned up—that's from high school. Another picture is from the prom. I have a then-fashionable bun made by a hairdresser. My mother sewed a blouse of white guipure and a skirt of black crepe for the occasion. I remember the prom as an evening when no one danced with me. Our class, made up of girls only, didn't invite boys. You could invite your boyfriend, but only a few girls did. The vast majority were alone and probably entered their adult life with disappointed hearts, like I did.

I still have my memory books with entries of my friends from primary school. I now read some of those "words of wisdom" with surprise. Some entries were serious and mature, some sentimental, some were funny and childish, some silly:

> I'm not a queen, I'm not a sage,
> So I put my name on the fiftieth page.

Patriotic elements were marked very strongly:

> If your heart ever bears a scar
> From being stung by a thorn
> Remember that more suffering
> Our homeland has borne.

> Autumn winds swoosh and hum
> And people's eyes so full of sorrow,
> So you must a light and hope become
> For Poland's better tomorrow.

Be a bold daughter
of the Polish nation!

I have three wishes to ask of you
But I shall not ask a lot,
Love God and your country
And forget me not.

As well as serious instructions:

Pray and work
And happiness will grow.

And words about the future, which have such a different sound now, that
many years have passed:

When we go apart
When we go away
I'll carry in my heart
Your face of today.
One day the words I wrote here, though few
Will remind you of me, too.

At one time at a later age
You will look again at this page
And then you will remember me,
The friend from group 5B.

When you end the time of school
And go seek out your own fate
Please remember with kind heart
Your friend from the sixth grade.

Everything comes back some time
In the strange ways of fate.
But youth's days gone by
Will not return or wait.

A time will come for dreams to stop
And we'll go our separate ways.
So let me now put here a tiny drop
To remember the good old days.

Where are my school friends from that time?...What remained of the dreams
of our youth?...

Twice I spent part of my summer holidays with Aunt Danuta (Danka),
first in Zwoleń and then in Dobre Miasto. She always lived comfortably. She

had a housekeeper, and enjoyed the privileged position of the "pharmacist" in town. She taught me to use cocoa butter. "For the sun, for sunbathing, it will always be good for you," she said. Cocoa butter is still my favourite cream. My aunt was generous and friendly. She had a lot of friends. I particularly remember a trip to the lake, where I spent more than a week. We were staying in a small summer lodge.

Aunt's housekeeper, an elderly, grey-haired woman, told my fortune for the first time in my life. Looking at my palms, she said I would be "rich and happy." She gave me some herbs which she said to brew or add to tea and give to a man, who would "later fall very strongly in love with me." I always kept the little box with the pinch of herbs somewhere in my drawer. The box wasn't tightly closed, the herbs spilled about and then I gathered them back with care. Aunt's housekeeper made delicious crepes with cottage cheese, and tasty fruit preserves.

During summer, Father gave me stacks of new books to read. Childhood tales ended, adventure began, with discoveries of the world and its dangers. Father told us we should read "the right books at the right age". As a child, I read the tales of the Grimm brothers and Andersen, the poems of Brzechwa and Konopnicka.[4] I read *Co słonko widziało (What the Sun Has Seen)*, the gloomy tales of Little Red Riding Hood, Baba Yaga,[5] the mysterious Snow Queen, the moving *Heart* by Amicis. I liked Makuszyński's[6] *Bezgrzeszne lata (Innocent Years)*, or *Awantura o Basię (Argument About Basia)*. Then came adventure and travel books. My brothers and I loved *The Adventures of Tom Sawyer*, *Wspomnienia niebieskiego mundurka*[7] *(Recollections of the Blue School Uniform)* and *Przygody Samowara (Samowar's Adventures)*,[8] Molnár's *The Paul Street Boys*, Robert Montgomery Bird's novel on Indian fights *Nick of the Woods*, *Kiddi the Scout* by Robert Leighton, in Olga Małkowska's translation.

White Fang, Kazan, Winnetou, Cora, Uncas, Chingachgook and Old Surehand[9] were our dear friends. Such were also the husky dogs from London's novels, the Sioux, Dakota, Comanche, Mohicans. There were the riveting adventures of Count Monte Christo, the three musketeers, Robin Hood, Robinson Crusoe and Gulliver, the protagonists of Jack London, James Fenimore Cooper, Jules Verne, Karl May... They aroused the imagination and inspired dreams—dreams of travels, faraway lands, unusual adventures, interesting life. Father said that books were something great. They are the life, heart and centre of the passing time. Many people lived for books and died for books. Books were their lives. Father gave me a notebook, which we called the "book of golden thoughts." In it, I wrote there the thoughts of authors of the books I'd read and been particularly fascinated with. I kept it for many years, and in those years the entries changed. Just like my handwriting. You can see there how the books affected my view of the world and of my future: from an idealist approach to disquieted thoughts on reading Thomas Hardy, or Joseph Conrad.

"Young hearts are unforgiving," wrote Conrad in *Lord Jim*. And in the same novel:

"There is never time to say our last word—the last word of our love, of our desire, faith, remorse, submissions, revolt. The heaven and the earth must not be shaken, I suppose. (...)"

Conrad's protagonists faced difficult life situations. They lost, they won, but they always fascinated. The words of truth weren't beautiful, and beautiful words didn't ring true. For quite a long time, it was easier to see things in black and white. The world in that time was simplified. Whatever I disliked—I hated; whatever I liked—I loved. When more complex protagonists started to appear, I slowly changed my views and judgement. The world grew richer through the complexities of human characters and behaviour. I remember thinking that people should live twice: once on a trial basis, and the second time for real. Some sentences, poems, thoughts of the authors would dwell in my mind for a long time, and some still do.

"I thank Thee for (...) Green Gables; and please let me be good-looking when I grow up..." During school, a particular favourite was *Anne of Green Gables*, actually the whole series with Anne. Those books shaped my emotions, my feelings, my dreams. Lucy Montgomery was my favourite author then. The topic of Anne returned many years later in Canada. My friend, Zdzisław Przygoda, had part of a park in Toronto named after Lucy Montgomery. Another friend of mine, Barbara (Basia) Wachowicz, went to Prince Edward Island, following Anne's "route", and gave me a very picturesque account of the trip.

"... Oleńka, it's the most beautiful place on earth—you have to go there with Norman..."

A separate period was that of Henryk Sienkiewicz. I started with *W pustyni i w puszczy* (*In Desert and Wilderness*) and later went on to his historical books. For long days, with a burning face and bated breath, I read about the adventures of Skrzetuski, Kmicic, Wołodyjowski.[10] I didn't care for eating, I didn't care for sleeping, I wanted to read. And then the terrible awakening and regret when the Trilogy ended and there was no more! Then came the time of *Krzyżacy* (*The Teutonic Knights*, or *Knights of the Cross*). I still remember the beginning words: "At the Wild Aurochs, an inn belonging to the abbey at Tyniec, several men were sitting, listening to the tales of war and travel being related by a veteran knight who had come from distant parts."[11]

Our whole class went to see Ford's film.[12] I fell in love with Zbyszko[13] played by Mieczysław Kalenik. I didn't know how to explain to myself the fact that after the death of Danusia he fell in love again, this time with

Jagienka. At that time, I thought you loved once and forever. But I liked Jagienka, so I thought it over and finally accepted her as his second love.

Years later I met a friend of Basia Wachowicz—Wiesia Czapińska-Kalenik. I wanted to ask about her husband Mieczysław (the actor), but we always talked about many other issues, and never about husbands.

Once I finished reading Sienkiewicz, my father—a historian and great lover of Polish history, gave me the historical books by Walery Przybyszewski, Karol Bunsch, and all works by Kraszewski (my favourite one was *Stara baśń* (*An Ancient Tale*)) to read. Those were several volumes that taught me Polish history. Did they shape my opinions on history, and my approach to it? I am sure they did so at that time. Mother read Rodziewiczówna's[14] novels and wanted to talk to me about them.

My school friends fell in love with boys, and I fell in love with literary protagonists. When I started going to the cinema, the circle broadened to encompass actors, or maybe it'd be more precise to say: the characters they played. All my classmates fell in love with the actor who played *Szatan z siódmej klasy*[15] (*Satan from the 7th grade*)—I can't even remember his name now. An actress playing in that film, the pretty Pola Raksa, lived in Łódź then. Krysia Małowiejska always knew more about everything, because she had television. I read a lot of news in periodicals: *Przekrój, Ekran, Film.*[16]

Each week, on Saturday, Father brought periodicals he'd subscribed to, which we then read for long hours. We read among others *Tygodnik Powszechny, Polityka, Forum, Mówią wieki, Poznaj świat, Panorama Północy, Panorama Śląska, Panorama Polska*, a Wrocław weekly *WTK.*[17] Father collected issues of a monthly *Ameryka*. Next to films, it was for us one of the sources of knowledge about that country. At home we read books, press, listened to the radio and to recordings. We also went to the opera and operetta, and to the cinema.

I remember going to the cinema for the first time. I must have been really little, because Father took me in…under his coat. Small children were not allowed, and so he had to smuggle me in. I don't even know why he took me then. Maybe he had no one to leave me with? I remember other people looking at me, and it made me feel self-conscious. Years later, in America I saw people bring infants to the cinema. Nobody protested. When they started to wail, their parents calmly left the room. The first film I'd seen in the cinema was in a foreign language—French, I think—and I couldn't read the subtitles. I remember a group of young girls going in a carriage and singing. It took place in a very beautiful, large estate. The young ladies had pretty dresses and parasols. I have no idea what the title was. I returned home half-feverish with excitement, dreaming of wonderful parks, elegant carriages and of beautiful, laughing, elegant people.

Father purchased season tickets and each of us went to see a new film every week. That was the time of westerns. Westerns built my image of

America: *High Noon, From Hell to Texas, 15.10 to Yuma, The Big Country*. Followed by the far away Texas, Alamo, and its beautiful story. When I saw the young Ricky Nelson singing the ballad about a horse and rifle in *Rio Bravo*, I developed a huge crush on him. Krysia Małowiejska learned the lyrics and shared them with me. I hummed them quietly to myself, while she sang them to us before Physical Education classes. In some film magazine, I found the California address of Ricky Nelson. Using a dictionary (I had English classes, but I didn't speak any English), I wrote a few sentences of awe over the film. In response by mail, I received Nelson's large colored picture, and on the reverse it had a few polite words. The picture came just before Christmas. I placed it on the tree and gazed at it with glittering eyes. I wrote a reply, and it was followed by the very same picture with the very same text on the reverse. I cooled down, as if I was given a cold water shower over my head, and I felt cheated. I realized that some agency was sending the same pictures with the same text to everyone.

I have no idea what is happening to Krysia now. I'm sure she didn't become a singer, although she had the talent and courage for that. I was shy and introverted. I hated public performances. When I played an angel in a Nativity play, I went out on the stage slowly, as told, recited my lines and then rushed off the stage almost at a run. Sister Halina criticized me quite sharply, saying that "Angels walk slowly and with dignity."

I started my theatre experiences with Nativity plays in the church of the Salesian Fathers on Wodna Street. I was terribly scared of the Death and the Devil in the plays. Together as a whole class, we went to real theatre performances. We most often went to the Teatr Powszechny (Public Theatre) to see plays that were obligatory reading: *Śluby panieńskie* (*Maidens' Oath*), *Zemsta* (*Revenge*), *Dziady* (*Forefathers' Eve*), *Dom otwarty* (*Neighbours: Open house*).[18]

Once I started collecting pictures of actresses. They set the canons of beauty, fashion, behaviour, gestures. Like most of my friends, I acquired the pictures from various sources—I usually cut them out of magazines—and pasted them into a separate, large notebook. Brigitte Bardot, Jane Mansfield, Gina Lollobrigida and Sophia Loren were in fashion. I remember that Father was particularly annoyed by this "base" hobby of mine. He thought there was something unhealthy in such staring at beautiful actresses and handsome actors, and that it took too much of my time. And so one day... he burned the notebook. I was hurt by that for a long time.

The end of primary school brought the first emotions connected with a boy. His name was Zygmunt. He waited for me in front of the school and carried my bag as he walked me home. My first kiss was with him. However, apart from the pleasure in someone finally taking an interest in me, I had no other feelings for him. He was not the love of my youth, and after a few times I tried to avoid him. Then he... cut his wrists. He didn't do it seriously, but he showed me his wrist with slight cuts from a razor blade. I know he confessed his supposed feelings towards me to Sister Halina who taught us religion. Many years later, Sister Halina told my surprised fourteen-year-old son Tomek, about the event. He couldn't believe the story about his mother. I remember being quite embarrassed with the whole issue at that time, and carefully hid it from my parents. I decided that it was easier, simpler and more beautiful to fall in love with book or film protagonists.

Soon I started high school. I liked history, Polish and geography classes the most. In the fifth grade I started learning German and, in separate courses, English. Once a week, I went to religion classes in the afternoon at a religious education room in the Good Shepherd's Parish. The classes were taught by Father Włodzimierz Michałkiewicz, not Sister Halina anymore, and later with Father Wiktor Harbich, the parish priest, who also taught ethics in high school.

School brought plenty of problems and anxieties. I always had the feeling that I didn't devote enough time to learning, and I was afraid of tests and the atmosphere in some classes. For me, the teachers made a subject interesting, and then I learned gladly, or if it was difficult and boring, I shunned it.

A few of my friends from primary school went to the same high school as I did: Krysia Knapik, Bożenka Nowak and the very talented Ania Gwizdka. Ania was great at mathematic, and very friendly. I liked visiting Ania in her apartment. She gladly explained mathematical tasks to me, and I watched the family life in her home with high interest. She was, if I remember correctly, one of six children. Her youngest sister was three. There was always something going on in their home. At that time, I nearly envied Krysia and Bożenka, who didn't have siblings. I thought it was great to have your parents only for yourself, without sharing their attention with your siblings. That didn't last long, though. Never before and never after did I imagine my life without my brothers next to me. Now I realise that women who have brothers expect and accept male sensitivity. From primary school, I also remember Tadzio Węgrzycki, a delicate, talented boy. But he went to a different high school, and I lost contact with him.

I had the closest and most pleasant contact with Jola Chrzanowska. Mainly because I liked her home, she was well-read, learned music, and she was also modest, almost shy. I wasn't drawn to condescending girls and their problems. I liked Krysia Knapik and Bożenka Nowak, but they were interested in sports. They devoted much time to additional training. I was never fond of sports. I didn't like our Physical Education teacher. She was arrogant and noisy, and soon left our class.

Unfortunately, I never developed a love for sport. I frequently regretted that later in life, and often I would hide the fact that, for instance, I couldn't swim. After Norman—who swims and skis—proposed, I only confessed to him in a letter that I was completely incapable of doing any sport. He wrote me it was alright. "But I count on you going with me to the pool and to the mountains. I'll teach you everything..." In Utah, he gave up skiing to give me much loving care and help me ski down a small hill. For swimming, I was intensively taught by Tomek. He still has a mark on his heel from trying to help me stay afloat but in turn hurt his foot in the Gulf of Mexico.

I remember in primary school I was selected to participate in an inter-school running competition. I felt I was wasting time. I stopped coming to training; I ignored it. I was reprimanded, but I was stubborn and finally they left me alone. In primary school, I was also selected to the school choir. I went to those classes regularly and really liked them. In choir, I learned the lyrics to many songs, among them the Latin hymn *Gaudeamus igitur*. I inherited the admiration of good voices from my mother. Possibly, if I had trained my voice—in the words of one of the priests—I would be able to sing as nicely as my mother.

I didn't belong to the highly popular school scouts. Already in primary school, Father forbade us to join the "Communist scouts," although I had a particular sentiment to the meetings and the whole atmosphere of scouting. In high school, it was led by Ms. Gryzelda Markiewicz, who was very de-voted to the issue. Girls joined in large numbers, went together to summer camps and became close friends. Jola and I always kept away from any sort of group, cautioned thus by our fathers, and likely also due to our inherent and well-honed individualism and need of privacy. We didn't participate in the Labor Day marches. I wasn't afraid of the consequences, having the support of my family. And as luck would have it, I faced no consequences.

One day Aleksander Kamiński,[19] author of *Kamienie na szaniec* (*Stones for the Rampart*) and *Zośka i Parasol* (*Zośka and Parasol (Battalions)*), was invited to our school. Also invited were Zośka's sister and Alek's mother (Zośka and Alek[20] being war-time heroes of Szare Szeregi—Grey Ranks). Aleksander Kamiński, who lived in Łódź since the end of the war and taught in the Department of Pedagogy of the University of Łódź, was highly re-spected in my home. I was friends with him for many years. As a student, I went to his lectures in pedagogy, which were additional classes, met his wife Janina, visited them at home. On retiring, Aleksander Kamiński moved back to Warsaw. After that, I visited him and his wife several times in their home on Kochanowskiego Street. In 1974, I took him to meet the writer Melchior Wańkowicz in the latter's home on Studencka Street. They'd never met before. Wańkowicz's daughter, Krystyna, pseudonym Anna, was a liaison officer for the scouting battalion *Parasol* during the Warsaw Uprising. She was killed on the sixth day of the Uprising in fights in the Calvinist cemetery on Młynarska Street. Her body was never found. I expected it would be an extraordinary meeting for both those extraordinary people. However, Wańkowicz was ill and just had a serious surgery, and Kamiński was calm and quiet as usual, and the meeting didn't cause them to have a closer contact.

In high school, I continued German classes, stopped taking the additional English course and started learning Russian. During Russian lessons, I remember our teacher, with tears in her eyes, telling us that President John Kennedy had been killed in Dallas, Texas. It had to be 22nd November 1963. I recalled that scene twenty years later, in Washington, talking to friends. We tried to recall what each of us was doing at the moment when we learned about the assassination. They were surprised that a teacher of Russian in the faraway, then-Communist Poland, was moved to tears by the news. Many other people were also deeply affected. The American myth was already strong.

When in high school, I liked Hitchcock films and the colorful films with Shirley McLaine, Doris Day and an elegant world.

I liked and admired our history teacher, Bronisława Kawecka. History, which was so revered and loved in my home, was taught by her in an interesting and honest way. She never told us lies. Father warned us that the teachers of the Communist regime did not reveal the truth about past history. She didn't discuss certain topics, but neither did she give us the official versions of such controversial issues as Katyń or the war of 1920.[21] She taught us to love ancient Greece and Rome, mythology, archaeology. During that time, I read many books: *Zeigt mir Adams Testament* (*Show Me Adam's Last Will*) by Herrmann, *Tristes Tropiques* (*Sad Tropics*) by Claude Levi-Strauss, *The History of the Decline and Fall of the Roman Empire* by Edward Gibbon, to name a few. Krzysio was enthralled with the *Ceram series*,[22] telling us for the first time about the book *Gdy słońce było Bogiem* (*When the sun was a god*), by Zenon Kosidowski. We were all interested in the times of Napoleon—Father instilled this interest. I started learning Polish history thanks to Paweł Jasienica's books,[23] which were collected in our library. I also valued Władysław Pobóg-Malinowski's book *Najnowsza historia polityczna Polski 1864–1945* (*Modern Political History of Poland. 1864-1945*).

Professor Jadwiga Banasiak taught us geography. She wore her hair smoothed back and was strict and demanding. Thanks to those lessons and some additional reading, my world broadened very much from the age of fourteen to eighteen. I read Conrad's works and dreamed of foreign lands. I studied a two-volume *World Geography*. We were taught biology by Professor Wiesława Stępińska; we called her Ducky. The biology room was well equipped, and the pupils were involved in interesting experiments. I remember dissections of the frog and the earthworm. I read Maurice Maeterlinck's *La Vie des fourmis* (*The Life of the Ant*), and I was fascinated with the book. I admired the organized character of the ants, as well as the bees. Then came books by Konrad Lorenz. I had a strong inclination to biological sciences and for a while I considered studying medicine or veterinary science in the future. Yet I decided I would study literature. High school brought new books and new fascinations. There came the period of Romanticism. Father bought me *Dzieła wszystkie* (*All Works*) of Słowacki and Mickiewicz, as well as volumes of the later poets: Asnyk, Kasprowicz, Tetmajer. Delight in poems by Herbert[24] and Miłosz[25] came later. Earlier I rewrote Pawlikowska-Jasnorzewska's poems in a separate notebook, and they satisfied my need of love for poetry. Slowly I became acquainted with the novels by Reymont, Żeromski, Prus, Orzeszkowa.[26] Żeromski was the favourite writer of Gryzelda Markiewicz and she could talk of him to us in a captivating way. Then I read the stories by Maupassant, the novels by Balzac and Zola. Then was Sigrid Undset, Hemingway, Romain Rolland. I remembered *Jean-Christophe* and *The Enchanted Soul* so well that later I told them to my friend from studies, Ala, in instalments. *Biblioteka Boya*[27] with lots of translations of the masterpieces of French literature gave many interesting topics for conversations and reflections.

The writer who became the closest to me—and I think he's still my favourite today—was Thomas Hardy. In my library in America, I have his books in English, and in Warsaw the Polish translations: *Tessa d'Urberville*, *Far from the Madding Crowd*, *Jude the Obscure*. The film with Julia Christie, based on the book *Far from the Madding Crowd*, remains one of my favourite films. At this time, I started to consider the role of coincidence in human lives. If Fanny hadn't been late to church to marry soldier Troy, if Gabriel hadn't lost all the sheep on one day, what choices would Bathsheba have made? The ifs, the ifs...

When I was ill with angina and had to remain in bed a few days, Father gave me a book to read which then turned out to be a very special story: Margaret Mitchell's *Gone with the Wind*. My cheeks burned with excitement as I devoured the story of Scarlett O'Hara, I admired Rhett Butler and was pulled into the war between the North and the South in the United States. The Southern States, depicted by the author in such a wonderful way, left a warm trace in my heart. Later my brothers and I went to see the film with my parents, when it finally was shown in Polish cinemas. I identified myself with Scarlett very strongly, and placed quite an affection for Clark Gable. I remembered Vivien Leigh when she starred in one of the most romantic and moving films: *Waterloo Bridge*. When I was grown up, my Father gave me Margaret Mitchell's novel in two volumes nicely bound by the bookbinder. Little did I know that the book and its protagonists would play a role later in my life.

Meanwhile, I faced the choice of studies. I was worried by the problems with the teachers of Polish. During high school, they often changed, and none were the best of teachers. Father gave me the book by Ignacy Chrzanowski[28] to study literature, and it helped me considerably. In Reymont's High School, chemistry ranked at an undoubtedly high level. A particular figure was the school's deputy head and teacher of chemistry, Grażyna Mościcka. Elegant and handsome, demanding and strict, she successfully prepared candidates for chemical studies. I wasn't fond of chemistry, I was never well prepared. I also think gratefully about the teacher of mathematics—the headmaster, Stanisław Zawadowski. He actually asked the pupil who was best at mathematics in the whole school, Władysław Kamiński (currently a professor at the University of Łódź), to explain the more difficult things to me. Zdzisław Chruścicki, a teacher of Polish, was an extraordinary individual, and a man of great knowledge. Unfortunately, he didn't have regular classes with us, he taught us only as a substitute teacher and for a year we had introduction to philosophy with him. He was Henio's teacher, and Henio told us about him at home. I had to prepare by myself for the entry exams to the University of Łódź's Department of Philosophy and Literature. I was likely saved by my knowledge of books and good preparation that I gleaned in primary school (Ms. Bronisława Salska gave us solid foundations of grammar and literary analysis). A teacher who knows the art of teaching, who is demanding and has extensive knowledge, is a winning lottery ticket for pupils. I often spoke with Jola about that; she was preparing for entry exams to the law department.

The love for history we learned at home made my older brother want to study history. I remember the conversations with Father, who opposed the idea, giving himself as an example. He said that in Communist Poland, history studies were, as he put it, mendacious, and didn't promise a future for honest people. Henio started studies at the Department of Mechanical Engineering of the Łódź Polytechnic Institute. When my turn came, I applied to the Department of Philosophy and Literature at the University of Łódź. My great love for literature, instilled in me by my father, had won.

In my next to last year of high school, I was summoned to the Security Service. Because I was underage, Father was summoned to come with me. The men from the Service had seized the letters I'd sent to the program *Rendez-vous at 6.10* broadcast daily by Radio Free Europe. Thanks to those programs, young people could listen to the newest Western hits. The program lasted for an hour and ended in "listeners' choice"—certain songs were repeated as requested by the listeners. The station kept giving new addresses to send letters to, stressing that if you sent them immediately, they would reach the radio. After a few days, we were told, the given address was intercepted and the letters were confiscated. Usually Paris and London addresses were given. I remember well the afternoon *Rendez-vous at 6.10* programs, which my brothers and I listened to as we were doing our homework. They were hosted by Jan Tyszkiewicz, Janusz Hewell, Barbara Nawratowicz and sometimes by Tadeusz Olsztyński (Nowakowski). A few of my letters reached the addresses, and I was happy to listen to a song broadcast at my request. Certainly, however, a few of my letters never reached their destination.

During that meeting, my Father and I were reprimanded for listening to Radio Free Europe at all. They threatened and "warned" us against doing so in the future.

Soon the unrest of March 1968[29] started. Students were involved, but the unrest didn't reach schools. Once I walked down Piotrkowska Street with my father, and we saw young people forcibly dispersed with truncheon blows by the militia.[30] I was shaken and didn't understand what was going on. I felt a certain helplessness and broad ignorance. I remember Father discussing current events with an old friend of his—from before the war—Jurek Sokołowski. They were both skeptical and saw actions and provocations of the authorities in all public addresses. Yet in our house, we did not focus on current political issues, but lived and breathed historical books obtained by Father in various ways. Politics was a subject reserved to Father and a narrow circle of his friends.

We lived in great symbiosis with the Church. In the summer before my final grade, my mother and I took part in the annual walking pilgrimage to the Jasna Góra monastery in Częstochowa in August. The pilgrimage took ten days—we went four days to the city, then spent two days in Częstochowa, and returned to Łódź in another four days. The pilgrimages were perfectly organized, and the experiences left a meaningful impression for many years. After the morning mass we set off, singing elements of the Little Office of Our Lady.

> Let our mouths praise Virgin Mary, so holy,
> Let them sing her unimaginable glory.
> Our Lady of Mercy, free us when we cower
> From the mighty foes' overwhelming power.

The sun was slowly rising as the day broke. Such early awakenings and beautiful mornings I admired a few years later on a ship. When the grey surface of the ocean grew silver, and the sun's golden sphere rose into the sky, you stilled your breath and praised the Maker. The awareness of God's existence is strong in me; maybe it is a kind of grace? Faith, religion, church rituals—all of that I grew up with. Neither as a very young person nor now did I experience any great doubts, breakdowns, or any great rapture. I accept God's existence naturally. Among my friends there are people of various religions.

I remember an anecdote I'd heard a long ago in Canada. I found it to be an interesting outlook.

There were two Frenchmen, strangers, sitting in a café, sipping coffee, reading papers. One of them spoke up to ask the other:

"Say, you like Jews?"

"No," was the reply.

"Well, you like Catholics?"

"No." The other man didn't as much as raise his eyes from his paper.

"Do you like Americans?"

"No."

"Do you like the French?"

"No."

"Well, then who do you like?"

The man finally raised his eyes for a moment.

"I like my friends," and he returned to the paper.

During the pilgrimage my mother always got up early, and I was sulky and miserable. Only after breakfast and setting off, did I recover as we went. Mom always says that I couldn't be bothered to talk then, as I always snapped or grunted. During the pilgrimage, I made friends with two people with whom I'm still friends today, and I highly value those friendships. In Częstochowa, Mother and I became friends with a Pauline father, Marian Lubelski (later prior of the Jasna Góra monastery in Częstochowa), and in Łódź, with Bishop Jan Kulik. Bishop Kulik told me how full personal happiness of a human was dependent on moral order. Nobody, he said, shall recreate the whole internal struggle and tragic nature of life more truly and convincingly than the one who dares consciously go against that order. Yet at the same time, the Christian concept of the world assumes the possibility of collaborating with grace and improving oneself in each specific situation in life. A person who is rooted in a particular family, environmental or social relations, connections, relationships has a chance to improve, and his or her seemingly grey and pointless efforts and everyday work have their aim, sense and supreme point of reference...

Under the influence of the conversations I had with Bishop Jan, studing at the Lublin Catholic University became my preference. Mother was encouraged for me to follow that route by the Salesian Sister Aniela Olczyk. The bishop gave me a letter of recommendation to Professor Zdzisław Papierkowski, Vice-President of the university. We went to Lublin with Father, and considered the possibility of my studies there. But we finally abandoned the idea, mainly for financial reasons. Scholarships were rare, and there was also the important fact that I lived in Łódź, which is a university city.

For my eighteenth birthday Mom organized a party. She gave me her mother's engagement ring, with a real red ruby. The ring was delicate and modest. To my party, I invited Jola Chrzanowska, Ania Gwizdka, Anka Kubacka, Romek Sokołowski, as well as Wojtek Tomczyk, Henio's friend from studies. They both studied at the Department of Mechanical Engineering of the Łódź Polytechnic Institute. We listened to records of Elvis Presley and Paul Anka, and also to Czerwone Gitary with their song *Matura*.[31] The singers Karin Stanek and Helena Majdaniec reigned supreme in Poland at that time, but thanks to *Rendez-vous at 6.10* my brothers and I were *au courant* with the newest world hits. Wojtek had a motorbike and often drove Henio home. He sometimes visited with us. We watched each other closely. He was a handsome boy, dark-haired and fair-skinned, with a moustache and a beard. He lived close to the Łagiewniki Forest. He invited me for walks. We went by motorbike. I was afraid of riding it, but I liked the wind and the speed. As we walked—we walked together more or less once every two weeks—he said next to nothing. He seemed shy, and awakened my curiosity. He brought me small rings and mini-baskets made of straw. We both liked the song *Wspomnienie (Memory)* with lyrics by Julian Tuwim, sang by Niemen. [32] Once he kissed me and then started talking about himself. He seemed to be full of protest against his parents and all the other people around.

Entry examinations to studies were always a big event in my home. This particularly concerned my brothers, because if they didn't pass, they faced obligatory service in the army. In my calendar, I noted events of the day, and these were for instance: "Henio: final school exam," "Henio accepted by the Łódź Polytechnic Institute." I was very concerned for the fate of my older brother. When I took my entry exams, the Polish Communist authorities had introduced so-called additional points, which you gained as a student from a peasant or working-class background. My intelligentsia background helped me none, and I had to pass the exam well enough to be accepted. I remember reading loads of detective novels between the particular exams, waiting for the results. I was out of touch with reality then, and didn't lose my nerve waiting. A later custom developed that at times of tension and waiting, I asked Father to bring me a good detective story. When I was informed of acceptance into the University of Łódź's Philosophy and Literature Department, I went on another pilgrimage to Częstochowa with Mom. I liked the discipline, concentration and rhythm that we had to follow. We felt good together, got closer, made plans for the future. I was happy I'd be studying my favourite subject: literature. How little did we know then of what awaited me in the coming years.

Chapter Six

University—Marriage—
Birth of Thomas

The greyness of the first weeks of autumn had come, and the days were getting shorter. Wojtek and I were returning from a motorbike trip. I wanted to make it home for supper. The weather was windy, cool and quite unpleasant. The wind blew my hair about, as I had no safety helmet on. Wojtek had said he would drive carefully on short distances, so he put off the purchase of another helmet as a convenient savings. I regretted not having a warmer sweater on, and thought about hot tea waiting for me at home. Then I felt the motorbike turn sharply, felt an impact, heard a noise, then strong shock. I rolled with great force over the road, there was pain, the hardness of the asphalt turned into the softness of the shoulder, and I rolled and rolled in some enormous rush, pulling tufts of grass with my fingers. There seemed to be no end to that rolling towards the unknown. Then there was silence, and it was broken by a voice. "Is she alive?..."—"I'm here..." I said. "What happened?..."—"It's a miracle you're alive, I saw you roll across the road. And there's that pole just a step away from your head, if you hadn't stopped..." continued the unfamiliar voice. "Oh my God, how are they?" asked someone almost in a lament. The voice was that of the owner of the horse and cart that held a mower. He was returning home from the field, and had forgotten to put a light on his cart.

Not waiting for an ambulance, a private car took Wojtek to the closest hospital in Zgierz. In good faith, the driver wanted to provide immediate help. By ambulance which arrived twenty minutes later, I was taken to a hospital in Julianów in Łódź. They cleaned the open wound under my knee and put some stitches in. I asked to be taken home. I needed its peace and quiet.

Wojtek had a double open (compound) fracture of his left leg, a concussion, and bruises. A week later, his leg in a plaster cast he was brought to the hospital on Kopernika Street in Łódź. His mother, a known pediatrician, ensured he had the best care and the best doctors. In contrast to him, I came through the accident almost fine. My survival was a near-miracle, since I hadn't been wearing a helmet to protect me. I stayed in bed for two weeks, half-conscious. At nights I was delirious. My whole body was black and blue. The injury below my knee healed. Three weeks later, I went to the hospital to visit Wojtek. He was lying in a private room with his leg in traction. Cuts on his face were healing. He looked pale and tired. As we talked, sudden tears started to flow down his cheeks.

"They said I couldn't have another motorbike, that they wouldn't let me drive..."

"Who?" I asked, not understanding. "The doctors?..."

"No, my parents," he complained.

I looked at him, immobilized in bed, sentenced to the same position for hours, for days and weeks. Wojtek's mother visited him each day, and I also tried to come often. He cheered up on seeing me. I brought him books to read, sometimes some oranges. He read the books, liked some of them, then we talked about them and somehow I was finding my way back towards him. The predominant feeling was great sympathy, and out of nowhere there appeared a certain sense of guilt...that I was fine, that I hadn't been hurt in the accident, that I had a normal life. I even thought that if he had been alone, without me, he would have chosen a different road and never met that unlighted cart. Almost every day I saw how the hospital and the immobility exhausted him, and I almost felt responsible for his suffering. I don't know why I couldn't, and still can't, analize the reasons for such feelings.

He finally left the hospital returning home. I still visited him and brought new books. I began and was able to know his family. He had two younger sisters: Elżbieta, who took classes in piano and in foreign languages, and Joasia, always laughing and ready to play. Hania, a deaf-mute woman, lived in a small room upstairs. She was once a caregiver of Wojtek's grandmother, who now did various heavier work in the house and in the garden. His father worked in an office. He was a forestry engineer and liked hunting rabbits. He was tall and lean, while Wojtek's mother was rather short, with a pleasant, fair, open face.

Wojtek began to feel better, at least mentally. He was waiting for the plaster cast to be removed, but that was put off for another month. And I had more and more work at the university and missed the calm evenings at home. I lacked time to read books for pleasure. I started to think about the time when Wojtek would return to normal life and continue his interrupted studies as if freeing myself of some promise and obligation. I wanted to look at everything both directly and indirectly and have time for reflection. The life around me was interesting and engrossed me with growing intensity. Wojtek, his problems and his surroundings were not my own. On the contrary, a feeling of growing distance towards them began to develop within me. I noticed, however, that he felt much closer to me emotionally and while critical towards others, he was idealizing me. Once the plaster cast was off, he started to slowly return to normal life, and spent much time with me. I understood I'd become an important part of his life, and I was also very attached to him. He was the first boy I fell in love with. We showed much tenderness and warmth to each other. I remember our moving trip to the forest in Łagiewniki, to the small Franciscan chapel of St. Anthony, where we promised love to each other. Next to the chapel there was a small well with crystal clear spring water. We went for a whole day to Warsaw, bought records of our favorite songs, spent a lot of time together, but at the same time, I saw a distancing process in myself. In my commitment, I saw much idealizing, fantasies, exaltation and a desire to be loved. Deep in my heart, I felt that I wanted to love and be loved in a different way. I didn't know how to name the feeling, how to describe it. I think I was still waiting for true love. I was not yet in the spring of my life—it was still the time to dream, too early for love. But I don't think I realized it then. And I was so impatient.

My parents, particularly my father, gave a suspicious eye to my commitment. They had nothing against Wojtek, but they thought that neither he nor I should spend so much time together, that our "children's play," as they put it, would lead nowhere. I remember my conflicts with Father, who told me flatly and strictly to commit myself foremost to my studies.

I learned well. I finished the first semester with A's. I ploughed through the difficult exam on the grammar of Old Church Slavonic language. I remember the literature theory lectures of Professor Stefania Skwarczyńska as particularly interesting. She was a lady of great knowledge and wisdom, surrounded with a particular myth at the university. My father knew her husband, a pre-war colonel. Classes in literature theory were conducted by Teresa Cieślikowska, and in theatre—by Stanisław Kaszyński. Extremely captivating were classes in logic with Professor Ija Lazari-Pawłowska, author of many studies on ethical issues, as well as lectures in culture sociology held by Professor Antonina Kłoskowska. I struggled with Latin, taught by Łucja Macherowa. The assistants were young doctoral fellows, among them Sławomir Świontek, Jerzy Poradecki, Tadeusz Błażejewski, Jerzy Rzymowski, Wojciech Pusz, Aleksandra Budrecka.

During my first year, Professor Jan Dürr-Durski who came over from Warsaw to Łódź to teach Old Polish literature, suddenly died. Professor Skwarczyńska lost her daughter in an accident in canoeing. My mother was deeply affected by the terrible blow to Mrs. Bieniasowa, whose son Danek had a fatal accident on a motorcycle right before final school exams. Mother had been friends with her for a long time. Her daughter Ala used to scatter flowers in the church like I did. We had the First Holy Communion together. Mrs. Bieniasowa broke down completely after her son's death. She spent whole days at his grave. My mother and I visited her there, at the cemetery in Doły. Only with great difficulty was I able to recognize the once cheerful woman as the grey-haired figure in black. She was always a beauty, and now her face had a tragic expression, like a figure from Greek mythology. I heard that Ala was being taken care of by her grandmother, because her mother couldn't focus on anything.

Those first months of my studies, when I went by trolley to Narutowicza Street, were exceptional in that during a break between classes—sometimes even an hour or more—I visited with my grandmother Genowefa, who lived on Tuwima Street. She served me tasty soups, cake and tea with lemon. Grandmother liked talking to me and showed me much affection. She hoped for a good life for me, and a good husband. "Maybe you'll marry some Swede, like my friend's daughter did. He loves her and they're doing quite well..." She always had some new presents for me. I was given leather winter gloves, golden earrings with corals, a golden bracelet. I became her beloved granddaughter. We went for walks, and she was planning a summer trip for us together. I liked this new relationship with my grandmother, with whom I hadn't been close as a child. But she soon started to have health problems. I visited her. She wanted to be with me then and plan our trips. In a way, for her I was a return to normal life and a kind of hope that is sometimes given to older people by another's youth.

There was an aura of sadness at home, and of waiting for what fate would bring. Mom visited grandmother each day, and cried after those visits. After spending frequent and regular time with Wojtek, I stopped seeing him. My time was taken up by classes at the university and visits with my seriously ill grandmother.

At the same time, I was going through a time of tension and expectation myself. I could not believe that my conjectures might be true, but time inexorably confirmed them: I was with child. I went to see Wojtek, who "consoled" me that I might be wrong and that I just needed to...wait.

Grandmother passed away. The funeral was on a cold, rainy day. I remember the grief of my mother and her siblings, and how my father, who had lost his own mother as a teenager, stood over the grave. At some point in prayer, I asked my Grandmother for help...to help me in my own situation, which paralyzed me and woke me up at night. I remember spending my days in classes, at the university, with my friends there, going asleep tired and waking up at night—frightened and helpless. I saw no way out. Years later, whenever I recalled that period, it always seemed to me one of the most difficult times in my life.

"Do as you wish, the decision is yours," said Wojtek.

I decided to tell Mother. But I delayed it. Days were passing, and I was waiting for a moment when there would be the two of us at home. On that day, my mother was making pasta in the kitchen, and I sat next to her. I remember the conversation very well. In particular, I remember Mom's face—surprise, disbelief, despair...on the same day she went to Wojtek's mother. They talked, and both had tears in their eyes.

I wasn't so terribly alone with it now. I asked her, naively, not to tell Father immediately. Those few days seemed normal, I went to classes, returned, studied at home. On the third day or so, I turned to Father with some question. He didn't answer. I looked at him and saw his changed face. I quickly left the room.

It was as if nothing had changed, and yet, everything was different. I never talked to my brothers Krzysio and Henio, and they didn't say a word about my situation, but they knew. They were quieter, almost disconcerted. Father changed the most. He stopped conversing with me. If he did talk to me, it was only to issue some instruction, almost a notification. We communicated, but never conversed. It was painful for me, but I accepted it with certain humility. Mother, in turn, took exceptional care of me. Each day I had a fresh egg, fresh butter and a piece of meat. I was favoured, but my brothers didn't protest. They accepted that as a fact related to my condition, something indisputable.

On one March 1969, I married Wojtek in the registry office. I was nearing twenty, and Wojtek was four weeks short of his twenty-first birthday. He needed a special permission from the court to be able to marry those few weeks early. Our civil ceremony took place without our parents, or anyone from our families. Wojtek's friend was the witness. I wore a navy blue costume. We didn't even have the wedding rings yet. I believe we were the most modest pair, and the clerk gave us a suspicious look. When it was over, we went to our classes—Wojtek to the Polytechnic, I to the university.

Our church wedding was on sixth April, in my parish, the Good Shepherd's Parish. The day was warm and beautiful. My mother prepared a small party for the closest family. I remember that in the morning I sat on a bench in the garden. The sun was warm. I was flushed and almost feverish. My father was sitting next to me with a book, but he wasn't reading. We sat there in silence. I was looking as if from the sidelines at the whole situation, at myself, and I felt like crying. I knew that changes were taking place which would impact my whole life...How different had been my dreams of the wedding I would have. Nobody knew what I was thinking, and I don't think anyone cared.

I had a long dress of white guipure lace and a long veil. The dress was made by the *Telimena* Fashion House. My mother said I couldn't wear a myrtle garland,[1] of which she'd always dreamed of for her daughter. Aunt Danka powdered my face, amazed that I never used cosmetics. In the church,

Schubert's *Ave Maria* was played on a violin, and a choir sang. Three priests married us—one who'd baptized me, and two who'd taught me in religion classes. Wojtek was moved and excited with the whole situation. To me it seemed that I was taking part in a ceremony which didn't affect me personally, but at which I had to be present.

On the next morning we went by train through Zakopane to Krynica Górska for five days. In Zakopane we changed to a bus. Tired from the trip, we searched a long time for a free room, and finally found one in a villa. We liked the area very well and enjoyed many long walks. I constantly felt tired and slept a lot. Returning rested, our faces were well tanned. Each of us returned home. I was still living with my parents and brothers, and Wojtek with his family. Our parents believed it was most important that we continue our studies, so *status quo* came first. Soon, exams started. I completed the first year of studies with good grades. The 1960s brought the fashion for high-waisted dresses with a flared skirt, which concealed the figure. They hid my changing figure, and few people at the university knew of my pregnancy. The last weeks of June and July I sat in the garden all day. I was reading the obligatory readings for the second year of studies, and waiting for my child to be born. The child was to be born in the year when Neil Armstrong—the first man to set his foot on the Moon—said: "*That's one small step for man, one giant leap for mankind.*"

When I thought about the coming baby, I thought of a boy. "If I am to have a baby at such a young age, let it be a boy." Like Fleur, the protagonist of *The Forsyte Saga—End of the Chapter*, I spoke of the unborn child: HE. I believed that a girl needed special attention, tenderness, plaiting braids, dressing up. A girl needed complete motherhood, and I wasn't ready for being a complete mother. A boy would have been different, a child that you could have without all those grand expectations, preparations and female activities. I remember at the time, I paid particular attention to the lectures by Maria Zygadlewicz on child psychology.

My mother carefully prepared the layette for the infant in two colours: blue for a boy, and pink for a girl. She trimmed the diapers, baby caps and tops with hemstitch, embroidered the little pillowcases with white thread. She made a long pillow of real feathers for the baby, then ordered another one—as suggested by Wojtek's mother—made of seagrass. Supposedly, it was healthier. A baby carriage, crib and pacifiers were bought. Mother was very excited about the coming baby. She returned from work full of ideas about what else she could prepare for the baby's birth. She was full of enthusiasm and goodwill. Still young, always full of love for us, she decided to support me wholeheartedly in my difficult situation. She devoted all her free time after work to the challenge, often prolonging it until late at night if she wanted to finish all the work. Neither Mother nor my brothers ever said a bad word about me and my situation. My situation was particularly difficult for Mother, a very religious and honest person, to hear the comments and questions of the neighbors, friends, even our own family. She was mainly loyal towards me, her own child, and such she always remained. For Father, who was always quite introverted by nature, it was not easy to accept the whole situation, and he didn't show me as much enthusiasm and tenderness as Mother. She took me to visit a midwife she knew, Mrs. Stefania Dzięgielewska, who'd assisted at the birth of both my brothers and me, and whom Mother really trusted. Mrs. Dzięgielewska, with a nice, kind face, gave me a good, close look and stated that I would have a boy. So a boy I expected, and thought only of boys' names.

There came the calm, lazy August days. I spent whole days in the garden. There was always one of my brothers at home, per Mother's instruction. Wojtek visited me during the day. He came by motorcycle and spent an hour with me. His house was empty as his mother and sisters left for vacation to the Bulgarian seaside, and his father spent long hours at work. Wojtek invited me to his house. He had a room upstairs, where he listened to the radio and amateur radio operators talking. By the house there was a big garden with vegetables, currant bushes and fruit trees. The garden was taken care of by the deaf-mute Hania, who always weeded it. I took a book with me and spent many hours with Wojtek.

Finally the day came.

At noon, Saturday the ninth August 1969, Tomasz (nickname in Polish: Tomek; in English: Thomas) was born. I remember the moment of silence when I held my breath, waiting to hear that it was a boy and a healthy one. I immediately thought: of course it was a boy.

I was lying in a two-bed room with a sixteen-year-old girl, who had just had a daughter. The next door was open, and I saw older (as I viewed them) women in their thirties. They complained about husbands, the "hard life" of women, etc. At some point I felt as if my world had been taken away. There I was, a mother, just like those women, and issues were catching up to me that I had never before been concerned with or that I was interested in. I felt at least ten years older, and as if I'd lost something irretrievably. The thoughts of the future were terrifying. I remember that after those thoughts I cried long and hard over myself and my life. At night, I cried into the pillow for a long time.

On the same day that Tomasz (Tomek or Thomas) was born, in faraway California, Manson's sect murdered Sharon Tate and her friends. She was pregnant, and soon to give birth. I only comprehended the cruelty of that crime much later. At that time, I didn't know of it happening yet.

The nurse brought flowers and a letter from Mom. She wrote me that Wojtek had come in the morning with the news that I was in the hospital. She went to work, but took the day off and came at eleven to the hospital, where she was told I would "have the baby soon." My good Mother waited for news in the corridor downstairs, saying the rosary for me. When she learned I had a son, she went home. At the hospital's entrance door, she met Krzysio, who told her he was coming to see me. Excited, both returned home, sending the flowers up to me. I also got a bunch of roses from Wojtek's father. But I didn't have any sign from Wojtek for quite a long time. It turned out he had spent the day in the market square, looking for some motorcycle parts. He didn't think I would have the child "so quickly." I also got a nice letter from Ala Lasoń, a friend from my school days.

My first emotions soon erupted over the little bundle with my son inside it. After feeding he opened his beautiful blue eyes wide and it seemed to me that he was looking intensely at me. I touched my fingers to his little fist, admiring the delicate little fingers. He opened the fist and grabbed my finger. My new emotions couldn't compare to any others I ever had: overwhelming joy and elation, tenderness and affection. I was seized with indefinite happiness, and wanted time to stand still.

August and September passed. In October, Mother took a monthly leave to take care of the baby. I started my second year at University. I tried to be home often and long. I went only to the most important classes, and often returned home in the middle of the day to feed Tomek. When you're a mother, you're never alone in your thoughts anymore. You think of yourself and the child each and every moment.

The choice of the name caused some problems. Wojtek's father wanted the baby to be named Teodor, and my family firmly opposed it. Also Tadeusz was suggested. For a long time, Wojtek and I wanted to name him Michał, and that name was opposed by Wojtek's mother. Wojtek and I liked one more name. Finally, he was entered into my identification record and received a birth certificate for the name of Tomasz (nickname Tomek, pronounced: *tomik*) Józef Tomczyk. The middle name came from his two maternal great-grandfathers.

The christening took place in the Good Shepherd's Parish on twelve October, St. Stanislaus Kostka's day. The godparents were my brother Henryk and Elżbieta, Wojtek's sister. It was a sunny, exceptionally warm Sunday.

On the second day after the christening—at my mother's request and according to an old tradition—I went again to the Good Shepherd's Church with my son wrapped in a long pillow, "offering him to God" and asking for his blessing. Father Wiktor Harbich said the prayer for the child and me the mother in the church's sacristy. I found the words of that prayer years later:

> ...Almighty, eternal God, through the birth of our Lord Jesus Christ of the Holy Virgin Mary you have changed the pain of believing mothers into joy. Please look kindly upon this servant of yours who comes full of joy to your temple to

give her thanks. Grant that after worldly life, through the merits and interces-
sion of the same God's Mother, she and her child attain...

He also said a beautiful prayer to bless the child:

...Lord Jesus Christ, son of the living God, eternally begotten, in the worldly
life you wanted to be a child, you love the innocence of that age, you embraced
with love the children you blessed. Surround this child with the sweetness of
your blessing, do not allow anger to change his mind, and keep it growing in
years, wisdom and grace so that you are always pleased with it...

Later, as Tomasz grew up, I often prayed for him with similar words.

November came. Tomek, as we also called him, was three months old. My
mother's monthly leave ended and she had to return to work. Help in the next
month, at first on a trial basis, was offered by Krzysio, who had classes in the
afternoon and for a few days a week could stay with Tomek until three pm. I
arranged my classes at the university so as to be able to return home in time
and stay until five pm, when Mother returned from work. One day a week,
beside Saturdays, was free for students and meant for reading and homework.
Then I could stay home with Tomek for the entire day. There remained four
days with the hours between three to five pm not covered. We carefully
divided the time between us. I managed to shift many classes to earlier hours.
Wojtek's mother didn't want him to participate in our scheduling. She was
worried– he failed exams and found learning quite hard, and she didn't want
to burden him with any additional duties.

My friends from studies were delighted with the news of the first baby
born to one of my student group. I became close friends with Ala Lasoń, a
slender girl, diligent and always prepared for classes. Ala helped her older
sister raise the latter's little son, Pawełek, and now was happy to listen about
little Tomek. For my friends, the second year of studies was also a time of
romance and love. I had a husband and wanted to go with him to special
occasions. But Wojtek didn't like going out, he didn't dance and practically
avoided people. I tried to go out with him for walks or to the cinema. I
enrolled for a course in Morse code, conducted at the university in the department of physics by Jerzy Dresler. I believed we should both make efforts to
make our marriage harmonious and, particularly as we didn't live together, to
have frequent contact and possibly much in common.

Years later, Wojtek chose to immigrate and settled far away in Australia.
His older sister chose Sweden.

The first vacations with my son I spent in a nice village near Skiernie-
wice, known from Reymont's novel[2] —in Lipce Reymontowskie. Here Tomek took his first steps, learned about animals and enjoyed the warmth of the

ripening corn. I took him to the forest or to a meadow and when he slept, I read successive volumes of Proust's *In Search of Lost Time*.

After the summer, I returned to the university. Tomek again stayed with Krzysio in the mornings. As usual, we made schedules for the week and the month, and time flew.

I learned well and with pleasure. Some classes and lectures were particularly interesting. My friendship with Ala thrived. We returned home together, and I told her—in instalments—the story of Sylvie and Annette from Romain Rolland's *The Enchanted Soul*. Discussing professors and public persons, we even told each other of the films we had seen. Both of us were so anxious for experiences and for the outer world. Each slightest echo of the other's affairs left us with an accelerated heartbeat. Individually, neither of us had experienced much of anything, in a way, and we yearned for great joys and serious problems. Both of us admired Clark Gable, and spun tales of him like two schoolgirls. One day we went together to the library on Matejki Street and ordered pre-war editions of the weekly *Film*. Doing a terrible thing, and I'm still ashamed of having done so– we tore out a few pages with the actor's photos and then fairly divided the hauls. I, taught by my Father to respect book and periodicals, committed such a crime! I didn't feel good about my transgression, and when the occasion arose, I immediately confessed to the library's director, Michał Kuna, what I had done, and suggested to him that the mutilated annual volumes of the weekly needed to be supplemented. Michał Kuna, always helpful, always ready to share his time, encouraged me to join the Book Lovers' Association (Towarzystwo Przyjaciół Książki) in Łódź. There I met many passionate book readers, among them Janusz Dunin and Jerzy Andrzejewski. Michał Kuna lent my Father books which were under a publishing ban, and I could borrow from him the immigration editions of the Paris *Kultura (Culture)* monthly the titles of which were in a separate index. My friendship with Michał Kuna lasted for years.

Both Ala and I chose the history of French literature as our specialty. The lectures were held by a great expert in the field, Professor Kazimierz Kupisz. Most people chose Russian literature as their specialty—it was considered "easier"—and a few people went to lectures in classical literature. The lectures of Professor Kupisz had only four students in total. The Professor didn't mind. He spoke in such a captivating manner that we were absolutely awed. Montaigne was my favourite author then. I liked the sadness-filled poetry by Alfred de Musset and the sixteenth century hymns by Ronsard. When the sonnets of Louise Labé, called La Belle Cordière (The Beautiful Ropemaker), were discussed, we listened to the lectures almost with shivers of emotion. Professor Kupisz loved the literature and openness of the French and passed much of his passion to us. I still have a thick notebook with notes from his lectures. A few weeks later it turned out that the teacher of Russian literature resigned, and as a result most people had to change to the lectures of Professor Kupisz. The room was then bursting at the seams, but the small group of people who'd initially chosen the specialty in the beginning were particularly nice and faithful to the Professor.

I spent all the sunny days in the garden with Tomek. There I read the books for the fourth year, and considered the topic of my Master's thesis. The garden and its inhabitants, mainly the dogs, were now a source of joy for my son, like they had once been for me. In the evenings I showed him cartoons on slides on the projector at home. He would cover his face with his hands in particularly dangerous moments. Even when he was somewhat older, he kept doing that. He hid his head under the quilt and asked: "Did they kill him yet? Is it over?..." He snuggled up to me for comfort.

Once I read that the joy of having a child was so natural that you didn't feel it. I think that you do feel the wonderfully beautiful moments, for instance the waking. On Sunday mornings, when I could sleep in, Tomek laid on cushions of the bed, covered with his quilt, and always woke up first. He calmly lay there, keeping his eyes on me and babbling: guh, guh...He didn't protest when I slept longer in the morning, and he spotted my waking immediately. When I opened my eyes and looked at him, he responded with such a beautiful smile that my heart overflowed with happiness. When I closed my eyes again to catch at least ten more minutes of sleep, he didn't let me. He started to demand my attention aloud. He decided that since I was awake, it was time to take care of him. I liked it when he still had that smell of sleep about him, and liked his pyjamas with the pattern of building blocks, sewn by my mother...Mom always repeated that I had to be understanding towards him, but also perfect to some degree. A mother not only needed to *be*, but also had to *seem* flawless to her child. Otherwise she wasn't good. She could have no fault...In comparison to me, my dear mother had such a simple, transparent life.

Wojtek had another month of professional training and military training ahead. He visited us on a regular basis. He came on the motorbike and brought a bottle of milk for Tomek, "fresh from the cow." He showed us much tenderness, but I think he mainly dwelled on his own affairs. He was worried by failed exams—he was repeating a year. I realized we were drifting apart, but I didn't think much about it.

Mother started to prepare my "full trousseau" for that future independent life: she bought sets of towels, pots, plates, spoons, teaspoons, knives and forks, food processors, mixers, etc. She shared her beautiful crystal glass collection, giving me glasses for tea and for wine, as well as grandmom's coloured goblets. In the evenings, she did some machine embroidery with white thread on duvets and pillowcases. I was given exactly a dozen of them. To that she added sheets and blankets, and ordered feather and woollen quilts. Table cloths she embroidered separately, with colourful thread. She didn't want her daughter to start life like she had, having just a few necessary things, but she wanted me to have many useful and pretty things.

In the fourth year of studies, our group was joined by Jacek Bierezin and Witold Sułkowski. They both wrote poems and exhibited a nonchalance in behaviour and a specific atmosphere they created around themselves. Janusz Maciejewski, a Ph.D coming from Warsaw to Łódź every now and again to conduct classes in modern literature, devoted much of his time to them. Maciejewski stayed with them after classes and together they had discussions. Neither Sułkowski nor Bierezin were friends with any student from the group. Older than us, they kept close to each other, but soon dropped out of our class.

Only after quite some time, I learned they were active in politics and that they had trouble. They joined the intellectual and poetic movement called today Nowa Fala—New Wave. The movement, related to a large group of older poets, was characterized by anti-totalitarian attitude, visible in their works and manifested in their lives. In the beginning, the formation was a fronde of a mainly social and café character. I learned about it much later. In 1976, during the events in Ursus and Radom,[3] Jacek Bierezin was the Łódź liaison of the Workers' Defense Committee (KOR).[4] A year later, he and his friends opened *Puls*, an irregular literary quarterly, which later became one of the best periodicals of the pre-Solidarity underground. By August 1980, twelve issues appeared, each of over a hundred pages. It was in *Puls* that Adam Michnik wrote (he reprinted the essay later in *Lektury więzienne—Prison Readings*) that the correspondence between Wańkowicz and Miłosz that I published was "one of the most significant events of Polish freedom," a publication of "Polish Solidarity." After his internment in 1982, Jacek Bierezin immigrated to France. He was involved with the poet and writer Anka Kowalska. Witold Sułkowski immigrated to the United States, and worked in the Voice of America radio. Only much later, in Canada, did I see a volume of poetry by Jacek Bierezin. Titled *Wam* (*To You*), and issued by *Instytut Literacki (Literary Institute)* in 1974, it was a proclamation of the generation's rebellion against totalitarian authorities.

Later, in the United States, in Dallas, I heard about Jacek's tragic death in Paris. In New York's *Przegląd Polski (Polish Review)*, Witold Sułkowski wrote a tribute to him. Among other things, he wrote that Jacek Bierezin was a born athlete and in those last days before his death he passed an examination for a sports instructor, and he'd dreamed of working as a coach for years. He had great hopes that it would be a new start and a rebirth, but he never stopped talking of death, either.

Allegedly, Jacek threw himself in front of a car. They said that after he was hit, he got up and threw himself in front of another car, this time dying instantly.

Such cases of political involvement and awareness at the Łódź University were rare. What struck me most at that time was the lack of any kind of information about modern immigration writers. They weren't mentioned in classes, and their works were unavailable. A great part in making me aware of the writers and accessing them was instigated by my father. I was aware that many girls who studied with me didn't know the names of Czesław Miłosz, Herling-Grudziński, or Józef Mackiewicz. Once I talked to Ala Lasoń and used the expression "Soviet occupation," as my Father used to say. "What are you talking about?" she was amazed. "What Russians? Where?" When I told her of Katyń, she almost refused to listen in terror. She told me her parents had told her that it was only thanks to the Communist system that they could get an apartment in a block, with water supply, gas and electricity, and that she, a daughter of manual workers, could study.

Although under the Russian "yoke," Communism did not flourish in Poland. Collectivization was not enforced, and private enterprise existed. Russian military was not seen on the streets, and no symbols were displayed. The Churches were fully attended, and it was the only country under Soviet influence that regular people (not being involved in anti-government activities) could travel abroad. For example, East Germans or Czechoslovakians could not go abroad.

When my younger brother, Krzysio, started studying at the Łódź Polytechnic Institute, he was unable to devote as many hours a day to Tomek as he had. Our shifts with him became difficult to schedule. But I had more time for my own reading, and fewer lectures. Krzysio earned some extra money, just like Henio, by working physically in his spare time in the students' company Puchatek. I remember Henio buying jeans and then adjusting them to the current fashion—he rubbed them with pumice to get the desired faded colour, cut them, sewed them, and by doing that he broke many a needle in Mother's favourite Singer sewing machine. When Christmas came, Krzysio bought a rocking horse for Tomek as a gift. He spent his hard-earned money not on himself, but on his nephew.

During studies, Krzysio met his future wife, Ania Golańska. They spent their free time together. They went for bicycle trips and often took Tomek with them. Tomek loved his uncles—my brothers—and called them by their first names. He grew up almost like our youngest brother. My father was an authority to him. Tomek listened to him and had obvious respect for him.

Tomek brought me closer to my father again. Our time returned for discussing books that he gave me to read as he once used to. As an adolescent, Tomek was always obedient and disciplined in my father's presence. Slowly, they grew to be very good friends. During examination periods—one in February and one in June—each year for the last three years of my studies, Mom or Dad alternately took Tomek for a two-week holiday—to give me "some peace to prepare for the exams." They did that also for a few years after I graduated, when Tomek grew up from a baby to a boy. They went into the mountains and to the seaside, sent me postcards and came back even closer to each other. Tomek often recalls his trips with Grandmom and Granddad. Preparations started at least a week prior. He remembers getting up early in the morning, going by trolley far to the Kaliski train station. Together, Henio, Father and I (when it was Mother leaving) saw them off. Tomek says that Grandmom looked for a compartment with many older people, because she felt safer travelling in their company.

My mother was constantly knitting something for Tomek, and he wore beautiful sweaters, caps, coats. All his pillow cases were starched and a blinding white. Wojtek's father was a hunter and gave us furs for a coat for Tomek. In it my son looked like a big rabbit.

I was brought colourful baby clothes by a friend from France, Sonia Barylak. She studied Polish literature as a foreigner. She came from a Polish immigrant family from Lyon. Sonia was a very warm person. She visited me at home, and she liked Henio very much. I was friends with Hania Stefankie-wicz for a while. She was a sad blonde-haired girl, constantly lost in thought, living in the dorm. I often invited her home. She told me of her sick mother in Uniejów, and of her older brothers. She somehow clung to my family. For reasons completely unknown, suddenly Hania started to avoid me, or so it seemed. When asked about it, she gave an evasive answer. We lost complete contact, and I even stopped seeing her in class. I heard she wasn't in our class anymore, but I did not know why.

Years later, in the States, Hania suddenly called me. I learned that she'd married and had two boys, and they all lived in Illinois. Soon they moved to Connecticut. They had immigrated to the United States during Poland's Solidarity period and were quite pleased with the choice. Hania told me that back then in Łódź she had a lot of personal problems with her ill mother and little money for studies. When I asked why she'd suddenly broken off our friendship without any explanation, she said that… in a sense she'd been envious of my family, of the atmosphere of warmth and love, and she'd preferred to be alone with her problems. Now, in a new situation, being happy, she very much wanted to keep up the renewed contact.

Ala Lasoń had another friend, the quiet and sensitive Iwona Szewczyk, so I also knew her. We both liked Ewa Kołodrubiec, a calm, delicate girl. Our interest was awakened by Alina Socha, a girl older than us who appeared at the university in our third year. She wore careful make-up and fashionable clothes. She was a model for *Moda Polska (Polish Fashion)* company and had little time for classes. Soon she stopped coming. She had a low voice, was very tall and attractive.

Another interesting group were three very able students, all three by the name of Ewa: Jażdżewska, Chmielewska and Miller. Whenever we met in lectures—sporadically—I was always left highly interested, but we were in different groups for classes, which would allow for more regular meetings, and we never became good friends.

During the penultimate year I took Tomek with me to some of the classes. He could sit there quietly, drawing on paper. Once when we had classes with the professor in pedagogics, Tomek looked at him coming into the room and cried in surprise: "Mom, he's got naked hair!" For the first time he saw a bald person. After his loud comment, I froze in horror, my friends quietly giggled, and the teacher, Piotr Bąk, started classes, which he conducted as always with calm and dignity, as if he'd never heard anything.

Chapter Seven

Melchior Wańkowicz

In my fourth year of studies, I chose the non-fiction and documentary work of the great Polish writer Melchior Wańkowicz for the topic of my Master's thesis. In my opinion, Wańkowicz is Poland's Ernest Hemingway; his life and writings are bigger than life. My advisor, Professor Zdzisław Skwarczyński, grimaced with reluctance on hearing my choice of the topic. [1] He tried to discourage me: "You will have no access to the writer's work published outside of Poland. Maybe you'll consider this obstacle and decide to take a different topic?" I replied I had access to the books by the author of *Kundlizm (Mongrelism)* and that I didn't want to search for another topic. Wańkowicz was a writer much respected in my family home, and his books—generally unavailable—were obtained by my father Henryk, a devoted literature lover. He had many of them in his collection. He highly valued the three-volume Rome edition of *Bitwa o Monte Cassino (Battle of Monte Cassino)* and *Drogą do Urzędowa (The Road to Urzędów)* issued in New York. My father's respect and appreciation for the writer grew particularly after the latter's political trial in 1964. I was also hoping to gain access to some books through the help of the then director of the University Library in Łódź, Michał Kuna, a generous and helpful person. He often enabled one to gain access to books listed separately as not available to everyone due to their political message or their anti-communist authors.

I prepared to engage my topic carefully and systematically. I started with reading the pre-war books by Wańkowicz, such as *Strzępy epopei (Rags of an Epic), W kościołach Meksyku (In the Churches of Mexico), Szpital w Cichiniczach (The Hospital in Cichinicze), Opierzona rewolucja (The Fledging Revolution), Sztafeta (Courier)*. After the war, only *Szczenięce lata (The Puppy Years)* and *Na tropach Smętka (On the Trail of Smętek)* were reissued. I read of the critics' reaction to the books and their reviews published

69

both in pre-war and post-war papers. I wrote a separate essay on *Strzępy epopei* and the book *Moje wspomnienia* (*My memoirs*) by General Józef Dowbor-Muśnicki. Then I read the books: *Wrzesień żagwiący, (September Aflame) Dzieje rodziny Korzeniowskich (The Korzniewski Family Saga), Kundlizm, Drogą do Urzędowa, Tworzywo (Matter), Ziele na kraterze (Herbs at the Crater).* I had trouble accessing *De profundis* issued in Tel-Aviv, and *Polacy i Ameryka* (*Poles and America*) issued in New York.

Finally—I wrote a letter to the writer, in which I carefully outlined my problems. The address wasn't difficult to find. Soon I received an answer inviting me to Warsaw for a short afternoon meeting. He set the day and time: twenty of May 1972, at five p.m.

I was excited and was looking forward to the meeting awaiting me. I came to Warsaw early in the afternoon, took a streetcar, disembarked earlier and walked slowly down Marszałkowska Street. The last half-hour I spent drinking tea in a café, just opposite the Wańkowicz's home, at the corner of Puławska and Rakowiecka Streets. The café was adjacent to the *Moskwa* cinema, that was torn down after 1989, and where a trade and banking center now stands.

To reach the apartment No. 35 on 10 Puławska Street, you took the elevator to the sixth floor, then you had to take the stairs to go up one floor. When I rang the door bell, the door was opened by Wańkowicz himself. He invited me to the sitting room, beautifully furnished with period furniture including a period couch, armchairs, a writing desk, a secretary, on which stood a Philips box radio, a small table with a TV, a divan with a hand-painted *toile de Geneve* canvas hanging above it, an antique table with a chair, and a small folding Chippendale table. Above the couch, two historic sashes were hung (richly embroidered garments once worn by nobility), a copy of Walenty Wańkowicz's[2] painting *Mickiewicz na Judahu skale,*[3] a framed inscription and signatures of people gathered at the fiftieth wedding anniversary of Zofia and Melchior Wańkowicz. Almost the whole floor was covered with a carpet. Many family pictures in decorative frames stood on the shelves and tables.

I was offered coffee and a chocolate cake from Wedel[4] served by the housekeeper on a small silver tray in the shape of a leaf, and observed everything curiously, mainly Wańkowicz himself. Having a broad face, and rather long, disheveled hair, his heavy-lidded eyes were lively and sharp. He seemed large and obese to me, but his moves were light-footed, and thus he avoided the impression of being heavy. There was something dignified, something of a nobleman, in the moves of the large framed man. An aura of coldness, impatience and weariness seemed to envelope the writer.

"Which of my books have you read?" he asked me. "Tell me directly with what problems you have come to me. I have no more than forty-five minutes. This is how much time I usually give journalists visiting me."

"I know almost all your books," I replied. "I also know the critics' reactions to some of them. I have many questions, all of them written down..." I opened a large, academic notebook.

He looked at my notes.

"Have you read them? Even the pre-war ones, not re-issued after the war? Do you know *Opierzona rewolucja* and *Strzępy epopei*? Do you know my books published outside of Poland?..." He asked questions one after the other.

"My father has in his collection, for example, *Drogą do Urzędowa*...I have brought a few of my essays prepared for university classes, concerning your books, for instance on *Strzępy epopei*..."

"Could you show them to me?..." He interrupted our conversation, took my typescripts and started to read. The first ten minutes passed. I drank the coffee, ate the cakes and glanced at him. He seemed completely engrossed in the reading, and paid me no attention. *I hope I can reasonably use the time left*, I thought.

"You are capable of critical thinking," he said, interrupting his reading and giving me a close look. "You have prepared yourself carefully and read my books and their reviews. I've forgotten about some matters, and thanks to you I'm recalling them now."

Wańkowicz grew gentler, his voice became warmer, and the whole atmosphere changed from tense and impatient to warm and pleasant. He asked questions, one after another and seemed pleased with my answers and maybe somewhat surprised by them.

"You know, I am approached by students who write their Master's theses on my work, and then it turns out that they have come to me with scanty knowledge. They know just a few books, as if they'd come across them by chance, and give all sorts of explanations. And I feel as if they want to see me like some monkey in a zoo. As if my time didn't matter to them. And my time is very dear to me."

He started to talk about himself, about a new book, which he hadn't titled yet. He planned to share in it his observations from his whole life, concerning work and the very process of writing. He still needed to collect much material for it.

"At my age, when I don't travel anymore and don't collect materials for reportages, I would like to tell others how I used to do it. The old heron, he laughed, cannot fish anymore, but it wants to tell of it and it may teach others something. I need many examples of how others did it and still do it, both writers and artists, creative people. What the creativity process itself consists of, if there is inspiration or not, what the greatest obstacle on the outside is, what dangers reside within us. What conditions are needed to write, if we impose them ourselves, or submit ourselves to them. For instance, Hemingway wrote while standing at a writing desk and liked the smell of apples being dried."

An hour passed, then another one. Wańkowicz suggested that we have supper together. It had been prepared by the housekeeper in the kitchen. The kitchen itself was spacious. It consisted of two sections: a dining part with a large table and a glassed cabinet, and a section for preparing and cooking the meals. Supper consisted of cold meat and salad. Wańkowicz kept asking new questions, also about me and my family. After supper we went to a long, narrow study. By the window stood a desk, and at the desk a huge, comfortable armchair on wheels was positioned. From the window and the door leading out onto a small balcony, Puławska Street could be viewed. Next to the desk, a glassed bookcase stood, a table, and another, smaller one. There were many pictures, including four portraits—of the writer, his wife, and daughters: Krystyna and Marta. A beautiful Mexican saddlecloth, embroidered mainly in red and golden threads, drew my eyes. Both the longer walls were covered by shelves that reached the ceiling with each shelf tightly packed with books. Wańkowicz was clearly pleased to show me his—as he put it—aids: two tape recorders, and cameras including his famous Leica. He liked technological novelties. I can imagine how he would have appreciated the computer and the Internet.

We sat on small sofas opposite each other. The study seemed cramped, but also carefully furnished and cozy. Wańkowicz talked much and while talking, looked at me closely. I discovered features in him that were new for me: patience, softness and some authentic openness.

He told me then of his unpleasant experience with a researcher, Aleksander Horodyski-Kotecki, who helped him gather materials for the book *Wojna i pióro* (*War and Pen*) and later wanted to be considered as co-author.

"I now suggest that you gather for me the materials I need for my newest book," he said.

He showed me a precise plan he'd prepared of chapters with working titles, with subheadings and additional notes. He gave me copies of the plan and explained that he expected me to prepare quotations on "notesheets". The notesheets were to be of a particular size about one-half of a standard page, and have the number of the main plan, subheading and chapter written in the corner. The quoted fragment was to have a full bibliography of the quoted source. I was to use mainly books that were monographs and biographies. The writer offered me an advance payment of five hundred zlotys, quite a sum for my student pocket. I was to define independently the hours I worked. If the cooperation went well, I was to come to Warsaw twice a month with new material.

I was honored and pleased with the proposal. The whole meeting surpassed all my wildest dreams or expectations. Wańkowicz asked me to come the next day, Sunday, at ten a.m., to accompany him to the book fair, during which he had two hours to sign his books. I happily agreed to his invitation and stayed overnight at the student guest house at Warsaw University. In front of the Palace of Culture, bookstalls of renowned publishing houses presented novelties and titles published within the last year. Usually whole crowds of people gathered there who wanted to buy books and use the occasion to obtain an autograph from their favorite writer. That day, in front of the PIW[5] publishing house bookstall, who had organized the meeting with Wańkowicz, a long queue had been standing for the last hour. Each of the people in the queue had brought from home several copies of the writer's books, planning to also buy some re-issued titles at the fair and acquire a signature on each book. The PIW publishing house had issued a collection of the writer's articles, *Przez cztery klimaty. 1912-1972 (Through Four Climates. 1912-1972).* This was a new title, and everyone wanted to buy it. When Wańkowicz's characteristic figure appeared, he was immediately surrounded with a crowd of people. He was clearly pleased with that. He talked to some people, showed interest in their affairs. He sat down in the chair and, not raising his eyes from the books, he silently signed his name on the copy put before him. I was sitting next to him; he asked me to write the date.

He became tired. After an hour, his pen moved slower and slower with each signature. The queue was moving slowly, and it wasn't certain if Wańkowicz would be able to sign the books for all the interested people on that day. At some point a woman holding a boy in her arms said: "Start reciting, Piotruś..." The little Piotruś began to recite fragments of *Ziele na kraterze*. Wańkowicz stopped signing the books for a few minutes, but then he noticed people were getting impatient, and came back to signing, paying no more attention to the reciting boy. The mother, clearly offended with his indifference, took the boy away, mumbling something to herself.

I was dazed by it all, also with the sad event. I felt sorry both for the boy and for his ambitious mother. I understood it was difficult for Wańkowicz to find a way out of the situation without hurting someone's feelings, but I expected him to show perhaps some more understanding. When I returned to the subject later, the writer told me how people tired him more and more, and how difficult it was to meet the often importunate and unpleasant requirements and expectations. He was glad to meet people, he needed them, but at the same time they often tired and annoyed him.

After the book fair, we had dinner in the Palace of Culture, in a Russian restaurant *Trojka*. Following our dinner together, Wańkowicz took me to the train station. We agreed that I was to come in two weeks with the first portion of the materials that I had gathered. I was taking a true treasure with me to Łódź: a few books with his inscription, and also I was taking one of the files from the writer's archives. So that I could read its contents at home, he lent it to me with the admonition, "You've come to gather materials for your Master's thesis—seek them in my archives yourself."

Only after some time was I able to fully appreciate the gesture and the trust placed in me by the writer. I saw how reluctantly, distrustfully, he allowed others even a peek in his archives materials on site...and he allowed me to take them to Łódź!

Now, after years, I think that after his unpleasant experience with the researcher Aleksander Horodyski-Kotecki who judged himself a co-author of their book, when Wańkowicz saw in me such an "eager beaver university student," he thought he might obtain material for a new book not fearing that the student researcher would come up with a similar idea.

I returned home with lots of enthusiasm as to my plans for the near future. At once, I borrowed some biographical books about writers and artists and started reading them with regard to the book that Wańkowicz was preparing. I didn't have to spend time in the library searching for materials for my thesis. With the materials I'd brought from Warsaw, I could work with them at home.

After the two weeks had passed, I came to Warsaw and brought the materials I'd collected on cards. Wańkowicz read them and decided that he was "employing me as his 'researcher.'" I returned the file from his archives, and took another one to Łódź. My Master's thesis was developing well, I read many books and wrote the quotations onto the notesheets.

Regularly, every two weeks, I came to Warsaw by train on Saturday. Nearly every week there came a letter, sometimes two, informing me what my employer-boss was expecting of me. Work on the book went smoothly. The writer decided to prepare two volumes. He also gave the book a final title: *Karafka La Fontaine'a (La Fontaine's Carafe).* He chose it to emphasize the diversity and objectivism of his view and opinion. At that time—as well as later—he very much stressed the feature, which he'd come to value particularly. The title came from an anecdote. La Fontaine was once asked to settle a dispute arisen among the revelers gathered in the inn. In the middle of the table there stood a crystal decanter with wine. Sun rays were coming through the window and reflecting off the carafe. One of the revelers said they were reflected red. Another denied, saying it was blue. The third one said it was pink. When asked, La Fontaine went around the table and said that each of the men was right: depending on the side you were looking from, as the sun refracted in the carafe it showed different colors. What was most important, as he said, was to see all the colors together, to understand there wasn't just one.

The second volume of *Karafka La Fontaine'a* is dedicated to me: "To my Assistant, Aleksandra Ziółkowska, without whose committed cooperation this book would most likely have been worse than it is."

This dedication to me was an extraordinary gift, just like bequeathing his archives to me in his last will had been one. I believed then—and I still do—

that I owed a debt of gratitude towards the hope pinned on me, towards the confidence the writer had placed in me, and that I ought to pay that debt in any way I could. I have always endeavored to do so, and I always will do so.

For the first money I'd earned and saved, I bought a winter sheepskin coat, which I was very pleased with. Spring passed, summer came, vacation was slowly coming on. Wańkowicz sent a letter to my parents. Asking that I stay for two weeks in the Artists' Retreat in Obory near Warsaw, he wrote e.g.:

> ...In closing, in the foremost I should like to express my remorse towards the Mother. I am somewhat more certain of the Father due to his interests. We would find much in common: I knew personally Dmowski, Balicki, Zygmunt Wasilewski, was a correspondent of the Warsaw Gazette (Gazeta Warszaws-ka) etc. I would be extremely pleased if, visiting Warsaw, you would be as kind as to accept a dinner invitation, and by that occasion I could show you my archives and my (truly modest) library, in the case of which I would like to ask your advice. I shake your hand, Sir, and kiss the Lady's hands—Melchior Wańkowicz. 9th August 1972.

I spent two weeks in the Artists' Retreat in Obory near Warsaw, working on the book. Before I even completed studies and defended my thesis, Wańkowicz had offered me a permanent job as his secretary and assistant. Knowing I wanted to write a doctoral thesis, he himself phoned Professor Julian Krzyżanowski asking him to be my guidance counselor.[6] Altogether, from that day we'd met, when I was completing studies and coming regularly to Warsaw for a year, then as I moved to Warsaw and worked permanently— until the writer's death in September 1974—two years and four months had passed. Such a short time, and so important. So vitally important.

For long days, Wańkowicz was working on the book, which fully en-grossed him and which was the most important matter to him. He required much of me, and I think I submitted to his authority. To watch and to some extent participate in the book's creation was for me a truly fascinating expe-rience. I felt tremendous awe, respect, and almost girlish admiration for the writer. He had a fascinating personality. He always had a great sense of humor. Life lived next to him was nearly a run of interesting events, conver-sations, often surprises. He gave much of his attention and time to me. Noting that I was very anxious to absorb all and very grateful, time was taken to explain to me things I didn't know or hadn't done before. Having much patience for me, almost as if he was placing much hope in me, the eminent writer spoke of the need to learn, to gain as many "skills" in life as possible.

"You never know when you may need them. And it's also worth knowing well something that is very practical. Each person," he said, "should have their own selected discipline about which they know a lot, about which they want to learn something new all the time. Have a passion. You cannot know

the whole literature. Choose one writer, but get to know his works thoroughly." (Years later, one of my friends added to it: "You may choose one title,
one book, but learn everything about it. I would choose *The Magic Mountain*
by Thomas Mann.")

Wańkowicz told me about himself, his life. Sometimes it seemed to me
that he did it to make me think in new categories. I think he wanted to show
me that life wasn't grey or rosy, that it often had the color and sense that we
gave to it ourselves. "Aim high." I remembered a Japanese proverb: "When
you fall, never get up empty-handed." Wańkowicz added a Polish one: "If
you're going to fall, let it be from a high horse...The heavier you fall, the
stronger you will bounce back..."

Years later I learned one more saying: "If you aim high, you'll get high.
Even halfway up it is already high. If you aim at an average level, you'll
attain less. If you aim low, you'll attain nothing..."

He told me much about the hardships in his life and how he overcame
them later. He spoke of the significance of hardships, difficulties, challenging situations in human life.

"After years, some good may come out of them for you," he said. "You
might not understand that yet, but remember this. It is important how you
treat them. Whether you yield to them and surrender, or struggle up and
make them a value."

There is often in our lives one event that everything begins from and everything comes back to. One experience which gives this special psychological
hue. One day which makes you see the world and yourself in a different light.
It may be an illness you or someone close to you suffers, death, love, child-
birth, an artistic experience, a journey, a meeting. Later, although there are
some greater and more important things that came, events are divided into
"before" and "after."

For a long time I used to say that something happened "before I'd met
Wańkowicz"...

For a long time now, I haven't said that. So many years have passed that
almost everything qualifies under "after meeting Wańkowicz."

The work with Wańkowicz opened areas to me of which I had only
known from obscure accounts of others. Wańkowicz and his work, his surroundings, everything fascinated me. A two-and-a-half-year period began in
my life when I was staying in the immediate proximity of the writer. There
are board games for children where a pawn standing on a specific field
moves several places ahead. Something like that happened in my life as a
humble student of the Łódź University at the moment I met the author of
Karafka La Fontaine'a. When I started working for him, my life gained pace
and excitement. My observations began to concern issues that were important, serious, that required manifold sensitivity. I was also aware of myself

being a subject of processing, creating, molding by another, powerful personality.

I didn't mind that—on the contrary, it impressed and pleased me. I was at an age where it might be the easiest to accept and soak up learning and criticism. I submitted myself to the atmosphere, the requirements, the discipline of work, the rhythm of the day imposed by the writer. As he said himself, he had less and less time left, and he very much wanted to do something sensible with it. Writing was his job, life choice, passion and love. In me, he saw a person committed to him, one who knew his books and their topics well, and who had much respect, esteem, sometimes admiration for them. Yet the said admiration was not as childish or irritating as to disturb his work, but rather allowed him to push the work forward. I was committed to him and didn't protest when he imposed sometimes difficult working conditions, particularly as concerned the number of hours we worked. Maybe if I had been older and had a more settled private life, it would have been more difficult for me to reconcile my work for Wańkowicz with my personal life. When we grow up, we often start—be it right or wrong—to value ourselves in some stubborn way. We often refuse to devote ourselves fully and with dedication to anything. We either have no time for that, or life itself tempts us too much and distracts us in the possible choices. Wańkowicz taught me to work, focus, pay attention, concentrate, to use the time well.

> Don't waste time, don't waste the days. If you work, commit yourself to it. When you feel tired, rest, but plan your leisure. Be aware of the passing of time. Have no empty days. Fill them—with work, reading, play, or sport. But try to watch what is happening with you. Don't spend days doing nothing...Learn life, and get to know people. When Adam and Eve, expelled from Paradise, caught their first breath of earthly air, they were able to know love, jealousy, deceit, meanness, envy, desire and weakness. And such are whole generations of people. Look at them, and that knowledge will support you and add to your own strength.

He said: "Get tight and tough. Watch, and try things yourself. But whatever you see or do, do it for future topics. Don't let anything pull or suck you in. Someone changed into a tree cannot paint it. To paint a tree well, you have to take a good look from up close, then turn away and look from afar..."

Thus, *Karafka La Fontaine'a* is a book very close to me. As is the lesson that light often refracts in a different color for each person, and that a writer tries to see them all. I also came to understand the great difficulty of grasping and naming what the creative process actually is.

In Obory, Wańkowicz read the newest volumes of Czesław Miłosz's poetry, lent to him by Grażyna and Andrzej Miłosz. We sat at the table together for meals. Wańkowicz joked with the attractive Grażyna, calling her his "little squirrel," and asked Andrzej about his childhood. I listened with particular interest to stories about the area of Nevėžis, a river in Lithuania, also close to the brothers Czesław and Andrzej Miłosz. Nevėžis, joining into the Niemen River, flowed through Kėdainiai and Panevėžys. The estate of Nowotrzeby (Lith. Naujatriobiai), owned by Melchior Wańkowicz's grandmother, Feliksa Szwoynicka was on the Nevėžis River. The writer had spent his childhood in Nowotrzeby, and wrote about it in *Szczenięce lata*. In the evenings, I copied some poems by Miłosz too keep for myself. Among the guests in Obory, I remember the poets Ludwik Bohdan Grzeniewski and Janina Brzostowska, who translated Sappho. She gave me her volume of poetry with a tender inscription, which Wańkowicz looked at with funny fake suspicion. The writer was also visited by the editor-in-chief of the *Nowe Książki* monthly,[7] Zenona Macużanka, who brought him much fresh news about fellow writers and politicians. Also visiting were the lawyers: Władysław Siła-Nowicki, Olgierd Missuna, Adam Dobrowolski, or Stanisław Śniechórski, with whom he discussed the current trials in court.

Wańkowicz had filed three legal suits in total. The first, filed in 1972 (earlier the case was dismissed by the court without an explanation) against Tadeusz Walichnowski, concerned the book *Na tropach Smętka*. In his book *Warmia, Mazury, Powiśle,*[8] Walichnowski accused the writer that *Na tropach Smętka* brought about the death of many people, for which the author benefited from fame and money. During the trial, the writer proved that before the book was printed, he'd given the typescript to representatives of Polish organisations in Germany to read. The typescript had been read by Polish consuls in the East Prussia area of ethnographically Polish land— consul Zalewski in Olsztyn, consul Rogalski in Pisz, vice-president of the Union of Poles in Germany, staying in Warmia, Kazimierz Donimirski, who authorized the writer to reproduce the written threats of Nazi storm-troopers in the book. Then the typescript was assessed by the Institute for Study of Nationality Issues,[9] whose president was Leon Wasilewski. The latter's successor Stanisław Paprocki also read the book. Next, the book was given to the director of the Polish Western Association,[10] Bolesław Srocki, and then to the Foreign Affairs committee, where a report on it was presented by the department director, Drymmer. As a result, the research brought high appraisal of the book, which was deemed most beneficial. Finally, the typescript was presented to the Union of Poles in Germany, not only in order to gain a general opinion, but to define the final and complete list of names which could be given in the text. Names of people actively engaged were deleted. Names of old people, who passively expressed pro-Polish sympathies, were left in. Of all the other persons that would be worth mentioning, only the name of Kiwicki was left, who had bought a little shop in Działdów for ten thousand zlotys. The widow of the activist killed during the plebiscite, whose testimony was tragic, was offered a place in an old people's home in Pomerania. Names that were left in the typescript included that of the eighty-year-old Kajka, who had a Nazi family and refused an interview, the name of the missionary Barcz, whose religious missions conducted in Polish were so numerous and popular that naming him in the book was no revelation, as well as that of Kazimierz Donimirski, who himself suggested to use the interview with him. Wańkowicz obtained a statement from the head of the Union of Poles in Germany, Jan Kaczmarek, who used words stating that without any doubt the people and organizations in all areas in Germany suffered during the war just as much as in East Prussia and that the book did not bring about greater persecutions than occurred elsewhere. The suit filed by Wańkowicz against Walichnowski ended only two years after the writer's death. In January 1976, the Supreme Court decided that the accusations against Wańkowicz were groundless.

The second trial, against Strumph-Wojtkiewicz, concerned the times of *Rój*.[11] In his book *O własnych siłach* (*On Your Own*) Stanisław Strumph-Wojtkiewicz wrote that as director of the *Rój* publishing house the writer..."overprinted the editions, provided a figurehead aunt"...Earlier, Wańkowicz had written a study about him *Czaruś w grobowcu Szujskich. Polski Münchhausen* (*Czaruś in the Szujskis' Tomb. Polish Münchhausen*), which he published in the *Przez cztery klimaty* collection. In the study, Wańkowicz had pointed out the man's lies and hypocrisy. Now, deeply perturbed by Strumph-Wojtkiewicz's slander, he filed a suit. The author demanded the fragment be deleted from possible further editions, an apology issued in the *Życie Warszawy (Life of Warsaw)* daily and five thousand zlotys paid to the Red Cross. Wańkowicz won the trial.

I was present at one of the trials, when witnesses were examined. The court examined Henryk Ładosz, working in the Polish radio, who in the 1930s recited texts in children's programs as a "radio uncle." They also examined Jarosław Iwaszkiewicz, called as a witness by Strumph. Before the war, *Rój* had rejected Iwaszkiewicz's *Brzezina (Birch Wood)*. Wańkowicz said much later that it had been a publishing mistake. During the trial, Iwaszkiewicz and Ładosz said that they didn't remember those years so well and couldn't say anything in the case. Iwaszkiewicz was never a friend to Wańkowicz and surely he would gladly have said something against him.

Wańkowicz complained of having an exceptionally bothersome trait: he couldn't remember faces. It was true. Frequently, he would lean over to me and furtively ask to remind him of the name of the person he was talking to, and who spoke to him like to a good friend. Once we were given a ride by Danusia and Szymon Kobyliński.[12] Szymon had that characteristic face with the large beard, and a peculiar manner of expression...Wańkowicz asked me quietly, "Remind me of the name." I whispered it to him and he immediately "got it." He asked about Maciek, the son of Danusia and Szymon, about the dogs, which he remembered by names. He felt embarrassed with his inability to recognize faces, and tried to hide it. For people whom he saw often, his recollection was no problem. The Kobylińskis were quite frequent guests in Nadliwie and were always recognized. On one occasion, the Kobylińskis visited the author with an elderly lady, who said that during her youth she'd made a boat trip with Melchior. Danusia and Szymon were ready for an evening filled with memories. But Wańkowicz barely looked at the woman, and asked Szymon about various new things. The guest was nearly ignored. Wańkowicz didn't need her in terms of writing, he wasn't writing recollections of his early youth and would have considered talking to her a waste of time.

I wouldn't want to "demonize" that trait of not recognizing people. The writer said that he met new people all the time and later, seeing them again, they didn't introduce themselves. Wańkowicz usually didn't remember in what circumstances he'd met them, although their faces were familiar. He told me that in 1958 when he returned to Poland for good, many new people were introduced to him, and he was reacquainting himself with those he remembered from before the war. At one of the parties, he was approached by the known writer Jaroslaw Iwaszkiewicz, and they spoke to each other for a long time. Sometime later Iwaszkiewicz came to him about some issue. Wańkowicz interrupted him and asked, "Excuse me, would you reintroduce yourself?" Iwaszkiewicz gave him an icy stare and left.

The appearance of the name of Iwaszkiewicz in relation with the trial of Strumph-Wojtkiewicz had further repercussions. Somehow, they were related in a way with me. Marta Miklaszewska, a journalist whom Wańkowicz valued and was friends with, told us that on the trial in court Strumph's lawyer told her that "...the young blonde accompanying Wańkowicz is his wife."

"How do you know?" Marta was surprised.

"From Iwaszkiewicz," the lawyer said.

Certainly Wańkowicz was perturbed with the news he heard. The marriage rumours concerned my predecessor, the writer's secretary, Miss Alicja, but they were also transferred onto me. He told Kąkolewski about it in the exceptional interview-book *Wańkowicz krzepi* (*Wańkowicz Strengthens*).[13] (quote: "Glad that the gossips had their fun once and got tired, because there is no new gossip about my marriage. If so, then it must be those old rumours reaching the least informed.") Shortly thereafter, the writer wrote a letter to Iwaszkiewicz, in which he stated he was surprised with the man spreading false information, rehashing old rumours. He explained I was a "serious person", who wrote a doctoral thesis on his work, had a child I raised by myself, etc. Soon a letter came from Iwaszkiewicz. He wrote that he didn't understand why Wańkowicz was so upset with being suspected of a marriage with a young girl, that there have been cases of very late marriages of elderly writers and artists with young women. He even gave a few names. In the end, he noted that the word "rehash" was spelled differently. The next letter Wańkowicz dictated to me. He stated that he also knew many cases of relationships of older men and very young women, added a few names to the list given by Iwaszkiewicz, but that in his case no such circumstance had arisen and that he was surprised that the president of the Writers' Union spread such unverified information. In the postscript he added: "Thank you for telling me how the word «rehash» was spelled. I didn't know."

A few days after the death of Wańkowicz, Iwaszkiewicz read those letters at a meeting and made sport of them. The editors of *Szpilki*[14] *(Pins)* asked me to make those letters available to them. I believed it improper to print that correspondence a few months after the writer's death, and so I refused.

The third trial concerned a breach of copyright. The writer filed a suit against Władysław Machejek editor-in-chief of the Kraków weekly *Życie Literackie (Literary Life)*. Without reviewing it with the writer and seeking his agreement to it, Machejek printed the essay on war he'd been sent by the author, shortening it by a third, even summarizing certain fragments. "Those are ever more frequent practices used by papers, and I want to help young journalists with this case. Cuts without prior agreement infringe on the copyright. I would like people to respect us writers," Wańkowicz stated.

In Obory, I met Joanna and Krzysztof Kąkolewski for the first time. Later, I became good friends with them, and they became particularly close to me in Warsaw. Krzysztof came to authorize the typescript of *Wańkowicz krzepi*. Joanna and I went for a walk, and the men locked themselves up in the room. Joasia (Joanna), not much older than me, pretty, with long, dark, flowing hair, spoke of Krzysztof per "partner." She was so different, and attracted attention so much, that I looked at her with quite an interest. When we returned from the walk, I saw that the talks between the men did not end unanimously. Wańkowicz asked for the typescript to be left with him.

Wańkowicz spent several hours over it during the next days. He worked so diligently that above almost each statement he wrote by hand a new version of his own. When Kąkolewski came again, he was surprised and protested.

"But I have different statements in my notes, you said something else!" he exclaimed.

"Even if I said something else, now, in the final authorization, I have the right to change it. You speak differently during a meeting of several hours, and differently if the words are to be printed. My right is to give a final shape to my statements," explained Wańkowicz.

When the book was finally printed, Wańkowicz read in Kraków literary *Zeszyty Prasoznawcze*[15] (*Press Studies Brochures*) an essay on the contribution and work of the interviewer. The author (Paweł Dubiel) wondered if in the case of interviews should the fee be split in half—between the author and the protagonist of the interview. Wańkowicz tore out the pages with the essay and asked me to send it to Kąkolewski's address from Łódź, with the envelope addressed by hand. I did that. Wańkowicz thought it was a good joke, and expected Kąkolewski's reaction. Yet the man never responded.

Years later Krzysztof told me he had immediately guessed the article had been sent on a suggestion of Wańkowicz. While visiting him, he even noticed the issue of *Zeszyty Prasoznawcze* with the missing pages. "I guessed you did it per the writer's instruction...I forgive you," he added.

Wańkowicz krzepi became a bestseller, was reissued a few times, and was popular among the readers. At the same time, a biographical book on the author of *Bitwa o Monte Cassino* was being written by Mieczysław Kurzyna. Wańkowicz gave him some of his time and allowed use of the archives, and finally read the typescript of the book entitled *O Wańkowiczu—nie wszystko* (*About Wańkowicz—But Not Everything*). The typescript was also read by Marta Erdman, the writer's daughter, when she was in Poland. She had a very good opinion of it, much better than her father.

That summer I went for ten September days to the Artists' Retreat of ZAIKS[16] in Konstancin. Wańkowicz sent another letter to my parents, asking for their cooperation by caring for Tomek. The writer was full of energy and enthusiasm for the book he was writing. The first volume was finished, and we started working on the second one. Two chapters from the first volume, *Krytyka (Criticism)* and *Cenzura (Censorship)* Wańkowicz shifted to the second one. Anticipating there would be problems with the censors, he wanted the first volume to be already in print. In Konstancin, we sat at a table with the poet Jerzy Zagórski and his wife. Wańkowicz conducted an amusing argument for the right to a few hours of quiet with Witold Małcużyński, who regularly practiced on the piano. Finally, the two gentlemen set out working hours when they were supposed not to disturb each other.

In Konstancin, I met Roman Rodziewicz. He came to Poland from England and called Wańkowicz, whom he always contacted when in Poland. He visited the country every few years.

"You will meet an interesting man. I met him when he was a boy, and I was travelling in Kresy [Borderlands[17]] before the war. I stayed for a time in an estate belonging to his uncle, Ławski Bród, located amongst fjords, mountain passes and precipitous routes. As one of the most beautiful Polish landscapes (*Zabrzezie commune, Volozhin district*[18]), I named it *Polish Switzerland* in my reportages from Kresy. There, in that land, Polishness grew like a hundred-year-old oak grove, the language there was juicy and soft, and people were always ready to sacrifice. For several centuries, the land belonged to the Rodziewicz family, of Tartar roots, with a quiver and an arrow in their Tarnawa coat of arms. I met Roman again in Italy, after the war. He was an adult by then. I was introduced to him by Mrs. Papée, wife of the ambassador and sister of Major Dobrzański, Hubal.[19] He told me the history of Hubal's unit, which he had belonged to from the very first to the very last day of its existence. He is a noble man, and a great soldier. I wrote the book *Hubalczycy* (*Hubal Soldiers*) based on the story he'd told me. I wanted to share my author's fee with him, but he refused. When you meet him, take note of his hands. He has the large hands of a working man. He works very hard..."

Roman was accompanied by another Hubal soldier, Józef Drabik. We all went to the *Świerkowa* restaurant in Konstancin. We ordered crayfish, and Roman told us many stories. In some way, he was still reliving the details about Major Hubal himself, his death, the history of his unit. Roman was straightforward and noble. I watched him with interest. Little did I know at the time that we would become friends, and I would write a book based on his life.

Since the news spread among my friends that I was working with Wańkowicz, many people approached me with various agendas. The easiest thing was to obtain the writer's autograph. More difficult was inviting the author of *Ziele na kraterze* to an author's meeting. For a meeting with scouts organised by Bohdan Kosmynka in the Łódź Youth Community Centre, he agreed to come. My friends, Ala and Sonia, came too, along with Henio and Krzysio with Ania, his fiancée. In a picture from the event, we are all happy, and I have my arm linked through one of Wańkowicz, who seems to be in a brilliant mood. Ala is standing on his other side, and Sonia is talking to Henio, clearly happy.

Wańkowicz told me of a funny event, or actually of a reaction to it. For my twenty-third birthday, on fifteen April he took me to dinner in the historic Hotel Europejski. The time was late, people started dancing, we drank some champagne, had dinner and left. A few days later, the writer was told that Stanisław Stomma, a Catholic columnist, reported he had seen Wańkowicz in a restaurant "late evening, with a chick." The writer immediately retorted: "And what was that pious person doing in that place at such a time?"

I started the fifth year of my studies—the last one. I had fewer classes, more time for writing my thesis, and thus more time to spend at home. Tomek grew up with the image of his mother reading till late at night, and typing during the day. Playing next to me, every now and then, Tomek would demand I focus on him. His independent nature was gaining shape, becoming somewhat stubborn and sensitive.

Tomek usually played alone, created battlefields and acting out battles. He was preoccupied with his LEGO blocks, drawing and painting. Krzysio taught him to play chess, just like he made him interested in photography years later. After a while, chess became Tomek's favorite pastime. He wanted and asked me to play with him, but I dodged it. Chess required time, focus, and constant exercise. I wasn't fascinated by chess, and Tomek was very upset about that. Thus, he played against Krzysio and against himself. He was able to play alone. I remember teaching him his first abstract word: "loyalty." Once I told Mother about one of his stunts and he gave me a look full of disappointment and cried: "You're not lolal, you're not lolal" (for a long time, he couldn't say "yell," always saying "lell"). Since then, the sense of loyalty was very important and observed between us.

He kept on creating new words. Children's neologisms are so remarkable: to uncell (to free someone), to port something (to anchor something), a holdinger (a hand).

He had strong protective urges in himself, and sometimes they did have very moving effects. He didn't want to go for a walk holding my hand—he broke free and ran ahead. I told him then:

"Look, it's so uneven here, so many holes, I might fall in them..."

"Are you scared?" he asked.

He took my hand then and led me. He was taking me for a walk.

I started to publish my articles in a Łódź daily. The first time I went to the associate editor, Stefan Kotlarek, and showed him an article about my struggles with learning to drive. He acted kindly, and I was very happy when he printed the text I gave him. I started to bring him features about a photographer from Łódź, Mr. Mirecki, reviews of Wańkowicz's book *Wojna i pióro* the visit in Gniazdów, in the beautiful house of Danusia and Szymon Kobyliński. I remember the kindness of Mr. Kotlarek towards me with gratefulness. A Łódź weekly *Odgłosy* (*Sounds*) printed my interview with Wańkowicz concerning Łódź themes in the book *Tworzywo* and the writer's new plans. The interview was severely shortened without any agreement with me or the writer, but it was strongly publicized. Further texts I published in a Warsaw monthly *Więź* (*Bond*) and the weekly *Literatura* (*Literature*).

My trips to Warsaw and the increasingly better collaboration with Wańkowicz gave me a lot of satisfaction. Once—at the writer's persuasion— I took Tomek with me. We all went to the Warsaw zoo. The boy was running about and enjoying the trip. Wańkowicz made pictures of him with his Leica. We all came back tired, and Tomek started to act weary and sleepy. Although tired, Wańkowicz found the strength to tell him about the pets of his childhood as a good night story. The child regained his strength and good humor and demanded more, and finally absolutely overcame the writer and me.

When Wańkowicz's daughter and son-in-law, Marta (called Tili) and Jan Erdman, visited Poland, I was able to meet them. I imagined Marta's appearance differently. Always it seems that the protagonists of books and films (and she was the protagonist of the books *Na tropach Smętka* and *Ziele na kraterze*) seem different to us, taller, younger and more beautiful. Marta turned out to be a rather short lady of my mother's age, usually wearing broad pants. She had greying hair, smoothed back, and wore large glasses. Yet her eyes and look were youthful. When she spoke, you immediately surrendered to her charm. Marta was a true lady. She could talk to anyone and please them with the conversation. She went to the train station to collect me, left her father on the platform and hurried about by herself, trying to recognize me from pictures. Frequently talking, she would interrupt herself by laughing a lot. She drove a huge lemon-yellow car, joking all the time. Marta planned to take a trip around Europe with Jan before returning to the States. She was very charming and immensely open to other people. After dinner we went together for a walk in the Łazienki Park.[20] She broke off in the middle of a sentence and stopped, fascinated:

"Look, what a beautiful tree!"

She smiled in awe.

"I am sometimes so fascinated with the Polish language. For instance, "puchaty" (downy)...it's not "puszysty" (fluffy), it has an entirely different meaning..."

Revealing the news that she didn't intend to stay in Poland with her husband when retired, she confided that the news disappointed Wańkowicz. "He told me he would ensure the environment for me and so on. When I met some of the people he'd told me about, I thought I wouldn't want to stay among them. They are loud and presumptuous..." She said her father had reproached her: "How much you have to hate a nation to prefer living in tight financial conditions and not staying in it." Marta had answered: "On the contrary, how you have to love that nation." Wańkowicz, in turn, repeated with bitterness the words of Marta's husband, Jan Erdman, who'd told him that each person was free and chose to live where he wanted. And that he himself didn't intend to choose Poland as his place to stay.

The writer showed me an issue of the Paris *Kultura* with Marta's article *Obojnaki* (*Hyphenated people*), which she published after her visit to Poland in 1960. He saw the text as a camouflage for her attitude towards Poland. He was astonished and hurt by the words: "My dear, you are wrong in the very assumption. I am not Polish anymore."

In her story, Marta quoted her mother's arguments that "people did not die in the Warsaw Uprising to have their children lose their national identity now." The protagonist grimaced on hearing that, and claimed that "a person grows like a beanstalk, on the bed on which fate had thrown them." In Marta's thesis—an echo of her father's convictions that "you cannot raise your children in a vacuum," she refuted him with her belief how you lived depended on the person, and not on latitude. Her father claimed you could not raise your child to be someone you are not. You could not then give them what each American mother or father automatically gave their chil-dren..."You will impoverish your children if you don't raise them to be Poles, to be who you are." What is the answer of the story's protagonist? Her stance is clearly negative. It is almost as if the author put her own reflections in the woman's mouth and considered her personal problem. At the same time, she was aware, and knew, that the blow was too painful for her parents, and was unable to deal with it herself. She spoke her mind only indirectly. The reply of the literary character created by Marta in her story sounds sharp and cruel:

"But I am not Polish anymore. I am not an American just because of the passport, and only for convenience. I love this country. I miss it when I leave. I am angry with what is wrong in it. I have lived here for most of my life. Here I have studied. Here I have fallen in love and married. Here I have worked. Here I have had my children. Here I have a home. It is my country."

Wańkowicz told me he had never written or spoken about his feelings after reading the text. He chose silence. After the writer's death, Marta asked me if I knew anything about her father's feelings. She hadn't dared ask her father.

I finished my Master's thesis and submitted it to the Department of Polish Literature, and I was nearing graduation. I had one more, final exam, the defense of my thesis. In the nearest future, I intended to pursue an academic career and write a doctoral thesis. My parents clearly approved of those career plans. My personal life with Wojtek after four years of marriage was almost non-existent. We weren't living together, we had our own, different interests. Wojtek still had two years of studies ahead. We didn't really know how our common life would look like, which we kept on postponing for "later," when we would both graduate. Once we lived on the hope of graduation, to be able to live together. We spent less and less time together. Four years of marriage in which we weren't living together definitely played their part.

At that time, just before my graduation, Wańkowicz offered me a permanent job—as his assistant and secretary.

I thought the proposal was great, and accepted it enthusiastically. In a way, it continued what I'd been doing for the last year. However, it required my moving to Warsaw permanently. Knowing I was raising Tomek, the writer invited us both. Wańkowicz had much enthusiasm and many plans for his future. He bought a car, a red Fiat wagon that I was supposed to drive, but foremost he decided to build a house which would offer enough space for everyone. His apartment on the fifth floor of the tenement, comfortable and nicely furnished, started to tire him. The writer wanted a house where he wouldn't have to climb the stairs. He started planning a house with a garden and a large study. Starting a careful search of potential locations which he informed me of in frequent letters, he finally bought a lot on Studencka Street, a side street of Wilanowska Alley, in the district of Mokotów, and found a crew that agreed to build the house in a few months. Proudly showing me the architectural plans, we discussed together what the house should look like in detail. To manage the construction of his new house, Wankowicz chose Jan Sawa. Jan was married to Elżbieta, the youngest daughter of Hania Morawska (born Wańkowicz) and the writer's sister-in-law Maria's grand-daughter. Wańkowicz confided in me that for a long time his conservative family objected to the marriage proposal of Jan Sawa, who came from a different class, from a peasant family. Wańkowicz intervened on behalf of the young people and they married. The couple remained grateful to the uncle. Jan Sawa, a graduate of pedagogics, was a very industrious person and was skilled in many things. He gladly accepted the task of supervising the building for an agreed payment, and Jan excelled at his task. The house was built at a lightning pace, considering the conditions in Poland at that time. The construction costs were expensive, but the writer did not spare the money. He wanted it to be completed as soon as possible. He wrote me in a diverting manner about the peculiar ceremony of laying the foundation act. In a copper tube a parchment sheet was placed with a statement on it that the house was built in tribute to a great writer. The tube's contents included the books *Szczenięce lata* (with the note: "A book on what life was like before the First World War"), *Ziele na kraterze* (with the writer's note: "What life was like before the Second World War") and *Przez cztery klimaty* ("...since the Second World War broke out"). The house stood after six months, and the interior was being furnished.

He bequeathed his apartment on Puławska Street as a privately-owned one to his granddaughter, Ania Erdman, who on graduating from medical studies in Warsaw married Tadeusz Walendowski and they have a son, Dawid. After the writer's death, on the initiative of the young hosts, the apartment became a centre for meetings of intelligentsia, meetings of political opposition, and it was also there that the meetings of the Flying University[21] took place. Ania had another son, Eliasz, but due to the increasingly difficult political situation and constant harassment of her family, she finally returned to the States.

While the house was being furnished, between June and September 1973, Wańkowicz rented a holiday house near the picturesque Liwiec river in Nadliwie near Wyszków. A beautifully situated house on a hill in a forest, spacious and nicely designed, its owners, Maria and Janeczka Wolińska, lived in two rooms. Wańkowicz stayed there with the housekeeper, Marta Karaban, her daughter Anna, me and four-year-old Tomek. He bought bicycles for Anna and me, and we went with Tomek for cycling trips in the forest. Also, Tomek was taken for a few hours daily to the nearby scouts' camp. A few weeks after moving to Nadliwie, we were joined by a dachshund pup, black, with yellow markings and a perfect pedigree. A dachshund lover, Dr. Kazimierz Ściesiński brought the dog to us. The dog evoked all of our affection, and we each tried to win his favor. With an official pedigree name: Dedi-Smętek, the inspired Wańkowicz—at first in jest, but then more and more insistent on keeping the new name—gave him a name which we all got used to, but which always stirred a certain sensation and made people smile. He called the dog Dupek (*Assjack.*) When the author of *Monte Cassino* appeared in the TV programme *Tele-Echo*, hosted by Irena Dziedzic, with a dachshund in his lap which he called by the name Dupek, the mass of viewers accepted the name without any reservations. Some remembered the writer's feature *W obronie niewyzwolonej (In Defense of the Non-Liberated One)* and now re-called it in conversations.

The dog brought joy to all of us. Once Wańkowicz decided to try and see whom the dog loved most. When walking in the Las Kabacki forest, we separated, going in opposite directions. The dog ran along the usual route, taken by Wańkowicz, but then looked around and spotted me going in the opposite direction. He ran after me, looked back again, turned around and ran up to Wańkowicz. Then again he ran to me, and finally in desperation and being miserable, started barking loudly and angrily, and with that he finally called us to order. Later, it was difficult to keep Dupek in the garden. He'd known freedom in Nadliwie, where he was free to walk without a leash, and now he was very upset about the restriction. Thus, he constantly dug tunnels under the fence and made long trips out into the surroundings, from which he was brought back thanks to the ID address tag placed on his collar.

We took Dupek for walks in the park in Wilanów. During one of those walks, he sniffed out a hedgehog. To the dog's surprise and to my and Tomek's joy, Wańkowicz allowed us to take the animal home. The hedgehog lived for a few weeks in the pergola, and sometimes we let it out into the garden. But one day the hedgehog set off on some longer trip and neither we were able to find it, nor could the desperate dog sniff out its hiding place.

Tomek kept fish in an aquarium in his room. At first he kept shells in a jar, telling me there were snails inside. He brought them leaves and talked to them. Then I bought him an aquarium and one fish to start with. Coming back from the shop, he held the fish in a jar in his lap, all smiles. We tested the water. It turned out that the water was good, so we bought more fish and some plants. Tomek secretly fed them additional portions. I told him that their bellies would burst from overeating. He didn't enjoy the aquarium for long. When he let in snails he'd found in the park—for company—the fish didn't survive the experience.

Dupek was happy when Tomek had a cold and had to stay in bed. The dog accompanied him non-stop. He kept chewing and gnawing at things—slippers, Tomek's fur coat, blankets.

Chapter Eight

House on Studencka Street

The house on Studencka Street was spacious and comfortable. There were eight rooms, two bathrooms, and an additional toilet in the cellar, which was cleverly and carefully designed. I had a darkroom for developing pictures. Also there was a pantry, laundry room, store and a garage. The largest room was the writer's study, with a door to the terrace, adjoining my office and—from a different side—Wańkowicz's small bedroom. Two pieces of furniture stood out in the living room. On a decorative shelf, all editions of the writer's works, carefully bound by Polish and foreign bookbinders were prominent. The other part of the house was comprised of: a kitchen with a window to the dining room, my room and Tomek's. Tomek's room was tiny, but very cosy. I remember an amusing "incident" concerning the furnishing of my room. On the wall I had hung a colourful Mexican saddlecloth (shabrack) and a small icon. Wańkowicz saw it and took the icon to his bedroom.

"That magpie takes everything to her nest," he complained in jest.

In a dejected tone I said, "Maybe let's hang the shabrack somewhere else, too," I said.

"Maybe the sabre, Marshal?" he joked. Then he told me a story of how Marshall Piłsudski was sick and received General Iwaszkiewicz, commander of the 3rd Division. The latter told him in details of how he was honoured with a sabre for valor. Piłsudski was silent all that time, and finally the General, slightly alarmed, asked: "Maybe [you'd like] the sabre, Marshal?"

From the dining room you could go out to the pergola, almost completely cloaked with the expansive branches of an apple tree. The front of the house was covered with a wooden roof down to the gate. The idea was later used by our neighbours, and currently in the very same street there are several buildings with a roof extending down to the entrance. Wańkowicz's house was surrounded with a large garden. Part of it had been adapted by the former owner for his purposes. There were cherry trees and peach trees. With the gardener's help, decorative bushes were planted, among them rhododendron, hedges, flowers. Marta used a small part of the garden to grow vegetables.

In the garden, Tomek played with the dog and kids from the area. Tomek brought activity and adventure with him. He spent his mornings in a kindergarten on Odyńca Street, and his afternoons and evenings were spent frolicking in the house and the garden. Wańkowicz, who was actually irritated by children, tried to be patient and attentive with the little boy. I remember that once he told Tomek that he was all "in parts" and could disassemble himself, like a wooden soldier toy.

"Hmpf," the child pouted with disbelief in such nonsense.

"Then I'll show you that I've got everything movable," said the writer, and to the boy's astonishment he took out his lower teeth, then his upper teeth...When he held his head with both hands in order to "unscrew" it, as he said, the child ran to his room screaming in fear. I had to calm him down for a long time.

The writer had his own child-raising methods and was glad that I didn't fault them. Now I recall them with some surprise. He frightened Tomek that a militia man would come for him, punished the boy by not taking him for a walk, but also awarded a daily "order of the black cookie" to him for good behaviour. When the neighbours complained that Tomek fought with other kids, I was surprised by Wańkowicz's support for "the boy that won't be pushed about."

Tomek and I liked cycling together very much, and we often went for trips along Wilanowska Street and Sobieskiego Alley, on special cycling paths. I have tapes with fragments of Silly-Billy-Goat's adventures read to Tomek by Wańkowicz. The writer would stop reading and make a digression: "Do you know how a wolf howls?" And then imitate the animal in a great, full voice. Tomek loved it when I read Brzechwa's poems to him. It was a pleasure to learn them by heart:

> Crocodile: "Where are you from? Crocodile!"
> "I am from the River Nile,
> Let me go out for a while,
> I'll take you to the Nile."

> Elephant: This is Bombi.
> An elephant, I suppose.
> He would like to play on his nose.
> Don't ask him why,
> Because he is very shy. [1]

When Tomek reached age of four, he became inquisitive and asked many questions each day:

"Why does snow disappear?"

"Because it melts," I said.

"And why does it melt?"

"Because it's getting warmer."

"And why is it sometimes raining, and sometimes snowing?"

Once his Granddad told him a story of why the dog dislikes the cat, and the cat dislikes the mouse. My father started saying:

"It was a very long time ago, you were not born yet, your mother wasn't born yet..."

"And were you born?" asked Tomek.

"No, I wasn't born yet, either."

"So how do you know?" inquired the child.

"Because I've read about it," replied his grandfather, clearly amused.

It was also a period of showing exceptional tenderness and love.

To me: "I love you so much that I can't stop looking at you," he said.

"And me?" asked his grandmother, present when he said that.

"I can stop looking at you," he replied cruelly.

During holidays in Świnoujście with Grandmom, Tomek made an eating competition: who would finish first. "Even if she's last, my mommy will still always be first, me second, and Grandmom last." To that, my mother strongly protested.

On a different day: "My Mom is the prettiest, even though Agnieszka said in kindergarten that her mom was prettiest. My Mom is my diamond and gold!"

I don't know where he got those comparisons from. When I bought him training shoes, I called him Adidassy, and he called me Rubby (I wore rubber boots).

"You are the queen and I will draw you," he said seriously, drawing my and his silhouettes in straight lines. When I felt ill, he told me to sit in the chair and put pillows behind my back. He remembered that when Wańkowicz was ill, he had pillows put behind him in the armchair. Wańkowicz was sometimes quite delighted with Tomek, although he disliked small kids as a rule and was very critical if the boy deserved it.

When an interview was recorded for *Tele-Echo* with Irena Dziedzic, who visited the writer on Studencka Street and carefully prepared for the program (she said: "I believe only in prepared improvisation"), I met Barbara Wachowicz for the first time, in the TV building on Woronicza Street. I remember she leaned over from behind and covered Wańkowicz's eyes, asking: "Maestro, do you recognize me?" She looked very fetching: a light blonde with locks of curly hair, wearing a short violet leather skirt and violet leather boots that reached above the knee. She spoke beautiful Polish, and made quite an impression. She introduced me to "her moustache-man," as she'd named him, Ziuk Napiórkowski, a young, tall, handsome man, a stage designer and her husband. Wańkowicz brightened on seeing her and at home he showed me a beautiful letter from her, in which she informed him of her marriage with Ziuk. Barbara's style followed the stylized Old Polish from Sienkiewicz's books, written in a violet marker, in an even, beautiful hand. There were several other letters. In one of them, among other things, she referred to a comb lent by Ziuk to Wańkowicz, which the writer used to comb his hair before the interview. She wrote: "...the comb with which you combed your hair during «Tele-Echo», now named Melchior's, rests in a place of honor in my dear husband's sanctuary, next to my letters!!!"

Wańkowicz's book *Wojna i pióro* was in print and facing new difficulties. I witnessed a few talks with a representative of censorship. The publisher from the Ministry of Defense showed the writer fragments questioned by the censors. When writing the book, Wańkowicz introduced what he called "huge elephants" by quoting earlier writers: "we are governed by plain rabble" or "we've been flooded by red plague." They served his purpose of "haggling" (negotiating) "I will give in on this fragment, but I can't yield on the other..." Thus he cleverly kept the fragments he really wanted.

Before he started talking with a censor who was—if I remember correctly—vice-president of the Control Office[2] on Mysia Street, a young man was sent from there to talk to Wańkowicz.

"He nodded to everything, made notes, but he was unable to make any decision by himself—he had to ask his superiors," Wańkowicz told me. "So I demanded someone who would stand high enough in the hierarchy to make his own decisions. I didn't want to waste my time with others." Then a Mr. Adamiak came (I can't remember his given name). The writer's housewife, Marta Karaban, brought snacks for the guest, Wańkowicz offered drinks, the talks were slow but brought results. Some of them I remember particularly well.

The sentence was questioned: "Going into attack, the soldier doesn't say: Long live Poland. He may at the most swear: f**k it."

The writer was surprised. "What do you mean? Are the dear lips of the Polish soldier so delicate that the word will not come out?"

"No," replied the censor. "But you see, the f-expression in Polish is grammatically feminine, and the word fatherland is also feminine. The reader may become suspicious. We must intervene here."

Or the words: "The war of the United States in Korea."

"But the press wrote about that war," the writer was irritated.

"That's true," replied the censor. "But you're not taking a stand towards that war. You should write: "The imperialist war of the United States in Korea.""

The house on Studencka Street was visited by many people. A regular guest was Michał Radgowski, with whom Wańkowicz played chess. The first time he came to visit us with Tadeusz Drewnowski, was on New Year's Day 1974. The writer had been telling me of that excellent journalist earlier, and gave me a collection of his features *Gafa za gafą (A Gaffe After a Gaffe)* to read. Michał Radgowski visited us with his wife Krystyna and a brown dachshund Mała—Little One.

Aleksander Małachowski also visited, either alone or with his wife (wheelchair-bound)—he was a tall, handsome, interesting man. He was planning to go to Peking with his wife, who was suffering from multiple sclerosis. They were hoping that Chinese acupuncture would help her recover.

Beside writers and journalists, editors were also regular guests, like Andrzej Kurz director of *Wydawnictwo Literackie* (*Literary Press*), or Zbigniew Borówka director of the *Instytut Wydawniczy PAX* (*PAX Publishing Institute*). Wańkowicz was very active, new editions of his books and new titles were published continuously. He maintained extensive contacts with creative people, active people. The writer was always interested in such people, regardless of their beliefs. He didn't always see them as friends, but they captured his interest. Very few people were on a first name basis with him. He told me that once, after a drink, writer Wojciech Żukrowski suggested they be on a first name basis. Wańkowicz waited for a moment, then replied: "But Mr. Wojciech,[3] we're not really that close friends..."

The house on Studencka Street was visited by the writer's peers and friends—graduates of the Chrzanowski (now Zamoyski) High School, whom he teased about being "old coots," but he truly liked them and often joked with them. During one of such conversations about years gone by, I grabbed a recorder and recorded it. Later I wrote it down and quoted in my book *Blisko Wańkowicza* (*Near Wańkowicz*) in the chapter *Rozmowa po latach (Talking Years Later)*. Other visitors came who were participants of the Monte Cassino battle, the former soldiers of General Anders's 2nd Corps, or Hubal's soldiers. Out of the latter, I'd had a chance to meet Roman Rodziewicz earlier—he stayed with us in the house on Studencka Street when he was in Poland in the summer of 1974—as well as Józef Alicki, Marek Szymański, Henryk Ossowski, also former Hubal soldiers.

Another welcome guest was the journalist Zbigniew K. Rogowski, always cordial and kind. He brought news and much excitement. He spoke of his contacts with Jan Kiepura[4] and Martha Eggerth.[5] He published memoirs of what happened in the writer's house in the *Mieszanka Firmowa* section in *Przekrój* and *Stolica* weeklies.

I always kept in contact with my family in Łódź. On twelve January 1974, Henio married Marysia (Maria) Dominiak. Kazimierz Kowalski, a well-known bass, sang during the reception. I danced with my little Tomek, who felt quite special. I brought *Ziele na kraterze* with Wańkowicz's dedication as a gift to the young couple. Later they both visited me in Warsaw, just like my parents. Wańkowicz wrote a beautiful dedication to my father and was happy to talk about Roman Dmowski with him. (Wańkowicz wrote an essay *Niech żyje Dmowski i Piłsudski (Long live Dmowski and Piłsudski)*.

During this period, my family lost our house on Franciszkańska Street. Four neighboring houses: ours, that of the Skoniecznys and two of the Dyjaczyńskis, together with big gardens, were taken by the city for a construction site. The trees were cut, and a large building erected. We received a small compensation. In that time, similar actions were quite frequent. My parents moved to a three-room apartment on Murarska Street. Henio and Marysia acquired an apartment in the same block, in another stairwell. The enjoyment of having the garden was over. The house I missed was no more. Now I visited my parents in the small rooms they had. Father took one room for all his books. He put them in two rows, and even used the place under the window, where he installed additional shelves.

Our pets seemed to sense the change that was about to occur. Aza, our big yellow dog, passed quietly away in his doghouse shortly before we moved, and Psotka, my little black shaggy dog, ran away from the new place at the first opportunity. She found the direction instinctively. She found her way among the blocks, ran across the busy Łagiewnicka Street and ran up to the old house. When I visited my parents for the first time on Murarska Street, the dog wasn't home. Mother and I went to Franciszkańska Street. The dog was sitting there staring blankly ahead. We took her away from there, but she never accepted the new conditions, and the lack of freedom. A few months later, Psotka also died.

Meanwhile, my life in Warsaw was extremely intensive. I started collecting materials for my doctoral thesis. I planned to write it on the works of Melchior Wańkowicz. Professor Julian Krzyżanowski agreed to be my supervisor. He gave me a free hand in writing, and encouraged a flexible work schedule. I visited him regularly in his house on Miączyńska Street. He offered me red wine and stories from his own literary experiences. In the 1950s, in the first collected works by Sienkiewicz, issued by the PIW publishing house, the book *Ogniem i mieczem* (*With Fire and Sword*) was missing[6]. There was much ado about it, and the book immediately appeared in photocopies. The authorities were afraid of a private trade developing, and also one of the high state dignitaries of the USSR stated he liked reading Sienkiewicz. Thus, the first part of the Trilogy was finally issued.

My days were full. There was work on the successive chapters of *Karafka La Fontaine'a*, collecting materials for a new book, writing features, and caring for Tomek. In the last period there were also the visiting doctors: the long-time friend, Professor Stefan Wesołowski, doctors: Stanisław Leszczyński, Tadeusz Lewiński, Maria Waśniewska, Kazimierz Nowak.

The writer was an avid theatre (e.g. Adam Hanuszkiewicz sent him invitations to premieres) and cinema goer (he valued each new film by Andrzej Wajda). Together we viewed the premiere of Bohdan Poręba's film *Hubal*. We went to lectures, meetings, to the History Institute in the Old Market Square, to the Pietrzak club on Piękna Street, we were also at the Pietrzak award giving ceremony in the Staszic Palace.[7] Sometimes the author visited people. I remember visiting with Zbigniew and Swietłana Załuski, or Zenona Macużanka. Wańkowicz himself was visited by old friends from the United States and Canada. Regular guests, almost household members were Joanna and Krzysztof Kąkolewski, Aleksander Małachowski, Mieczysław Kurzyna, Michał Radgowski. Some of the people I met at that time became my friends. Some offered me much kindness and help after the writer's death.

Wańkowicz read extensively. He often asked about a young reporter from the *Polityka* weekly, Hanna Krall, in whose reportages *Na Wschód od Arbatu (East of Arbat Street)* he had taken a particular interest. He enjoyed Redliński's *Konopielka* novel, and a few stories by Marek Nowakowski. The last book he read before his death was *The Gulag Archipelago* by Solzhenitsyn. He read it in Russian. Strongly impressed by the book, he told me much about it. Wańkowicz worried, as he said, about the Russian soul, stifled for so long. He saw no hope for big changes in that country. On reading Jerzy Łojek's book *Powstanie Listopadowe (November Uprising)*,[8] he wondered how many wise, open-minded, educated, righteous people we would need to fill all key posts in Poland and inspire a revolution. I remember well visits from Jan Olszewski, Marta Miklaszewska and Jan Józef Lipski. Wańkowicz gave some money to bail out students arrested by the militia for participation in political movements. In his book *Opozycja polityczna w PRL 1945–1980 (Political Opposition in the People's Republic 1945–1980)* Andrzej Friszke quotes the words of J. J. Lipski, saying that the writer had offered a substantial amount of money in 1965 to the "aid fund for repressed oppositionists and their families." During one of the last visits of Olszewski and Lipski, in 1974, the writer gave them a then considerable amount of money. He wanted the funds to be used after his death to help people in political trouble. Jan Olszewski was then a well-known lawyer who defended young participants of political actions. Later, after the writer's death, when KOR was established, he became an active member. He was one of the prosecution lawyers in the trial for the murder of Father Popiełuszko.[9] Olszewski was later to become the Prime Minister of Poland.

In February 1974, the house on Studencka Street heard talks about the possibility of establishing a movement or organization which would group brave people striving for introducing changes in Poland. There was no such organization earlier. (KOR, the Workers' Defense Committee, was established in June 1976, after the Radom events.) Wańkowicz was worried that "Poland is flooded by Eurasian sand," and concerned for the country's future.

He offered his house as the meeting place. He spoke of drainage of the Polish culture and the need to act. He gave as an example the forest fires in America. There are some small fires, spreading until the fire engulfs the whole forest covering huge areas.

"If only everyone here would create such small fires around themselves. I don't demand the impossible, but only for each of us to fight in our own backyard for things that can be created. Not to assume in advance that it can't be done, that they will "remember" you. We must fight disinterested stupidity, own cowardice and self-censorship."

The topic of the first meeting was to discuss Polish culture impoverishment, the attack on Polish culture that was not done through violence, but through drainage. Names of people to invite were singled out: Małachowski, Lipski, Olszewski, Dziewanowski, Zanussi, Wańkowicz, Herbert, Marta Miklaszewska, Jakub Karpiński, Łojek, Marian Brandys, Wielowieyski, Bartoszewski. That such assemblies were very necessary was agreed by all, and were to occur without any strict discipline and oaths. Wańkowicz took it upon himself to invite people without the form of an organization. Yet the writer's progressing illness prevented any action.

Chapter Nine

The Writer's Illness

The repeated X-rays showed cancer. Immediate surgery was vital, it could offer a few more years to live. For the writer the doctors wanted what they thought to be the best solution. They suggested he go to the Wythenshawe Hospital in Manchester, England where they knew an excellent surgeon, Gordon Jack.

Wańkowicz took the news of the illness calmly.

"I never was in a situation in life where I wouldn't tell myself that both ways out of it were good. When in 1964 they wanted to put me away for a few years, I told myself it was good, it was an asset for me. If they didn't, it would give me publicity. Many times in my life I knew how to find two opposite solutions to a case. Now my life is ending, actually almost everything is completed. It would be a nice ending, even, without coming apart, decomposing in old age and illness...But on the other hand, I'd like to live. I have a great curiosity about life and would like to live at least some two more years, to give you Aleksandra the time to start out on your own. You need me..."

Before going to the hospital, he asked a lawyer, Stanisław Szczuka, to come to him and prepare his Last Will. He sent the completed second volume of *Karafka La Fontaine'a* to Wydawnictwo Literackie, with its dedication to me included.

While in England, where we went for the surgery in March 1974, we attended an interesting meeting in a house in Ealing, organised by his cousin, Karol Wańkowicz. I had the opportunity to meet Stanisław Gliwa, a graphic artist, who designed the cover for *Monte Cassino*. He lived in New Eltham and had his own printing house. Once, right after the war, Zofia and Melchior Wańkowicz had lived in Ealing, together with Gliwa. To our meeting, Karol Wańkowicz invited Wacław Zagórski, Stanisław Grocholski, Teresa Lechnicka, Piotr Yolles (whose pen-name was Michał Sambor), and Zbigniew Racięski, a Free Europe journalist for London and New York press, called Róbcuś. Racięski showed me London with its most beautiful sights and the Polish Club Ognisko. I also met his wife, Stanisława. The acquaintanceship developed into a friendship of many years. In the Polish Club and in the Polish Ex-Combatants Association in London, I was given many books from immigrant publishers, and I was very happy with them.

Jarosław Żaba was a man well known among the Poles in Manchester, and he visited the writer a few times in the hospital with his wife Zofia. During those visits, interesting comments were exchanged on Poland and the immigration. Wańkowicz stressed the great significance of Giedroyc's *Institut Littéraire* in Paris, and of Fundacja Kulturalna (Polish Cultural Foundation) and Veritas in London for the continuity of Polish culture. Żaba spoke of the resentment of Poles living in Britain towards the writer for agreeing to have *Monte Cassino* published in an abridged version.

"They don't resent your return to Poland, although all of us—the immigrants—became weaker without you, but the *Monte Cassino* thing..."

"I published one volume, but huge and illustrated. I took the position that the truth about Monte Cassino should be shown to the nation, even if I pay for it with abridgements. But I understand that it is a controversial matter, particularly among immigrants...I believe that in particular the immigration of carpenters, engineers and doctors is a great loss for the country. Roman Rodziewicz, a son of a land-owning family, became a turner in England, and I'd prefer him being a turner in Poland," said Wańkowicz.

Bocianowski, an immigrant also from Manchester, told the writer when visiting him in the hospital that once he also thought that immigration should be small, an elite. But that intelligentsia often accepted the status quo too easily. In 1941 in Vilnius, Polish intelligentsia started speaking Russian. It was the janitors, simple people who cried and didn't want to yield.

Roman Rodziewicz came to Manchester from Sheffield. He made a bet with the writer that if the latter survived the operation, he would buy Roman a bottle of cognac. "And for whom will you buy a bottle if I don't survive?" asked Wańkowicz.

Rodziewicz invited me to his home for a few days. I met his friend Staszek Rysztogi, who had his studies in Polish literature at the Jagiellonian University interrupted by the war. He had been a soldier of the II Corps, and settled in Sheffield after the war. I met many others: Helena and Stefan Nowodworski, Jan Wyszyński, Ryszard Koziełł-Poklewski, Władysław Wieteska and Józef Zyss. There were many stories circulating about the latter. He was a handsome former RAF pilot, with perfect manners, who married a rich Englishwoman after the war and started his own company. He made a lot of money, but his wife left him. Zyss lived alone and sought the company of other Poles, who—while they were slightly jealous of his money and good looks—liked and valued him, because he was a generous person.

I missed Tomek, whom I'd left in Poland, as it was the first time we were separated for a longer time. In London, I bought him a set of soldiers and some clothes.

A great help in those weeks was the presence of Marta Erdman. We became friends during our long night talks. We shared a room in the Post House Hotel, near the hospital. I asked Tili why she wasn't writing.

"It's not easy, being the daughter Wańkowicz," she replied. "It was easier to make a debut in *Płomyk*,[1] but writing a book is a different matter. What am I to write about? About my childhood? Father has already done it, and better than me. I cannot mess about "the inside." Will I write a book about my father? Oh, no! Certainly not! I wouldn't want to..."

Before the surgery, Tili and I prayed in the hospital chapel. Flower bouquets already had been laid in the hall next to the chapel.

"Is that to thank the doctors?" I asked.

"No, these are mourning bouquets," she replied.

Doctor Gordon Jack said he was technically pleased with the surgery. After the doctor left, Wańkowicz told us:

"For the first time in my life I can't do anything."

"What are you saying? For the first time in your life? Then you are an exceptional man," Marta was amazed.

"The first time that I can't fight it."

Doctor Jack expected a year and half of peace. It turned out that the writer had only six more months to live.

Soon after Wańkowicz returned from England, he had a visit from Barbara Wachowicz and Zofia Nasierowska who made a series of pictures. The pictures show the writer's face much emaciated, almost suffering. Jan Molga painted him with similar countenance. Wańkowicz gave me a copy of that painting as a gift. He doesn't resemble the man who was usually bursting with verve and curiosity. His appearance was apathetic, weary and sickly. He was sometimes like that in the last months of his life. I particularly value one of the three portraits by Wiesław Śniadecki. The painting has a warm atmosphere in it—maybe that is why I like it. This painting hangs in the living room of my Warsaw apartment.

One day I brought Marian Brandys to Studencka Street. The writer knew him, and valued his books particularly. Wańkowicz, very ill, was worried about Brandys' state of health, like many other friends who were ailing. The author of the *Koniec świata szwoleżerów* (*The End of the Light Cavalry World*) cycle had acute asthma and spent a lot of time in hospitals. When I was driving the guest back to his place on Marszałkowska Street, Brandys confessed he was glad that Wańkowicz had devoted people around him, because it was easier to take the suffering then. He seemed truly concerned and friendly.

Wańkowicz worked almost every day until the very last day. On 8 September 1974, I was playing with Tomek on the terrace when Wańkowicz came, saying he had strong shivering fits. He laid down and was given some hot soup. He received guests from New York: Ludwik Seidenman, a lawyer, and his wife. They didn't stay long, seeing how ill he was feeling.

On the nine September he felt decidedly ill. In the evening the doctors recommended that he go to the hospital. The writer asked to wait until morning, but the ambulance was called. Wańkowicz asked me to go with him, but I wasn't allowed by the paramedics. A reporter, Barbara Seidler, was in front of the hospital and heard him call me.

"Oleńka will be with you in a moment," she soothed him. Then she called me. "You must come, he needs you."

I arrived shortly at the hospital, Kąkolewski having driven me there. When I entered the room, the writer spoke:

"Oh, you're finally here! Tomorrow early morning, bring me: slippers, pyjamas, mineral water..." He saw the doctor had come, and motioned us to leave.

"Goodbye," he waved at me, and smiled as usual when I was leaving.

At home I couldn't rest. I tried going to sleep. At half past four, I called the hospital. They told me Wańkowicz had died ten past four. He'd lost consciousness right after I left and never woke up.

There are people who passively let the waves carry them on, and even see a sense of some necessary security in that. Wańkowicz was different. He tried to direct both himself and his environment. Only death was able to snatch that significant and sometimes incomprehensible ability from him. The writer's interests turned both to himself and to others, to great causes of the time in which, despite his age, he participated with all his zeal and deep insight. Neither old age nor illness managed to isolate Wańkowicz from life. Vitality and awareness were great gifts of his nature. Life near Wańkowicz was never dull. It was always intensive, imbued with color and meaning.

I owe much to Wańkowicz. I remember his geniality and affirmation of life, as well as a strong tendency for jokes, and for that he always found the strength. When I received an invitation to a wedding from the Dean of the Polish Philology department, Stanisław Kaszyński, Wańkowicz made up a rhyme which he advised me to send as a telegram. He was already very ill, but jocularity never left him. I don't know how Dr. Kaszyński reacted upon receiving the following text:

Though hopes were dashed
Of our future relations

I shall have a bash
At congratulations.

I remember his visitors, and his conversations. They were sometimes difficult, as they were consciously provoked by a man facing death. He told me
two stories from his life. One he revealed in parts in the house on Studencka
Street, the other he told me and Marta Erdman in the hospital in Manchester.
We both listened in amazement and later sleep eluded us for a long time in
our hotel room. I talked to the writer in the hospital, right before he had
surgery, and I told him how he'd affected me with that confession, how I
couldn't understand a lot of things. He grew pale and said:

"Maybe I shouldn't have told you, you might be too young to understand..."

He returned to the topic after the surgery, seriously ill, in a hospital bed.

Both stories are personal, very private and very human. After the writer's
death, spending over two years near Wańkowicz, I was richer in experience
and less carefree.

Before I moved to my own apartment on Kmicica Street, I lived with Tomek
in the house on Studencka Street for a whole year. According to the last will
of Melchior Wańkowicz, we could stay there until I obtained a place of my
own.

According to the will, I was to oversee the series of *Collected Works*,
receiving a monthly salary for my work taken out of the writer's fee. The
series was started by two publishers who divided the titles among themselves: PAX and Wydawnictwo Literackie in Kraków. The writer lived to see
the first volume published: *Czerwień i amarant* (*Red and Amaranth*), which
included *Szczenięce lata* and *Opierzona rewolucja* (with some fragments
missing; the whole works were published in 1993 by the Polonia Publishing
House).

According to the will of Wańkowicz, I also became the official, lawful
owner of the writer's valuable archives. Next to the dedication for me written
by the writer in the second volume of *Karafka La Fontaine'a* (as I quoted
earlier: "To my Assistant, Aleksandra Ziółkowska, without whose committed
cooperation this book would most likely have been worse than it is")—he
sent it to *Wydawnictwo Literackie* asking to add it to the manuscript—that
legacy of the whole archives was the most beautiful present from the writer. I
highly value the enormous trust placed in me by Wańkowicz—again. The
contents of the archives were a subject for speculation and conjecture, suppo-
sitions and rumors. I wrote about it in the books *Blisko Wańkowicza* and *Na
tropach Wańkowicza* (*On Wańkowicz's Tracks*). I allowed only a few people
access to the archives: Professor Marcin Kula, Robert Jarocki (to materials
concerning Jewish issues), Kazimierz Wierzyński's letters I have shown to

Paweł Kądziela, Zofia Kossak-Szczucka's correspondence—to Mirosława
Pałaszewska, Westerplatte[2] -related materials to a doctoral student, Krzysztof Zajączkowski, and general materials to Anna Malcer-Zakrzacka from
Gdańsk, who was writing her doctoral thesis on the author of *Szczenięce lata*,
as well as a few others.

Chapter Ten

Burial of Wańkowicz

Wańkowicz died on ten September 1974. On the next day, Mother came with Henio. They took Tomek to Łódź for two weeks. I had a call from Izabela Szafran, who worked in Moda Polska, and who offered to make a dark dress for me. She knew my size, so she cut and sewed it by herself and brought a finished dress to Studencka Street. Marta Erdman came from the United States for her father's funeral, and stayed in Poland for over a month. Together, in Wańkowicz's house, we settled many issues. Our conversations then were special, held long at night, after the writer's body was brought in the covered, simple, light-colored, wooden casket. The drawing room was filled with gladiolas, long sword lilies, the flowers he liked in particular and which bloomed in September. Candles were lighted, as well as side lamps. The light refracted, casting golden shadows. There was silence and a sense of peace.

As they were taking him to the hospital, he told me: "I'll come back here..." When the casket was brought in, I sobbed emotionally remembering those words.

People came from early morning, such as were known and unknown by the writer. There was no obituary in the press yet, but people already knew and came to Studencka Street. The press informed people of his death, and then about the funeral. The Writers' Union's delegation of several people, led by Lesław Bartelski, came to talk about the funeral. Marta was asked if she agreed to a state funeral, with the casket lying in state in the Primate's Palace on Senatorska Street. After some consideration, she refused. She said her father would have surely liked a more private ceremony. People who were to speak at the cemetery also came: Mieczysław Kurzyna, Aleksander Małachowski, Lesław Bartelski and Jan Józef Lipski.

On the day of the funeral—fourteen September—the casket was brought to St. John's Cathedral, and after the Mass, at three p.m., it was to be taken from there to the Powązki Cemetery. Marta and I came to the cathedral around noon, and we sat down in one of the pews. Centrally, stood the casket; former soldiers from Monte Cassino and Major Hubal's partisans took turns standing guard over it. People came up to the casket and placed their flowers on it. Soon the casket was all but covered with small bouquets. Beside it there stood stately wreaths, constantly new ones were brought in, from organizations, associations, groupings, officials. At some point, I went to the casket to rearrange some flowers. I left my handbag in the pew, next to Marta. When I came back, she whispered to me that a woman had approached her, saying: "Please watch Tili's handbag, so that she doesn't lose it..." (Tili was her nickname; her father used it in his books.) Marta was clearly amused with that remark. She often said that people wanted to see her still as a young girl, such as she was in her father's books. Even on the day of his funeral, readers did not want to accept the passing of time, even though I was even younger than his granddaughters.

The cathedral and streets leading to the Old Town's Market Square were filled with people. The Mass was celebrated by Bishop Zbigniew Kraszewski. The fact that a bishop said the Mass himself was rather surprising. Probably the Church decided so out of regard for a great writer, although he didn't attend church and privately called himself an agnostic. He was very attached to tradition. Brought up as a Catholic, he passed the faith to his daughters. He said that nothing could equal the beauty of a traditional, Polish, Catholic funeral. That was how he buried his wife, and asked for such a funeral for himself. Mieczysław Kurzyna told me that Wańkowicz asked him to cross out a sentence in the book on himself which defined him as an "atheist." He changed it to "agnostic." "I do know that God exists," he said. He liked looking up fragments in the Bible and translating them for himself. "Do you believe that angels came down on earth?" he reportedly asked Kurzyna. Marta believed, in turn, that her father was not lucky enough to meet a partner in religious matters in his life. She gave the example of the great theologian, Father Jan Zieja, an exceptional man. Reportedly, Zieja advised her he had been told to go to Wańkowicz when the latter fell ill. The Father replied that when a man suffers, a priest's coming is not human, so it is not divine. He was not a priest who "went for the soul while armed with a spear." He waited hoping that maybe Wańkowicz himself would ask him to come.

Many years later, I was embarrassed to hear a remark by an employee of the Museum of Literature. The employee was showing the writer's study to a group of young people and indicated the kneeler that bore clear signs of wear as an example that the author of *Szczenięce lata* prayed on his knees...Actually, Wańkowicz kept that kneeler next to his armchair and used it as a...footstool.

After the requiem Mass, in a large crowd and with some difficulty, a bus was provided for family and friends. Wańkowicz was to be buried in his family grave in the Powązki Cemetery, where for over five years the body of Zofia Wańkowiczowa lay, along with her two brothers—Stanisław and Kazimierz Małagowski, Polish Army officers, killed in 1919 within three weeks of each other. The grave had a low relief on it that had been pierced by a bullet during the Uprising in 1944. The writer had asked not to repair it.

From the gate, the casket was borne by, among others, Krzysztof Kąkolewski and Jan Józef Lipski. At the head of the funeral procession walked Bishop Kraszewski, priests, and a Dominican father representing the parish church on Dominikańska Street. State television, which transmitted the funeral, took great pains to avoid showing the priests. The Bishop said the prayers, then speeches began. Jan Józef Lipski spoke, reading the text he had shown us earlier, in a trembling, quiet voice. On behalf of the Writers' Union, Bartelski spoke first, then Mieczysław Kurzyna. Then we heard a cry of anguish. A grave beside collapsed and some people fell into the excavation. (Marta paid later to have the damage repaired.) At the end, standing over our heads on the base of one of the gravestones, Aleksander Małachowski spoke in a sonorous voice. On behalf of the late writer's family he thanked Bishop Kraszewski for coming to the funeral.

Małachowski's speech caused much misunderstanding and distortion later. Reportedly, the authorities imputed to Małachowski that he had not thanked everyone, meaning the distinguished officials who'd come, among them the Minister of Culture (or the American ambassador, who had also come to the funeral). Next day, the daily press printed notes that carefully listed the names of the officials who'd been to the funeral.

Before the grave was covered, a new voice was heard. A man, standing near the grave, read a few sentences written down on a sheet of paper. He said that we should all remember Katyń and observe its anniversary. Later on, Marta and I learned that the man was Wojciech Ziembiński, who later was to be a member of KOR.

Soon after the writer's death a censorship regulation was imposed. From that moment on, no texts could be printed about the late writer (*Polityka* managed to print a beautiful short text by Michał Radgowski before the regulation, exactly on fourteenth September, the day of the funeral). My long-accepted text to be printed in the *Literatura* weekly was withdrawn. Western papers (including American *Time*) published comments and notes, always stressing that Wańkowicz had been given a political trial in 1964. A great Polish writer died, and Polish literary papers weren't allowed to print any occasional texts. They couldn't use words like "great writer, brave man." You could write about him, but sparingly and with restraint. After the years, I found the actual text of the regulation: "Any publications concerning the person and works of Melchior Wańkowicz that go beyond the sphere of technique and literature issues (naming him a man of great courage, politician, activist, national hero, etc.) must be stopped and directed to the management of GUKPPiW[1] (13.09.1974)."

Soon there also appeared some incredible news concerning the writer's last will. The revelation said he had given a substantial sum of money to the Katyń case. Or, that he had left "a note in his will to have a Mass said for him each year on every seventeen September." The news was even repeated by the Paris *Kultura (No. 11, 1974)*. That note, according to *Kultura*, was the reason for the ban on press publications concerning the late writer. Marta Erdman protested in reaction to that letter, expressing her surprise that *Kultura* would repeat a rumor which had repeatedly been denied. She ended with the words: "*Making 'grand gestures from the beyond' would not be my father's style. Instead, he valued highly what he had managed to accomplish in his life.*" There was also much speculation about the writer's possible wealth and its division. Marta Erdman, who stayed with me for nearly a month, heard all such news with much surprise. At the same time, we saw astounding things. The house on Studencka Street was watched day and night by two cars parked nearby, mysterious men sitting inside. One day I was asked to come and see the vice-minister of culture, Aleksander Syczewski. During the meeting in the ministry, Syczewski told me that many people were "concerned" about the security of the writer's archives. He suggested placing the more valuable documents in the ministry's building, where "they would be safe." I replied that I did not intend to hand the archives over to anyone. The writer had bequeathed them to me, and I was their lawful owner. I was writing a doctoral thesis and intended to use the materials in my research. I remember that Aleksander Syczewski did not insist, and in general he was friendly towards the writer's case. The Minister of Culture, Józef Tejchma, had earlier shown his goodwill towards the writer, as he intervened when the publication of *Opierzona rewolucja* was hindered. After the writer's death, he complied with the family's request not to have an autopsy done (Wańkowicz didn't want one). After the meeting in the ministry, Andrzej Kurz, director of the *Wydawnictwo Literackie* came to the house on Studencka Street. He tried to persuade Marta to convince me to agree to hand the archives over to some "safe place." Of course, Marta was against it. She thought that had her father wanted to offer his collection to some institution, he would have done so himself or left instructions to that effect. Probably the support of many people made the topic of the archives finally subside. I, on the other hand, was given a real safe. Minister Tejchma gave it to me with the advice to keep the "most explosive" materials in it. He said he was afraid of other groups—security services, who might try to "steal" the materials.

Some incredible people came to our house. One day, Marta Karaban, the housewife, came to the room where I sat with Marta, and informed us with a mysterious expression that "some woman has come and said she was the daughter of Wańkowicz, and what am I to do with her?" Marta went to see the stranger and spent about half an hour with her. She returned deeply affected, but she was also laughing.

"You wouldn't believe what kind of a woman she is! She came from Świnoujście, a large, fat, pocked-faced woman, as father would put it. She showed me her birth certificate (1931, in Kobryń), where her father's name stood clear as you please: Melchior Wańkowicz (mother: Zofia Bekman, and her own name was Krystyna Malinowska). She claimed to be the daughter from his first marriage. She came...for her inheritance."

"And?" I asked, still not understanding.

"And nothing. I told her that father had never mentioned an illegitimate child, she could go to court if she wanted, and actually, where was she all those years? Besides, her birth date doesn't fit father's biography (he married Zofia in 1916—author's note). Aunt Marieta would have known, she knew everything about family matters. Do you remember? I asked father in the hospital in Manchester if I should expect any "illegitimate offspring" of his to appear. He laughed and told me I absolutely shouldn't, and that I shouldn't make fun of a sick man. And long ago, he'd mentioned he had a peer somewhere with the same first and last name, who was wanted for slander."

Marta repeated the whole conversation to Mr. Stanisław Szczuka, the lawyer who'd prepared the writer's last will. He said that a birth certificate from the other side of the Bug River[2] was easy to forge, and not to make any deals...The woman did not go to court, didn't appear again, but she left a trace...in the cemetery. On the grave, under a rock she put a piece of paper which said she was the daughter of Wańkowicz. Whom she wanted to inform of the news in such a complicated way, we did not know. Reportedly she'd also gone to the Writers' Union. Years later, when I was in Gdańsk, someone told me with conviction that "Wańkowicz's daughter" was living on the Polish coast, showing her birth certificate, and people believed her.

A few years later, in my Dominican parish in Warsaw, one of the fathers told me that in the *Służew nad Dolinką* housing estate (where I was also living with Tomek), the grandson of Wańkowicz also lived.

"What grandson?" I was amazed. "His grandson is just a few years old and left long ago with his parents to the States."

"But Miss Aleksandra," the father was quite irritated with me. "He certainly is the writer's grandson, and besides he's got his grandfather's talent, and writes beautiful essays in school."

It was a warm, golden autumn. I often went with Tomek to the Powązki Cemetery. He wanted to talk to me. It was his first contact with death. In his daily evening prayer he said: "Dear Baby Jesus, please make Mr. Wańkowicz wake up and play with us again, tell stories, give black cookie medals, and write books."

He asked me:

"Will I also lie in a grave like that? When? And who'll be first, you or me?"

I said I'd be first.

"Gosh, and who will cook dinner for me?"

"You'll marry, you'll have a wife."

With Marta I took Wańkowicz's clothes to the Sisters of the Resurrection. The nun who took the clothes wanted her to help build a church. She also complained about the room for religion classes being too small.

Marta and I decided to give mementoes after the writer, mainly his library and study furniture, to the Adam Mickiewicz Museum of Literature in Warsaw. The museum's director, Janusz Odrowąż-Pieniążek, promised a permanent exhibition: giving one of the rooms for public use. The museum already had rooms with keepsakes after such famous writers as Maria Dąbrowska, or Julian Tuwim. When director Pieniążek showed me and Marta around Maria Dąbrowska's study, he showed us immigration books which the writer had in her collection, and which were hidden furtively behind a curtain. He didn't display them, he stressed. Soon after that, one of the museum employees called us to say that certain books from Wańkowicz's library—for instance those concerning Katyń—would not be displayed, so instead of keeping them in a cellar, it was better to return them. In this way, my private library was enriched with particularly valuable collections.

To the museum we gave the black oak bookshelves, library, desk, armchairs, typewriter, pictures. On the desk, everything lays as it did when the writer was alive: the file with an unfinished chapter he wanted to add to *Karafka La Fontaine'a*, writing tools. I also gave them the first issues of Wańkowicz's books, including the valuable three-volume Italian issue of *Bitwa o Monte Cassino*.

The writer left the archives to me, and with me it stayed. Wańkowicz's last will was made by the lawyer, Stanisław Szczuka, before the writer left to England for the surgery. A few years before his death, Wańkowicz gave typed manuscripts of many of his books to the Ossolineum Institute[3] in Wrocław, and I wondered if I shouldn't add to the collection of that highly respected institution, and leave just the writer's study, or the keepsake room, in the museum.

The official opening of Wańkowicz's study on sixth November attracted many people. Writers, journalists and publishers came as well as the writer's friends. Official authorities were represented by the vice-minister for culture, Aleksander Syczewski. I met for the first time some people that the writer had told me much about, and whom he valued and whose work he followed, like Kazimierz Dziewanowski. When seeing the exhibition right before the opening, Marta was amazed to see a few valuable items from her father's collection missing. On the wall, there was the cross from Monte Cassino, made of shrapnel from a shell which had hit Wańkowicz in the shoulder. In the writer's home, that cross always hung next to the framed legend-explanation of what it represented, signed by General Anders. When we asked director Pieniążek what had happened to that framed statement by Gen. Anders, he briefly replied: "Censorship."

I remember coming home utterly appalled. It must have been my upbringing, and the years of working with Wańkowicz, that gave me the courage and evoked a healthy reaction. I looked up the phone number of the censor from the Control Office in Wańkowicz's notebook and called him. I said I knew that censors had confiscated a few mementoes of the writer from the Literature Museum, and I wished them to be returned to me. He replied he knew nothing of the sort, but he would immediately ask about and call me back. After an hour, he called with the information that...there was no intervention by the censorship in the Warsaw Museum of Literature. Soon I was also called from the museum, with the caller informing me in a frightened voice that they had had a call from the Censorship Office...

"That was after I intervened," I said. "I was told certain mementoes had been confiscated..."

"No, there were no censors involved," was the reply. "It was us, we took them away just in case...anticipating a possible intervention."

Wańkowicz's room in the Museum of Literature that opened so quickly after the writer's death, was—however—closed after a few months, and all materials were locked in the storage room. They waited for a different room to be renovated to put them back on display as a permanent exhibition. Meanwhile, months passed, then years. Each time she visited Poland, Marta worried greatly that the study was not yet open to the public. The room was opened after nearly nine years after the writer's death. Now it is a permanent exhibition. Shortly before her death in 1982, Marta brought some of her father's letters and gave them to the museum.

Twice I gave some of the writer's archives to Ossolineum. The Ossolineum Library in Wrocław has a complete collection of his typed manuscripts, including the last book, *Karafka La Fontaine'a*. The remaining materials, mainly the whole correspondence, are still with me. I decided to hand the particular materials over to the Ossolineum collections successively, after preparing their final versions.

After the writer's death, I called the people he valued and liked, and suggested they add his books to their collections. They gratefully accepted. I avoided new contacts, although I was quite popular at that time, and got many invitations. I felt honored by the friendship of two married couples. I spent my evenings, often until late at night, in the apartment in Washington Alley, with Joasia and Krzysztof Kąkolewski, and long afternoons were spent on Chełmska Street—with Krystyna and Michał Radgowski. Kąkolewski was working on a new chapter for his interview-book *Wańkowicz krzepi*. Once he invited me and Stanisław Dygat for a trip to the forest in Konstancin, and afterwards we went for tea to the house of Dygat and Kalina Jędrusik.[4] The author of *Jezioro Bodeńskie* (*Lake Constance*) spoke of his stay in the United States. Once, when we visited again, he returned to the topic. "There is so much comfort there," he said of America. "If I were to inherit a legacy there, I would drink away some of it, and give the rest away. I wouldn't know how to use it. I wouldn't be able to get used to full luxury."

The Radgowskis gave special names to many of their friends (*Neighbour, Long One, Gardener, Lady*). They called me "Miss." Michał bought recordings with classical music, and greatly contributed to my musical knowledge. Thanks to him, I grew to like Vivaldi in particular. He also tried to win me over for Bach and, as he put it, more serious and difficult music. Later, a tradition developed which was maintained for many years: on Sundays, we all went to the Las Kabacki forest—together with Tomek and our dachshunds—for a long walk. I took Krysia and Michał in my car (Michał took over driving in the forest,) and after the walk we had dinner at their place. During those walks, often lasting for hours, they told me of their friends, of political matters, of the Poznań events, of the events of 1968.[5] They both had a flair for politics and a strong sense of reality. Krysia repeated to me what Hanna Krall had said about her—"with her, I could do time." Michał, being the assistant editor of *Polityka*, had much information about current political life. I really valued our friendship, and treated those talks as classes in modern history. Krysia was also knowledgeable about art, liked talking of fashion and she cooked delicious food. Her suppers and receptions had menus with seemingly simple dishes, but refined and artistically done. Both she and her younger sister Wanda, a biologist, had in their faces something of the female sweetness shown in Botticelli's paintings. Krysia was a sociologist, and worked as an editor in the PIW publishing house,[6] in the exquisite department of Modern Thought Library. She dabbled in Sunday painting, as she put it. Her painting collections: flowers, fairy-tale birds, abstract ones, were finally exhibited in the Zapiecek art gallery in the Old Town. I have a few paintings from her, which hang in my apartment on Kmicica Street. One depicts a girl sitting under a tree. The tree has roots which intertwine around the globe. There is no distinction into states or nations.

In one of the meetings on Chełmska Street, when I spoke of Wańkowicz and his last months of life, the Radgowskis told me: "Instead of telling us, write it all down. If there's enough material, write a book."

I started working on it the next day. I soon had the first chapter, and left it with them, asking for their opinion. They called me to say they liked it and that I should continue writing. They supported each new fragment faithfully, and it is to the Radgowskis that I owe my adhering to the idea until the end. I wrote the book almost constantly, for whole days. I started writing it in October 1974, and finished on the last day of December. I unburdened myself of many memories, many scenes from my daily communing with the writer. They were very vivid and sharing them was a sort of relief, a form of therapy. I wanted to record moments which quickly blur in memory. I didn't consider whether I was impoverishing any myth or maybe creating a new one. I did not want to synthesize one life, but rather to show many common days from the last years of life of a great writer. I thus showed some images from the life of a man I knew personally: Wańkowicz and his writing, Wańkowicz and his home, Wańkowicz and his environment. The book became a record of events and anecdotes from life beside the writer. I believe I wasn't guilty of undue nosiness, and didn't "sell the writer out to the public." I tried to be reserved, but not secretive. I kept a certain style in the book— maybe irritating, but both sweetness and crudeness were foreign to that man. The stronger epithets used are only a matter of convention. I often write of trivial matters—but I think they did not lack in significance and value. They were, in a way, threads of a tapestry the weaving of which surpasses the abilities of one person. Funny scenes are interwoven with tragic moments. Moments of hope stand next to loss of it. In many pages of the book, the writer himself speaks—in his letters. His image is painted also by the letters addressed to him.

In any memoirs there is the danger of the recollecting person shifting to the forefront, as if they enviously granted themselves more space than would follow from the circumstances. I tried to avoid that and instead focus on the atmosphere, the climate of the writer's life.

When I wondered how to title the book, I recalled the advice of Ryszard Kapuściński.[7] "You must put the name of Wańkowicz in the title. The title shouldn't be long, so add just one more word, for instance: beside, close to. 'Near' sounds better."

I named the book *Blisko Wańkowicza—Near Wańkowicz*. I selected the pictures and suggested publishing by a renowned Kraków publishing house: Wydawnictwo Literackie. Shortly I received a reply confirming the decision to publish the book. It was issued a year after the writer's death.

At the same time, PAX Publishing Institute made a proposal that I prepare a book of recollections about the writer. I liked the idea and after some consideration I gave to the publisher a list of people whom I would like to ask to write the texts. Wańkowicz surrounded himself with various people, who often represented opposite beliefs and convictions. I wanted this book to show the variety of his acquaintances and contacts. Thus I put together a list of various people, also artists, also people who were staying abroad as immigrants. During the talks in PAX, I noticed that my set of names wasn't accepted.

"We can't print texts written by Górnicki, Małachowski, and some others," was the reply. "And we would like to add some people from our institution, among them some PAX editors. We'd like more of our people, from PAX."

"Wańkowicz didn't surround himself only with people from PAX, and the book would break the proportion. I'll sign the contract if I concur to the list of names attached to it."

Meanwhile I received recollection texts from Szymon Kobyliński, Stanisław Gliwa (mentioned earlier graphic artists for the book *Monte Cassino* living near London), Karol Wańkowicz, texts from Zofia Romanowiczowa, a writer from Paris, who'd delivered the text publicly after the writer's death, from Hanna Pieczarkowska, who had worked with him in *Łącznik Pocztowy*[8] and still remembered the pre-war time. Many people knew of the project of the book and were very enthusiastic about it. Yet the matter of agreeing on a list of names was no closer to being solved. Ryszard Kapuściński advised me to remain inflexible. And he advised me to write a different recollection book altogether: reporters about Wańkowicz. To have the texts written by: Kapuściński, Kąkolewski, Dziewanowski, Andrzej Mularczyk, Stefan Kozicki, Wiesław Górnicki, Aleksander Rowiński, Barbara Seidler. In conflict with PAX, I wanted—for my reportage notes—to talk to Bolesław Piasecki himself. He was long absent in Warsaw, and I was seen by his deputy, Zygmunt Przetakiewicz. He tried to be nice, didn't commit himself to the matter, nothing was arranged. Soon I was sent the contract to sign, with a quite high remuneration proposal. I didn't send the contract back, wishing to solve the matter of the list of names first. Since that never came about, I still have that contract in my collections.

Years later, Józef Szczypka, a writer and PAX editor, told me: "We crossed swords over Górnicki, among others. Now we could print him." It was 1983. Górnicki stopped being a journalist, and became what he called a state official, the main adviser to General Jaruzelski.[9] Wańkowicz once told me that after his return to Poland in 1958, he had many young, ambitious journalists introduced to him. He met them and followed their articles. One of the questions he asked them was: "Do you belong to the Party?" Most said: "Yes, I do, you know, I have a wife and kids..." Górnicki was the only one to reply: "Yes, I do, because I believe in the system."

"I thought that was more honest," the writer told me.

In the writer's archives there are many letters from Górnicki, very open in their content. In many of them he complains about the censors thwarting his writing freedom. My friendship with Sławek, as he was commonly called, was quite interesting. He came to my name's day parties with his wife Murka. I have beautiful inscriptions from him in his books that he gave me. One of them, titled *Zanim zaczną rządzić maszyny* (*Before Machines Start to Reign*), was withdrawn from bookstores and destroyed. Allegedly it was about the following fragment:

> A coup d'état doesn't necessarily have to start with the sudden arrival of tanks with shells loaded into their gun receivers before the presidential palace or the government's seat. Neither does it have to end in total triumph or total defeat of the conspirators. Very often—more often than we think—it starts with seemingly minor shifts in the lower state machinery, from having various lousy buffoons enter the stage, to ending only in taking over the key points of resistance, while leaving a broad area to those who think that they've obviated the danger of a coup, or even that they've succeeded.

I haven't talked to Wiesław Górnicki for many years now. I don't know how he lives and how he views his complex life. Years later I read in Jerzy Giedroyc's *Autobiografia* (*Autobiography*) that he valued Górnicki. That remark gave me a sense of relief.

After the death of Wańkowicz, I had my author's meetings, among others in *Towarzystwo Przyjaciół Warszawy* (*Society of Friends of Warsaw*), and in the *Pineska* (*Thumbtack*) students' club of the Warsaw Polytechnic Institute. The first one, I believe, took place in the academic students' club *Stodoła* (*Barn*) in the Mokotów district. Other guests were Barbara Wachowicz, Krzysztof Kąkolewski, and Mieczysław Kurzyna. We were to share our recollections of Wańkowicz. Before I made my speech, I met the grandmother of Basia[10] Wachowicz. She saw how nervous I was before speaking to the public, and when I finished, she approached me and said: "You did well, I see a great future ahead of you..."

Those friendly, comforting words I remember in particular. The more so as her granddaughter, Barbara, was a master of the spoken word and her author's meetings and speeches evoked unforgettable emotions.

Time changed greatly after the death of Wańkowicz. I sometimes felt lost and lonely. Now I was suddenly free to decide about my own time and activities. I continued working on my thesis, and worked on editing further volumes of Wańkowicz's *Collected Works*. I gratefully accepted invitations from the writer's friends and acquaintances who wanted to talk about him and his books. I had so much to say. There was always much sensation around Wańkowicz, and that aura intended to reappear, even among his friends. I also remember that my parents were deeply affected by adverse enquiries and comments of some of their neighbours.

Chapter Eleven

Fortune Teller

After the writer's death, another story continued from something that had happened to me while he was alive. In January 1974, one of my friends told me that there was a fortune teller in Warsaw who said highly interesting things. Wańkowicz encouraged me to go there, and offered the man's phone number. I told him I was afraid of augury. Wańkowicz was listening to us talk.

"Why don't you go to see something you don't know? It might come in handy one day as a topic."

He called it entering each topic, each case, "observing for landscapes." "Take a look, watch it, try yourself, but always remember: you're watching it only for the landscapes."

I phoned as instructed. A woman answered, asked for my name and set the day and time.

On the set day, I was full of anticipation. I even wondered if I should take a tape recorder with me. However, after some consideration I abandoned the idea. Precisely at the given hour I pressed the bell at the door. It was opened by a pleasant, elderly woman. She checked my name on the list. I sat down on one of three chairs, next to a young girl. From behind a glass door came a soft, quite monotone voice, but I couldn't catch words. We started a whispered conversation. The girl told me about her earlier visits to the fortune teller.

"I came here two years ago. He told me then that I would give up my studies, go abroad, and would have two men courting me and I wouldn't know which one to choose. Just imagine that I gave up my studies, and although I had no one abroad, I still went there. I've been in Poland for two months now. Before I left, two men have proposed to me. I came here to ask—what happens next..."

The door opened, and a woman came out, pensive. The girls sitting next to me sprang out of the chair and disappeared behind the glass door.

The woman looked at me. "He always speaks of my children, never about me. As if there is nothing I can expect..." She left.

I waited, focused, slightly nervous. After a while the door opened slightly and the girl left. Now it was my turn to enter the adjoining room.

The room was long and narrow, with tall windows. Pots with flowers stood on the window sill. At the back stood a desk covered with dark green oilcloth. Next to it there was a lamp lighting the room. I sat on the hard, plain chair, facing a man who had his eyes lowered. He wasn't looking at me and was smoking a cigarette; the opened pack lay beside him. Hunched he was shuffling cards looking weary. His hair was going grey, it was worn in a crew cut, but it needed trimming. Deep wrinkles, bags under the eyes, oriental features. "A Tartar, possibly?" I thought briefly. I sat so in silence, holding my breath. He finished shuffling and put the cards in front of me.

"Please cut three times to yourself."

He put the cards together, tilted one to take a glance, and started laying them out on the desk. The cards were colorful, stiff, lacquered. There were colorful drawings, numbers, symbols on them. For instance, there were images of a girl, a boy, a cat, a coffin, lightning, a stork. I later learned it was a deck of Tarot of Marseille and that it consisted of seventy-eight cards showing allegoric images with numbers and names. Then he started speaking.

"You have a strange road ahead of you, more male than female, typical of strong and outstanding people, brave ones. It's also a hard, difficult road. In the field you choose you will receive an award. Your sign is tempestuousness. You have an interesting life ahead of you, full of sense, work, successes, joy and pain. Much suffering, too. The heart. You put a lot of heart into everything you do, in what you're engaged in, this adds, helps—but one day you will put a lot of yourself into something or someone and that will break you, betray you. That will be your defeat, your pain, but you will return to your road of life, you'll straighten after that. You are a woman of action, strong. You approach a person with a catalyst which creates or frees nonexistent values almost as you speak. You can be grateful—for everything, for appreciation, for attention, for understanding, for a smile. Many far travels here. Learn French, Italian or Spanish, because you will spend a few years in warm countries. Soon, in a short time, you will go abroad. You have five difficult years behind you, it will last one more year, then a break and you'll start a good time. With the new year—but not the one people usually take for the beginning, because the planetary year starts on twenty-first March, when the Sun starts a new trek. In twelve months it will get better. A problem, but you must solve it yourself, you must make a decision yourself. Your little son won't help you, he's too small, neither will your brothers, because they're too far. A few times in life you will feel that despite many friends and acquaintances you're alone. You'll also die alone, in a way. But then, each man dies alone...

"Do you want to know anything else? Do you have any question?"

"Have I chosen the right way? Shouldn't I turn back?"

"There is no turning from your path, even if you tried, you'll come back to it anyway. Everything that happened earlier, is past. You have a whole life ahead of you. You're still very young. Do you want to know anything else, anything special?"

"No, thank you, this is enough."

At home I told it all to Wańkowicz.

"I don't believe in such things, the people are usually swindlers. The only specific thing he told you was that you had a small son and brothers. That is interesting. And where are you planning to go abroad?"

"Nowhere."

"Exactly."

Wańkowicz, who for some time had been having health problems, feeling sleepy and under the weather, consulted various doctors. To one of them, Kazimierz Nowak, he repeated the fortune I'd been told, as an anecdote. The doctor listened and said he viewed those matters with some reserve, but that his mother had an incredible gift of foretelling the future. Two years before the war's outbreak she came to her children crying and said that she saw in cards that in two years her husband would die, the orchard would be cut down, and the pigs slaughtered. And all that happened, his father was killed in 1939.

Wańkowicz, in turn, told me stories from his life which he did not understand, and was unable to explain. One was from his early years, the other from later years. That other story happened in the States. He was driving on a California freeway, and his wife, Zofia Wańkowicz, sat next to him. At some point she said: "Stasiek, Kazik...(those were the names of her brothers, killed in 1919). Stasiek is here, he touched me." The car stopped in the middle of the road. "I don't know what happened, I didn't understand it. I turned the key and the engine started. I drove on. My wife couldn't explain her reaction, either." (He also told the story of that event to Kąkolewski, who included the story in *Wańkowicz krzepi*.) Once Wańkowicz told me half-jokingly that whichever one of us left earlier, he or she would try to let the other know how it is on the "other side."

I remember that on our return from England, Wańkowicz reminded me of the fortune teller.

"Remember, he said you would go abroad in a short time. Go to him again. He may tell you something completely different and you'll know he's a swindler."

I didn't feel like going. The prophecy of being lonely, of feeling it in particular, stayed with me for a long time. I didn't want to hear similar words which would again take away my peace of mind for a while. Wańkowicz urged me:

"Go, what's the harm in trying, you'll see what he says this time."

It was August 1974. I was a bit upset to again be with the fortune teller.

"Either you focus, or come some other time. You clearly don't want your future told."

I asked him to try once more.

"I am sorry," he begun. "All cards show the nearest six, or even three months of your life. Not for the whole life. The layout is bad, it's called 'the devil's laughing and rubbing hands with glee'...It would seem a dead-end situation. Many tribulations—blackmail, envy, unpleasant stories with some letters abroad. Many problems, serious ones. Next to you there is death of an elderly person, trouble of some official nature, maybe political. Neither your life nor that of your son is in danger, but you must be strong. You'll be close to breaking down. If I can help any with what I see, look here, at the end you have a good, sunny card. You'll come out of all the trouble, everything will turn out well."

I told Wańkowicz some of what I'd heard.

"I don't understand any of it. I am eighty-two years old, I've lived through so much, seen so much. I don't believe in any fortune telling. Once I told you the strange stories from my life which I couldn't explain. There weren't many. You know what, I'll go to that fortune teller. Set a date with him for me."

I was alarmed. There would go a very ill man, whose face was known to everyone. He'd lost thirty kilograms (66 pounds). That would make a depressing impression on people who remembered him in better shape. And what did I know about the fortune teller, about what he was like? What would he tell him? Maybe he'd say that in a few months, or in two years, the writer would die? He didn't need additional distress at a time which was still so bad. I didn't react. Wańkowicz had a habit of placing notes with his instructions on my desk. I still have some of them today. From the end of August, two instructions were: Biblioteka Narodowa (National Library), check...I have: the fortune teller. Underlined. He was irritated I'd forgotten.

"If he reminds me once again, I will have to arrange the visit. It is his decision, I cannot change anything, I can't decide," I thought. He never got to do it. (He passed away in a few weeks.)

Mr. Mustafa told me my fortune a few more times. I have all his predictions written down. Maybe I'll come back to them after some years?

Under the name of Józef Marcinkowski, Mustafa published a book *Pamiętnik jasnowidza* (*A Clairvoyant's Diary*). He was very happy with a

Pole being chosen for the pope. When a picture of the pope with his hand reaching out was published on the cover of *Paris Match*, Mustafa told me that he saw blood on it. That the pope was in danger.

In our conversations, the issue of predictions which gave people hope returned. They allowed one to endure a bad time. It cannot be good if people somehow direct their lives to adjust them to the predictions they hear.

"If someone has a strong will," said Mustafa, "he can change a lot. You can direct your fate, it's only the destiny that you cannot change. You can reach the same destination by various ways. The choice of the way depends to a large extent on ourselves."

Under the impact of our conversation I wrote a text. I called Mr. Marcin-kowski and we arranged to meet. I wanted to show him the story before I could use it. I read it out loud to him. He listened carefully, interrupted me, made corrections and additions. He allowed printing, but we agreed his name shouldn't be mentioned. He was ill and didn't want to be advertised, as that would drive crowds of people to him.

I left Poland and lived in Toronto. In a Canadian weekly *Związkowiec* (*The Alliancer*) I published fragments of that text, then the next ones in the Warsaw *Express reporterów* (*Reporters' Express*). I sent him cuttings through a person who was going to Poland. She told me later that Mr. Mar-cinkowski's wife asked to thank me. Her husband had died of a heart failure a few weeks earlier. Mrs. Marcinkowska sent me a short letter. I still have it.

The full text about the fortune teller and his philosophy, his reflections, was included in the collection *Moje i zasłyszane* (*Mine and Overheard Stories*) with the title: *Mówią o nim, że jest Tybetańczykiem* (*He is said to be Tibetan*). He'd chosen that title himself.

He was one of my most remarkable acquaintances. I brought a few people to him, some others came on my recommendation. Each of those visits is a separate story. Each is interesting, like Mustafa himself.

If people trust predictions too much and take each word to be true, they renounce their own free will. Fortune tellers usually don't indicate to their customers how the latter could free the potential energy and possibilities. With the information given, it depends on the person what he or she does.

Mother Antonina Ziółkowska

Father Henryk Ziółkowski

Aleksandra, her older brother Henryk, and her younger brother Krzysztof

Older brother Henryk Ziółkowski

Younger brother Krzysztof Ziółkowski

Aleksandra

Thomas and his dog

Thomas Tomczyk

Aleksandra and Thomas, Warsaw

Melchior Wańkowicz and Aleksandra, June 1972

Warsaw, 1985, Aleksandra and Canadian Senator Stanley Haidasz

Zbigniew Brzezinski, NN, Aleksandra, Warsaw

Roman Rodziewicz and Aleksandra, Warsaw

Aleksandra at Warsaw Kmicica apartment

Writer Ryszard Kapuściński and Thomas Tomczyk, Warsaw

Thomas Tomczyk, May 1993, graduation in Architecture, University of Arkansas

Aleksandra and Thomas, Wilmington, Delaware

Thomas

Aleksandra and Norman, 1990

Aleksandra and Norman, Mount St. Helens National Volcanic Monument, Washington State

Aleksandra in Rio de Janiero, Brazil, 1991

Aleksandra at home in Wilmington, Delaware

Barbara Wachowicz, Norman, and Aleksandra, Philadelphia, 2000

Aleksandra and Norman at Woodlands

Chapter Twelve

England Again

Marta Erdman leased the writer's house on Studencka Street to an English family, Ann and Peter Lagoe. The date when I was to get my own apartment and move out was constantly postponed, and in effect we all lived together for a few weeks. My room and Tomek's remained unchanged as oases of the past for a few more weeks. Ann was a cheerful young woman. She had two daughters: Sara and Katie. We all became friends.

At that time thanks to the efforts of Mr. and Mrs. Racięski, I received an invitation from the British Council and I left to England for a two-month scholarship. In London, I visited the writer's cousin, Karol Wańkowicz, and his wife who belonged to the famous Romer family, as well as Zbigniew and Stanisława Racięski. They showed me the towns of Woodstock, Chipping, Camden, Banbury, and also Stonehenge and the Winchester Cathedral. Mr. Racięski drove me to Oxford, where in Brasenose College I took English courses and lectures on the British theatre. We made a few trips to Stratford-on-Avon and saw a Shakespearean play. I felt wonderful, as if I was a student again. Under the influence of a young couple from Switzerland, I became interested in the issue of Zodiac signs. I bought a few books about horoscopes, which I brought to Warsaw. In Oxford, I made friends with people from various parts of the world. Our British teachers were always available and gladly spent their free time with us. Graeme Tytler, a professor of English grammar, always in a stiff white collar, took us for walks. After my return to Warsaw, we corresponded for many months.

I became friends with the Cousins family. They took me on trips and invited me to dinner in their home. Jean, Brian, Lynda and Janet introduced me to their friends. They were all curious about the world, and travelled much. Brian took me to a yachting club in Abingdon on the River Thames. Near the district of Old Marston the Cherwell River flows, and from there into the Thames. We sailed a few times. I remember walks in the romantic Donkey Bridge, and visits to pubs.

In South Hinksey Village, in Manor Road, in a picturesque part of Oxford, the house of Stefania and Edmund Piechowiak was located. They were Poles, with whom I spent a few pleasant evenings. In Pembroke College, I met Professor Zbigniew Pełczyński, who invited me to his study. With a broken leg in plaster, he showed me his historical works on Poland. He told me about his way to Oxford. Born in Warsaw, raised in Grodzisk Mazowiecki, he fought in the Warsaw Uprising in the Mokotów district as a soldier of the *Baszta* regiment of the Home Army. After the defeat of the Uprising, he was taken to a POW camp. Later he fought in General Maczek's 1st Armoured Division. After the war, he took a course in law and obtained a Master's degree at St. Andrews University in Scotland. He then obtained another Master's degree and then a doctoral degree in political philosophy at Oxford University. Since 1953, he taught political science in Oxford, in Pembroke College, and was also invited to lecture at Yale, McGill, Harvard, Jerusalem, and Tokyo. In the 1960s, he was the teacher of an American scholarship holder, William Clinton, the future President of the United States. Professor Pełczyński helped many Poles to study at one of the best universities in the world, in Oxford. He carried out his program in the 1980s thanks to George Soros, an American billionaire of Hungarian descent. The Stefan Batory Trust was established to support the studies of Polish, Hungarian, and also Czechoslovakian and Russian academics.

I missed Tomek, who was being taken care of by my parents and—for a few hours a day—by the Salesian Sisters. An elderly sister Wanda took him to the nunnery garden, in which she weeded and took care of the flowers and vegetables. I bought him another set of toy soldiers, some clothes, and a figure of an American soldier, which later became one of his favourite toys.

At Oxford I received letters from Marta Erdman, and also what I believe to be the nicest telegram I have ever received: "Love you and miss you: Joanna, Krzysztof, Przema."

Przema I met thanks to Krzysztof Kąkolewski. He called me to say that there was a young sculptress who was carving Wańkowicz's head and needed suggestions. I visited her in her study on the fifteenth floor of a block on Grzybowska Street. I saw a giant clay head worked on by a petite girl of oriental features. She laughed heartily, readily, and loud. She was a year older than me, and had a pretty daughter named Wandzia. Przema was born and raised in Sopot, a resort city on the Baltic sea. Her father, Zygmunt Karolak, was a professor at the Academy of Fine Arts and a known painter. In Warsaw, Przema had a flat and a study. Her husband, a journalist, was living in Gdańsk. We both had similar lives—our husbands were away from us, and we both had children. I think we both shared a zest for life and interesting people. We became friends and grew close. On Saturday evenings, we had long talks over the phone (for instance, if love yielded to circumstances. *Cedit amor rebus*). Przema was greatly talented and hardworking. I admired her sculptures and her drawings. She could stop in the middle of a street looking with awe at some monstrous man: "What a great head he has!"

I showed her the writer's pictures, gave some advice, and soon the great sculpture of the head of the author of *Monte Cassino* was completed.

Przema valued art and believed it to be worthy of great sacrifices. At that time, I was reading Józef Szczublewski's book about Helena Modrzejewska,[1] where the author quoted a letter written by the actress in 1895. What she had written seemed also highly interesting to me: "Art does not give happiness, because you always seek something in it that you can usually not find; then, it gives no rest, because you always need to rush ahead so as not to be left behind; finally, it breeds ambition, and ambition devours you. But then, we are not born solely to happiness."

Przema carved the head of Krzysztof Kąkolewski (whom she fancied quite platonically), then mine (the posing was very tiresome to me, I could not talk, because it distracted the sculptress). I introduced Przema to Krystyna and Michał Radgowskis, who came to like her very much, and introduced her to other friends of theirs. Soon the assistant editor of *Polityka*, Jan Bijak, asked Przema to carve the head of his attractive daughter Anna. Yet I believe my greatest achievement was bringing Professor of philosophy Władysław Tatarkiewicz[2] to her, who agreed to pose for a sculpture. The Professor was 90 then. He looked well, was fit, and his mind worked clearly and unfailingly. He was a man of gallantry and refinement. If I wanted, for instance, to help him out of the car, or hold the elevator door for him, I had to do that discreetly, so that he would not be piqued with the offered help. When Przema finished her work, the Professor turned to me with a request:

"I have looked well and healthy for many, many years. I've looked that for most of my life. Could your friend possibly rejuvenate me somewhat? Her sculpture emphasizes all the signs of old age in me, and those have appeared relatively recently. Why is my head to immortalise the period which is last and likely brief?"

Przema snorted at me, saying she would not rejuvenate the Professor's head, that all those wrinkles were beautiful (that was how she saw people), and that she had to show the whole truth as it was.

On completion, the Professor asked to be able to keep the head for a week in his apartment on Chocimska Street. He wanted to get used to it. He would either buy it for himself, or return it. He chose the latter.

Once Krzysztof and Joanna invited Przema, me and Waldemar Kosiński, a journalist from Poznań, to a supper at SPATiF[3] on Aleje Ujazdowskie Street. I went to Przema's flat to get her, took little Wandzia (she was Tomek's senior by two years) and brought her to Studencka Street, to Tomek.

The house was spacious, the garden blooming. The children were to stay together for a few hours, accompanied by Ania Figlewicz, daughter of the neighbors across the street. The supper in SPATiF was delicious, and the conversations interesting. Time flew, and I started to remind my friend that our children were waiting for us and it was time to go home.

"They'll surely go to bed," she assured me.

"Maybe even together?" Krzysztof joked.

When we returned home, we saw two small pale creatures, motionless with fatigue. They were waiting for their mothers. I promised myself never to have that situation repeated. Home was important. You had only one child-hood and I wanted Tomek to remember it as a good and interesting one, and wanted to spend as much time with him as possible. I had great pleasure spending my time with him, as it were. He grew up, asked many questions, and slowly a strong friendship was being born between us. Przema sometimes made fun of my—as she put it—bourgeois approach to raising a child.

The English friend of mine, Ann Lagoe, belonged to the club of diplomats' wives (Peter was on a trading post there). These ladies wanted to visit the studios of artists and popular people. Ann asked me if any of my friends could show them his or her studio. I thought of Przema, contacted her, and we both prepared carefully for the wive's visit. Przema tidied up the studio, pulled out dozens of her drawings, and we prepared *passe-partout* frames for them. The ladies were to come in two groups, each of at least twenty people. When the time of the visit was near, we heard the squealing noise of high-pitched voices—we called it "eek-eek"—in the corridor. We opened the door and saw a colourfully dressed group of women at various ages, laughing. They seated themselves on the chairs, stools, and cushions available and were all ears. Przema showed how she carved, showed her drawings and paintings.

"Was she that talented already as a child?" asked the ladies.

"Oh, yes. She showed exceptional talent as a child," I said with conviction.

Ann Lagoe had a beautifully framed drawing by Przema in her living room, and told her friends she'd invested in a young, talented painter.

Wandzia, Przema's daughter, was to go to the First Communion, but it turned out that her mother had not baptized her yet. Thus we held a christening party, and guests included Krzysztof and Joanna, Professor Tatarkiewicz (it was the time when he posed for Przema's sculpture), and Przema's sister Jagusia. I was the godmother and very much excited with the role.

Earlier, I became the godmother of my nephew Michał (Michałek), the son of Henio and Marysia. Michał Ziółkowski was born on second October 1975. My dear older brother was deeply moved with his son's birth. I went to Łódź and brought the young mother cradling the child in her arms from the hospital.

On my return from Oxford in the autumn, when I was still living on Studencka Street (with the Lagoe family), a woman called me. She introduced herself as Wanda Kazimirska and very much wanted to meet with me. She sounded a little mysterious, but pleasant, and she wasn't pushy. I set a meeting in the *Mazowia* café on Marszałkowska Street. When I arrived there, I saw a relatively young woman, pleasant and neatly dressed. She took a black and white picture out of her purse and gave it to me, asking:

"Do you recognise the person in this picture?"

I looked at it with surprise. I saw the face of Wańkowicz—thin, thus from the last period of his life. The picture was black, no background, just that face, with some strange grimace.

"This is Wańkowicz. Where do you have the picture from?"

She told me that her friend's daughter and her fiancé were developing a film with pictures from their visit in a zoo. Some frames were badly lighted, but they were particularly curious about one of them—it seemed very contrasting. On removing the print from the water, they saw only a head. They didn't know who was in the picture. It scared them. Mrs. Kazimirska, whom they showed the picture to, recognized Wańkowicz's face. It turned out that the pictures were developed on the tenth of September, exactly on the first anniversary of the writer's death. They decided to contact me. I showed the pictures to photographers, Krzysztof Fus and Lech Suchcicki, who took pictures of Wańkowicz when he was ill. They didn't have such a frame in their collections. They offered various explanations for how the picture could have appeared, for instance as an accidental exposure when the film was handled, perhaps of an image from TV. But they couldn't fully explain all the circumstances. Meanwhile, Mrs. Kazimirska, who had contact with a Warsaw spiritists' group, encouraged me to take part in their meetings among whom a significant role was played by Eugeniusz Jasiewicz, a known esotericist. I was asked to prepare questions to Wańkowicz to which the writer's "spirit" was to give answers in the future. I left them three questions the answers to which could be known only to the author of *Ziele na kraterze*. I wasn't given specific answers, however, what I was given was an extensive epistle written in verse (I was told that the medium was a poet) in which (among others) the writer's "soul" granted me each and every authorization to act in his name, because he was already engaged with other, more mundane matters. I answered that I could hardly believe the writer's "soul" would have become so boring and expound such jibberish that I was not interested in the whole matter.

Meanwhile, ever new copies of the said poem circulated in Warsaw, many new versions appeared concerning the topic, and some people approached me, asking for a comment. I didn't give any.

In Dallas I received a letter from Barbara Wachowicz. She wrote to me from the spa in Busko Zdrój:

I am now in Busko—using the burn-ups and soak-ins, as Mr. Melchior would say. They have a nice habit here of making a small exhibition concerning my humble self—there is also a picture with the author of *Ziele (na kraterze)*—and lo and behold, today some biddy assaulted me with a suspicious glint in her eye—if I know that Wańkowicz (sic!) has written twelve letters from the beyond to his sister...

I expressed my surprise at his having taken such pains when the addressee was quite at hand—since she'd passed to the other side before her brother and assuredly awaited him there. Then I advised her to visit a library and find a book by Oleńka Ziółkowska *Na tropach Wańkowicza* and read of that netherworld event...I couldn't possibly remember the versed epistles the Grandad was supposed to send from heavens above (whatsoever—light-bright, sky high,) but I quoted to my ladies (Alusia Damroszowa and Monisia Olbrychska) your great comeback that should Mr. Wańkowicz turn such a scribbler upon his death, you have no wish of meeting again!

See how tales are spreading...

Chapter Thirteen

Apartment on Kmicica Street

In October 1975, I moved into my own apartment purchased in a huge 10 story building (called "block" in Poland) on Kmicica Street. The block stood alone on the edge of a large housing estate consisting of detached houses with gardens. Approachable from Wilanowska Alley, the block could be reached by turning onto Wernyhory Street or Studencka Street, parallel to each other and only four streets apart. Earlier, when walking in the neighbourhood, Wańkowicz and I watched the block being built. The writer joked—what would happen if I was to obtain aa apartment in that very place, so close. I was surprised when it turned out that his jokes came true: my apartment was about ten minutes walking distance from the writer's house. The area is called *Służew nad Dolinką*. Surrounded by greenery, at that time it was considered one of the prettier and neater home properties in Warsaw.

I was very happy with the apartment. Although being rather small, the apartment was well planned with three rooms, a kitchen, a large hall, a bathroom and a separate toilet. Particularly attractive was the square balcony with its outer walls featuring two large planters for earth. When I decided that some modifications were needed, Krysia Radgowska recommended a Mr. Jan Pytel, a worker who'd earlier refurbished her place. I provided Jan the keys to my apartment, and he worked long weeks alone, but also employed additional workers. Michał Radgowski jokingly said that the apartment was built anew. The workers tore off the PVC floors, installed beautiful hardwood floors in the living room and bedrooms, tiled the kitchen, bathroom, toilet floors and walls, built in wardrobes, cupboards, and shelves. On the largest wall in the big room, Jan built a huge bookcase. I had the impression that he actually liked the apartment and worked at it with his heart and ideas. When I moved in with Tomek, the rooms were full of boards and screws for many more weeks, and renovation continued. When my mother visited me, she wrung her hands in despair for my son and I living in a quasi-carpenter's shop.

The hardships of those few months paid off; the apartment had become functional and pleasant. Jan wainscoted the hall, shifted the lighting, and added many improvements. Those were the 1970s, the years under Gierek, [1] and in the shops everything you needed was available for the modifications I desired. In Henryków, I bought some Biedermeier style furniture. I already had two valuable antiques: Chippendale table and XIX century chest. Przema, my artist friend, helped hang up her drawings, and with Krysia I bought a chandelier. In February, for my name's day party (the day designated to the saint, like February 26: Saint Aleksandra), I invited friends to the newly furnished abode. They brought good wishes and presents: the Kąkolewskis brought a decorative tin bowl, Szymon Kobyliński his drawings, Teresa Jonkajtys-Sołtanowa her paintings on metal, Professor Tatarkiewicz old porcelain, Ryszard Kapuściński a Coptic cross, the Radgowskis a silver-plated tray, Aleksander Małachowski artistic, handmade birds, Basia Wachowicz her book *Marie jego życia* (*The Marias of His Life*) with a tender-hearted inscription...and so on. As time passed, the apartment became filled with mementoes, the more valuable that they were gifts received from talented people whom I valued highly and liked very much. In my bedroom, I had separate shelves for books given to me by my friends who had provided inscriptions inside. I remember various funny moments—for instance, once when I had a problem with the overhead light in Tomek's room, and Mr. Małachowski had to stand on a stool for a long time to repair the light. Each year, for my namesday in February, I would invite a large party, sometimes up to thirty people. I planned the party a few days ahead, and my friends helped me prepare for it.

A funny story is connected with the elevator in the block on Kmicica Street. My rent included an additional fee for using the elevator, however, for me to use the elevator was impractical. For access to my apartment on the second floor, I could traverse the corridor and walk up two flights from ground level or I could ride the elevator up three flights traverse the corridor and walk down one flight. It was much simpler and quicker to traverse the corridor and take the stairs, which started at the ground or entrance level of the block. However, the entrance was not the most elegant, and with time it became outright squalid. When moving in, I was charged additional fees for the laborious effort of carrying furniture up the stairs. Since the elevator was unavailable to the inhabitants of the two lowest floors, I decided not to pay for it, and I sent a letter explaining the situation to the management of the housing cooperative. The housing cooperative management's reply letter contained threats of elaborate sanctions against me for failure to pay the "impractical elevator fee." Unexpectedly, help came from Michał Radgowski, who knew the situation. In one of his weekly features in *Polityka* he described the whole situation, mocking the "impracticality" of using the elevator by some of the residents. He named the street and quoted the threatening reaction of the housing cooperative. Two weeks after the article was printed, the janitor knocked at all doors at my floor and granted the residents an official "dispensation," deducting the elevator fee from our monthly rent.

As years went by, the nice, neat and freshly painted block slowly grew more and more rundown and unkempt. Broken window panes were replaced with plywood boards, the front door didn't close properly, mischevous play by children caused burn out of the elevator buttons. The appearance of our block reflected the situation of the collapsing country more and more, and its dwellers presented a cross-section of the society. Many nice and neat people lived there, as well as many slovenly types and troublemakers—a situation incomprehensible in other countries, where usually the slovenly types and troublemakers stay together (as in the old saying *birds of a feather stick together*). These types tend to make up their own neighborhoods and are carefully avoided by other city dwellers. My neighbors from another floor, the well-known actors, Marek Walczewski and Małgosia Niemirska, whose apartment was robbed, often exchanged grim remarks with me about such new incidents in our block. Another couple of actors, Piotr Cieślak and Jadwiga Jankowska-Cieślak, moved out after a few years. A poet, Zbigniew Bieńkowski, who took his dachshund for walks with his wife Adriana Szymańska, also a poet, usually spoke of all and any joys of life rather than about the appearance of our block. The whole housing estate, with its greenery and neat and pleasant look, was disintegrating. Pipes burst and flooded flats. Water was switched off sometimes even for a few hours. When visiting, friends from abroad wondered why I was living in the slums. Their bad impression faded away on entering the apartment. In most blocks of similar kind, the occupants carefully furnished their flats, had elegant furniture and china, and they tried to create an aura of coziness and homeyness. Everything outside—corridors, elevators—belonged to no one, and no one cared to keep them clean and nice-looking. Occupants often installed another front door lock or even an additional front door, often of metal. Fencing oneself in, an occupant lived in the conviction that everything was fine and the falling apart of the block didn't concern him. Some of the residents of higher floors separated themselves into sections, installing barred doors and additional locks. Later I learned that there were a few places in the world where inhabitants would have four or five locks on their door. I saw similar precautions when I visited Brazil and Argentina. In the United States and in Canada, I had one or at the most two keys to the flats and homes I stayed in. Corridors in apartment buildings in Wilmington on Pennsylvania Avenue, and in Dallas on Turtle Creek Boulevard or McKinney Avenue were covered with carpets. Delicate lights, porters, separate elevators for moving furniture and taking dogs for walks, glass doors, quiet music and flowers, sofas and armchairs, the spaces clean and large. My block in Warsaw was gradually partitioned and locked off into fortified sections, secured against possible burglaries. Everyone made certain to secure their front door, without the slightest care for the "no-man's land" of dirty and shabby corridors. When you looked from your balcony to the neighboring blocks, you would wonder whether they were part of the apartments, or of the no-man's territory. With heaps of old furniture, boxes, TV sets out of use, the blocks being viewed were haunted with mess and dirt just as mine was. Like others, I traversed the long, squalid corridor to my apartment and once inside, I forgot about its surroundings. The windows overlooking the gardens and greenery of Wernyhory Street on one side, a lawn and sandpits for children on the other side, and Wałbrzyska Street further away, gave an impression of cosiness and an illusory sense of comfort. Years later in early1990-ies, the building was renovated, modernized and beautifully landscaped. The new time in Poland had arrived.

Chapter Fourteen

First Book: *Near Wańkowicz*

Soon after I moved to Kmicica Street, when my Mom was visiting me, a harbinger of spring came by mail: the first copy of *Blisko Wańkowicza* (*Near Wańkowicz*). I remember that I turned the pages and looked at the pictures again, and again. I started to receive invitations to the radio. I recalled McLuhan's theory—it divided people and media into hot and cool types. According to him, radio belonged to cool media, and television to hot media. However, radio favored hot types of people, and the TV, cool ones. The cool ones are people who are in some way elliptical, undefined, and the viewer can add to them much of himself and as much of what he wants. Steve McQueen was a cool actor with a poker face. Kennedy won the elections appearing in TV as a cool type. In Polish television, Aleksander Bardini[1] belonged to the cool type, while Zygmunt Kałużyński[2] was a hot type. The latter often seemed to irritate people. They called his fierce speeches boorish. All hot discussions were viewed as deviating from the norm. And the norm was a certain dullness. I cannot say to what type of people—according to McLuhan's theory—I belonged. But I liked the radio and never refused the invitations.

One day, when Jan the craftsman was drilling some holes, and Tomek was in bed with a cold, someone knocked at the door. There stood an ominous appearing creature of a man. He showed me a Security Office card, entered (without invitation), sat down on some piece of board and took a look around in surprise. Without any preliminaries, he lectured me on how in my book I had mentioned a Mr. Zbigniew Racięski from London, who is an "enemy of the People's Poland." Racieski being a high-ranking employee of Radio Free Europe, the newcomer warned me against contact with that man. Finally, he gave me some slip of paper to sign. The document stated that I would not say anything to anyone about the visit. "I will not sign it, and quite the contrary—I will tell a lot of people," I replied. The man stared at me in amazement. Jan was hammering away in the adjoining room, and Tomek was crying a little in his room. The man left without as much as a goodbye. He never came back. When I told Krzysztof Kąkolewski of the whole matter, he stated that if they agreed to my not signing the note, it was not a dangerous visit.

My book was popular. The funniest note about it was published by the weekly *Tygodnik Powszechny*[3] (20 V 1976) The first reply to the weekly's mini-competition of our column (topic: "How I obtained a bestseller"):

> I obtained *Blisko Wańkowicza* by Aleksandra Ziółkowska thanks to a friend I work with. His friend—knew another friend who knew another friend who was working with the *Dom Ksiazki* bookstore, and he left one copy under the counter for my opportunity to collect. And all that worked because this year that friend is getting the successive issues of *Tygodnik Powszechny* from me once I read them—and feeling indebted, he activated that chain of contacts."

After *Blisko Wańkowicza* was published, as the author, I was invited to various promotional meetings. Thanks to them I was able to visit various parts of the country. Twice I was invited by *Międzynarodowy Klub Prasy i Książki* (*The International Press and Book Club*) in Szczecin, Świnoujście, Międzyzdroje, Łódź. I visited Gdańsk, Katowice, Zabrze, Zamość, Nysa, Kluczbork, Strzelce, Hrubieszów, Biłgoraj, Starogard, Nowogard. When I was absent on these travels, my father came to Warsaw to take care of Tomek. I could always count on my parents' help and understanding. Father had a deep affection for all of us, which he expressed in his typical, calm and quiet way. Proudly, he obtained books, academic aids, and drawing instruments for us. Always watching Henio, Krzysio and me coping in life, our father was very concerned with our problems.

Before each speech, I was very nervous. I remember well how difficult a task overcoming my shyness. I had better and worse days. I usually spotted some friendly face in the first row and imagined that I spoke to that person. I couldn't talk to a crowd—crowds terrified and paralysed me. After a while, meetings went better and better, and I established good contact with the audience. I think that all my meetings were in a way private with someone, despite so many people being present. I remember the organizers of many of my meetings. They were almost as excited as I was, and their cordial approach endeared them to me. The meetings in Katowice and Zabrze were organized by Xenia Popowicz, one of Wańkowicz's faithful readers, who wrote many interesting letters to me after his death. The friendship born in that way has lasted for years. Frequently, on later visits to Silesia, I stayed with her and we talked long hours. I know the important issues of her life and we are still in contact. Also in Katowice, there lived a former soldier who'd taken part in the Monte Cassino battle, Tadeusz Szumański. When

Wańkowicz's *Bitwa o Monte Cassino* was reissued again, he gave the publisher access for use of the photographs in his rich collection.

Twice I was invited to the Zaolzie region, to Český Těšín. I lived in the hotel *Piast*, formerly *Polonia*, the picture of which I knew from *Sztafeta*. In the Main Centre of the Polish Cultural and Educational Union,[4] I met journalists working in Polish papers issued there. The monthly *Zwrot (Turn)* has been issued since 1949 and always with particular care; the publishers showed me Wańkowicz's inscription he'd written when delivering a series of lectures in 1958. Most people didn't know the chapter of *Sztafeta* titled *Fanfara Zaolziańska (Zaolzie Fanfare)*, or the *Chciejstwo (Wishful Thinking)* chapter from the second volume of *Karafka La Fontaine'a*, which showed a different view of the writer after many years on the case of Zaolzie.[5] I had author's meetings in Třinec, Jablunkov, Orlová, Ostrava, Mosty, Těšín and Karviná. With Halinka Kowalczyk, a journalist, we traveled to Ligotka, and in the *Kozieniec* hostel in Guty had tea together. "Again and again, we have to make choices, have to be for or against something. Constant choices...my husband and I have so many problems, normal, daily ones. When I think that we'd have another one, if my children should call me *mamusia* or *maminka*[6] ...then it's better to avoid it and marry a Pole," said Halinka.

The misfortune of the people of Zaolzie is that they were born in a territory that constantly changed the state it belonged to. Marshal Piłsudski, the chief of state of Zaolzie, once said to a delegation from Těšín (Cieszyn) Silesia: "Wait with faith, and persevere. I repeat, we shall not renounce you."

I took part in a two-day autumn seminar in Kosarzyska, visited a Polish library, saw a play in the Polish Theatre in Zaolzie. I met many people, among them Franciszek Swider (painter), Karol Piegza (designer of monuments in Karviná and Třinec, teacher, collector, folk poet and painter), Kazimierz Kaszper (poet) and Władysław Niedoba, head of the Polish Stage (Scena Polska). We passed Milíkov, the Olza and Lomianka rivers. Everywhere there were Polish clubs, hundred-years-old former Polish schools with church turrets, because once it was the priest who taught children. Viewing a shrine from the 15th century, we saw an elderly, stooped woman in a colorful folk headscarf, waiting for the evening Mass. I was in the capital of the highlands, in Jablunkov, which was compared by Wańkowicz to Dubrovnik. I made new friends. I wrote the text *Zapiski zaolziańskie (Zaolzie Notes)*. I left with admiration for the beauty of the entire area and the treasures it held.

After *Blisko Wańkowicza* was published, I received a letter from Iwo Jankowski, a young man from Toruń, a topographer by education. He shared a funny story with me. Being a pupil of primary school, he learned by heart a fragment of *Tędy i owędy (This Way and That)*, in which the writer quotes curses he'd hurled at a Warsaw hackney driver when still very young. On hearing those "bad words," Iwo's teacher forbade him to come to school and summoned his mother. Explanations by Iwo and his mother that it was a quote from a famous writer's book did not satisfy the teacher. However, finally Iwo returned to school, and his mother wrote about the whole incident in a letter to Wańkowicz. The writer sent the young boy a book with the following inscription:

> Sonny, don't say naughty slang
> or you'll get another spank.
> Once your schooling's done and closed
> I'll some more to you disclose.

My correspondence with Iwo lasted for many years. He followed all editions of Wańkowicz's books, knew about the writer's letters that I was preparing for print, and collected all the issues very conscientiously. Once, when he was staying in Warsaw for a few days, he visited me in my apartment on Kmicica Street. When he saw my collection of editions of the Paris *Kultura,* he asked me to lend him some titles. From these titles, he was able to read *Cancer Ward* and *In the First Circle* by Solzhenitsyn, among others. Iwo later told me that during that Warsaw visit, the group of military topographers who were with him also read the borrowed books long into the nights.

After reading *Blisko Wańkowicza,* a journalist and writer, Alicja Grajewska, approached me. She owned a small house with a garden near Bielany forest in Warsaw. I often visited her with Tomek, who ran in the garden and discovered birds' nests. Alicja owned a German Shepherd dog named Mate, however, Tomek managed to twist its name calling it: Check. In the summer, Alicja organized small parties for her name's day; in autumn, traditional St. Andrew's Eve fortunetelling parties were her venue. At the end of November, the day before St Andrew's day, in the last evening before the Advent, Alicja invited a few friends for fortunetelling. We all dropped some hot wax in the water to tell us our fortune. Sometimes it was difficult to read the fortune. Tomek and I constantly read what appeared to be exotic animals, which the hostess infallibly interpreted as travels to faraway countries. Alicja's guests for this party were warmed by a fire burning in the fireplace and by the sipping of red wine. Alicja, called the Gardener or the Heiress by the Radgowskis, was a very talented person. She wrote under the name Krzysztof Narutowicz. One of her books was *Konstelacje* (*Constellations*) that included interesting essays on the works of Mauriac, Wańkowicz, Parnicki, and Irzykowski. Being spiritual and somewhat unreal, in her company she made you feel relaxed and very special. Alicja could talk about her garden, flowers, butterflies, birds or the mole in an incredible way. For her, all living creatures were important, and she "humanized" them in a way that made you feel about them as she did.

After the death of Julian Krzyżanowski, I had to contact a new professor for a supervisor of my doctoral thesis. I turned to Professor Janina Kulczycka-Saloni, whose works on the "positivist period" (the end of XIX century) in Polish literature I valued in particular. She agreed, and regular appointments began for me. At first, we met at the university, then in her apartment on Foksal Street. I would bring my son, who patiently waited for me playing with the Professor's black Dachshund named Bella.

Chapter Fifteen

Ship Cruise

The time neared when Tomek would start school. I thought long and hard where to take him for a last vacation before school began. He went to the seaside and to the mountains interchangeably with my parents. I wanted to have a trip which would make a particular impression on his memory. After much consideration and many inquiries, we decided on a cruise by a ship of the *Polska Żegluga Morska* (*Polish Steamship Company*). Not many people knew about such trips, but they were relatively inexpensive and very well organized. They guaranteed peace, beautiful weather in the summer, often attractive places and international ports. We sailed on the ship *Kopalnia Zofiówka*, which was to stop in Italian ports and then went to the coast of Africa. The journey was an extraordinary one. Life gained different dimensions: another time, distances, deadlines, duties, work. The unusual colors of the Mediterranean Sea and the Atlantic Ocean reigned: the emeralds and the manifold shades of greyness. Never before and never after have I seen such sunrises and sunsets, when the sun rolled over the sky, first dazzlingly silver, then turning golden, and in the evening it took on purple robes and vanished in the ocean's depths like a red exotic fruit.

The ship had a shipowner's cabin, which was taken by passengers if there were any. For our cruise, the cabin was mine and Tomek's. The cabin consisted of three parts: a hall, with a door leading to a bathroom with shower, one leading to a small living room, holding shelves, a table and armchairs, all fixed to the floor, and one to a bedroom, filled with two beds by the walls and a small table with a lamp between them. Our ship accomodation was not roomy, but cozy, and very functionally furnished. The windows let in much light, and the rooms were flooded with sunshine. In the living room, I placed my typewriter and tried to devote some time each day to the most laborious chapter of my doctor'a thesis, the materials for which I had taken with me. I brought a few books with me, among them *Polski dowcip językowy* (*Polish Linguistic Humour*) by Danuta Buttler, and *The Neurotic Personality of Our Time* by Karen Horney. The daily schedule on the ship was constant, dictated mainly by the four meals: breakfast, lunch, afternoon snack and supper. Films were shown three times a week. There were two showings, so that sailors working on various shifts could partake of them. The ship also had a small gym and a library.

Beside us, the only passenger was the captain's wife, Majka Pałkańska, with whom I became friends. I remember repeating to her the opinions of Karen Horney, whose book I found highly interesting:

> It is, in reality, not so terribly important that people in general should like us. It may, in fact, be important only that certain persons like us—those whom we care for, those with whom we have to live or work, or those on whom it is expedient to make a good impression.

And another one:

> [The person] has no clear conception that this is his own life, and that it is up to him to make something out of it or to spoil it, but he lives as if what happens to him were no concern of his own, as if good and evil came from the outside without his having anything to do about it, as if he had a right to expect the good things from others and to blame them for all bad things.

The ships of the *Polish Steamship Company* were designed to accommodate only a few passengers, and their cabins were not isolated from the sailors' cabins. Passengers were not isolated from the sailors. They could be either accepted by the sailors, or rejected and left alone. Tomek and I were treated almost like members of the crew. During the cruise, the sailors were particularly protective of Tomek, and devoted much attention to him. I had the chance to see the sailors' work, habits, existence at sea. They gladly talked of their families, waited for phone connections, and worried if no one answered the phone at home. They missed their wives, children, families. When we stopped in ports, they ran from shop to shop with lists of what their wives and friends asked them to purchase. Often they sought my advice as to whether they'd made the right choice. Majka told me that when at sea her husband wrote letters full of yearning for her and for their son, that there was great joy and excitement whenever he came home, and then after some two weeks, they were both looking forward to the time when he would set sail again and the house return to its "normal" life.

Above all, the trip brought soothing peace and quiet. The constant breeze gave pleasantly cool air. For the first time in my life I saw dolphins. They swam in a school just next to the ship, clearly pleased with the attention they were getting. They could jump up, turning their heads towards the people watching them. Dolphins are always friendly towards people. If there are accidents at sea, they often help by pushing people towards the shore, and they will drive away sharks attacking humans. The sailors told me a story of a dolphin in Rotterdam that led ships into the harbor during the war, serving as a kind of guide. The brave dolphin was later given a monument.

I remember the extraordinary sight of Messina from the Messina Strait as we crossed it—a mountainous area with white houses protruding fom it. We stopped for a few days in the Marghera port in Mestre near Venice. From there, we made trips to the utterly wonderful city of Venice. By waterbus along the Grand Canal, we reached the center of Venice. Flooded with spring sun, Venice seemed to me a city taken out of a beautiful dream. We explored its narrow streets, visited the churches, and gazed at the paintings of the great masters. Tomek also succumbed to the singular atmosphere of the city. We rode gondolas and drank cold juice in *Piazza San Marco*.

To leave the gem of Italy was sad for all of us. I promised myself to visit Venice again one day. Years late I considered that next to our native Kraków, San Francisco and Haifa, it is one of the more beautiful cities I have ever visited.

The day after we left the port, Tomek saw a boy hiding on board. He ran up to me, excited, and said that a passenger was coming with us, a small boy, and that "we will take care of him, first of all bring him food." I couldn't understand what he was talking about. Finally I went to investigate it, and indeed, among the ropes I saw a huddled boy. He appeared nine or ten years old, and looked at me with a mixture of fear and trust that maybe something would change for the better in his life. I returned to my cabin, wondering what would happen. When I told the captain, the ship was immediately searched. Finding the boy confirmed that we had a stowaway on board who wanted to work and earn some summer wages. Our stowaway was a Yugoslavian lad named Borys, fourteen years of age, who lived in Nova Gorica, a town 140 kilometres from Venice. Polish law forbade such employment, and the ship had to return the boy back to Italy. He gave us reproachful looks, unable to understand why we didn't want him. Tomek was also upset that we couldn't take the boy with us.

For the following days, we ate fresh Italian fruit and bread on the ship. In each port the ship stayed in, shopping was done to add variety to our meals with fresh products.

When the ship neared the African coast, twe noticed its sun-burnt soil with surprise. How bleak the mass of earth looked after seeing the green coast of Italy.

In the Moroccan port of Safi, we were warned against wandering off on our own, so we always shopped in a group. I was amazed by everything—the dark faces of Arabs, the smell of fish in the air. I gazed long at a potter's work, and finally I was tempted enough to buy small hand-painted fired vases. On my return I gave them away to friends as gifts. We went for a walk in the souk (market), passing colorful stands with leather goods, mats, cotton. The Arabs knew a few Polish words they'd picked up from sailors. I learned the question: *Kayf haalek il-youm?*—and the answer: *Sucran. Sahatiy zayn.* (How are you today?—Thank you, my health is good.) Tomek bought a camel leather belt for himself, and helped me pick a blue cotton dress and fitting shoes. They were the world's most beautiful things to me.

The return to the port of Świnoujście and then the trip by train to Warsaw were like a glass of cold water to cool us down, and a return to reality. The memories of the trip stayed with us for good, and they were so strong that when Tomek completed high school, he claimed he wanted to be a sailor to "travel and see the world."

In Warsaw, we were welcomed by Michał Radgowski and a huge pack of correspondence he'd collected for us while we were away. ("Never in my life have I seen such an amount of letters," he joked.)

After my lectures on the northern coast, the director of the publishing house *Wydawnictwo Literackie*, Andrzej Kurz, told me that people from the Security Service visited him as the publisher of my book, repeating some of my "not so cautious words." He mentioned his encounter in a conversation almost in passing. Stating that he was not threatening me, Kurz advised me to be cautious. At that time, the workers' strike in the Ursus factory began. Prime Minister Jaroszewicz had announced a considerable increase in prices. In Ursus, there was a strike, and railway tracks were blocked. In Radom, there were riots in the streets. The militia crushed the workers. All my friends and I could talk about were these events. I drove to Łódź as was my custom, and together with the whole family listened to Radio Free Europe. My invitations to author's meetings stopped. I worked more intensively on my doctoral thesis, and I had the regular monthly remuneration (bequeathed to me by the writer) for work on the series of the collected works of Wańkowicz. New titles were published successively.

Chapter Sixteen

Radziejowice—
Professor Władysław Tatarkiewicz

Summer was only starting. On 17th July 1976, my brother Krzysio and Ania Golańska were married in Łódź. They had just graduated, but their nearest future was still veiled. I then had the idea to invite them immediately after their wedding to my Warsaw apartment and to use it for their honeymoon. At the same time, I had a planned trip to the writers' retreat in Radziejowice with Tomek. For a month of that hot summer, we were there. Long walks to the nearby meadows were enjoyed, as were boats trips on the canal of the Radziejowice Park. Tomek picked wild flowers and made bouquets which he then gave to me. Having started such a nice habit when he was just a small boy, he maintained it for many years.

I often spent the time after supper walking around the park with the well known philosopher Professor Władysław Tatarkiewicz (mentioned earlier). We all ate at separate, small tables. The Professor ate alone, since his wife was in a hospital at that time. A retreat's assistant came up to the Professor after the meal and leaned over to ask in a sweet voice:

"How did you sleep, dear Professor? Did you like your potatoes? Was the meat tender?"

After a few days of those questions, we heard an answer. The Professor reacted in a stentorian voice:

"Ma'am, I do not like such affections in public!...And do not address me like you would a child, I have long since stopped being one!"

The whole room fell silent, and the woman left without another word. She never came to ask any more questions.

In Radziejowice, I was visited by my doctor's thesis supervisor, Professor Janina Kulczycka-Saloni. Earlier she had told me that Professor Tatarkie-wicz's biographical notes were about learning optimism, but it was the opti-

141

mism of a wealthy man who never had financial trouble. In his house, there
was always wealth and order. And that he was never engaged in anything
"unsuitable."

I soon received from Professor Tatarkiewicz his three-volume *Historia
filozofii* (*History of Philosophy*) with the inscription:

> As I am signing this book for Ms. Aleksandra Ziółkowska, I feel as if I were
> signing it for my granddaughter, because she is studying under the supervision
> of Professor Kulczycka-Saloni, just like the Professor studied under my super-
> vision. But this doesn't mean that I feel old. Two generations have passed very
> quickly.

He revealed to me:
"When I was young, I liked women like you."
"And now?" I asked.
"Now I like other ones as well."
He also told me:
"You always look as if freshly showered, which is a great compliment."

He gave me another book, *O szczęściu (About Happiness)* with a curious
inscription: I think that a man's happiness lies in the right woman, and I
believe that Melchior Wańkowicz was happy.

The book contained many wise thoughts about happiness, and I read some
of them with keen interest. For instance, Democritus believed that a happy
life was one that was felt positively and with which a man was satisfied.
What was important in life was not what you had, but how you felt about
what you had. Aristotle, in turn, believed that happiness consisted in having
the most valuable thing. If knowledge is the most valuable, then happy is the
man who has knowledge; if it is valour and bravery, then happy is a brave
man. Boethius asked: Why are you looking outside of yourselves for happiness which is in you?

Years later, I remembered the words of Father Józef Bocheński: that a
man should seek the cause of his happiness or misery in himself, that he
should find joy in small things and do his job—and happiness will come.
That you shouldn't be interested in other people, unless they are your enemies or may be useful, or you are responsible for them, or you can help them.

Professor Tatarkiewicz told me about a sculptor who'd died recently in
France, August Zamoyski. The Professor gave me a printed version of the
correspondence they'd exchanged. Zamoyski had a highly interesting life: he
was born in Podlasie, graduated in Warsaw, studied law and economy in
Freiburg, and philosophy in Heidelberg. In Berlin, he married Rita Sacchetto,
a singer of world fame. They lived in Vienna, then in Zakopane. His philosophical background gave him a high level of artistic consciousness. He
sculpted, wrote, was active in sports, and lived a full life. At the end of the

1920's he left for Paris, where he had a relationship with a singer, Manet Radwan, whose face he immortalized in the sculptures *Venus* and *Ewa*. During the Nazi occupation, he left for Brazil, where he remained for fifteen years with his second wife, Isabella Paes Leme, a painter. In Brazil, he sculpted a monument of Chopin, one of Chateaubriand, and a statue of John the Baptist. In the mid-1950s, he returned to Paris, and after a short stay in a Dominican monastery he married for the fourth time, his new wife being Helena Peltier, a teacher of Russian literature at the university in Toulouse. They lived in the country, in Saint-Clarde-Riviere. His works from that time had a religious character: *Pieta, Ból istnienia (Weltschmerz), Ludzki krzyż (Human Cross), Zmartwychwstanie (Resurrection)*. By the end of his life, he sought an answer to the "mystery of existence" in mysticism. Professor Tatarkiewicz spoke of August Zamoyski with great fascination.

A few years later, in January 1994, I learned that August Zamoyski's sculptures were exhibited in the National Museum in Warsaw. The exhibition was arranged by Krystyna Zachwatowicz, who along with Andrzej Wajda[1] are said to be great enthusiasts of Zamoyski's works.

On one occasion, Professor Tatarkiewicz discovered that I was a Zodiak Aries, as he was. Comparing himself to Wańkowicz who liked people, he too liked people, but sometimes did not know how to "rid himself" of them. "I haven't come up with a way, like Wańkowicz, to say that 'Mr. Małachowski is coming,'" he said in reference to the anecdote I'd quoted in my book *Blisko Wańkowicza*. A few times we travelled from Łódź to Warsaw together. His wife was in a hospital, and he visited her every few days. Once we were returning in a heavy rain, when he presented me with a copy from *Kwartalnik Historii Nauki i Techniki (Quarterly Journal of the History of Science and Technology)—(For Ms. Aleksandra Ziółkowska—with thanks for a beautiful ride in storm and rain)*, titled *Zapiski do autobiografii (Notes for Autobiography)*. Issued later as a separate book, I remember many remarks from it, which I repeat here in no particular order. Writing of his life, he stressed things that were important to him. That he was not a sociable man, Tatarkiewicz admitted, although he liked parties. Being able to meet many interesting people at a party, and arranging for another meeting with some was a challenge for him. The Professor avoided meeting the same company regularly, because repeat of the same news. As he wrote, it was better and more productive to walk away and read an interesting book. Often he couldn't make a choice himself, and he allowed life itself to suggest the best solution to him. Tatarkiewicz believed that his fate gave him a generally positive balance and a general satisfaction. "I owe it," wrote the Professor, "to a certain ease of forgetting any hurts and little tendency to worry in advance. I expected little: if I was satisfied, it was not because of the future I expected. Although I know that future has in general a greater impact on a man's being than the present and the past. But that was balanced by the ability to forego thinking about the future, a sense that I would somehow make it. That was the factor of my satisfaction in life. And also, what is sometimes called the optimistic tendency of memory, that is, the tendency to remember things in more rosy colors than they really were."

Such outlook on life was very close to mine. The Professor asked me about my impressions on reading his work. I allowed myself to say that he never mentioned women in his life and their important role.

"You are right. I could add that no one knows why we love a particular kind of woman. This is a mystery. It's surely not the prettiest or the nicest. No one knows why we love certain ones, and other ones we do not. I never had an ideal image of a woman; each one had different values. I feel unsatisfied to an extent from my relationships with women, but I believe that it is better to remain unsatisfied than to be satiated."

When asked which of the philosophers he valued the most, he named Aristotle and Pascal. "Aristotle valued common sense or, on the other extreme, 'sheer folly,'" he observed. Repeatedly, he reverted to the *Meditations* by Marcus Aurelius. His own early philosophical dissertations read after many years were written in a style foreign to him. They were not his style yet, but that of his professors. When I praised his simple, clear language in the *Historia filozofii* he said he'd developed his own style by writing that very book. The book took him five years to write, although when he signed the contract with the *Ossolineum* publishing house, he thought he would finish in half a year.

The Professor spoke of the shrinking of time. Citing his observations mentioned in *Zapiski...:* Only astronomical time flows evenly. Human time constantly accelerates (although, it slows down temporarily with every anticipation). An old man's year is much less than a year of a child, or even a young man. "That concerns not only the present," wrote the Professor, "but also the future: an old man has disproportionately and unexpectedly little time. This is a typical small human tragedy: a young man thinks he has immeasurable time ahead of him, and then it turns out that he has little of it—not only because part of his time is already gone, but also because the time that is left turns out to be shorter than it had seemed. Time shortens in two directions: it is not only the future time left to the man, but also the past one, which is already gone—and it also seems to grow shorter."

The Professor valued the time of his retirement, because he kept doing what he had chosen and what he valued in life. He stopped being competitive, so he had no opponents or enemies, and then life was—as he said—much more tolerable.

Wańkowicz spoke similarly of time and old age to Krzysztof Kąkolewski in the book *Wańkowicz krzepi*. The author believed that a child's year was like five years of a fourteen-year-old, and ten years of a sixty-year-old. Since there was no future, nothing bad could happen to a man anymore. He saw the lack of youth's anxiety as an advantage of old age.

Ryszard Kapuściński wrote in *Lapidarium* that as life passes, it becomes more and more a trip inside our own past, i.e. inside us. Thus, we care for newcomers to the world less and less, because they're not coming for us.

Professor Tatarkiewicz valued human kindness the most, and he preferred politeness to honesty, not liking those who told him he didn't look well or he had written a bad article. For him, the greatest post-war year's events were his two trips to North America. The Professor thought California to be the place made for a man: not too cold, not too hot, not too dry, not too humid, flowers all year round, and the beautiful city of San Francisco. New York City with its elegant Park Avenue ranked equally high for Tatarkiewicz.

Joanna and Krzysztof Kąkolewski also visited me in Radziejowice. To them, the Professor remarked: "You writers are so close to life. We—the academics—only sit over books." Krzysio and Ania dropped by for a weekend during their honeymoon. They were so much in love, they couldn't take their eyes off each other, and for me, it was a pleasure to see them. Joanna and Krzysztof Kąkolewski brought our artist friend Przema with them. In Radziejowice, we learned of Antoni Słonimski's[2] sudden death. From among his many valuable feature articles, I particularly remember the last one on Sandauer.[3]

In Warsaw, on my return, the Professor and I went for walks in the Łazienki Park or met in the *Mokotowianka* cafe near his apartment. He invited me for tea at his home. A few times, Tatarkiewicz also graced me with his presence in my apartment on Kmicica Street, along with others as a guest to my namesday party at the end of February.

We talked of everything, like...writing with a Pelikan fountain pen (his favorite), he would travel to Hamburg especially to obtain the special pen...the Professor was amazed by once being ranked first in a competition for the most popular academic of the last thirty-five years, organized by *Trybuna Ludu*.[4] He highly valued Dąbrowska's four-volume novel *Noce i dnie* (*Nights and Days*)—and particularly the two middle parts. For him, the film adaptation failed—in the film, Bogumił is boorish, coarse, and that was not the author's intention, her protagonist was a sensitive insurrectionist...Nałkowska was a personality, not a writer. The Professor found Nałkowska rather haughty, pretty enough, but not beautiful. Neither did he believe her sensuality to be as great as it would seem from reading her *Dzienniki (Journals)*.

"When you're old," he said, "you find fewer and fewer good books. You've read too many good ones before."

I remember a few visits on Chocimska Street with the Kąkolewskis. During one of them, the Professor showed us the American edition of *Analysis of Happiness*,[5] saying that the book was beautifully published, but only in a limited edition, and with no advertising it was not very popular. I also remember Krzysztof telling us about his barber who had visited him at home. At some point, Krzystof claimed the barber was an "outstanding man." The Professor replied: "My barber also comes to visit me, but he has nothing special about him."

I remember lending Tatarkiewicz's *Zapiski* to Aleksander Kamiński, the author of *Kamienie na szaniec*[6] who later shared his opinion with me.

"I read it with huge interest. I remember the Professor's lectures. We valued them very highly. I took my exam in logic with him, and was graded with a C. He was not patient, but that was no wonder, having over a hundred students to examine. On reading the book, I was struck by how much he was carried along through life. To me, it would seem that someone who made his life great, gave a lot of himself, and bent life more to himself. However, he writes as if it was not so. I missed notes on his personal life that should have been included throughout. Never writing about any financial difficulties—I can only presume he never had any. Certainly dryness prevailed, and what seems to be—superficiality. He liked the company encountered only in big banquets, but then seemed to only be "halfhearted" as he engaged in them. His life apparently was one without great friendships. Interesting are his words that people can be tired with life. I think the Professor will have a sudden, quick death. I envy you that acquaintance, "He is a great man."

Two months after that conversation, in March 1978, Aleksander Kamiński died. Professor Władysław Tatarkiewicz survived him by two years. He was ninety-four.

On return from Radziejowice to Warsaw, Tomek went to Mielno with my father. The last months before starting schools were shrinking, but were rich in various impressions.

Chapter Seventeen

Thomas' School

On 1st September we both went to Tomek's new school. All mothers waited in the corridor for their kids to complete that first day in school. A new period in life was starting, and everyone was aware of that.

I remember one conversation with Tomek:

"Son, you don't know how to put sounds and syllables together!"

"If I knew, they wouldn't be teaching me," he answered with a sulky face.

A sailor friend of ours, Zbyszek Skrzywan, who travelled much, but was also a little superstitious, kept a box with earth in his car.

"Why do you keep this here?" asked Tomek.

"That's earth from Jerusalem. I have it to prevent me from having an accident," replied Zbyszek seriously.

"Lend me some, I'll keep it with my bike so that the chain doesn't fall off," asked Tomek.

A few days later, I noticed a box in his school bag.

"What is that?" I asked in surprise.

"This is Polish earth, I carry it so that I don't get F's at school," answered my first-grader.

There were constant notes from the teacher in his record book...that he left the classroom through the window, played tag during the break and gave himself a bump on the head. Tomek brought new notes every few days and was always worried and a little scared when he shyly gave them to me to sign.

He was not a model pupil, but he managed well. One day he returned from school very excited and as happy as a lark. He told me it was the most beautiful day of his life.

"What is going on?" I asked.

"I won't tell you, because you'll worry all night long."

"Please tell me, I'm already worried."

"Okay," he agreed. He clearly wanted to share. "What does Krzysio have?"

"What?...I don't know."

"Well, who does he have?"

"Ania."

"Exactly...I'll only tell you the word: blackboard. And I can't tell you anything more, it's a secret. I'll tell you in seventeen years."

"What is it? Will something happen to you?"

"No, no..."

"Are you in love?"

He blushed furiously: "Yes."

"Then don't worry. I'll be your friend."

"So, it's Ania. Maybe I'll marry her. She only has A's and just a few B's. I don't want the others in the class to know, so I didn't vote for her today, but for another girl. I don't want gossip, like the others do."

"You must now be neat and take care of yourself,"...I started...trying to achieve my goals.

"No, no! They'll notice. I must look as if nothing was going on."

He told his grandmother of his affections. She asked him:

"And what do you like about Ania? Is it her pinafore?"

"Come on, Grandmom," he replied, indignant. "I like her eyes."

Children can be crystal clear at times. Rarely does an adult express the essence of their childhood feelings in an equally direct manner, lacking any shade of stylization.

We spent New Year's Eve together, just the two of us. I treated the ending of the old year and the beginning of twelve new months ritually and philosophically. On that day Tomek and I liked looking through family photos, I answered his questions about his earliest childhood, and we summarized the past year and planned for the future. At midnight, we drank a glass of champagne and then danced to the mazurka from TV. Dressed in nice pyjamas, we watched a late night film. In the morning, after breakfast, we went to church in Dominikańska Street.

During a school break once again, we went to Radziejowice with our Dachshund, Dupek. After Wańkowicz's death, the dog grew sad and much more serious. He didn't want to part from us, and we tried to take him everywhere. On one very sad occasion, when walking with Tomek in Łódź, in Łagiewniki forest, Dupek was painfully bitten by a large dog. He needed surgery and tender care. Fat Thursday[1] was coming, and I decided to spend the evening with Przema and our kids. I also took Dupek. Przema and I wanted to go to the cake shop nearby to buy some donuts. The children stayed with the dog. When we came back, we found Wandzia and Tomek all in tears, and the dog was nowhere to be seen. They told us that when I left, the dog raced to the door. When they opened the door to see if we were back, he slipped out and ran into the corridor. They waited for us, crying. Przema and I ran down thirteen floors, stopping at each and calling: "Dupek, Dupek..." We hoped someone had taken him into their apartment and that the dog would hear us call. Doors did open, surprised neighbours peeked out, but the dog was not to be found. We returned to the apartment and wrote thirteen notes with our phone numbers, asking the recipients to return the dog. We pasted them beside each elevator at all floors. We also left a message with the lady in the news-stand outside, who said she had seen a small black dog with a collar that ran outside.

Tomek and I returned home crying. The house was empty, and we felt lonely and sad to be there. The next day I posted an ad in daily newspapers. People started calling. One lady said she had seen a black Dachshund near some cars in the parking lot, and that "some man picked the dog up, looked around furtively, then carried it towards a bus stop." Next day, I posted another ad in the newspapers: "The man who on...at...Street took care of a black Dachshund is requested to contact the number...The dog is under medical treatment." I hoped that the man who'd "taken care" of the dog—i.e. the thief—would be scared by the thought of the dog's treatment and would return him in exchange for a reward. Later, after three days, during which time I never left home, sitting by the phone instead, a stranger called. The "culprit" said he had the dog and asked for a 500 zlotys reward and Wańkowicz's book *Monte Cassino*. I ran to the kitchen, where Tomek was eating fried apple scones, and told him the news. Still with a scone in hand, he ran to the car with me, and we drove by car to the other end of Warsaw and the Grochów district.

The emaciated Dupek stared at me in misbelief. He sat on a couch. I took him in my lap, and the dog put his head on my shoulder and looked at me. Tears fell from his eyes...This is true. Never before and never after have I seen such emotion in a dog. He didn't bark, he didn't jump, Dupek just looked at me. I didn't know dogs could cry like people: with happiness.

The man said he'd "taken" Dupek to keep his son company, but the dog didn't want to eat, was dejected and sad, and was unhappy in the house. The "culprit" simply became bored with the dog he'd stolen, and I, instead of calling him all sorts of names, paid the reward, took Dupek in my arms and, we all quickly came back home, happy. After his tragic experience, Dupek changed his attitude towards people and was not so friendly and trusting any longer.

The dog was very unhappy when we moved from a house with a garden to a second-floor apartment in a large block. He didn't like staying alone, but wanted constantly to be with me. Dupek enjoyed riding in the car, because it was a link to his old world. The move to our new residence was a strong shock for the dog, and his only solace was walking along the familiar areas near Studencka Street. The dog always liked, and continued to enjoy, walking in the park in Wilanów, or Las Kabacki. The locales reminded him of familiar routes from the past. So we went there again—not with Wańkowicz anymore, but with the Radgowskis and their brown Dachshund called Mała. A few months after his "kidnapping," Dupek returned to his old self and felt free and trusting, as before. Not accustomed to a leash, Dupek hated the restraint it imposed and always showed us his dislike. We unleashed him, and the dog ran towards Studencka Street, sniffed around the gardens there and returned home. One day he didn't return. Repeated adverts in the daily press didn't help this time. No one called. Dupek was a particularly beautiful dog. Small, of almost miniature build, he looked like a delicate pup and not a grown dog. At that time, I took a pup from Dupek's last "relationship," which I wanted to give to my parents. However, Tomek and I decided to keep the pup for ourselves. We called him Bisio. On seeing him, Jerzy Witlin, the houmorist, said he "encored Dupek" (in Polish: bisować). I remember our trips with the new dog to Las Kabacki. The Dachshund rummaged about in the bushes, and Tomek collected sticks which he later brought home. Bisio joined us when Tomek was seven, so—according to experts on animals—they were peers and certainly they had great fun together.

Earlier I gave one of Dupek's pups as a gift to Władysław and Irena Mirecki, a pair of photographers from Łódź. I was grateful for their beautiful pictures of Tomek and of me. I had previously agreed with Mr. Mirecki that he would bring the pictures to me in Warsaw, where he planned to meet his wife at the airport and to remain a few days to visit their son. In the morning, he called to tell me he had the pictures in an envelope, and would call me when he arrived in Warsaw. That evening, I received a call from a Militia Commissioner. After introducing himself, he asked if I knew a Mr. Władysław Mirecki, and if he was a relative. I said he was a good friend, gave them the number to his son and asked why he'd queried me if I knew Mirecki.

"Mr. Mirecki had a fatal car accident. In his briefcase, we found an envelope with pictures, your name and phone number."

I was deeply affected by the sad news. In a phone conversation, I learned that the daughter of the Mireckis, Halinka, who was travelling with her father, was in the hospital, unconscious. Her father had a heart attack while driving. Two weeks later, Irena Mirecka visited me. She told me more of the sad story and how it continued. When she arrived from Italy and her husband was not at the airport, she was worried. Irena called her son and he immediately came for her. It was only late in the evening that they learned of the tragedy. She arranged for her husband's funeral in Łódź, then returned to Warsaw and each day went to the hospital to visit her daughter, who awakened after a week. Irena asked her what had happened to their dog—was it killed in the accident? No one knew anything. With her son, she went to the road near Radzymin, and they stopped at the accident's site. At the nearby village, Irena questioned the local inhabitants if they remembered the accident. Responding affirmatively, they said they did, and that they were still affected by the tragedy. "And have you seen a small black Dachshund?" "Yes, there was some black dog roaming about and coming to the site of the accident." Irena went to a grove near the accident site and to her amazement, there was the dog, scared, emaciated and chilled. She returned home with the dog, and it recovered. Later visiting me, Irena shared the story of the miraculously recovered dog. Her daughter's health was also improving.

Once I went by car to visit Father, who was staying with Tomek in Krynica Górska on holiday. Bisio was with me. The summer was exceptionally hot, and I was tired from the drive and the heat. Near Grocholice, I stopped the car close to a forest, sat in a tree's shadow and closed my eyes. Bisio laid down next to me. The road wasn't very busy, but I heard cars pass by from time to time. At some point, I heard a strange sound as if something was hit. I looked at the road and saw a car drive away, and my dog rolling from side to side, as if convulsing. I wrapped him in a blanket in my car, then quickly drove to the closest town, Grocholice, where the local veterinarian treated him. Bisio recovered, and we took him with us to Nieborów in the winter.

Chapter Eighteen

Nieborów

My friend, Robert Jarocki, a writer, who regularly went to Nieborów to work there. He encouraged me to write an application to the National Museum for permission to spend two weeks there. The applications were considered by Professor Stanisław Lorentz[1] himself. Robert, who'd written a book about Lorentz, interceded for me, and I was granted permission. I knew the tradition was that if I "proved myself," I'd be able to write directly to the museum's custodian, Włodzimierz Piwkowski (who wrote a book on Nieborów), and book a room. Since my first trip there with Tomek in the winter of 1977, almost each February, we have gone together for a winter holiday in Nieborów. The palace and its customs, elegant meals served in the dining room, walking in the forest, solitude, refinement, harmony, beauty—all allowed us to rest like you could not rest at any other place. When walking in the park or the vast forest areas, you could see deer and sometimes wild boars, and admire birch alleys. From time to time, a fire was started in the fireplace in the library of the Radziwiłłs[2] and the guests gathered there. In the library, I was always fascinated by the two huge globes from Venice (Earth and Heaven). There weren't many guests, but they were always extremely interesting people.

The one most strongly attached to Nieborów was a professor of neurosurgery, Jerzy Szapiro, who came there regularly. He took me for a walk a few times. We went with hoods on our heads for cover from the falling snow. The professor, who treated all the locals for free, talked non-stop about his experiences as a Jewish boy hiding in a trunk during the war. He also elaborated about his experiments and new techniques in brain examination methods. A few times the Professor organized meetings to show the guests the phenomenon of levitation. He gathered a few people and chose one to sit on a chair, and the lights were dimmed. Four other people and the Professor first held their hands over the sitting person's head, and then put the hands on his or her head in a certain order. Everyone was quiet, the Professor decided for how long. At his sign, the chosen person was lifted by the fingers of the four under his armpits and knees and was raised upwards, "light like a feather" (sic!). I was the "raised" person, a "raiser," also as an onlooker. I cannot explain how the mystical trick was performed. The experiment, called a physical phenomenon by the Professor, remains inexplicable to me.

Frequent winter guests at Nieborow were Stanisław Fijałkowski, a painter, professor of the Academy of Fine Arts in Łódź, a graphic artist famous in many countries, and his wife Waleria, a great-hearted woman. He read old prints (you could borrow them there), and shared his impressions with us. He had an exceptionally clear, sharp mind. Other guests included Professor Wiesław Juszczak, Jacek Sempoliński (painter), Janusz Zakrzewski (professor of physics—Tomek says that due to our extended acquaintance, I wanted him to become a physicist as well and an extraordinary figure), Professor Aleksander Gieysztor, Professor Alina Kowalczykowa, Alina and Stanisław Ozimek (whose Dachshund once caught a hare)...I had long conversations with a professor of economics, Jerzy Rutkowski. He often brought taped records of classical music and we listened to them in quiet concentration in the library after supper. After lunch, occasionally all the guests went together to shops in Łowicz or nearby villages and brought beautiful pots, colorful stockings or other trophies. The supplies in Polish shops were getting poorer all the time, and near Nieborów we bought products difficult to purchase in Warsaw. The atmosphere of the palace helped work. In Nieborów, I wrote my book *Moje i zasłyszane (Mine and Overheard Stories)*, among others.

Tomek skated over frozen canals and ponds. One day, just before lunch, he ran into the room wet and terrified.

"Mom, I almost drowned," he confessed. "I fell through the ice into waist-deep water, I was so surprised that it was like a movie, and not my own story. I grabbed a branch and pulled myself out of the water..."

The adventure ended well, as he didn't even develop a fever. In Nieborów, I met Doctor Janina Salwa, a later protagonist of one of my stories. She was a woman with exceptional eyes. You remembered their look forever. She ran a rehabilitation center in the hospital on Szwoleżerów Street in Warsaw, where various disabilities are treated, and for many patients with limited mobility. Doctor Salwa took care of them patiently, believing in the effectiveness of the rehabilitation. Once she was disabled herself and now, as she told me, she understood her patients better. She knew from experience how important the relation of the doctor, as well as the family, was to the patient; how much the patient needed kindness. In Nieborów, she told me the story of her accident. How she overcame it seemed so exceptional to me that I titled the text about Doctor Salwa—*To Live Anew (Życie na nowo)*.

Chapter Nineteen

Zakopane

Each year with Tomek, usually in July, I visited Zakopane, and we lodged in the "Halama" house of ZAiKS by the ski jump. Usually it rained the first week, and the following one was clear and sunny. When Tomek was still in the early grades, we were given a room in the *Orlik* house next to *Halama*, which had rooms for families with smaller children. When he grew, we were promoted to *Halama*. The atmosphere and habits of the house in Zakopane are known in the world of Polish writers, musicians, journalists, artists: breakfasts brought to rooms on trays, delicious lunches and suppers cooked under the supervision of Ms. Rózia, a highlander from Podhale.

Before I left to Zakopane, Michał Radgowski gave me some tourist advice. He was a great enthusiast of walking the Tatra Mountains. Every day I visited new valleys: *Białego, Strążyska* up to the Giewont Mountain, the gorgeous, vast, light-filled *Chochołowska*, the long and picturesque *Kościeliska* with the *Ornak* hostel, and *Dolina Małej Łąki*. *Halama* catered to a number of outstanding guests, many writers, artists, composers and actors. It was also visited by Wojciech Młynarski,[1] who had a house of his own in Zakopane.

I usually left the dog Bisio in Łódź for the time of my vacation. The dog was happy with the brief change, my parents indulged him and were also happy. Tomek went for additional vacations, still under the care of his grandparents. My father showed him as much wisdom as he had shown earlier to my brothers and me. He gave Tomek books "for his age," which made him into an avid reader.

In 1977, I started working in the Warsaw TV theatre. I was accepted for the position by Jan Paweł Gawlik, former director of Teatr Stary (Old Theatre) in

Kraków, that was made famous by theatrical producer Konrad Swinarski. When interviewing me, he asked:

"Do you belong to the Communist Party?"

"No, I do not," I replied.

"Good, neither do I."

Gawlik's query was the first time in my life that I was asked about belonging to the Party. My generation was in a better situation than the generation of my parents, who were harassed with questions, and some of them yielded to the pressure.

TV theatre enjoyed a deservedly good reputation. The most eminent directors and actors showed the works of world and Polish drama. Polish TV plays, valued in Poland, were also awarded in European contests. I worked in the repertoire editorial section. We looked for new titles, organized competitions, adapted literary works, presented well-known plays in new renditions. I prepared literary texts for a director with an exceptional sense of imagery, Stefan Szlachtycz, for Andrzej Kotkowski (he made such films as *Olimpiada 44 (Olympics 44)*. Always interesting were the meetings with Agnieszka Holland, or Ryszard Bugajski, who later directed the *film Przesłuchanie (Interrogation)* and the Canadian made *Clearcut* (which was an adaptation of M. T. Kelly's book *A Dream Like Mine*).

Thanks to my TV work, I had the chance to see many premieres, and many interesting performances. I edited the bulletin *Polish Television Theatre*. The bulletin was printed in several languages and sent to theatres in Poland and in Europe. Juliusz Burski, the deputy of Jan Paweł Gawlik was a great expert on theatre, The theatrical team of Polish TV included many talented people.

My son turned out to be a regular viewer of TV theatre. I was amazed to see him with his eyes fixed on ambitious theatre plays, also on the Olga Lipińska cabaret.[2] "What an eccentric he's going to be," wondered Michał Radgowski.

Among the candidates for directors was a young Pole of Japanese origin, Bernard Ford Hanaoka, who some years later created his own fashion house. I became friends with two very talented journalists who hosted a popular science series *Sonda (Probe)*: Kurek and Kamiński. Together with them and Wanda Konarzewska, I occasionally had coffee in the president's café named *President's Whim*. Concurrently, I met Małgosia Holender, who started working in another editorial team and who became a friend. She was very sensitive, wrote songs and was full of surprises.

Usually, each year I went to England, where I had friends. In London, I stayed in the small Shellbourne Hotel. I went with Zbyszek Racięski to the National Gallery to view the Italian painting exhibition, with Titian, Raphael, Botticelli, Tintoretto. We explored the city. One day he brought me to the Gunnesbury cemetery, where I saw a Katyń memorial. I also went to a meeting dedicated to Adam Ciołkosz, a socialist who died in 1978. I saw great faces and noble features of now elderly people. The Poles living in England were formed by the cream of interwar Poland—you could see their class in each move. Stanisław Baliński signed his newest book titled *Antrakty* (*Intervals*) for me: *For Ms. Aleksandra Ziółkowska—asking to be kept in good memory and after reading the book, asking her not to criticize our difficult life in London (the first and last feature).*

At a reception at the home of Stanisława and Zbigniew Racięski, Irena Delmar sang songs about Lviv with Włada Majewska, accompanied on the piano by Bernard Czaplicki. We talked of the future of Poles in England and predictions what would happen in sixty years. Włada Majewska said that a United States of Europe would be created under the aegis of America ("Not USSR, heaven forbid..."), that people still remembered the war and didn't want to see it again. Majewska believed that in sixty years the Polish organisations abroad would be taken over by the children of the current activists, or maybe by the British. The British might show some respect for the Sikorski Museum, but slowly all organizations would be closed.

It was October 1978. None of us ever thought what would happen in Poland and in the world not in sixty years, but in just a few...Stanisław Grocholski told me of the global convention of Poles abroad in Toronto. Enthusiastically he developed the visions of a strong environment ("We need more such people as Brzeziński...").

I visited Jędrzej Giertych, who gave his books to my father. He questioned me sternly about my private life, which discomfited and irritated me.

In Sheffield, I saw a close friend, Roman Rodziewicz, protagonist of my book *Z miejsca na miejsce*, and Staszek Rysztogi, a traveller thanks to whom I saw many interesting places, among them York and Birmingham. We traveled to the latter for his son's graduation. An affection for England always remained in me, although it did not inspire ardent feelings such as I later experienced in Canada or the United States. But Poland provided much new excitation and thus gave hope for changes.

The day of my doctoral defense drew nearer. After passing all exams, the date of thesis defense was announced in *Życie Warszawy*. A large party came to the public defense, among them many friends of mine. Their presence made me terribly self-conscious and I had a bad case of exam nerves. On finishing and hearing the final successful result, my prevailing feeling was one of total relief. I'd completed many years of studies. The doctoral degree later helped me greatly when I applied for scholarships abroad available to people with a list of academic publications and an advanced degree.

My parents and brothers came to the ceremony of diploma award with the title of a Doctor of Humanistic studies of the Warsaw University. Tomek sat with them in the room very quietly, and later told me he understood little of what was happening. My parents were deeply moved, and I took particular care of them that day. For many years they had given me their emotional support, and helped in each situation when Tomek needed care, never hesitating to devote their time and effort.

Around my doctoral graduation time, I became friends with Aldona and Zbyszek Kubikowski. Zbyszek, a writer and journalist, was the editor-in-chief of the Wrocław monthly *Odra*, which he brought to a high level. He printed among others Kazimierz Moczarski's *Rozmowy z katem* and Hanna Krall's *Zdążyć przed Panem Bogiem.*[3] He was brave, intelligent and talented. Zbyszek was later dismissed and moved to Warsaw, where he worked as the literary manager of the *Teatr Popularny (Popular Theatre)*. He was also active in the Writers' Union and put forward many brave proposals. Aldona was a pretty dark-haired woman with slanting eyes. She worked as the editor in the *Ossolineum* publishing house. We lived nearby and I liked visiting them. I remember their warm hospitality and also their love for animals. Once a large shaggy female dog from a shelter looked at them "with longing" eyes. The Kubikowskis and their son Tomasz were enraptured by the dog and immediately adopted her. Newly named, Warka quickly adjusted to her new home and loved the whole family faithfully and with devotion.

An event of enormous historic significance was the 16th October 1978—the election of the Polish pope. I remember listening to the radio as they said that the archbishop of metropolitan Kraków was elected by the College of Cardinals for the Bishop of Rome and that the new Pope took the name John Paul II. Excited with the news, I called to Suchedniów to the Kąkolewskis (they still remember that call), then to Basia Wachowicz. "Oleńka," she said, "it's like they'd elected a king for Poland..."

Like many others, I sent a congratulatory letter to the address of *Città del Vaticano*. I got an elegant thank-you note in reply. The Mass, broadcast in TV, I watched with great emotion, as most Poles did.

When in 1979 John Paul II made his first visit to Poland as the Pope, I was there in the Mass in the *Victory Square* in Warsaw. I remember how deeply affected I was with his presence and his words: "Let your Spirit descend! And renew the face of the earth. The face of this land!"

I went with Tomek to Częstochowa, where a Pauline father, Marian Lubelski, found a place for us on the monastery fortification walls during the Mass celebrated by the Pope. Later, we were also at the Papal Mass in Kraków. In those days, I almost didn't recognize the people around me: gone were gloomy faces, joy and laughter appeared. Some breakthrough occurred. Poland became "the Pope's nation."

His famous words: "Be not afraid" meant so much to everyone.

A joyous event in our family was the birth of Małgorzata Maria, daughter of Krzysio and Ania, on 9th May 1979. The couple were still waiting to acquire an apartment, staying first with our parents, then with Ania's parents. I was the godmother of little Małgosia. A nice period was evident when the family grows and everyone is healthy. Remembering that time after many years is also a joy.

When she visited Poland in 1979, Marta Erdman gave me the then newest book by Zofia Romanowiczowa: *Sono felice*. "You know, this book is about Father. He is not named as such, but the book is about him. There are clear references—to Monte Cassino, etc. I think that Zofia has paid a certain debt that she definitely had with Father. A kind of dues. You'll see it yourself."

Wańkowicz told me about Zofia Romanowiczowa (born Górska) as he was reading her new book *Groby Napoleona* (*Napoleon's Graves*) which he'd received a few months before his death. He told me of a young, fearful girl he'd met in Italy near the end of the war. She was a former prisoner of the Ravensbrück concentration camp. The girl found temporary shelter in one of the Roman monasteries. Wańkowicz, who had daughters her age, took care of her, and employed her as his secretary while writing *Monte Cassino*. With his help, she had her debut in 1945 with a story titled *Tomuś* (*Tommy*), published in *Orzeł Biały*, a weekly of the 2nd Corps. In *Karafka La Fontaine'a* he described coming with Zofia to Germany, visiting the camp in Dachau, and her reaction to it. Before leaving to England he helped her— arranged for a place in a school in Paris, founded a scholarship. They exchanged letters for many years. Zofia graduated from the Sorbonne University, got married, settled in Paris, had a daughter. She and her husband, Kazimierz Romanowicz, founded a publishing company *Libella* . She sent Wańkowicz all her books: *Baśka i Barbara, Przejście przez Morze Czerwone, Szklana Kula, Łagodne Oko Błękitu, Skrytki.* [4]

I was very curious as I settled down to reading the book I'd been given. I knew other books by the author and found them valuable. Still impressed by the author and what I'd read, I wrote the story *Powroty* (*Returns*), which was later included in the book *Moje i zasłyszane*. In the text by Romanowiczowa, I also found many truths stated by Wańkowicz, which he'd taught me, as well.

In the late 1970's, I took many trips, among others to Budapest, Zagreb, Opatija, Rijeka, Trieste and Venice. Budapest was colorful and lively, Zagreb—affluent and bourgeois, Opatija sunny and green. I liked Rijeka, a port town shifted by the hand of history back and forth between Italy and Yugoslavia. I saw Venice for the second time, but this time, I found the extraordinary city to be mainly crowded. Tourists from all over the world moved slowly through the narrow streets. *Piazza San Marco* was filled with masses of people. The canals gave off an unpleasant odor. Combined with the heat, humidity, and crowds, this was not the Venice I saw in spring, romantic and colorful.

I also went to Istanbul, where I visited Jola and Alex Pawłowski. Alex, an American of Polish descent, worked for PanAm airlines in Warsaw. I met them when I was staying on Studencka Street after the death of Wańkowicz. The Pawlowskis came to rent the writer's house. Marta Erdman was then in the process of advanced talks with Edward Piszek, a famous American philanthropist and businessmen, who was interested in buying the house. At that time, however, Piszek's house in Pennsylvania burned down, and he gave up the idea. For a few years Marta rented the house to a British family, Peter and Ann Lagoe (whom I wrote about above), and finally decided to sell it. Wańkowicz's house was finally bought by Piszek's secretary and representative in Poland, a film-maker by education, Stanisław Moszuk. He changed it after a while and added another floor. The new house did not resemble the writer's old one.

Alexander Pawłowski, with whom I stayed in touch over the years, had an extraordinary life, with an impressive episode as a RAF pilot during the war. As a PanAm employee, he lived in many places in the world. From Warsaw he was sent to Turkey with his family, and that was where I visited them. They were living in an elegant district of the city, Bebek, on the Bosphorus. Thanks to Alex and Jola, I was able to see much of Istanbul.

I was awakened in the mornings by the voice of the praying muezzin. Seeing the city's sights, the wonderful mosques, the palace with its harem, was eclipsed with the everyday sights of the great metropolis: dirt in the streets, men urinating by the walls, noisy, importunate merchants. Somehow I couldn't yield to the charm of the city, so fascinating in itself. Maybe the fault was mine?

Adam Mickiewicz, one of the most eminent Polish Romantic poets, died in Istanbul on 26th November 1855. The house he lived in burned down. A new one was built in 1955, and it now holds the poet's museum. Mickiewicz came to Istanbul through Smyrna, Dardanelles, and the Bosphorus as an envoy of the French government and of Prince Adam Czartoryski to talk of forming a Polish legion. There were two military units in Turkey then and many Poles. In the whole Grande Rue de Pera, today named Istiklal, it was said you could always hear Polish spoken. Now in the Polish St. Andrew's Church, Italian priests hold a Mass with a Turkish sermon.

I very much wanted to go to the Polish village of Adampol near Istanbul, which was soon to be visited by Pope John Paul II. For many years, I have been very interested in Polonezkoy, earlier named Adampol, a Polish settlement founded by Michał Czajkowski and soldiers of the November Uprising of 1830–31 with the help of Adam Czartoryski and French Christian missionaries, the Lazarites. I knew from my Father that in the cemetery next to the grave of Ludwika Śniadecka, a Polish activist in Turkey, there was a grave of the Ziółkowski family. The progenitor was Paweł Ziółkowski (1878–1939), who arrived in 1902 from Poznańskie. As the borough leader and teacher, he played a significant role in propagating Polish language and culture. He wrote the first and until 1981 the only book on Adampol (same-named), published in French in 1922 and in Polish in 1929. However, I never learned more details from Father concerning that branch of the Ziółkowski family. The Pope was to visit Maryem Ana. Located high in the mountains above Ephesus, where St. John the Evangelist once taught, there is a small temple adjoining the cavern where Christ's Mother spent the last years of her life. As a pilgrimage site sought not only of Christians, other pilgrims come there for the 15th August, the Assumption Day, connected directly with the site.

To be in Turkey and not visit Polonezkoy, that little patch of Poland in Turkish land, was almost distressful for me. But Jola and Alex told me they didn't move outside of Istanbul themselves. They knew that busses were stopped by groups of thieves who robbed everyone's luggage, pulling watches, jewellery and even shoes off the passengers.

I had an unpleasant experience happen to me. Jola and Alex took me to some shops so I could purchase famous Turkish leatherwear. In an elegant shop, I found a black leather suit that was very striking. The leather was as delicate and fine as a glove, the jacket and skirt were fashionable and well-cut. The suit fit me nicely and I liked it so much. The suit cost around one hundred dollars.

The shop's owner, a young Turk, walked about and touted and suggested other clothes, as well, such as sheepskin and leather jackets. He watched us carefully. When he realized we spoke Polish, he proudly said he knew some expressions in Polish, too. A lot of Poles came to Turkey at that time to buy coats and jackets, which they then sold in Poland at a profit. The Turk loudly stated his admiration for me in the suit, and then he said in a whisper, so that my friends wouldn't hear him:

"If you come alone in the evening, you'll get it for free..."

I couldn't believe that he would speak to me so brazenly, and said I wanted to pay him one hundred dollars to buy the suit.

"No, come later," he said firmly.

Jola and Alex realized what was going on, and said to me:

"Let's leave."

Out in the street, Alex said:

"Don't worry, you'll buy a similar suit somewhere else," he comforted me. "He won't sell it to you."

We entered other shops, and finally it was time to return to our hotel for supper. Seeing my sad face, Alex had an idea.

"Let me pay for an idea, and you pay for the suit."

He approached a group of four Poles (two women and two men) and asked them for a favor. "I'll pay you twenty dollars. Please go to that large shop on the other side of the street and buy the black suit. There is only one."

He explained to the group of Poles why the Turk didn't want to sell it to us. The women became excited with the situation, and they were likely pleased as well with the opportunity to earn some money. One of the men stayed with us, and the others went to the shop. Alex, Jola and I sat on a bench at the other side of the alley and waited. Darkness came slowly. You could see the brilliantly illuminated shop's entrance from afar. Alex advised us to sit there quietly and not show ourselves. Fifteen minutes passed, then half an hour, and finally forty-five minutes. The Turk came out of the shop and took a good look around.

"He's checking if we're not behind the action, he's suspicious," explained Alex.

Finally, after an hour, the women and the men left the shop and took a detour to meet up with us. Reaching us, one of the women revealed, "We have the suit, but there was so much trouble buying it...the Turk told me to try it on, said it was too tight, then I said I was buying this for my daughter. He gave us suspicious looks, went out the door to look around, sensed deceit. Finally, becoming bored too, we decided to quit. Then he sold it."

The next day, I asked my hosts if it wasn't worth putting the suit on and going to the Turk's shop for a minute. Alex immediately reacted negatively to my suggestion. "Don't you dare think of anything like that! If he saw you in that suit and saw you had outsmarted him, he'd cut the skirt with a knife or pour something on it to destroy the suit. He wouldn't give up."

I left Istanbul with relief such as I rarely ever felt. I usually grow attached to places and regret having to leave them.

Chapter Twenty

Roman Rodziewicz

I maintained friendly, warm contacts with former soldiers of Major Hubal's unit. I visited Marek Szymański and his wife, Cezaria-Kaja, a participant of the 1944 Warsaw Uprising and an architect by profession, in their lovely Warsaw house on Słoneczna Street. Kaja told me of Krystyna Krahelska, pseudonym Danuta, who posed for the statue of the Warsaw Mermaid.[1] Also a poet, she was the author of lyrics to a song of Warsaw Uprising participants: *Hej chłopcy, bagnet na broń* (*Hey Boys, Fix Bayonets*). Krystyna Krahelska was killed in the Uprising. Kaja was full of life and wit and could sometimes talk of her war experiences in such a manner that she made me...laugh till my sides ached. In my apartment on Kmicica Street, I hosted Henryk Ossowski from Borowiczki, adjutant of Major Henryk Dobrzański. He organized horse trips "along the route of Major Hubal." Another of my guests was Józef Alicki from Kamień on the Iława River. Józek, a fearless soldier of Hubal, harassed after the war by the Security Service, determined and peasant-like stubborn, he withstood the persecution. Working hard, he repaired a nearly crumbling house formerly owned by Germans and restored it to a like newly built condition. He and his wife Irena bred chickens and turkeys, and they worked hard from dawn to dusk. The Alickis bought a scenic piece of land, including a forest, and kept some horses, which—in his words—delighted the eye. They traveled to Italy, then to a far cousin in America. "I saw how well others lived, how normally, and with a heavy heart I thought of our oppressed country," he said. "I couldn't stay there longer than a few weeks, and I came back home. I pitched up and worked hard. That's the only hope for all of us..."

I visited the Alickis often with Tomek and with Roman Rodziewicz, when the latter visited Poland. A few times, Tomek spent part of his summer vacations with the Alickis, becoming friends with the animals that Józek bred at his farm.

Roman Rodziewicz stayed with me whenever he came to Poland. Wherever we went, he was always happiest speaking of his service in Hubal's unit. Roman spoke little of his life in England. For him, time stopped during the war. When I asked about his childhood and youth, Roman spoke of those years in a vivid manner, by revealing with melancholy a yearning for what passed but never would return. Raised in a land estate in Kresy, he had been groomed for managing a farm. Although born in Ławski Bród, Roman spent the first years of his life in Manchuria. His father, Antoni Rodziewicz, graduate of the Riga Technical University, as a young engineer taught in a technical school, but he also secretly taught Polish history to children, and for that he was exiled to Siberia in 1903. Roman's father obtained permission to come to Poland for two weeks to marry his fiancée, Natalia, and then they journeyed to Manchuria together. The Poles who lived in Manchuria at that time were mostly exiles and their children. A three-year Polish school was organized with Russian as the language of instruction (Natalia taught there). The Rodziewiczs lived for a few years in Qiqihar and then in Harbin. Each and every one of the two hundred Polish families living in Manchuria took great care to celebrate their national customs and traditions. The regaining of independence was celebrated the 3rd of May.[2] Children were taught patriotic poems and were constantly told of their home country. Roman yearned to see Poland, which was mythicized and beautified in the stories. His mother sang Polish patriotic songs as she played the piano. Their thoughts were constantly in Poland, and every letter they received from Poland was read several times over. In 1922, the Japanese occupied Manchuria, and they immediately began to show favor towards the Poles living there. The Poles were granted various privileges and the Japanese authorities even announced that they would provide any help required if the Poles wished to return home. The Rodziewiczs decided to send their children to Poland: Roman and his two sisters joined a large group of others also returning. Roman's parents were to sell their house and turnover their jobs to their successors. Little did Roman know that his departure from Manchuria would be the last time he would see his mother and father. His mother Natalia died of a heart failure at thirty-five years of age and was buried in Qiqihar. His father Antoni postponed the trip, took care of the funeral, and erected a brick tomb. A day before departing for Poland, after a farewell party for the Poles leaving Manchuria, he suddenly died of a heart failure, like his wife. In Poland, at Lawski Brod Roman was taken care of by his uncle Leon, whom the boy loved and respected like a father. On graduating, Roman joined the Suwalska Cavalry Brigade. He also had some farm training with his family in the Porzecze estate, and returned to Ławski Bród after two years. In 1939, when the war started, he reported to his regiment in Wołkowysk (Volkovysk). There he met officers and fellow soldiers, with whom he later lived and fought in the unit led by Major Henryk Dobrzański (Hubal).

Roman's service with the Hubal unit was continuous from the beginning to the end. Hubal's soldiers gained renown and recognition. The myth and fame were fueled by books, mainly the one written by the then war correspondent in Italy, Melchior Wańkowicz. Roman met Wańkowicz in Italy, where Roman ended up after many war hardships, among them a stay in the German concentration camps in Brzezinka and in Buchenwald. In Rome, he met the sister of Major Hubal, Mrs. Papée, the ambassador's wife. Through her, he was given contact to the writer, who had visited Ławski Bród before the war. Wańkowicz was fascinated by the story of Hubal, and the book *Hubalczycy* (*Hubal Soldiers*) was born from stories disclosed by Roman. The writer always stressed Roman's contribution to the writing of the book.

When I met Roman, I also yielded to the beauty and excitement of his story, to his unusual life. Together we went to Anielin, to the place of Major Dobrzański's death. We also went to Auschwitz. Involuntarily, I started to take part in his life. I witnessed his meeting with his ex-fiancée after over thirty years. Having no news from him, she had married her commander from the Warsaw Uprising (whose life she had saved after his injury by leading him to safety through the sewers of Warsaw), and just two weeks later she received a letter from Roman saying that he'd survived the war. Thus, he had no home, no land, no fiancée. Like other soldiers, he stayed in England. He settled in Sheffield and undertook many and various physical jobs, which finally cost him his health. He worked as a locksmith, a turner, in a coal mine. He married an English woman and started a family, but it gave him no happiness. He separated and divorced his wife, and his children are not interested in their father's homeland. The only highlight in his life are the visits to Poland, visiting friends and talking about Hubal.

I decided to write about Roman, created his life story, and I titled it *Z miejsca na miejsce*, meaning *From One Place to Another*.[3]

Wiktor Żak said he was a Belarusian. He lived in Minsk. One day, I received a letter from him which evoked my interest and immediate reaction. The sender wrote about his brother, Anatol, who'd been killed at Monte Cassino. He died as a Pole. Wiktor Żak asked in his letter whether I knew anything about that battle, for in the Soviet Union there was no information about it. He'd written to *Trybuna Ludu* and thus he learned about Wańkowicz. Later he somehow found me.

I was moved by Zak's letter. In the full edition of *Bitwa o Monte Cassino,* I found a picture of his brother, and even a fragment describing the circumstances of his death. In my response, I sent him the Polish edition of *Monte Cassino*, retyping the fragment about his brother which was missing from that particular issue and informing him that the original version had a picture of Anatol. A reply came quickly. Zak wrote with emotion that his mother was moved to tears on learning the details and the date of her son's death. He asked me very ardently to copy the picture, because among family mementoes, he had no picture of his brother from the last period of his life. I went to Michał Kuna from the university library in Łódź to ask for his help. He took the matter to heart and made a few copies in a photographic studio. We sent those to the Żak family in Minsk.

Since that time, I gradually became very friendly, sometimes receiving effusive letters from him. He visited me with three other people: his wife, his son, and a friend, a Pole from Białystok. We talked for a long time. He understood Polish, but preferred to answer in Russian. He was impressed by my library, particularly Solzhenitsyn's books: *Cancer Ward* and *In the First Circle*.

On another occasion, I received a phone call from a man who claimed to know Roman Rodziewicz. The man introduced himself as Jan Głowacz. He said he was a son of a Hubal soldier with the pseudonym Lis—Fox. He wanted to give me materials about his father, so that I could read them and write about Lis in the future. We met in a café that revealed a thin, nervous, middle-aged man. He looked like a clerk, and seemed to be completely immersed in his father's past. Głowacz showed me people's accounts about Lis's actions that he had collected. Wańkowicz wrote in *Hubalczycy* about his "outlaw boldness," about a "patriotic-outlaw" guerrilla war that he led on his own, etc. Głowacz showed me letters from Józef Alicki, Marek Szymański, Roman Rodziewicz. He passionately fought for a praiseworthy memory of his father. I found his story highly interesting. The sad tale portrayed a picture of a boy growing up in an orphanage, who learned about his father only when he was nineteen, by chance, on reading Wańkowicz's book *Hubalczycy*. He had a father to be proud of, a father who was a hero of the war, who was described in a book. The memory of his father, collecting materials, seeking any traces of his activity became the goal of his life— more than that, these activities changed his life. They gave him an identity and courage. He graduated from school, married, settled in Warsaw.

I was very moved with his story and decided to convert it into words. But the story was not about his father, but about himself. I still needed a few details, so we met again. Among other things, I asked about his current life, what he was doing now. He hesitated and was silent for a while, and then said: "I am a militia officer. I work in the internal affairs department of the security service on Puławska Street..."

I was struck dumb.

"You? The son of a Hubal soldier!?"

"Why the surprise?" he said, but without irritation, seeking no excuses. "It was the only way to move to Warsaw, to achieve something in life. I believe myself to be a decent man. I don't hurt people. I don't take part in any dirty things. My friends, my father's friends are decent people. If it ever comes to a coup in Poland, they will testify that I'm a good man. They are my alibi in case of any changes of government in Poland. I have a hideout in the Kielce forest. If it should come to anything, any changes, I'm not taking part in the unrest, I won't hurt anyone. I'll hole up in the forest and wait it out."

"Why do you work there?"

"For my family. If I were alone, I'd be different. My director is an ignoramus, a Stalinist. I'm afraid of him."

When I said I'd finished the text but that it was mainly about him, he asked me to change his first name (even now I'm using a false one).

"They won't find me out easily," he wondered. And he asked me to write that he was working in the "internal affairs resort" rather than in the Ministry of Internal Affairs. For him, there was a huge difference between those organizational definitions. The text about him, titled *W poszukiwaniu tożsamości (Seeking His Identity)*, I published in the collection *Moje i zasłyszane*.

He called me a few more times. On the first day after I returned from Canada in 1980, he called me to ask about Roman Rodziewicz.

"I know you've come back today, that's why I'm calling..."

"How do you know I returned today? I was absent for over two months..."

"I know," he said quickly.

The conversation broke off. He called me a few months later.

"My son has immigrated to Belgium. What is happening in Poland?...They talk with the strikers, but no one treats them seriously. Perhaps we could meet?"

I refused. He didn't call again.

I was strongly affected when Przema, my artist friend, left Poland with her daughter. She was marrying a Frenchman she'd met while she was in Paris, and now she was leaving us. I knew I was losing a very close friend. After a "bon voyage party" by a large group of friends we saw her off at the airport. Both dressed in pretty capes and hats Przema and her daughter attracted the eyes of people around us. We hid our sadness and exuded joy for Przema. When we were analyzing our loss, Krzysztof Kąkolewski said: "She'll be fine, she'll be happy, and that should be the most important thing for us..."

I was sad to lose the closeness of my friend. We had shared so many confidential talks and plans, we'd had such a joyous, full life. Telling secrets is a proof of friendship. You create a friendship when your listener reacts in a way you like, in a way you expect. Talking about yourself, you promote acquaintances to friends. And such was our rapport for those few years of my intensive friendship with Przema, my talented, sensitive friend from the time of my youth.

Chapter Twenty-One

Canada

I wonder when Tomek and I were closest and needed each other the most. I think it might have been during our nearly three-year stay in Canada. As a twelve-year-old, he had left Poland with me, and in Canada he matured, becoming a teenager.

My earlier trip to Canada in July 1980, that lasted one and a half months, must have been the start. I was invited by Tadeusz Krukowski, a Professor of Slavic studies at the University of Ottawa. He was well-known in many academic circles in Poland, primarily as the representative of Canadian collaboration with the Catholic University of Lublin. He worked with Polish scholarship holders and academics that came to Ottawa. Krukowski also visited Poland, where he had friends (including the poets Artur Międzyrzecki and Julia Hartwig).

When we first met, Professor Krukowski told me about the tours of Canadian cities Wańkowicz had made in the 1950's. They'd been organized by the Poles in America to allow him to gather materials for a book about them. He advised me to write a study about how I saw "the country of the maple leaf" and about the next generation of people described by Wańkowicz in *Tworzywo*. Coupled with his invitation, the professor promised to help me contact people.

Before leaving from Poland, I wrote to Benedykt Heydenkorn, a Polish-American journalist, long-time editor-in-chief of *Związkowiec (The Alliancer)*, an activist medium of the Canadian Polish Research Institute. I knew that it was due to his efforts that Wańkowicz's *Tworzywo* was published in English in Canada as *Three Generations*. Heydenkorn wrote a short letter in reply, inviting me to Toronto. Through Krukowski and Heydenkorn, my connections in Canada proved to be remarkable.

I was fascinated by the life stories of many people I met: soldiers of the 2nd Polish Corps under General Anders, children who survived Siberia and left to India. The parents of Hania Gałko, with whom I lived in Ottawa, remembered the famine in Russia, so they gathered packed food "just in case" if the situation were to happen again. I appeared in a TV program *Panorama* and on the radio where I was interviewed by Karolina Kęsik. I met many people who remembered Wańkowicz: Tadeusz Stelmaszyński, who with his wife Aleksandra (Oleńka), managed a lovely motel in Niagara Falls. Stelmaszynski had been a soldier of the 2nd Corps, Officer Cadet, commander of the rifle squad that defended hill 593 of Monte Cassino. After the war, both Wańkowicz and Stelmaszyński attended a photography course in England. Hanna Dunczewska knew Wańkowicz and his wife, and made interesting observations about their relations with their daughters Krysia and Tili. Wiktor Szyryński, a professor of psychiatry in Ottawa, told me about his conversations with the writer. I remember an amusing anecdote. The author of *Ziele na Kraterze* turned to him with a dilemma. "You know, I am losing faith..." When the Professor delivered a lecture using the arguments he knew, Wańkowicz thanked him with the words: "I needed that for my book..." He then used those arguments in the discussions of Lewin, the protagonist of *Drogą do Urzędowa* (*On the Way to Urzędów*).

Benedykt Heydenkorn, one of General Anders' soldiers, and an expert on immigration, writer for Parisian *Kultura*, was an unparalleled speaker, and I became friends for long years with him and his wife Hanka—called *Pestka* (*Pit*)[1] (the couple having met during the war).

Professor Krukowski told me that many Polish Canadian immigrants were unhappy people, internally torn, tragic, somehow separated from their children by a huge language barrier. While the parents knew Polish better than English, the children knew English better than Polish.

I returned to Poland with my notes, captivated with the kindness and trust I was treated with, and also delighted by the nature and the beauty of Canada, which my friends did their best to show me. Nadzia and Antek Kotarba took me on a boat trip along the St. Lawrence River, Aleksandra and Tadeusz Stelmaszyński showed me the Niagara Falls. (I threw a coin into the Falls wishing to return there with Tomek, as is the custom.) All the coins I have thrown in different places of the world strangely have resulted in my return to the location). I could not believe my eyes that I could actually see the wonders that I'd learned about at school. Zdzisław Przygoda showed me the McMichael Canadian Collection and the Civic Center in Scarborough. We saw a Shakespearean play in Stratford. Andrzej Dukszta showed me the Japanese Gardens, the galleries, shops and boutiques in the Bohemian district of Yorkville. I went with Senator Haidasz for lunch at the CNN Tower, one of the tallest towers in the world, where I enjoyed a breathtaking view of Toronto. Józia and John Poweska from Brantford, Ontario (where a museum dedicated to the inventor of the telephone, A.G. Bell is located), took me to an Indian pow-wow in Ohsweken, Six Nations Reservation. On the way there, we crossed the Grand River.

Later in Warsaw, after telling Tomek about my visit to the reservation, he drew a picture depicting dancing Indians. I have a particular liking to that drawing. Tomek was always happy to spend time over a piece of paper with pens or crayons. Another one of his interesting drawings is one showing a soldier—the man has huge boots, likely the most essential thing for an infantryman. (I framed both those pictures.) I remember that in Poland, when I put on the Indian headband I brought from Canada, Tomek protested, saying that I caused too much curiosity.

I returned to Poland in mid-August 1980. August was a lesson in collective action for everyone. The time was one of strikes and great tensions in the society. Shops were increasingly empty. I arrived on the day when television showed Cardinal Wyszyński's[2] speech advocating people to work, which caused high emotions (it was a maneuver of the censorship, with some parts of a longer speech deleted). There were constant strikes on the coast, enormous tension in the country, anxiety, predictions...I could not recover my wits after all the news. In television, where I was working, there always was tension, but now the atmosphere bordered on hysterical. When a Solidarity trade union was created in TV, I joined it with great enthusiasm.

Socially there were many conversations with friends and family. I told people many differences I found, among them how different reactions were to compliments in Poland and Canada. For example, when you said to a girl in Canada that she was wearing a nice dress or looked good, she smiled and thanked you. In Poland, it was a bit more complicated. We didn't know how to or perhaps didn't want to accept a compliment, and we diminished or even rejected it.

"That's not true," my colleagues from TV disagreed.

"All right, let's do an experiment. Everyone can always be told something nice, so just listen to how they react."

One of the editors from another office came in.

"How pretty you look today," I said.

"Oh, definitely not!" she said. "I have these circles under my eyes, I did not sleep well last night..."

After some time, another person came.

"What a nice coat!" I said, admiring it.

"Not at all, it's old and has stains that won't wash off, look, here, in this place..."

We all looked at one another and started laughing. They had to agree with my observations.

Meanwhile, my friends from Canada wrote in their letters that they had successfully applied for a year-long scholarship for me. I was going to be invited to the University of Toronto, and also receive scholarships from the Canadian Polish Research Institute and the Adam Mickiewicz Foundation in Toronto. Knowing I would be going there with Tomek, I sent him to private English classes with Mr. Zbigniew Filipowicz, a teacher at the well known Methodist School in Warsaw, who lived nearby on Skrzetuskiego Street.

At that time, some of my Canadian friends began arriving in Poland: Benedykt Heydenkorn, Professor Tadeusz Krukowski, Professor Adam Bromke, Wojciech Krajewski, Andrzej Dukszta.

With Benedykt (also called Bumek) Heydenkorn, I visited the Wesoła village to see the church there. The interior was painted by Jerzy Nowosielski, a great master of religious painting in the Byzantine style. As the author of several works on philosophy and religion, he has also done the paintings in the church in Lourdes. I was particularly impressed by the Stations of the Cross in the church in Wesoła.

In the Stara Prochownia theatre, I listened to Bulat Okudzhava's[3] songs, performed by the actor Wojciech Siemion and the singer Sława Przybylska. Heydenkorn, who was staying in my apartment in Warsaw, was visited by Halina and Zbigniew Stolarek (the latter an excellent translator from French), Professor Władysław Chojnacki and Professor Adolf Juzwenko from Wrocław. So many interesting conversations took place at that time, and an atmosphere of excitement existed in the whole country that spread on to everyone.

Marta Wańkowicz Erdman came to Poland at that time. Earlier she wrote to me that...it was she who'd "drawn the shorter match," having been diagnosed with cancer, but unlike her husband Jan, there was not much of a chance for her...I was extremely upset with the news. After Melchior Wańkowicz's death, Marta was the liaison for his affairs, and we often wrote to each other and saw each other when she was in Poland. Marta was always warm and friendly. Her daughters, Ania and Ewa, were only a few years older than me, and she had a slightly protective attitude towards me. I felt close to her. When we met, she said that she considered the visit her farewell to Poland. Seriously ill, she wanted to conclude many things. She donated some of her father's letters to the Museum of Literature in Warsaw. She sold the house in Studencka Street and also the apartment in Puławska Street, which the writer gave to his granddaughter Ania and her family after he moved to Studencka Street. Marta was looking forward to Christmas 1981, which she was going to spend with Jan and the whole family: Ania, Ewa, their husbands and children. She told me: "The doctor promised me this Christmas."

Marta was glad that I'd be coming to Canada, that we would have a chance to see each other again. We talked about the events in Poland, which she was interested in, but she was mostly concerned with her own, very special problems.

With Adam Bromke, who taught political science at the University of Hamilton, I visited Bernard Margueritte, a long-time correspondent for *Le Figaro* in Warsaw. He lived in Zalesie with his wife, who was Polish, and their little daughter. He spoke excellent Polish. I remember avidly listening to his stories about Lech Wałęsa, who was for me a symbol, the myth of Fighting Poland. Margueritte talked about his meeting with Wałęsa, how he met his six children, the youngest of whom, Kasia, climbed up in her father's lap. In the room where he received his guests, a large portrait of the Pope was displayed, a rosary, and a picture of Piłsudski stood on the TV set. Margueritte admired Wałęsa saying that he answered his questions shortly, concisely and to the point. He passed over some questions. When asked about Kania,[4] he replied: "Kania? I don't know, he didn't introduce himself to me. But if he wants, I can have him join Solidarity...Do you think I'm not a weak man? They offered me a villa and cars, and I was tempted to accept them, but I went to church, took Communion and was blessed with the right perspective of the issues. For some time, I even hesitated if I should accept a bigger flat, but I was living with my kids in a 35 square meter one, so I accepted a bigger one..." When asked where he drew his strength from, he replied: "From the heart and faith..."

I also visited with Professor Bromke a correspondent of the *Washington Post*, and had the opportunity to meet the head of the Independent Publishing House *Nowa*, Mirosław Chojecki. He was rather silent and dejected, but I could not take my eyes off him, for he personified a legend. In *Teatr Powszechny*, we saw the play *Wszystkie spektakle zarezerwowane (All Shows Booked)* in which Zygmunt Hübner, the author, used the poems of Barańczak, Zagajewski, Kornhauser, and Ewa Lipska. After the performance, I joined Hübner and Bromke for dinner at the *Kmicic* restaurant in the Old Town. We talked of Poland and its situation.

My financial situation was not good at that time. I was worried about each day, afraid of the future, just like many other people in Poland. I knew we were earning money as a way out of despair. I remember Wańkowicz saying: "If you have no money, don't think how to save, but how to earn..." Censorship eased somewhat in that period, and almost anything could be printed. I edited and prepared Wańkowicz's correspondence with Miłosz, and that with Dąbrowska and Cat Mackiewicz for print (*Więź* published the correspondence with Cat). Slowly, I began to make copies of his extensive, 53-year correspondence with his wife. It was then published in parts by *Kontrasty (Contrasts)* in Białystok. Earlier, the literary magazine had published his letters exchanged with Maria Dąbrowska.

After preparing the interesting correspondence between Miłosz and Wańkowicz, I sent a letter to Czesław Miłosz in Berkeley, asking for his permission to print it. Miłosz replied that he wanted to first see copies of the letters. I made photocopies and waited for an opportunity to transport them, because I didn't want them to go by mail. I was able to arrange for them to be carried by a friend of my friends, Gene Simmons, an American visiting Poland. Soon I received the poet's reply with his agreement for the letters to be printed. I wrote an introduction, and I gave the materials to the literary monthly *Twórczość*, where they were accepted with enthusiasm.

Much was happening in my workplace, there were a lot of interesting theatre premieres. Agnieszka Holland and Laco Adamik staged Kafka's *The Trial*. Wojciech Wiszniewski, a very talented director, staged an adaptation of Fuks's book *Spalovač mrtvol* (*The Cremator*). The 35-year-old Wiszniewski died soon after the premiere, which was a great loss for Polish culture.

Although a Solidarity union came into being in Polish Television, censorship was tightened and many people were scared. I remember that when writing the introduction to Jarosław Abramow's play *Żaglowce, białe żaglowce (Sailboats, white sailboats)*, I quoted the words of its author, who'd said in a conversation with an actor that "...four of the actors are dead, and the fifth immigrated." Stanisław Dürr-Durski, an employee of the Television Theatre, asked me:

"Did you cut out that sentence about immigration?"

"Is the word "immigration" forbidden?" I asked. On saying this, I observed Henia Bogusławska's crimson face and the surprised faces of others. There was a kind of mass fear, and it wasn't usual to ask questions. I went into the censor's room and wanted to obtain the approval required for releasing the text. No one wanted to approve it; everyone was afraid of the responsibility. A few days later, director Jan Paweł Gawlik told me he received a letter denouncing me.

Queues in stores lengthened: for butter, meat, toilet paper, anything. A doctor and friend of mine provided me with a huge pack of cotton wool, which was not easy to buy either. Then ration coupons appeared; like everyone else, I often had to stand in several queues to purchase what they entitled me to. Having to stand in a queue for two-three hours to buy some gasoline, I would carry with me theatre scenarios which I had to review, so that I could read them while waiting. I tried to make good use of the time. My mother came from Łódź to spend a week with me, mainly to help me with shopping. Tomek was helpful and understanding; sometimes I had to leave him alone for hours. During this period, he behaved strangely in a way that worried me: he was easily offended, sulked often. He was very sensitive. At the same time, he showed me so much tenderness that I was very much affected and grateful. He gave me his drawings, which took a lot of his time to prepare. Playing his favourite game chess against himself consumed much of Tomek's time.

In January 1981, Tomek and I went for a winter holiday to our favourite palace in Nieborów. I needed a break, a change of scenery and place.

Nieborów always gave me a sense of peace and relaxation. I brought a lovely book about a family of Hungarian immigrants in Paris: Jolán Földes's *Street of the Fishing Cat*, and Dionizy Sidorski's book *Żywoty bagienne* (*Marsh Lives*) about wildlife on the Biebrza River. The stories about beavers made me feel just as good as those about dolphins or Maeterlinck's stories of bees. I learned, for instance, that beavers reached maturity in their third year of life, they were monogamous, and when a male lost his mate, he lived a lonely life and usually died sooner than other beavers.

Tomek brought Arkady Fiedler's *Zwierzęta z lasu dziewiczego* (*Animals From the Virgin Forest*) and told me of fish that moved over the ground by leaping. In the village library near the Radziwiłł Palace, I saw a book I was not familiar with, written by Marian Brandys, a writer whom I valued very much. The book was entitled *Piotr i Maria* (*Peter and Mary*) and was published in thirty thousand copies in 1950. I was amazed on reading it. I didn't know that the author of *Oficer największych nadziei* (*Officer of the Greatest Hopes*) wrote books in such "poor style" as *Piotr i Maria* in the Stalinist period.

The Nieborów library organized a drawing competition about the impressions of the village, in which Tomek was quite successful. The guests gathered in front of the TV to watch Polish daily news. We all discussed the situation in Poland. Almost every day at noon, we drove to nearby towns and did shopping for future use: washing powder, toothpaste, etc. There was a shortage of many products in big cities. Professor Szapiro gave me his sketch to read—*Postęp, kryteria i mistyfikacja. Refleksje nie tylko profesjonalne (Progress, Criteria and Mystification. Reflections Not Just Professional).*

Walks to the forester's lodge in Siwica, discussions in the library, the park and its canals, where Tomek was skating, the wonderful atmosphere of Nieborów, and the marvellous relaxation, all gave me a lot of strength and restored my well-being and vitality, as they had done on previous visits.

During the period, I had the opportunity to observe Czesław Miłosz who came to a meeting with students in Warsaw's *Stodoła* club. The enthusiasm with which the message of the Nobel laureate's arrival was received, and the lengthy queues in bookstores when a volume of his poetry was published, indicated that people would come in crowds to the meeting. And so it happened.

I sat in a room full of young people, and more were still arriving. There were not enough seats, even though you had to have an invitation, people were standing or sitting on the floor. I watched the fevered crowd of young people and felt their great excitement, the sense of waiting for something extraordinary, something wonderful. "Miłosz has a great audience," I thought with pleasure, looking around the room.

When the poet appeared, everyone became silent and kept their eyes fixed on him. He looked excellent, well-dressed, elegant, dignified. He began to read his poems. The silence was absolute. He read with great cadence, melodious, which I can hear to this day. Then came the second part of the meeting—young people asking questions. They were carefully prepared and showed their erudition and knowledge of the poet's works. The students tried, often in a very academic way, to interpret the poems, discuss them in depth. This seemed to surprise Miłosz. He answered the questions without a smile, rather impatiently, one could even sense some dislike in his voice. I could not understand that. One of the students quoted a fragment of a poem and asked if the criticism it included referred to Russia.

"Of course not," answered Miłosz impatiently. "It is about Polish immigrants in London!"

We all listened in amazement and did not understand it. *What a haughty man*, I thought. *Such a great poet, and yet so rude and unapproachable.* I was surprised by my own reception of the author of *Dolina Issy* (*The Issa Valley*). I'd heard that Miłosz was sometimes moody, that he could be unpleasant. I also remembered what I'd read in *Kalendarz i klepsydra* about Konwicki flying to San Francisco, planning his conversation with the poet on the plane flight, but not foreseeing that Miłosz might not want to see him.

Most of my friends and acquaintances passionately discussed the situation in Poland. At numerous meetings, different scenarios were considered. When meeting at Teresa Jonkajtys-Sołtanowa's, Kazimierz Dziewanowski and Jerzy Jaruzelski (the author of the book *Mackiewicz i konserwatyści* (*Mackiewicz and Conservatives*)) discussed the possibility of Russian troops' intervention in Poland.

On the other hand, a friend told me in confidence: "Everybody listens to the TV news, gets excited, while I use the time to enjoy writing. Don't tell anyone..."

The situation in Poland was infused with additional dread when on 13th May 1981, we heard about the assassination attempt on the Pope. In all churches, people prayed for his health for long days. A week later, Cardinal Stefan Wyszyński died. His funeral was on 31st May. Tomek and I went to the *Warsaw Victory Square (Plac Zwycięstwa)* where the funeral Mass was celebrated by the Vatican secretary of state, Augusto Casaroli. We watched the parade of delegates and representatives, color guards from the whole of Poland, including also Solidarity banners. The marchers included Lech Wałęsa, but also Jabłoński, Rakowski, Ozdowski. An elderly man standing next to us said: "You know, I saw Piłsudski's funeral, but this one is even greater. That first funeral was military, this one is national..." In St. John's Church, the Primate's will was read. The will described the Cardinal as being glad not having hated the Poles who had imprisoned him for three years in an isolated place during 1953-1956 period, proud for forgiving them all for his persecution, and feeling a degree of strength at having suffered their mockeries and lies. The words made a big impression on everyone.

Ania and my brother Krzysio had another child: Paweł Michał was born on 30th June 1981. I was in Łódź to see my nephew, but I left before I could take part in his baptism.

The necessary documents arrived from Canada, I received Tomek's and my passports and visas, and on 11th September 1981, a plane of the Lot Polish Airlines flew us to Montreal.

After our arrival at the Mirabel Airport, Professor Tadeusz Krukowski drove us to his home in Ottawa for the first few days. Later he drove us to Toronto.

While in Ottawa, Tomek had a TV in his little room. He was watching a lot of westerns and often asked me: "Mom, will you translate for me, I can't understand a thing..."

We went to the shops, where Tomek spotted a knife that he had dreamed about for a long time. He was amazed with the enormous choice.

At the same time, we were so lonely and unsure during the period that we talked about what surprised and amazed us in this new country. We did not understand everything new, and it all seemed quite foreign to us. Tomek asked me to bring him books in Polish. I borrowed them from the Polish Institute of Arts and Sciences, and so for the first couple of weeks he was reading Sienkiewicz, or Curwood. This was probably his seatbelt, a stay within his native language, when his mind travelled to the wonderful world of the *Trilogy*. Although having many funny and enjoyable moments, in general, we felt almost unhappy, reliant, dependent on others for quite a long time. I also longed for the convenience of my own home.

The day after arriving in Toronto, Tomek and I went to the nearby Catholic school. The woman who welcomed us was the chancellor of the school. She did not even look at Tomek's certificate of completing five years of education at a primary school in Poland. She told me that they would place my son into the sixth grade. If he could not cope, they would demote him to a lower grade. The following day, I received a phone call from the school. The spokesperson advised me that Tomek would have extra English classes, and I was asked not to worry because he would return home later than usual. Over the next few months, I observed Tomek doing additional language exercises, doing his homework, and learning phrases. He told me that beside him, there were a few more children in a similar situation, that he worked individually with a tape recorder, and that they watched movies. I could tell that he had little difficulty doing his homework. He was immersed in the language, which came to him from a variety of sources around. Soon I noticed that he was using more and more English expressions and abbreviations. I did not give much effort to keeping his Polish pure, which is usually a matter of concern for families staying abroad permanently, because I knew that my stay in Canada was temporary. After about six months, I was notified that Tomek would not have extra English lessons any longer because he was doing well, and although he still made errors, it was only a matter of time for improvement to occur. I was also notified that he was moved a year forward in mathematics due to his excellent results. Tomek achieved a higher grade syllabus in his sixth, seventh, and eighth grades. In the latter, which is the end of primary school, he and eight other selected students, did the high school syllabus.

Since the beginning, I was greatly surprised with the Canadian school system and the way students and parents were approached. On return to Poland, I wrote about it in the chapter called *Szkoła w Kanadzie* (*School in Canada*), which was part of my book *Nie tylko Ameryka* (*Not Only America*).

Many young people worked part-time and had their own money, whether they were primary or high schools pupils or university students. Whether they came from affluent or poorer families, they always did some work during their holidays. Parents funding a three-month vacation for a student who got "overextended" with studying were quite rare. During the school year, girls worked as baby sitters, boys mowed grass, shovelled snow in winter, packed goods in stores, delivered newspapers, delivered medicines ordered in pharmacies or meals for the sick. Many jobs were available during summer in the tourist industry, e.g. girls from high schools worked as guides in the parliament. In the first weeks of our stay in Canada, Tomek asked me to help him find a job as a paper boy. I called the administrative department of the daily *Toronto Star*, gave his age, the name of his school, our address and phone number. After about two weeks, we learned of news that there was a delivery vacancy in the next street and that Tomek was assigned to the route. A brochure was received informing us what were the rights and obligations of a paper boy and since then, every day in the afternoon, and at seven in the morning on Saturdays and Sundays, Tomek received a package of newspapers with a printed list of names and addresses for deliveries. On rainy days, plastic bags were additionally supplied, to prevent the newspapers from getting wet.

Paper boys are well-liked in Canada. Customers treat them accordingly and are often happy to give them small tips. Students list the work of a paper boy as an additional after-school activity in their CVs, when they apply for admittance at a school or university.

However, when Tomek wrote about his occupation to his grandparents, they sent me a letter to express their shock: "Are you already so badly off that you've sent your child to work?!" I had to explain everything to them to clarify the situation.

We stayed in two rooms in the house of an elderly Polish woman, which Bumek Heydenkorn rented prior to our arrival. Ms. Bryk, an immigrant from before the war, who never visited Poland, had her own opinion about her country of origin and its inhabitants. She very carefully watched Tomek and I preparing meals in the kitchen.

"You must have been giving him something special to eat," she said.

"Why?" I was surprised.

"Because he doesn't have a large head, like all Polish poorly nourished children."

The elderly lady believed all sensational news given in the press or television. She was nosy, but caring in her own way. In our absence, she came into our rooms, emptied the trash bins, without being asked, she washed our clothes in the washing machine, etc. In the evenings, she came to my room to talk. I knew that I had to either accept it or move out. I chose the latter and found two rooms in the same area, at Mr. Frank Nierodka's. We had more privacy there, but then it turned out that the host was having divorced and had to sell the house. I found a more expensive, but self-contained apartment which consisted of two rooms, a dining room, a kitchen and a bathroom. It was the upstairs of a house in a pleasant neighbourhood close to a very elegant district, where Tomek was soon delivering newspapers. The new apartment was unfurnished, but my Canadian friends quickly helped me furnish it by lending me all the necessary, basic furniture. Gustaw Szkoda lent us a huge desk and a bookcase, Andrzej Dukszta gave us a little table for Tomek's room, and Hanka and Bumek Heydenkorn, my good spirits throughout my stay in Canada, not only found beds for both of us but also lent us a lovely Mexican rug, tables and armchairs. Zdzisław Przygoda gave us a TV, which we put in Tomek's room and which likely contributed very much to his accelerated learning of English. One day, Professor Adam Bromke arrived from Hamilton with a big package. There were some clothes of his sons and several dozen toy soldiers. He placed the soldiers on the floor in Tomek's room. My son was delighted with the gift and accepted it gratefully.

Polish Canadians remembered Wańkowicz from the days when he lived in the States and came to Canada for author's meetings. He was gathering materials for his book *Tworzywo* at that time. He was friends with Franciszek Głogowski and Benedykt Heydenkorn. Stanisław Zybała, once a Polish Canadian journalist, who at the time was an employee of the Secretary of State in the Federal Government, told me how the writer had been attacked in the Polish Canadian press after meeting with the editor of the communist newspaper *Kronika Tygodniowa* (*Weekly Chronicle*). The details on that fact can be found in the writer's archives. "We all expended a lot of energy to concern ourselves with that," joked Zybała. Zybała also gave me an interesting example of the specific attitude of some Polish Canadians to some matters. Earlier, pianist Witold Małcużyński came to Toronto where he gave a few concerts. He played Chopin, and on a particular day it was not his best performance, so a critical review—actually a justified one—of the pianist's play appeared in

Toronto Star. There was an immediate reaction of Poles indignant that some-one dared criticize "the music of Chopin who is a national idol."

I gave several lectures on Wańkowicz in Toronto, Montreal, Ottawa and Barry's Bay. Professor Florian Śmieja, a poet and author of many volumes of poetry, organized my meeting with the Polish speaking readers in London, Ontario. The author's meetings typically had large audiences and sometime involved heated discussions. Lively debates were held over the subjects of the writer, his books, and his decision to return to Poland in 1958. I regularly wrote for the Polish Canadian *Związkowiec,* which was published since 1934 in Toronto by the Polish Alliance of Canada. Wojciech Krajewski wrote features for the cycle *A życie Polonii biegnie (Polish Canadians' life goes on),* Benedykt Heydenkorn wrote reviews of new books. *Związkowiec* was an interesting paper, greatly owing to its editors-in-chief. The position changed some three times during my stay in Canada. There were many disputes that had nothing to do with running the paper, but rather with the policies within the Polish Alliance. The echoes of the disputes reached me, but I was never involved personally in affairs which were new and occurred in a new territo-ry, not known to me.

On Saturday mornings, Zdzisław Przygoda came and took us to a farm near Toronto where he kept his horse, Jolanta. Tomek enjoyed the weekly riding lessons, and I went alone for long walks. We didn't have lonely weekends; we were often invited to dinner by Hanka and Bumek.

Bumek and I really enjoyed our discussions, which were often quite ab-stract. We talked about honesty in life, loyalty, about many acting out certain roles, consciously or not. At that time I was reading the book *The Games People Play* written by psychiatrist Dr. Eric Berne. We discussed, for exam-ple, that some people wore a disguise, as if playing the person they would like to be, a more perfect one. Thus, at some point in life, the person iden-tified so much with the character played eventually became the character. The innate qualities thus merged with the disguise: the game turned into action. After a period of trial, the soul adopted and recognized the disguise as its part. In all America, much was said then about self-realization, self-improvement, positive thinking, visualization. The conversations reminded me of our Warsaw conversations with Kąkolewski, who phrased his opinions about similar topics very cleverly. A doctor in Poland that I knew once told me that when people achieved a good position, a successful career...it was easier to be noble and right. "Then, for instance," he said, "people do not take bribes anymore. While professors earn enough to live in dignity, young doc-tors earn pennies and cannot afford to refuse a bribe. They have to reach a higher level in the hierarchy to "grow noble."

On one occasion, I took part in a competition in the monthly *Kontrasty*, to whom I sent a story *Once Upon a Time*. My heroine in the story was looking for excellent people to admire and to follow their example. Yet, her task became increasingly more difficult as she became more mature and able to make closer observations. Finally, she came to the conclusion that it was easier to rise high in life and "become a princess" by herself than to look for extraordinary things. People were then eager to become friends with her and she made them glow. Kąkolewski would call it "humanization". Bumek Heydenkorn wrote down the quotes of philosophers whom he valued and gave them to me, then he referred to them in our talks and was glad to have found an enthusiast for those kind of discussions.

During the period, I mainly clung to my countrymen, with whom I wanted to talk about the situation of my country. Ever worse news came from Poland; the Canadian newspapers wrote at length about the potential entry of Soviet troops. Polish-Canadian newspapers repeated the news of *Radio Free Europe*. Poles shared the letters they were receiving from their friends and relatives in Poland, read them aloud and discussed them. I was unable to analyze the situation in Poland or make any comments about it. I was irritated and hurt by a certain undertone frequent in conversations. Some people who were staying in Canada repeated the bad news from Poland with a kind of satisfaction. The bad news served to justify their decision to leave the country, where "you simply cannot live," as they put it. Once in a café, a Polish woman who had been staying less than a year in Canada, added sugar from a packet on the table to her coffee and said with a laugh:

"In Poland, people would have taken this sugar into their pockets..."

"In Canada, they would do the same if they didn't have it in the shops," I replied sharply.

I heard many stories about Polish friends who would ask you repeatedly to send them something useable, they would even give you a shopping list, or urge you to provide a legal invitation to come to Canada. I listened to such stories with distaste. I was Polish, as well. I felt a kind of loyalty to my country. The loyalty meant that I would not speak ill of Poland, but only with pain and concern. Today, I still have this attitude: I criticize Poland when I am in Poland, just like I criticize the United States when I am in the States. When I'm out of the given country, I don't do that. On the contrary—I defend it and I see its good sides. I become an ambassador for the country that I leave.

Our neighbourhood had a sports centre where Tomek went swimming, and I had yoga classes. In the nice apartment on Page Avenue, our life slowly began to settle into a harmonious schedule. We went regularly to the library, delighted with the wide selection of books and the décor. I discovered there many novels by Canadian writers, such as Morley Callaghan, Margaret Lawrence, or Margaret Atwood.

Tomek liked watching the *Magnum* TV series which starred Tom Selleck, and was set in Honolulu, Hawaii. He liked his school, and being a newspaper delivery boy, he ambitiously collected money for a bike with four gears that he was dreaming of. He bought a few things with the money he earned: the knife he'd wanted, a fashionable jacket, skates and electronic chess. The chess was extremely interesting and fascinated everyone. Tomek could choose from four levels of difficulty and play the game alone as he had previously done. His electronic opponent signalled the suggested moves with lights. At the fourth, highest level of difficulty, the device sometimes thought for half an hour what move to make. Laterm after our return to Poland, our friend, journalist Michał Radgowski became a big fan of it. He visited us in Kmicica Street and usually played chess with Tomek.

Krysia Radgowska, Michał's wife, sent me a note from Poland that the correspondence between Melchior Wańkowicz and Czesław Miłosz which I had left to be printed in the monthly *Twórczość* before I left Poland, after printing (issue 10/81) was confiscated and destroyed by the Communist authorities. Only a few dozen copies were saved. That correspondence is an invaluable resource for researchers of Miłosz's life and work. Included are several very long letters, most of them from 1952, which marked the beginning of Miłosz's immigration. During this time, the poet obviously felt miserable as an immigrant. Wańkowicz wrote to him reminding Miłosz that being a poet, as he claimed, his person was highly valued as even writer's daughters were. Wańkowicz wanted to help him, raise his spirits, or at least give some advice, since he had been an immigrant himself since the war. Miłosz's situation was by no means easy. Soon after his decision to stay in the West, the poet announced that he did not want to join any Polish organizations. He deliberately kept away from them. Poles that lived outside Poland did not trust him and did not want to forget that he had worked in the Communist Polish diplomacy for several years after the war. Polish immigrants of Canada joined the campaign against the poet that was conducted in Poland. Embittered, Miłosz shared his opinions on the subject in letters to Wańkowicz, and unveiled matters unknown to the general public. He also expressed opinions which may be viewed critically now, from the perspective of many years. In his letters, the poet wrote that "literature in exile is more or less a fiction and things can actually be published only in foreign languages." The reality turned out to be quite different, both for him and for other Polish writers.

Soon, Bumek Heydenkorn received a copy of that correspondence from Europe by mail, with enthusiastic remarks as to its value. Gustaw Herling-Grudziński mentioned it in his *Dziennik pisany nocą* (*Journal Written at Night*). Adam Michnik wrote: "I consider the publication of the correspondence of Czesław Miłosz with Melchior Wańkowicz to be one of the most significant events of the short Polish freedom" (*Lektury więzienne*). When Miłosz saw the reaction of many prominent people to his letters and the theories contained in them, he was likely horrified and regretted his decision to give me permission to print them. When he learned that the correspondence was reprinted, he wrote to me that he was unhappy with that, but when he later found out that the reprints were done by underground publishing houses, he did not protest anymore.

The correspondence is a remarkable document of the epoch time. Each researcher of that period and each of Miłosz's biographer should read it. The poet's image is devalued in the eyes of all lovers of his poetry. The right arguments were clearly given by the clear-thinking, wise Wańkowicz. The arguments of the poet, as the journalist Kot-Jeleński put it, "were unfair and marked by an unacceptable self-confidence and self-pity..." Miłosz's book *Rok myśliwego (A Year of the Hunter)*, published by Instytut Literacki in 1990 contains extensive sections concerning the correspondence. The poet examines and explains his situation in those years. I think it was good that he consented to its printing (even though later he regretted the decision and in *Rok myśliwego* called it "magnanimous"), because he had a chance to express his views after all those years, to give explanations. If that correspondence were published after his death, he would not have had the opportunity to defend himself. Then, the words and statements contained in the letters of 1950 would weigh even more negatively on his biography.

While I was reading a special issue of monthly *Więź* (7/83), dedicated to a discussion of immigrant literature, I recalled the words of Miłosz, who in the 1950's called the immigration literature "fiction". It contained opinions of various literary critics: Paweł Hertz, Jan Błoński, Czesław Hernas, Tomasz Łubieński, Andrzej Mencwel. Błoński stressed that immigrant literature came down to greater freedom of speech combined with writing for scattered, not very distinctive or even imaginary readers. Hernas stated that if that literature passed through the eye of the needle of criticism and opinions of its recipients, it would become a permanent part in the achievements of Polish literature, as had already been seen in our history. Hertz pointed out that the works banned in Poland—the immigrant ones—sometimes seemed more valuable than they actually were. The literature created in Poland, restricted for obvious reasons, might often contain thoughts and content of greater importance, but requiring more thorough reading. Łubieński wrote that Polish writers abroad found themselves in an indifferent world interested in its own affairs, so they faced being closed in a narrow environment or even an "allergic" reaction to such fate. Immigrant writers were running the risk of sentimentality, depriving themselves of the right to express their opinions, or, quite the contrary, revelling in their own moral luxury, judging and adjudicating—while being acutely in error. Mencwel argued that immigrant literature was a form of regional or community-specific literature, and rarely rose above what directly conditioned it. Although part of national literature, it was not necessarily valuable enough. Juliusz Żuławski noted that certainly it was not freedom of thought and perception that made immigrant literature stand out, because this was "possible everywhere"...

I often met with Bumek Heydenkorn in the *Meyr* café, halfway between our house locations. I borrowed from him and passionately read books from the Paris *Institut Littéraire.* I read books I hadn't had time to read before, I also read *Kultura* on a regular basis. I marveled at Czesław Miłosz's translations of Walt Whitman's poems. What also startled me were the opinions of Russians about Poland, as written down by John Danton, a Warsaw correspondent of *New York Times*, quoted by the Parisian monthly (*Kultura* 7/8, 82). A Soviet journalist said:

> No, we do not like Poles much. They have so much already, and we have so little, and now they want us to pay for them, to subsidize them. Each nation has its own character, sometimes stereotypical. Germans are effective, Hungarians are smart. As for Poles, they have two features: they are lazy, and they are aggressive small business people. They always smuggle various things, they buy gold, sell various goods. They always travel to other countries and bring something from there. They do not work hard but constantly complain.

Another Russian said:

> Poles are cosmopolitans. They look different, they are even ashamed of being Slavic. They look only to the West. Well, fine, they do not like our system. A lot of other ethnic groups in the Soviet Union don't like it either, but they keep working.

I found Anka Kowalska's[5] opinion printed in *Kultura* (7/8, 81) to be very interesting. In an essay entitled *Początki (Beginnings)*, she wrote about her involvement with the underground movement KOR. The author was charmed with Jacek Kuroń's[6] personality. She wrote about his appearance and the strength you could see in him. Kuroń and the people around him seemed happy and safe to her. Kowalska ended her essay with the words: "In short, thanks to Jacek Kuroń, I tamed my fear; I think it is very important."

Kowalska's statement reminded me of our discussions in Nieborów, where Professor Szapiro argued that women often engaged in political activity when fascinated by men...Back then, that opinion seemed very critical and unfair to me.

The Polish Canadian press published many stories of people who—in my opinion—neither were heroes in Poland, nor even attempted to be. Now, many of them made up grand theories about their lives and difficulties.

Some Polish friends of mine looked after a young couple from Warsaw, who had immigrated via Stockholm. The husband had been an assistant lecturer in Poland at the Warsaw Polytechnic Institute. The couple told me that they felt they were "political refugees." I asked if he was involved in politics.

"No, I wasn't even a member of Solidarity," he responded.

"So you are not political refugees. You are looking for another, perhaps better perspective of life, and that is economic immigration."

Thus, I was unable to avoid judging others as well, although usually I tried to escape subjection to it.

It was December 1981. Toronto was full of Christmas lights, and a huge sleigh with six reindeers and Santa Claus appeared on University Avenue, one of the most beautiful streets of the city. The feast of lights and the excitement in the streets made everyone feel wonderful. In the evening of 12th December, at Hanka and Bumek's house, we listened with Tomek to recorded Polish carols from their extensive collection. One of the recordings included the voice of the Pope singing with the choirs. I felt almost as though I was in Poland.

At night, the phone rang. I picked it up in the dark. I was groggy, feeling so rudely awakened.

"I'm calling you so late, because I want to tell you what happened in Poland," I heard the voice of Adam Bromke. "Cars came to the Solidarity building in Warsaw and took away all the members, in Gdańsk too, so it must have been in other cities, as well. There is unconfirmed news of movements of Soviet troops."

"Oh my God," I barely managed to speak.

"Don't worry, Poland has always existed and always will, each generation has its worries, but Poland has been and will be...Each generation must pay its debt with its blood. I feel a bitter satisfaction of having predicted it..."

I hung up and cried. It was one o'clock at night. I realized that the 16-month-long Solidarity freedom in Poland had been disrupted.

For the whole next day, from early morning, Tomek's and my time was filled with phone calls and listening to the news. We knew that telephone communication with Poland was disrupted and that correspondents couldn't send out any news. The presence of Soviet troops in Poland was ruled out, different numbers of those arrested were reported, and it was not known where they were held, but some guesses were that they might be transported to Russia.

Tomek cried, saying he wanted to go back to Poland. Over the next few days, he was constantly asked at school about Poland and whether he would stay in Canada.

"Mom, you will not stay here?" he kept asking anxiously.

During that period, almost all my friends tried to persuade me that I "should of course stay in Canada."—"I can't make a decision now, I'm all aching and I'm concerned for my family and friends. I cannot and do not have to make any decisions yet. It's only three months since I left Poland..."

Marianne Ackerman, a journalist from Montreal that I knew, told me how one could enhance his/her popularity by saying that you were politically persecuted. She gave the example of a Polish director temporarily residing in Canada, who said that one of his plays was not allowed in Poland, and thus he got jobs. (I remembered him from television, he did quite well).

Few people were able to keep calm and behave rationally while worrying about Poland. During my meetings with Polish Canadians, I heard many say that Solidarity demanded "too much." I was a member of Solidarity myself, and the opinions of some Poles in exile that "Poland had sufficient freedom" often annoyed me. There were also other reactions: spasmodic sobs about the "end of Poland."

I refused the TV people who came to me asking for an interview. I was unable to consider the situation dispassionately, and I did not want to show publicly what emotions I struggled with. I was in a particular state of imbalance, both cold analysis and wise counsel of my friends annoyed me. My home was in Poland, along with my family and my life. I could not think without pain about all that was going on there, and which we only knew from enigmatic news. For the first week, the news was unconfirmed, but repeated by everyone around, ominous, frightening, tormenting.

Wojciech Karpiński wrote in *Amerykańskie cienie* (*American Shadows*): "What prophetic signs shall we appeal to, whom to ask for help, for the gift of bravery, even purely spiritual, from which I am so far now when I note my concerns with a trembling hand, I the absent. Is it true, and if so, then how long yet? What price do I pay for this freedom?"

Tomek began attending judo classes and continued swimming, and I took up tennis and continued yoga. We both liked going to the Eaton Center, the chain of elegant stores which to us then seemed the most beautiful in the world. You could get there directly with an underground train, which stopped twice. Little restaurants, cafés, fountains, shop displays, all were under a glass roof. We bought ice creams, looked at puppies in a pet store, with especially fond looks at small Dachshunds, and we went to one of the cinemas. Eaton Center is a meeting place for many Canadians. Before Christmas, it was especially nice to wander along the shops, everywhere there were decorations and illuminated Christmas trees, Christmas songs were played...*I'm dreaming of a White Christmas....Just like the ones I used to know...Where the treetops glisten, and children listen...to hear sleigh bells in the snow...*

Just before Christmas, we were invited by our friends from the United States, to visit them in Florida. In a way, I escaped from the Canadian snow and Polish affairs to have a few days' rest feeling a need for companionship with Tomek. I could not be with my family in my country, where in all the past years tradition set the course of my life and the world had its sense. So I didn't want to be with anyone else.

The stay was relaxing, although my thoughts were with my family. We basked in the sun in the Gulf of Mexico, drove to Disneyworld in Orlando, and I saw the extraordinary city of New Orleans for the first time.

On return to Toronto, I received shocking news from Poland about prisoners who were kept in the cold and hosed down with cold water, who had to pass through a line of militia with truncheons. Terrifying news reached us, lists of prisoners were given. I found the names of many friends of mine. At parties and dinners organized by Poles, people analysed how "a historical moment has passed for Poland," saying that now "you can only pray for a miracle." Wojtek Krajewski held a party at his home and initiated a quiz to question if Solidarity had a chance of survival. Almost everyone (two people abstained) said it had not. Adam Bromke said: "Even before it was founded, it stood no chance."

Bumek Heydenkorn returned from Boston, where a campaign of aid for Polish prisoners was discussed. Czesław Miłosz, Wiktor Weintraub and Stanisław Barańczak were to be its leaders. In the December issue of Paris *Kultura*, I read a feature article by Stefan Kisielewski that seemed to predict terror. He wrote that Poland was poor, in a murky, intransparent situation, where you could see neither concrete nor understandable suggestions for overcoming the desperation, not even a general motto which would encourage people, give them the impulse to act.

I also remember a sentence from Adam Michnik's afterword written years later for the book *Kościół, lewica i dialog* (*Church, the Left Wing and Dialogue*): "What I learned living in that regime for 35 years is that it's never as bad as we fear, and it is never as good as we want to believe."

The Canadian Polish Congress, whose vice-president was a well-known architect, Stanisław Orłowski, organized a shipment of food, clothing and money for Poland. The reaction was spontaneous and massive. Prime Minister Trudeau said that the introduction of martial law was a purely internal affair of Poland. Jaruzelski's government reportedly quoted those words as a proof of support of their policy. Trudeau was opposed e.g. by a Canadian MP of Polish origin, Jesse Flis, who organized an *Emergency Committee* of Canadian MPs and publicly criticized the Prime Minister's attitude.

During that time, I appreciated my situation being a holder of an independent scholarship of Canadian institutions. I was free and didn't have the difficulties encountered by Polish scholarship holders. Anna Reczyńska from Krakow was staying in Toronto for a year. I met her through Bumek, who aided all scholarship holders. She was lonely, felt badly for being away from Poland, was constantly depressed, and cried over the weekends. Immediately after the news of the martial law in Poland, she called me, sobbing on the phone that she was panicking, that her brother was in the army, that she had to go to the consulate.

"You shouldn't go there, especially now."

"I have to," she kept on saying. "Especially now."

After a few days, Anna telephoned me again and said that she had gone there and had been advised to find a job with *Kronika Tygodniowa*, a Communist newspaper of the Polish community. The cultural attaché told her that many Poles gathered at the consulate, threw tomatoes and wanted to break-down the entrance gate.

The first letters started coming from Poland, all of them open and stamped "censored." The letters from my family gave me a lot of peace. My mother sent a Christmas wafer, Krysia Radgowska wrote that Michał was writing a journal to show me later, and that he hoped that someday we would compare our impressions from those days. She sent me a card with a bear, and wrote: "Live normally, for us, too, so more intensely than ever, and think of us fondly."

I learned the news that Michał gave up his job in *Polityka*. When Mieczysław Rakowski asked why he didn't want to work for the paper, where he had been working from the beginning of its existence, he answered: "I see no place for myself in this paper as long as my assistant professor is interned." The assistant professor—Docent—was an invented character from Michał's feature articles, and one who the readers grew to like.

I received letters from Małgosia Holender a colleague from TV, who sent them "by occasion," i.e. privately through people travelling to Canada. Her letters were very poignant, she described the situation so clearly, the moods so intensely, that I could not sleep at night, reading them over and over many times.

In Toronto, a Polish radio station was run by Karolina Kęsik. She made an interesting interview with me, one that I really liked. However, I heard a lot of funny stories from people about the quality of the radio. A few years before, there had been an explosion in the PKO Rotunda, a bank building in Warsaw. Ms. Kęsik played an "occasional" song, as she put it, she always chose a song. On the day of the explosion, she'd selected: *Oto dziś dzień krwi i chwały (Lo the Day of Blood and Glory)*.

I did hear her exciting news broadcast, the day the Pope revealed that seven members of Solidarity had been sentenced to death in Poland. Then, Ms. Kęsik reported that a demonstration outside the consulate was organized by Pietrzak. A few moments later she said: "I'm so upset ...not by Pietrzak, by Przetakiewicz."

Two days later, she broadcast a correction—the news was not from the Pope, but from PAP (*the Polish Press Agency*), and it was not seven, but three members of Solidarity, and they were sentenced not to death, but to three years in prison.

I wished for such news not about Poland, but perhaps Nicaragua, and not now but, say, two years ago.

Toronto also had a Polish TV station. I remember a discussion of Adam Bromke and Barbara Kasińska about Solidarity. Kasińska said that the generation who were now in their thirties in Poland had only the shackles to lose. There was no purpose, no future, and so there was a huge opportunity and greater determination.

At the end of January 1981, a film about Poland entitled *Let Poland Be Poland* was shown by American television having been made by the US International Communication Agency. The film included e.g.: President Ronald Reagan, Margaret Thatcher, Helmut Schmidt, Francois Mitterand, Pierre Trudeau, politicians from Japan, Norway, Spain, Italy, Portugal, Belgium, all talking about Poland and its situation. Frank Sinatra sang in Polish. Famous American actors: Charlton Heston, Kirk Douglas, Glenda Jackson appeared there, too. There were pictures of Warsaw, Poland, with fragments of the Pope's visit to Poland shown. The film also featured the diplomats Rurarz and Spasowski, who'd decided to stay in the West, and their decision evoked a lot of interest.

I was moved by the program, but one of my Canadian friends told me cynically that it was cheaper for America to prepare the program than to help Poland. Stanisław Gliwa from London, sent me a letter mentioning that the American program was not shown in Europe in full, only parts of it were shown, because it was received critically.

Wiesław Chrzanowski came from Poland to present a lecture about Solidarity and the situation of Poland (in Warsaw, I had given him the invitation, that Professor Bromke left with me to give him). He was sensible and calm. A lecture in Toronto held by Jan Nowak-Jeziorański promised to be significent event, as he was known to everyone as the *Courier from Warsaw*. Nowak-Jezioranski grabbed the audience with his enthusiasm and passion. He was a great speaker. Bumek and I went to a private meeting with him. Asking me if I intended to go back to Poland, I responded yes. "Your intention is a proof of heroism and patriotism," he said thus being the only man who saw my decision in that way.

The Canadian government announced that the Poles who were in Canada legally could apply for permanent residence. The procedure was simplified. Like many others, I submitted the required papers. I decided to stay in Canada longer, I wanted to wait for the situation in Poland to be clear. My desire was to actively work and make use of my time in Canada.

Several times Tomek and I went to Florida, and twice I went to San Francisco. I was fascinated by the United States, wanting very much to see New York and Washington, and soon I did. I remember an interesting situation on the Berkeley campus near San Francisco. I was sitting in a student café with a small group, when I suddenly saw the poet Czesław Miłosz. He came in, looked around for a moment, then left. How different he looked from the image I remembered from two years earlier in Warsaw. There was weariness in his face and, above all, sadness. He looked like an unhappy man. He clearly differed from the smiling American professors and the joyful youth. "What a poor man, what a price he had to pay for his independence, exile, for being different," I thought.

Tomek spent three weeks of July in Barry's Bay sailing with a group of boy scouts aboard a sailing boat called the *Baltic*. He'd attended their meetings for the whole year. I realized that for the first time he was going to travel alone, away from me and from our family. Previously, he went away either with me or with his grandparents. I saw whole families seeing their children off; they were noisy and smiling. The appearance of Tomek's forlorn look in the window of the departing bus taking the children stayed in my memory for a long time. I went home and cried into my pillow. I was sad that he was alone, that it was only me who saw him off, that our family was far away, and that in spite of our friends, we were very lonely in Canada.

About that time, I received the order of Constantine the Great. Constantine Knights are an organization similar to the Knights of Malta. The tradition of the order dates back to 314 AC and the time of Constantine the Great. Thanks to that award, I was able to afford the cost for additional courses at the university. There was one Canadian of Polish origin in the group of members awarding scholarships, whom I had known for a long time— Zdzisław Przygoda. He was a very well-deserved figure for Polish affairs, Canadian Poles and his new country, Canada. Przygoda was a member of the board that reviewed and sanctioned acceptance of foreign engineering degree certificates and also helped many engineers arriving from Poland to find work. He was involved in the project of building a monument of Kazimierz (Casimir) Gzowski, which was unveiled in 1968 by the Prime Minister of Canada, Pierre Trudeau. In 1973, Zdzisław Przygoda collected funds during the celebration of the Copernican year to purchase a spectrograph for the University in Toruń. Thanks to his initiative, a square in Toronto was named after Lucy M. Montgomery, author of the world-popular book *Anne of Green Gables*. A few years after my arrival, Barbara Wachowicz followed the Canadian traces of that author in order to gather materials for a book.

After a year, when my scholarship from the Mickiewicz Foundation and the Research Institute were completed, I started working at the Ministry of Higher Education. I was employed in the department granting scholarships to students. General Bruce Legge helped me find the job. He was a member of the committee granting the award of Constantine the Great, and Legge had written a letter to Minister Betty Stevenson to support me. For six months, until I received another scholarship, I worked as a clerk from 9.00 am to 5.00

pm with a break for lunch. Having colleagues, we went together to jointly organized events. I learned about the conditions for granting scholarships to students, and about the relations and behaviour at a workplace. I went to work dressed like everyone else, in a jacket and skirt, regardless of the season, always in stockings and covered shoes. Coming to work in tight jeans and a sweater, which were normally worn by many girls working in TV in Warsaw, was unthinkable in the Ministry of Higher Education.

I interrupted my work at the Ministry of Higher Education when I was granted a year-long scholarship by the Ministry of Culture in Ontario. The award constituted a great success for me and I was very happy with it. While applying for it, I was asked to find a non-profit organization of at least ten years of existence to support me. I was a foreigner, so they wanted to protect themselves. Were I not to successfully accomplish the project, the said organization would have had to pay back the money given to me by the Ministry. The organization that provided me with such a guarantee was the Adam Mickiewicz Foundation. I have very good memories of the Foundation, and of all the people who were engaged in that project and strongly supported it. Rudolf Kogler, Wojciech Krajewski, Benedykt Heydenkorn...it was thanks to their recommendations that I could focus on gathering materials and take the time to write a book.

My commitment was to write a book about Polish immigrants, about their lives since they arrived in Canada. I was going to show different people, different fates, not just the successful and happy ones. I intended to reveal those people who considered their life a success, as well as those dissatisfied with the new country, who clearly did not feel well in exile, or who remained skeptical, regardless of the environment and place in which they lived. I noticed that I reacted more to human hurt and pain than to success and prosperity. For me, the human tragedies were more dramatic. In the book, I kept the right proportions of attitudes, it had more people satisfied with their immigration than those who regretted their decision. The texts showed real characters and real events, and mainly concerned people who came to Canada after World War II and were living in the Ontario province. An important conscious decision was made not to present people who had come to Canada in recent years. I thought it would have been too early to write about their attitudes towards the new country and about their achievements. All stories are either a result of my direct conversations with dozens of people, or are taken from diaries and memoirs that I read, using e.g. the resources of the Canadian Polish Research Institute in Toronto and the National Archives in Ontario.

The scholarship covered the cost for a translator. The translator was Wojtek Stelmaszyński, a son of Polish immigrants, graduate of Slavic Studies at the University of Toronto, and student of Professor Louis Iribarne. His parents owned an inn and a motel in Niagara Falls, where I stayed with Tomek several times. The place was visited by many Poles coming from Poland, including Cardinal Karol Wojtyła (who was later to become John Paul II) from Kraków, who was visiting Polish communities at that time. A beautiful picture from the Cardinal's visit hangs in the large dining hall.

At the same time, I was granted a small scholarship to help me write a book about the first Canadian senator of Polish origin, Stanley Haidasz. His career, and entry into the world of politics, were a milestone in the history of Polish Canadians and that was one of the reasons why I found the topic interesting. His father, Piotr Haidasz, immigrated to Canada in 1911 at the age of thirteen. The parents raised their children in the Polish language and spirit. After graduating from medical studies, Stanley worked in the Polish community, as he'd been working for the community since his teenage years. A doctor by profession, he never denied his time or attention to people. Haidasz was popular and well-liked. Elected president of the Canadian Polish Congress, Haidasz was active and successful in its fund raising activities. The Funds prospered under Haidasz reaching over three million dollars, used to spread Polish culture in Canada. Being a doctor, he could be financially independent. Entering politics (without interrupting his medical activities) presented much uncertainty for Haidasz. His dedication was sincere and complete. When the need arose for him to take part in political life, there weren't many candidates who spoke English well, had completed university education, could represent the Polish community with ardor, etc. Senator Haidasz's career was a step forward in developing Canadian Poles' consciousness. Poles, like other ethnic groups, accepted their inferior position, and frequently persecution. Someone who was not of English or French origin, did not say out loud what their roots were, and did not have the opportunity to occupy any important positions. Haidasz was the first one to make his origin a public case, and he won it. He received full support. Also, other ethnic groups gave him their support, seeing it as a chance for themselves, for everyone. One of the doctors in Toronto, Roman Bladek, told me: "Living on one street with an "ethnic" didn't use to be viewed well. The Poles gave their whole "backyard energy" to a man who stemmed from that backyard. They gave their support. And that is in a way their creation, their achievement." Parties, banquets, performances, lectures, Sunday picnics were organized, and the collected money sponsored Haidasz's election campaign. A group of people committed to electing him went from house to house and encouraged everybody to vote "for Doctor Haidasz." The priest in St. Casimir's church urged people to vote "for our man". Polish ethnic press worked at its full capacity. Both *Związkowiec* and *Głos Polski (Polish Voice)* published fiery articles calling people to vote for Dr. Haidasz, stressing the common origin, nationality, culture of the voters and the candidate. There was a huge mobilization, everyone united with a common goal—to elect "one of them."

In 1967, Haidasz won the elections in southern Ontario as the only Liberal, while all others were beaten by the Conservatives. In 1971, he became the first minister for multiculturalism, a policy introduced by Prime Minister Pierre Trudeau. His speeches in parliament, particularly in the United Nations, were always excellent. The crowning achievement of his career was his nomination as a senator in 1978.

He participated in and singly organized many events to help Poland and the Polish community abroad (he has a great allegiance for the Catholic University of Lublin). The senator contributed to introducing and refining specialist spinal surgery for children with scoliosis at a hospital in Zakopane, Poland.

A younger and very active politician, a member of the Canadian parliament, was Jesse Flis, also a son of Polish immigrants. Jesse emphasized the great role of Haidasz in paving the way for the "ethnics" into the politics in Canada, which had always been and still was very conservative and harsh in judging immigrants. Zbigniew Brzeziński told me that making a career in Canada would probably have been more difficult for him than in the States, where your skills and talents were somehow more willingly recognized by others.

Jesse Flis, with whom, as with Senator Haidasz, I kept in contact over the years, introduced me to the then Prime Minister, Pierre Trudeau. He made an excellent impression on me, focusing all his attention on the interlocutor. Trudeau gave me a large photograph of himself with the dedication "For Aleksandra." Trudeau was the subject of passionate discussions. His pro-Russian sympathies, his constant stressing of how Canada was different from America even in the smallest gestures, aroused controversy. Many people, while seeing his extremely strong personality, strongly criticized him. But it was Trudeau who brought the constitution from England to Canada, introduced the green maple leaf symbol, and introduced the national anthem. He also dealt very skilfully with the French-speaking province of Quebec.

In his book *Trudeau*, George Radwanski quotes Trudeau's words claiming that he was never bored in his life because there were so many unread books, unheard songs, so many people to meet, things to hear about, things to do, see, find...Trudeau quoted Cyrano: "I may climb perhaps to no great heights, but I will climb alone."

When I was studying Polish language and literature, I understood that I should choose the work of one writer to know it particularly well. Now, being in Canada, I similarly slowly learned more and more about the country and made quite an effort to do so. I wanted Canada to be a country which (along with my own) I knew well: its history, literature, problems. To some extent I succeeded.

I liked Canada, I felt good there. I also rebuilt my social life there, like in Warsaw. I had many friends whom I could rely on. Janusz Dukszta, a psychiatrist and politician of Polish origin (for ten years a Member of Parliament on behalf of the NDP), owner of a vast collection of paintings, he supported artists and was a colorful figure in Toronto. He and his brother Andrzej, a dentist, contributed to my being a regular visitor at concerts, to the theatre, even to the opera. Many artists, journalists and writers visited Janusz. There I met the future leader of the NDP party, Bob Rae. The party won the elections in the Ontario province. Later, I met Austin Clarke, an African Canadian, author of *The Meeting Pot* and *Storm of Fortune* who had given lectures in the States.

My acquaintance with several people grew closer. I often visited Barbara Frum, a prominent television journalist. On one visit, I was introduced to a popular contemporary Canadian writer, Margaret Atwood, and her partner, Graeme Gibson, a literary critic, as well as a well-known journalist, Peter Kent. Janusz knew Professor Louis Iribarne from the University of Toronto very well. The Professor was Miłosz's student, and later translator of his books. I went to the cinema with William Killbourne, author of many books. I visited a very pleasant couple, Leah and Jack Ludwig, who turned out to be friends of Julia Hartwig and Artur Międzyrzecki. I devoted a separate chapter of the book to conversations and meetings with Marion Andre, director and founder of the *Plus* theatre, whose biography was quite unusual. Years later, Marion Andre protested against many articles against Poland by printing his letters in the Canadian press—he was a Jew, and he emphasized that his and his mother's lives were saved by Poles during the war.

Peter Gzowski was an interesting figure, well-known in the radio and television, who invited me to his farm in Rockwood. Gzowski was the sixth generation after Sir Casimir Gzowski, whose statue stands on Lake Ontario. Casimir (Kazimierz) Gzowski, a participant of the November Uprising of 1830 in Poland, came to the United States in 1833. In 1841, he moved to Toronto, where he found a job in the department of public works and that marked the beginning of his remarkable career. Extremely active, he greatly contributed to the development of Canada. His major engineering works included building the International Bridge near Niagara Falls, and creating a railway system throughout eastern Canada.

As for Peter Gzowski, the only thing Polish about him was his surname. He told me about his trip to Poland, during which his jeans got stolen from his suitcase in a hotel. Peter was tall, gallant, a little mysterious, he liked *Nonsense Novels* by Stephen Leacock, loved horses, and most of all, he loved his program *This Country In The Morning*. It was a very popular daily radio program.

Once, Gzowski told me he was going to New York to have an interview with Jerzy Kosiński. The press was full of gossip and conjectures. The gossip hinted that Kosiński did not write his books himself but his secretaries-assistants did it. He denied it, his assistants only confirmed that Kosiński dictated his books to them, telling them the plot scene after scene. The secretaries, for whom English was their native language, wrote his stories onto paper. On return to Toronto, Gzowski said to me that he did not like the author of *The Painted Bird*, and that he'd mentioned me to Kosiński. Some two weeks later my phone rang at eleven pm. The voice said "Jerzy Kosiński speaking." During our conversation, he asked about my plans, and invited me to visit him, gave me his addresses in New York and Florida. "If you decide to stay in the States or in Canada, please remember that you will miss meeting with friends in a café, chatting with them. Here everyone is busy, no one has time for one another. You will miss the Warsaw environment..."

I encountered June Chow, a Chinese, at the University of Toronto. She was a student of musicology, and loved Chopin's music. June was a small brunette with long hair, always laughing and very intelligent. Often together, we went to the O'Keefe Center to see *Evita* with music by Andrew Lloyd Webber and the famous aria *Don't Cry For Me Argentina*. I met some of June's friends, among them John Fraser and his wife, a journalist, Elizabeth MacCallum. They both spent several years in China as correspondents of *Globe & Mail* and were very impressed with the culture and people. June visited them and they liked her, as did everyone who knew her. John Fraser invited June, Tomek and me to the christening of his child, little Kathleen. We all met at his house in Bernard Avenue, and he gave me his bestseller book about China *The Chinese: Portrait of a People*, which was highly popular. June invited me several times to her small concerts organized in different places, such as nursing homes. She always played Chopin and did so with feeling and passion. When I was leaving Canada, June was planning to move to the United States. Unfortunately, I lost contact with her.

Gail Henley was known as the author of a book about Polish settlers from Kashubia (named after a region of Poland) in Barry's Bay. They were the first group of Poles who came to Canada in 1858. They settled in the Ontario province in the county of Renfrew. In time, the settlement became a truly Polish town. Barry's Bay area, rich in lakes and forests, was good for scout expeditions, Poles liked to build summer cottages there in which they spent the warm summer months. Gail was a young woman with great ambitions, which she didn't hide.

The petite and pretty Merle Shain was an author of books published in the States under interesting titles: *When the Lovers Are Friends*, or *Some Men Are More Perfect Than Others*. She invited me to her house and wanted me to tell her about myself. She didn't seem to have any secrets herself, and gladly talked about her life. When I returned to Poland, I read in a letter that she was suddenly diagnosed with cancer and died soon after. The American press often quotes her parables and bookstores still have her books appearing with colorful covers. Here is one of her parables about heaven and hell:

> And the Lord said to the Rabbi, "Come, I will show you Hell." They entered a room where a group of people sat around a huge pot of stew. Everyone was famished and desperate. Each held a spoon that reached the pot but had a handle so long that it could not be used to reach their mouths. The suffering was terrible. "Come, now I will show you Heaven," the Lord said after a while. They entered another room, identical to the first—the pot of stew, the group of people, the same long spoons. But, there, everyone was happy and nourished. "I don't understand," said the Rabbi. "Why are they happy here when they were miserable in the other room?" The Lord smiled, "Ah, but don't you see?" he asked. "Here they have learned to feed each other."

Mary and Graham Sinclair often invited us for dinner. Graham had an interesting hobby: he cut semi-precious and precious stones. He made jewelry and took part in exhibitions. He gave me a nice pendant as a gift, and I learned from him to look at jewelry in a different way, as a sign of taste and fashion trends.

I really liked the Glista family, Marina and her children: Greg, Joann, Alexandra, Caroline. They were fourth generation Poles who'd settled in Canada, and were very much committed to the affairs of Poland and the Polish community abroad. I knew Marina's husband, Ted, from my first visit to Canada. He was an educated, energetic man with big aspirations. He died suddenly of a heart disease just before Christmas. The news of his death reached me in Poland before my departure. When I came back to Toronto, we met up with Marina and slowly became friends. Tomek and I visited their farm in Beaver Valley near Toronto, lighted the fire in the fireplace and talked with each other until late at night. After the death of her husband, Marina took care of their children and continued her husband's business. She was always very generous for the Polish community and, among other achievements, she founded an award named after her husband. She knew Polish quite well and told me about its tasty nuances. "How would you, for instance, translate into English my mother-in-law's words about a friend of hers who'd visited: "Po co się do mnie ta baba przywlokła?" (approximately: "Why (on earth) did that hag drag her sorry self over to me?")" Marina enthused. "So many meanings are contained in those words, the whole attitude of my mother-in-law for that person..."

Ania Jurksztowicz introduced me to the charismatic movement "Born again Christians" in Canada. Many interesting Poles were interested in the movement, like Alicja Manterys, Irma Ihnatowicz-Zaleska or Fr. Edward Ewczyński. I wrote about it in my book *Dreams and Reality*—that was the title that I gave to my English-language book devoted to Polish immigrants in Canada.

Art Jasinski explained to me the philosophy of "positive thinking" that was becoming increasingly popular and attracted many people. Peter Roper, a psychiatrist from Montreal, told me funny stories. He was an Englishman who managed very well in Quebec, did not know a word in French and had a specific colonial attitude to the province. Charles Nobbe, a Harvard graduate, constantly on the way to Pakistan, Thailand or India, was the representative of CIDA (equivalent of the American UNESCO). He was interested in other cultures, and talked a lot about his exotic travels. A few years later, in Washington, I met his twin brother, Richard, a handsome, well-educated employee of UNESCO, open to other cultures, who'd spent several years in Paris.

I kept in contact with Marta Erdman by mail and by phone. She sent me a hand-drawn map showing how to get to the town of Middlefield in Otsego County, New York, where she lived. I was going to visit her, but put off the trip for the warmer months. When martial law was declared in Poland, she wrote that she was happy that both her daughters were with her in the States, and not in Poland. We exchanged opinions on the book *Moje przygody z historią* (*My Adventures with History*) by Marian Brandys, which I read in Canada. Brandys had written that the widowed Wańkowicz lived alone in a large, four-room apartment, but let his granddaughter stay in a crowded dormitory. I wondered where he might have found such information. The writer lived in a cramped two-room apartment with an alcove in Puławska Street. Living in the dorm, as he told me, was Ania's choice, because she preferred to be among young people, but she often visited her grandfather in his apartment and from time to time stayed there for longer periods. There were a lot of other inaccuracies, but most of all I was surprised by the unkind tone of the writer whom Wańkowicz valued and considered his friend.

After many years, in the archives of the Institute of National Remembrance (IPN)[7] I found Marian Brandys's letter to Anna Erdman (Marta's daughter), and her husband, Tadeusz Walendowski, in which he wrote about different "atmospheres" in the apartment in Puławska Street. I quote:

Warsaw, 13.8.79

Dear Ania, Dear Tadeusz, Dear Friends,

I read your beautiful farewell letter with a sad heart. I will miss you greatly, for I owe unforgettable moments to you. Your "day room"—as you call it—has really given daylight to my life in the worst, darkest days. I became accustomed to sending a kind greeting towards your windows when going along Puławska Street. Now, I will be very sad every time I realize that you are no longer there. The great, clear, bright atmosphere of your home that you were able to create I can appreciate so much more for having been present in that room at social meetings also at a different time.

Although your leaving hurts me, I fully understand and support your rationale. It would be reason enough that Ania will be able to work normally, and Dawid and Eliasz will not have to explain why they have such names.

I wish you luck and all the blessings in your new life, because you really deserve that. I thank you from the bottom of my heart for everything that I owe you.

Marian Brandys

Greetings on behalf of Halina, who is absent.

Marta thus wrote to me about Brandys's book:

24th March 1982

(...) I read Marian Brandys's *Moje przygody z historią* with kind interest, but I was slightly surprised with his unkindness to Father, which he transferred on to me, innocent as a lamb. Maybe he needed it in order to show the contrast between the "brilliancy" of Tadeusz's family and Ania's materialistic and alienated ancestors. As a literary trick, it is a method well-known and valued, yet there are a bit too many falsehoods and inaccuracies in there. And has it really never occurred to him to consider who it was who'd taught Ania to speak Polish, and to a large extent to think, which no one in New Jersey or Washington really needed!

I remember that Father liked and appreciated him. I thought that he was a friend to my father, as well...

When I returned to Poland and had the opportunity to contact Marian Brandys, I decided to tell him about Marta's and my reactions to his book. Mr. Brandys was not feeling well, he'd been ill for many years (already Wańkowicz worried about his health back when he lived). During one of our conversations, I promised to send him Wańkowicz's correspondence with Miłosz and my own *Kanada, Kanada* (published in English as *Dreams and Reality*). After a few weeks, I received the following letter.

15th May 1987

Dear Aleksandra,

I just got back from the hospital and am in such a state that a conversation, even by phone, is unthinkable to me. Thank you very much for the package. I read both the Master's letters and your Kanada with great interest and relish. The only thing I have not found was the copy of Marta's letter, which you read to me on the phone. You must have forgotten about it.

If I ever recover from this illness of mine, of which I cannot be sure, I shall call you.

With kindest regards,

Marian Brandys

In response, I sent the copy of Marta's letter, which Mr. Brandys had asked about. I received a reply from him that touched me with his honesty and straightforwardness. His words said a lot about the author:

Warsaw, 27th May 1987
Dear Aleksandra,
I am grateful to you for your last letter and for the sincerity with which you put this whole story matter. Of course, it was not pleasant for me and, although there were a lot of things which annoyed me in Wańkowicz (who was a strange mixture of Polish *Kresy* old-style bawdy gentry and an American businessman) I truly appreciated and admired him as "the first reporter of Poland" and the author of *Szczenięce lata*, and on reading his *Ziele na kraterze* (it so unfortunately happened that I read that beautiful book only after his death) I truly came to love him.

But it's always like that with me: I tend to exaggerate and see everything in two colors: white and black (which is why I felt so at home in socialist realism). It does no harm to historical books as it increases their transparency and dramatic effect. But when I write about friends, I have a tendency to go to extremes and incur their wrath and offense. Marta has rightly concluded that I was fascinated by the brightness of the young and, therefore, tried to contrast them at all costs with the old (I got detailed information about the Master's weaknesses from his friends and lackeys). Well, one more lesson for me, although I am already so far away on the other side of the hill that I do not know if I shall be able to make much use of it.

At the end, something nice (for you). Do you remember how you brought me to the Master after his return from England? When I was with him alone, he began to talk about you. At one point, he said with fervour which he had never shown before: "Know that Oleńka has been like Providence for me for these last years."

When I stand firmly on my feet again (if it actually ever happens), I shall call you.
Marian Brandys

Marta's disease progressed. She wrote that Christmas 1981 was special because it was spent with her daughters and their families. Ewa received my last call, and she stated that her mother had just returned from the hospital, that she had my phone number written down and stuck to her desk, and would call me when she felt better. Marta never called. In early November 1982, news came of her death. Marta Erdman, born Wańkowicz, called Tili by her father, died eight years after him, also from cancer. She was sixty-one years old.

About books, Native Americans and many other things, I could talk for long hours with Grace Kopec, one of my Canadian friends. Her parents were Poles, and her father a RAF pilot during the war. Grace's son, Piotr, a graphic artist, designed the cover of my book *Dreams and Reality*. Grace had a diploma in library science from the University of Pittsburgh, was well-read and had many passions and interests, which she willingly shared with others. Her parents had a pretty summer cottage on a lake near Parry Sound, where Tomek and I often spent weekends. We would talk there until late at night. "Perhaps we'll go now and see if we aren't in our beds," Grace used to say before we finally went to sleep.

Our trips to the lakes around Parry Sound were exceptional. A boat journey was required to reach the house on the island. As an entire expedition, we found much joy in the experience. Tomek loved the clear water and swimming, and I could not take my eyes off the water, the rocks and greenery. We fed raccoons, and watched a small red-haired fox which came to get some food. The lakes and islands of Georgian Bay are among the most beautiful views I've seen in my life. Grace and I went to "Festival of the Sound" concerts in the town of Parry Sound, Ontario.

Later in Toronto, we all went to the O'Keefe Centre to see a performance of Duke Ellington's famous orchestra. In addition to performing his own compositions from the musicial *Sophisticated Ladies*, his orchestra also played among others the ever popular Sentimental Journey by Les Brown.

With Grace, I saw New York for the first time!

Grace's daughter Isabelle lived in New York with her husband, Pierre Moeser. They had their internship there after graduating from medical studies. In an internship, the aspirant worked for two years almost all day in a hospital earning only a small salary. After the internship, one could possibly start his or her great career as a doctor earning better money. Isabelle and Pierre lived on Avenue H in Brooklyn, were extremely hospitable and very busy, and sometimes were gone all day.

We agreed with Grace that she'd take us in her car and drive to New York City. Unfortunately, Tomek suffered an accident just before our scheduled departure. Riding his beloved bike, he fell so awkwardly that he tore off some skin on his chest and had some deep bruises. An ambulance took him to hospital where he underwent several medical tests. That afternoon when I returned home from shopping, my Swiss neighbor was waiting for me in front of the house and said: "Your son had an accident, but everything's all right. A policeman came and left a message which hospital he was in..."

On phoning the hospital, I was immediately put through to the right doctor, who reassured me that Tomek was still having a medical check-up, but everything was all right and in two hours he would be at home. A policeman brought Tomek home. With him was his twisted bicycle. Being very sore, he had to spend a few days in bed. I remember the problem we had in distributing his newspapers—Tomek walked beside me, limping, and showed me where I should throw the paper. After a few days, he felt better, but Grace had already gone to New York, so we decided to go by plane and then return together by automobile.

Crowds, colorful faces of all the races of the world, exoticism, noise, big city life and provincialism, all together, one gigantic sprawl. My delight mingled with horror. In New York City, you can see how people have managed in their lives, who has been successful, who barely so, and who gave up any effort long ago. No other city in the world has ever before or after aroused such mixed feelings in me, not Paris, London or Cairo, Bangkok, Jerusalem, Istanbul or Honolulu.

There were many descriptions of the New York subway. I remember an interesting one from Wojciech Karpiński's *Amerykańskie cienie (American Shadows)*. After the clean subways in Toronto, Montreal or Washington, the one in New York seemed a stinking dumpster. The smell of dirt, urine, mustiness never left it. Although there were some stations and escalators which were refurbished and clean, they did not all have well-functioning air conditioning. People fought for seats, pushed others to get off or to get on. They were aggressive, and made sharp comments:

"Why aren't you sitting, what are you waiting for?" They had sallow faces. Only in the mornings and afternoons, when officials were going to work, I could see neat, well-dressed people.

Twice we saw scenes that seemed like ones from a movie. A black man crawled into the car, he didn't have legs. He crawled forward, shaking a can before each person, begging for some money. At another time, a man rushed into the car, his long hair dishevelled, and cried that he did not want to rob anyone, but he didn't have anything to live on, so he was asking for support. A few people gave him a dollar but most stared straight ahead, as if they had air before their eyes instead of a man. That look was characteristic of New York. There was no one who stared at others, no one who looked at another passenger's dress or shoes, it was unacceptable, it was a violation of privacy. Everybody wanted to keep their anonymity and expected it from others.

Isabelle and Pierre commuted to work at the hospital by subway and they were used to it. For me it was an exciting experience because I was only on a visit to New York City. But I remember my relief when I later got on the subway in Toronto, where air conditioning always worked, where you could travel in a white dress, you could wear smart clothes and didn't have to look around with fear. Iziula (as she was called by Grace) warned Tomek and me against longer trips. She advised me to take off my gold necklace and bracelet so that I wouldn't tempt anyone, but I didn't heed her advice. I went with Tomek by subway to different destinations in the city. We visited our friend Halinka Wiel who lived in the remote Bronx, and we came back to Brooklyn through Yankee Stadium station well after midnight. The subway train was almost empty, in some cars there were blacks sleeping, some of them glancing at us. My heart was in my mouth, Tomek was sitting next to me, silent. We returned without any trouble. Our boasting about the safety of New York trains, only challenged Isabelle to calmly aver that the stories about the subway were all true and that we just got lucky.

Tomek and I bought tickets for a day trip around the city. We saw Upper and Lower New York, Chinatown, St. Patrick's Cathedral, St. John Divine's Cathedral, the Harlem district, the Statue of Liberty. Our guide indicated where Katherine Hepburn, Jacqueline Onassis and Robert Redford lived. In the evening, we walked with Grace down Fifth Avenue, we went to Rockefeller Center, Tiffany's, Bloomingdale's (which later became my favourite store) and to great bookstores. On Sunday, we all went to lunch at the Fulton Fish Market near Brooklyn Bridge. New York began to fascinate me, and I knew that I would want to go there again. Grace liked the bridges of New York: Verrazano, Brooklyn. My son and I most admired the Washington Square, where we sat on a bench and watched various scenes. There was a black man in tight shorts on roller skates dancing to music, which he listened to on his headphones. He danced very skilfully. Next to us, on a bench, some old men were playing cards, in front of me two girls practiced dancing. The police pulled up, quickly handcuffed three African American people and took them away. Nobody paid any attention to anyone. You could do what you wanted.

Thanks to Grace, I heard for the first time of the concept of "your problem," somehow popular in America. I told her about my friend who'd had surgery....His scalp was somehow reversed front to back to make his thinning hair look better.

"Apparently, I had once told him not to comb his hair from the back towards the front, that he would probably look better if he showed his hair as it was. After what I'd said to him, he started to think seriously about his hair receding and decided to have costly plastic surgery...This is my fault, I feel responsible," I complained to Grace.

"Why are you feeling guilty?" She was astonished. "You just told him what you thought; you had the right to express your opinion. If he was so much affected by it that he decided to have surgery, it means that the receding hair was his problem. This is not your problem, the whole thing is his problem," she told me firmly.

On the way back from New York to Toronto, we took a roundabout way and stopped in Cooperstown near Albany, in the small town of Middlefield. I visited Jan Erdman there on Labor Day, 5th September 1983, almost a year after his wife Marta's, Wańkowicz's daughter, death. I'd informed him about my arrival earlier. I carried the plan with directions how to get there, which Marta had sent me. We drove for a long time along a country road until I saw at the end of the village, next to the cemetery, Marta's favourite location. She had written so much about it to her father. The house was modest and did not look like other American homes. Consisting of several outbuildings, you first came into the woodshed, then into the kitchen and living room. Next there was a guest room with a bathroom. In the upper floor, there was a bedroom and a bathroom. In a niche below the windows stood Marta's escritoire and Jan's desk. Many books, pictures and memorabilia of her father were displayed. A piece of paper with my Canadian phone number was taped to the escritoire, which really touched me. Jan Erdman, a handsome and tall man, had been suffering from cancer for several years and was under constant medical supervision. He was talking about Marta with tears in his eyes. "How could she do that to me, dying first...It was supposed to be the other way round, she was supposed to help raise our grandchildren after my death...I cannot cook, I can only offer you scrambled eggs. Marta did everything in the house," he said.

He showed us a bench in the garden with the names: Marta and Jan carved in it. He had refused to live with the family of his elder daughter in Washington D.C., wanting to stay in the middle of nowhere, in his last home...Did he want to stay with his memories?

Bumek Heydenkorn phoned to tell me that Professor Tadeusz Krukowski had died. This was a sudden and unexpected message. I remember him as a very kind man, very supportive of Tomek and I, offering good advice and warm affection. He came a number of times from Ottawa to Toronto to see us, he helped us twice to move to a new apartment. Krukowski had shared with me his memories, thoughts, and looked quite philosophically at the past and his life. I did not understand why he confided so much in me. I wondered why he was doing it. I didn't know that he was very ill and wrestling with his thoughts, analyzing his life and the decisions he'd taken. He reminisced about his mother, and regretted his decision to stay in the West. He looked bitterly at his family life, at the West which "will never understand Poland and will never be loyal, despite the attachment Poland shows towards it." He yearned for contact with someone from Poland, whom he could talk to about all that. I didn't know that he was aware that he had only a few months of life ahead of him. A few weeks before his death, he came from Ottawa and we went to Grimsby together, to a symposium on the importance of language. The professor looked ill and was driving the car badly. I asked if he was sick. Being wintertime, it seemed to me he had a very bad cold. I advised him not to sit listening to speeches, but to return home. Soon after, he phoned me from Ottawa to say he wasn't feeling well and he was lying in bed. I told him I was flying with Tomek to Florida again. "Do you know I've never been to Florida? I've made so many trips, always to Europe, and recently only to Poland. It was the only place I wanted to go..."

The third person that we sincerely liked and who died suddenly during our stay, was Józef Steinberg, Renia's husband. They were recommended to me by Marysia Drewnowska before our departure from Warsaw, and both were very helpful to us. They invited us to their home on Saturdays, and we often went together to have coffee in *Café de Paris* in Bloor Street. Thanks to them, I was able to know a group of Polish and Czech Jews, who immigrated in 1968, and learned about their grievances and bitterness. But Józef Steinberg had a strength and calmness about him, and he happily gave advice.

Receiving such sad news while you are in a new country is difficult. Someone offers you their kind heart and friendship, and then they suddenly pass away. Your thoughts return home then, to the country where those you love are waiting for you. You know how much you need them in your life, and you want to be closer to them.

I sometimes missed Warsaw so intensely that I imagined myself walking down Ujazdowskie Avenue. I recalled the entire way from my apartment in *Dolny Mokotów* district, then Idzikowskiego Street where you pass *Królikarnia* and the American ambassador's office. Then I'd remember driving along Sobieski Street, Belwederska Street, and Ujazdowskie until I got to the *Plac Trzech Krzyży* square, where I turned into Książęca Street and drove along Oboźna Street and the historic *Krakowskie Przedmieście* to get to the Old Town. I remember every turn and each light. I'd stop near Kiliński's[8] monument and walk along the streets. The views I dreamt about were most dear to me, and sometimes I was astonished at how much I was missing them. I yearned for instance to suddenly find myself in Warsaw for a few hours, drive along its streets, stop in a few places, call my friends, invite Rysio (Kapuściński) for a chat, Maciek (Czaplicki) for coffee, go with Michał (Radgowski) to the Łazienki park, with Marek (Nowakowski) to the Vistula River, stay with Krzysztof and Joasia (Kakolewskis) until late at night.

I remember discussions about Warsaw. Poles living in other cities didn't like it. I emphasized my personal attitude, as well as the historical importance of the city. After years I read in *Nowy Dziennik (New Daily)* an article by Marta Zielińska who wrote that people in Warsaw never trusted the reality, history, appearances of normality. This attitude was the only way to live and survive so much. Marek Jaroszewicz, a professor of architecture at the University of Florida in Gainesville, told me interesting stories about the capital. He remembered Warsaw from his youth as a lively city with well lighted streets, people on the streets until late at night. In his opinion, the new Warsaw had lost its character. It was rebuilt according to Corbusier's principles, divided into parts: commercial, industrial and residential. As a result, each of the parts lives its own life, with their activity decreasing during certain hours. New York has a similar character in the area near Wall Street. Marek Jaroszewicz said he didn't like Warsaw's gigantic twelve or thirteen storey "drawers" for people, built in undeveloped areas where there was a lot of mud and mess, without any gardens. That made a very sad impression. If a city is to be alive, it must be built like Paris with shops on the ground floor, one or two floors above dedicated to offices, medical clinics, lawyers' offices, and higher floors for apartments. As a result, Parisian streets are alive day and night, in the evenings people go out to restaurants or to the movies. For me, Warsaw was a city that was connected with many memories, where my friends lived, where I had my own nice apartment. I looked at it in a special way.

My Father and brother Henryk sent me a clipping from *Dziennik Łódzki (Łódź Daily)* stating the following: "The Dean and the Council of the Faculty of Mechanical Engineering at the Łódź Polytechnic Institute inform that Mechanical Engineer Henryk Ziółkowski has had a public defense of his doctoral dissertation in the Senate Hall...." My older brother worked as a lecturer at the Polytechnic Institute and a doctorate was a compulsory step in his academic career.

My parents wrote frequent letters, which I was always waiting for. My mother mentioned how sad she was and how much she missed us. Tomek also wanted to go back. Once the second year of our stay passed, he asked me more and more often not to put off our returning home. He walked about sulky and quarrelsome. Through his stubbornness and quarrels, he wanted to make me decide to return home. He liked Canada, he did well there—more than that, even his personality changed for the better, as he became more cheerful and smiling than in Poland. But he missed his family, the dog, friends, the apartment, Warsaw. Canada was our extended vacation, and he longed for home. In the summer of 1983 he once again went to the scout camp on the lake in Barry's Bay. He sent me a touching letter from there. I kept it as I'd saved all the writings and drawings from his childhood.

Dear Mommy,

I'm already yearning for you here something awful. This camp is terrible, but I manage. I can't wait to see you. I'd really like to ask you, and I hope you can come next Saturday and Sunday, and if you can, take me home. But it is not that important.

I'm standing guard while I'm writing this letter, that's why it's so crumpled, but I also hope that you haven't forgotten about me and you'll write something nice. If you could, I would like you to bring me some apples.

I've thought about a lot of things here, our return and many other matters important to us. I've had a lot of experiences here, I was canoeing for two nights and did about 20 kilometers. We have our own kitchen, so there is little food and I am often hungry. But in the third week, when people leave, I think I'll be eating in the large kitchen and it should be much better.

Everyone gets visits from their parents, and I'm standing there and trying to imagine them all being you. Well, I hope you're already crying. I have a lot to tell you, but I'll keep it for our meeting and for the next letter. If you want to

pick me up on Saturday or Sunday, you can do it from 2.30 to 5.00. I think that
after this camp we won't argue and we'll respect and understand each other
more.
Always yours,
Tomek

I visited Tomek on the following Saturday, and it was one of the nicest times
with my son. He was waiting at the gate, all yearning, when I came by boat
with Gail Henley, the writer, who had her summer cottage on the other side
of the lake. Tomek could not believe his eyes. Quickly he boarded his canoe
to get to me, and took me for a long trip on the lakes. I was really frightened
although I had a life vest, which Tomek put on me, but I was very happy and
delighted with the view of crystal clear water and green scenery. My visit
was one of the most pleasant moments that I spent with my son in Canada.
Tomek had become caring, attentive, and he really took care of me. When
children grow up, they usually want to be everywhere but with their mother
at home. This time, he focused all his attention on my visit, he had longed for
me and was good to me.

I enjoyed a particularly close contact with my Father during that time, as in
the old days. We wrote frequently to each other, and therefore knew a lot
about each other during that period. Father showed his feelings only in his
letters. He sent Christmas wishes for Tomek and for me written in verse. He
gave us advice, confided to us, remembered about things. My father normally
wasn't like that when I was near. He wrote to me:

> … I understand very well Tomek's longing for his country, because I'd also
> longed for Polish speech and writing myself during the German occupation,
> although in my own country among my countrymen (…). I think Tomek
> should be tempted to explore the world as much as possible, because it is the
> thing which will stay in his memory for a lifetime…

We left our Dachshund Bisio with my parents in Łódź and always asked
about him. We missed having a dog so much. We sometimes played together
as if Bisio were with us.

"Come to me," I then said, pointing to the couch, like I always used to do
when Bisio was with us. We hugged our imaginary dog and we somehow felt
better. When I wanted to put Tomek to shame, I said:

"Well, it's good Bisio isn't here with us, he would be very sorry to see
you talk back to your mother so audaciously..."

Such words disarmed him and we were friends again. Once my parents
wrote that the dog fell ill, they went to the vet but after treatment Bisio's
condition didn't improve. When we received a letter with the news that the
dog was dead, I cried my eyes out. Tomek came for lunch at noon, and when

he heard what happened, he sat down beside me and also started to cry. Then he said reproachfully that if I had not put off returning to Poland, it wouldn't have happened. Yet, good news also began to come.

We learned about the birth of Henryk and Marysia's second son: Łukasz Aleksander was born on 17th August 1983. My parents became grandparents for the fifth time.

We slowly started to prepare ourselves to return to Poland. I completed two books. *Senator Haidasz* was beautifully published by Century Publishing Company Limited. A big promotional event was organized for me with many people present. *Dreams and Reality*, dedicated to the Polish immigrants in Canada, was to be released in a few months.

Before returning to Poland, I had some interesting meetings and trips. On 22nd November I visited Zbigniew Brzeziński in Washington. I found D.C. a beautiful city with the loveliest perspective on the axis of the Capitol—Washington Monument—Lincoln Memorial. My visit coincided with the 20th anniversary of the assassination of President Kennedy and the press wrote much about it, shop windows were decorated with the President's photographs. A warm and sunny day, Washington turned out, to my delight, to be a very clean and green city. However, I only stayed in the center.

I published the interview with Brzeziński in the Canadian press and included it in the book I was working on. He told me about his Polish childhood, the war, when as a boy he watched all events with passion and attention, he saw daily messages of the *Polish Telegraphic Agency* (PAT), that his father brought home, he visited with him the military barracks in Windsor as a guest of General Duch, commander of the armed forces units formed in North Africa. He lived in suspense, watching the actions of the Polish Army, and kept a regular diary. The end of the war was extremely painful for him as he was aware that Poland was subjugated under Russian influence and that they would not return to the country with the whole family. He felt a connection to Canada only after the end of the war, he then starting to identify with it. After his studies at McGill University in Montreal, he wanted to work for the Canadian diplomatic service. He won a competition for a scholarship to continue his studies in England. At the last moment, however, the scholarship was not given to him because he still didn't have Canadian citizenship. Brzezinski then applied to Harvard University, where he was admitted and so began his American career.

My interview with Zbigniew Brzeziński completed an extensive section of my book that was dedicated to his father, Tadeusz Brzeziński, who at the time of my visit in Montreal told me the story of his life. He was a man who'd rendered great services to Canadian Poles. He supported many actions to help Poland and Canadian Poles, among others he contributed to the historic tapestries being returned to the Wawel Castle.

I kept contact with Zbigniew Brzeziński thereafter. We exchanged letters, I visited him in his Washington office, I sent him books that he wrote commentaries on. I not only greatly admire him, but I am also very grateful to him. He wrote many letters of recommendation for me while I was applying for scholarships. When I sent him *Kanada, Kanada*, the Polish version of *Dreams and Reality*, with the chapter about his father, he wrote:

> (...) I was delighted also to received the books, and I have already started reading my copy. It is written with genuine feeling for the very special circumstances that the Polish immigrants encountered upon settling in Canada and I'm certain that it will give the Polish reader a new appreciation of what the Polish settlers have accomplished. Needless to say, I was particularly gratified by the chapter regarding my father.
>
> I would be happy to send you copies of my most recent bookis, provided there was some way of making certain that they reach you. If you have a suggestion, please let me know.
> With kind regards.
> Zbigniew Brzerzinski, January 5, 1987, Washington, DC

Mother wrote me that I should bring some nice clothes, underwear, etc. with me because they weren't available in Poland, but that I shouldn't worry about food. All the newspapers as well as visitors from Poland said that there was not much food available in Poland. I believed these suggestions, as if I didn't believe Mom, and just before we left I bought four packages of ham and four large blocks of cheese. I was taking the food home for Christmas, wishing to share it with my family.

Most of my friends were very surprised with my decision to return and did not hide it from me. There were farewell meetings, talks, cautioning, advice. "Do come back at the first opportunity. After all, you have permanent residence in Canada, you have a permanent residence card..."

I was told that I was interrupting a cycle I'd started, that Tomek wouldn't cope in a Polish school.

We wanted to go home. All the more so, for in people's stories and newspaper articles, Poland sounded much different than we remembered it. I wanted to see it myself.

Chapter Twenty-Two

Return to Poland

When we in landed at the Okęcie (now named Chopin) Airport in the morning, it was still dark. A border service soldier looked through my passport for a long time. Tomek and I went to the baggage room and through the glass we saw dear faces: Mom, Dad, Henio and Krzysio. I fought to contain my emotions...We gathered our suitcases. One of them held mostly Jan Nowak's and Brzeziński's books, pocket editions of the Paris *Kultura*, and books published by *Instytut Literacki*. I knew if found they would be confiscated, since they were published outside of Poland by uncensored publisher. The customs officer considered which of the suitcases I should open. He indicated my electric typewriter and asked what it was. I opened the case, showed him, he wrote out a customs receipt. He pointed at another suitcase and told me to open it. I breathed a sigh of relief, it wasn't the one full of books. Among the clothes, he found two copies of *Senator Haidasz*. He greedily grabbed the prey, browsing through the books, and found pictures of Wałęsa. He left us for a while, and then returned with a colleague.

"What is that?" asked the colleague.

"This is my book, I wrote it."

He thought for a moment, returned the book and left. The customs officer let us go, without looking at the other suitcases.

Mother gave me flowers, all the family looked happy. They couldn't take their eyes off Tomek. He'd grown, he was taller than me. Leaving Poland as a boy, he returned a young man. We arrived at our apartment. It looked small to me, everything seemed somehow smaller than I remembered. I was cold. The place was spotlessly clean and had been recently repainted. My parents came with Henio for weekends to Warsaw and painted my apartment as a surprise for my arrival. In the fridge, I had provisions: ham and veal, which my Mother bought for us. I was ashamed of my packages with ham and cheese...The Poles in Canada who had news from home warned me that in Poland there was "no food"...I believed them, not her, who wrote that I shouldn't worry about food. Tomek was happy and radiant. Everybody gave him a lot of attention, asked questions. He answered, interspersing his Polish with English words, and sometimes stopped to find the right word. For the first time I actually noticed that the melody of his words had changed. This surprised me. I was tired and sleepy. My parents and brothers left to return to Łódź, and I planned to visit them in a week.

I received phone calls from friends who knew about the day of my return. I was confused, I couldn't concentrate on anything, couldn't answer their questions. I still felt cold. Tomek went shopping and came back delighted. "Mom, the saleswoman said to me: "Sir..."

I slept for a few hours. Then I walked around my apartment, looked in the cupboards, through the bookshelves. Delighted with so many things, it seemed as if I had obtained them anew. I felt so affluent and rich with my silver cups, colored crystal goblets, old porcelain, prints and paintings, a few pieces of antique furniture. So many family memories were associated with these treasures, as they evoked so many familiar faces. I had my familiar spaces here: the view from my bedroom and Tomek's room into Wernyhory Street with its gardens, the view from the balcony on our *Służew nad Dolinką* housing development. The surrounding trees that had grown, and there was a new playground for children. The place seemed to me to be the safest on earth, and my own. My return to Poland, to Warsaw, in a way gave me back my identity. I didn't leave the apartment, I unpacked my suitcases, found room for various things, put my new books on the shelves, and placed the photos of Tomek and me taken during our "extended vacation in Canada."

In the evening, I called a few friends. "You're really back?...What happened?"

"Is there no more place for our community in the West that you're back?...

I didn't know how to explain it to them. I felt the truth that I missed Poland wouldn't convince them. The words would sound maudlin and false. In the following days, people reacted much the same way: with surprise, amazement, sometimes indignation. People didn't want to hear that I had my family in Poland, that Tomek was always talking about coming back, that I wanted to see my country. If I ever decided to immigrate, I wanted to make the decision consciously, decide by myself. I wanted to give myself a chance to return and make a decision. Tomek and I now possessed the official cards for permanent residence, and I knew I could return to Canada whenever I wanted. No one would listen to my explanations, my emotional words wouldn't sound right. Almost everybody spoke to me in a strangely, terribly serious manner and explained their concern as "common sense." People seemed extremely bitter. I visited many of my friends during the next days, and we spent hours in conversations. No, they were not conversations, but just listening to their stories. The people didn't ask about Canada, about what it was like. They only wanted to talk about themselves. I listened to them, almost humbly, and a feeling germinated in me, which would grow stronger and more powerful in the coming months. They were all heroes here, sometimes great, true ones, sometimes ordinary, everyday heroes, but heroes they were, and I...I came from a different world and should be sitting quietly and be ashamed of the "wealth of the West." More than that, I should feel ashamed of the "callousness of the West." Perhaps I wouldn't even be able to explain to them how life was there, how people lived there, how Poles lived their lives, how they reacted to things happening in Poland? Nobody cared about that, and I had accepted such a reaction. I just listened to their words of resentment and bitterness, all kind of remarks.

"The money we earn now has only symbolic value. Thank goodness we don't have children and can eat anything we desire, we don't have to worry about kids..."

"Now it takes years to get anything settled officially, clerks are absent for some reason, they retire, the motivation to work is down due to the inflation. The Polish zloty is losing value from hour to hour...To achieve each thing requires presenting hundreds of certificates. In some ways, things have improved because a lot of things have cleared up...We are poorer by missing those years, it's a terrible gap in our lives. We're going downhill..."

"Talking of neediness is done at full tables with good wine...If you can't buy something in the shop, you'll buy it at the market square. I've always lived modestly, nothing has changed. If I see any changes for worse, it's that people have become more petty, me too..."

"Watch out for G. and S., because they informed on people and it's not worth seeing them. There's nothing to watch on television, the pubs are rotten. People keep reminiscing about the former director. Many people have disappeared from social life. Several groups have regrouped...Poles are now serious and boring...Writers' fees are low, taxes are high. It doesn't pay to write, to be a writer, the only thing that amuses is to go to bed with a writer..."

"Everything is difficult, but the most difficult thing is for people to get on with one another...People are so nervous, they are waiting for a miracle, that's why they freeze their ears off..."

"Popularity is given by crowds, but it's not important. I don't care about it. I've reached my optimum age, I have peace, I work, I don't care. This tragic situation increases the stake, now you know that principles are the most important thing. The war has somehow sharpened, made you realize...Everyone is infected, they fight with farmers, they shoot at workers, they dissolve intellectuals' associations..."

Aldona and Zbyszek Kubikowski told me about Zbyszek's arrest on the 13th December, 1981, the day the martial law started that broke the Solidarity movement. Aldona had had an extremely tough year, her father died, Zbyszek soon fell ill.

Professor Janina Kulczycka-Saloni, who was always very composed person, told me that she had seen through the window of her apartment on Foksal Street ZOMO officers[1] brutally beating people. People were hiding in the backyard, the caretaker locked the door, but the officers smashed the glass and threw tear gas shells inside. "A terrible disaster befell Poland. The violence inflicted on us cannot be undone...You should try to learn about everything, your stay abroad has made a gap, if you leave again, you'll get alienated in your own country," she advised.

Zdzisław Kamiński, popular because of his television program for young people called *Sonda (Probe)* that showed the latest technology achievements in the world, told me about his trip to the mountains in December 1981. While standing in a line to go up the Kasprowy Mountain, the usher told him:

"You don't know there's a war?"

"War? With whom?"

"With Jaruzelski. He declared war on us."

He went down from Kasprowy, filled his automobile's tank with petrol (you could buy it until noon) and returned to Warsaw. *Sonda* had been taken off TV by the authorities, but after three months, was back on TV. Many people spat on seeing him; he stopped receiving invitations to many homes. An apparent code had been broken, a code that said you do not expose yourself on TV since it was taken over by the "anti Solidarity regime." "Now it's over," he told me. "But I remember. After all, there were others who were more tactful. Wojciech Marczewski came to me and said that we resumed the program too early, but that generally it was a good thing, because the program was for the young, it showed them what was going on in the world of technology..."

Marek Walczewski confided to me that actors were not doing well..."I'm considered to be a really good actor, yet I barely manage. I won't find work in the West because I don't have any language skills...Poles in the West are often a medley of scammers, sometimes plain rabble. Wojciech Pszoniak told me that various "scumbags" clung to him and wanted to pull a few anti-Poland sentences from him...A woman from Belgium came to look for actors for her film, some colleagues were bending over backwards. She invited me to a café. The doorman told me: "You'll be making a film in the West..." She offered me a low daily wage, I looked at her cheap equipment, looked at her, and left. Others said I was stupid...But I have my dignity. I'm not conceited, but I know what I'm worth..."

A colleague working with Western journalists told me that they "cut the material" according to a pattern settled in advance. They were most interested in showing acts of violence, "beating old women," as she put it.

Maciej Karpiński (Wojciech's and Jakub's brother, from the very eminent literary family) told me that friends from the States called him and asked:

"Is it true that they beat old ladies in Poland?..."

Of course no one beat old ladies, but he said: "Let's not talk about old women, there are so many important issues," he interrupted.

Later, Karpinski's friends said that he had changed and become callous if he reacted in that way.

I lent Maciej Karpiński a beautifully calligraphed anthology of war immigration poetry, made by Staszek Rysztogi from England. When I called him after some time to have it back, he told me that during a search the work was confiscated. To this day I regret losing that valuable collection of poems from papers and occasional prints, for it cannot be recreated. Staszek Rysztogi, a great lover of poetry, had been cutting out poems from newspapers, then glued them in his notebook and added decorative drawings.

Aleksander Małachowski visited me. I treated him almost like a hero because I knew he was imprisoned on 13th December, 1981. At the same time, a colleague from the radio visited me. She had been fired in December. A very brave woman, she made her own archives of tapes with recordings of the December events. They met each other in my apartment. She looked at him in delight.

"You're my role model," she said. "How much you had to suffer..."

"I didn't suffer, I had good meals," he interrupted her almost impatiently.

When she left, not understanding why he was reacting that way, Mr. Małachowski said to me: "Such emotional women I call aunts of revolution, and you need to be on guard against them. Solidarity fell apart because of such people..." He told me that Solidarity collapsed on its own. I didn't understand much, but I remembered Mr. Małachowski such as I'd seen him before my departure to Canada. Having grown a long beard and wearing a cross on his chest, he looked like a prophet. Now I also saw that his appearance had changed.

I heard stories about friends, about people who were more or less familiar to me...about Wiesław Górnicki, who gave up journalism and became General Jaruzelski's assistant...about Artur Sandauer, who had argued that Russia is solid and could not be overthrown. Many people also shared with me their views about colleagues, friends who I thought were "on the same side of the barricade." They often said disgusting things about each other, many things from the distant past, or nuances from the present time. "He's no great writer, look at those sentences in his book, they sound like socialist realism," a friend told me about an acknowledged reporter. An important underground activist had been arrested and interred along with others, and I heard that he had a "very shallow mind of little worth." "But if you repeat to anyone what I told you, I'll deny everything," the friend cautioned me. I was probably more surprised by the latter words than by his opinion on the known activist's mind. In Poland, you could badmouth people and reveal their very private matters without any fear. The saying "If John speaks ill of Mary, there is something wrong with John, not Mary" did not catch on in Polish reality. In America, many people would keep away from people who spoke badly of others without much thinking, rightly fearing that such a person would later speak badly of them, as well.

I was confused and felt more and more acutely my absence at such an important time for the country.

"You were on a different train than we were and going in another direction. Our trains missed each other, that's why it's difficult for you, and you see it from a different perspective, maybe even critically," said one of my friends.

On one occasion, I phoned my parents and cried that I'd been standing in a queue to get some meat but was refused by the lady at the counter. Apparently my "food stamps" hadn't been registered (during martial law in Poland the stamps were required of everyone, since food was then rationed). My parents apparently discussed this problem with each other because in a few days Father visited me.

"Give us the stamps. If you are to be unhappy that you've come back, because of the food stamps, we'll help you..."

Thereafter, they did monthly shopping in Łódź using my stamps, purchasing portions for Tomek and me. Their help was a huge convenience for me and another proof of their extraordinary protectiveness.

"When'd you get so sensitive?" a friend asked in amazement when I told him I'd been standing for two hours in a queue to get some gasoline.

Michał Radgowski brought me his diary from that period.

"I wrote it with you in mind, so that you could read it when you returned. It was difficult for me to write about those days in letters..."

Several days were consumed in reading the typescript. Michał's words helped me to better understand the events of the past period, and caused me to lose sleep over them. I really wanted to learn as much as possible, to know, to understand everything.

The people in Canada had asked me to do things for them after my return to Poland. I visited writer Marek Nowakowski on Długa Street. Jola, his wife, a petite brunette, turned on Chopin's music. They seem to be calm and collected. Marek gave me a list of literary magazines that it was "fair to work with": *Więź, Znak, Odra, Tygodnik Powszechny, Przegląd Powszechny, Królowa Apostołów, W drodze*. Andrzej Mencwel and Antoni Libera visited him at the same time. When I was leaving the building, a man stopped me as I reached my car. He asked to see my documents and when I asked his intent, he mumbled something like from "secret service security." He looked at my papers, made some notes and calmly, wordlessly returned them.

For Christmas, Tomek and I went to Łódź. Mother was busy preparing Christmas Eve supper, Father had decorated the Christmas tree in the morning, before we woke up, and he turned on Christmas carols...The smells of baked cakes, fish, mushroom soup, dried fruit compote wafted throughout the apartment...I went to the bathroom and cried. I powdered my face before leaving, I did not want to show my being emotional.

Proudly, Mother told me that she managed to obtain all the food needed for Christmas "standing in long queues." Instead of feeling admiration for her and being glad, I almost choked on the food. When we shared the Christmas wafer, Mother wished I would never leave the country, and my Father, that I wouldn't "lose my Polish identity." Henio and Krzysio wished for me to live the way I decided and wanted to live...

Henio, Marysia and the boys lived in an adjacent same apartment building next to that of my parents. Tomek had been writing letters from Canada to Michał, and now they were talking about something in the corner. Łukasz, the youngest child in the family, needed great attention and Marysia did not let him out of her sight. We visited Krzysio and Ania. They had been waiting ten years for their own apartment by living with in-laws alternatively. However, they never lost that special, gentle attitude towards each other, that I so admired in them from the beginning. Father also highly praised the educational methods they used with their children. Małgosia and Paweł were taught that they should apologize to each other and apologize to adults when they behaved badly. When they wanted to play with the same toy and snatched it from each other's grasp, Ania would set the alarm clock and assign a "specified time" to each of them. Małgosia was growing into a beautiful girl, she had long legs and thick hair. She admired my hair and constantly asked to brush it.

We returned to Warsaw before the New Year. I started searching for school books for Tomek. In the department of education, where I received the necessary official permit for Tomek's return to school, I was told that the school would provide all books. Yet, the school teacher looked at me astonished. "Not only are you bringing your child to school in the middle of the year, you want us to get you the books, too?" she asked with shock and reproach. I returned to the department of education, somewhat desperate, asking for help. The secretary advised me of reportedly the easiest way.

"If you have your passport, go with it to the bookstore on Koszykowa Street. Tell them that your child is going abroad, no, tell them that he's just come back, and they'll sell you..."

In the bookstore I asked about books for the eighth grade.

"And do you have a passport?"

"Yes, I have one".

They recorded the numbers, but didn't check whether I was leaving, and I brought the books home. That I returned from Canada never occured to them.

Tomek faced some problems. The first day he went to school, he was happy and smiling, but after a week he became sad and confused. One day he was given three failing grades and almost started crying. Because he hadn't learned the subject: Patriotic Movement for National Rebirth,[2] he failed in history classes. Not only did Tomek not understand the new school, he didn't understand what was happening in it. When I attended the parent-teacher meeting, I became aware of the differences between Canada and Poland. The teacher didn't smile, didn't look at anyone, and all the parents were gathered in one room. She stared for a long time at the register, then started reading out loud, one after another, the names of the children who had bad results or behaved badly, the school admonishing their performances quote: "nothing but troubles with them." Every meeting attendee heard that Elżbietka S. didn't do well in mathematics, Jacek B. was often late for school, Zosia F. used bad words. All the comments concerned fourteen- or fifteen-year-old children. The children's mothers, when named, lowered their heads, blushed red with shame, and others looked at them with compassion. To obtain a more detailed report, and generally learn something specific about your child, you had to wait for the end of the meeting. I was sitting at a pupil's desk, waiting in the queue. Two mothers came up to me and said that their daughters...were delighted with Tomek. He was a sensation at school, he let the girls go first in the doorway, used polite expressions such as: "Would you mind..."—"All the children talk about him and admire him so much," they told me with contentment.

When my turn came with the teacher, I told her my son's name.

"Tomasz Tomczyk." she thought for a moment. "Oh, that's the one who returned from abroad," she identified him.

"Yes, that's right."

"Ma'am, he didn't stand up when we spoke to him."

"What do you mean, he didn't stand up?" I was amazed.

"Well, when we talked to him, he kept sitting at his desk...But now he does stand up," she comforted me. She didn't have anything else to say.

I remember that in Toronto, Tomek told me he stood up when the teacher entered the classroom, and how that behaviour caused a sensation. Now he caused a sensation by sitting at his desk...

"Tomek, that's how you show respect, when you talk to a teacher standing," I explained to him.

"But Mom, you don't know how badly the kids talk about the teachers under their breath or when the teachers don't see them. They don't show their respect at all by standing up, that's not true," he defended himself.

The school year was drawing to a close and Tomek was going to take entrance exams to high school. I realized that he had large gaps to make up. He tried to catch up with others by himself. At weekends and each evening he read the compulsory books for the course in Polish literature. Together we revisited Polish grammar. I tried to be very patient, but it was not always easy. I wasn't cut out to be a teacher. Tomek spent the winter holidays in Łódź, where Henio revisited mathematics with him. "He knows a lot of the concepts and almost all the material, but he doesn't know the Polish terms for them," my brother said, comforting me that Tomek would manage.

Tomek chose the well-known Tadeusz Reytan High School, with its rich traditions and a high level of teaching. Many people recommended the school: Aleksander Małachowski, Barbara Chodorowska, a teacher from the Zamoyski High School (where I once had a meeting with young people) who offered her advice to me at that time in many school-related matters. The school had difficult entry exams.

Waiting outside the school for the entrance exam results were difficult moments for me. As the first threshold of difficulty for young people, I'd heard many bad stories about it from my friends. "If he doesn't pass, I'll be paying the price for my travels abroad," I fretted. I advised Tomek to be careful with spelling, replace one word with another if he wasn't sure of how it was spelled. Tomek was given a choice of two topics, one about the literature of the XVIII century, and the second, more general: what book he would recommend to read. Tomek opted for the second choice and chose Orwell's *Animal Farm*, that was compulsory reading in Canadian schools and he knew it well. Krysia Radgowska said that the teacher may respond positively, or may be opposed to such a recommendation. The teacher likely responded in a positive manner, because Tomek passed the written exam in Polish with good results, and he was also successful in mathematics. Tomek was not required to take oral exams and was admitted to the Reytan High School to a class with a mathematics profile.

The high school admittance was a great joy for us. The warm summer of 1984 was beginning. In July, we travelled to Zakopane to the house *Halama*, owned by ZAiKS, the Polish writers and artist society that I wrote about earlier in the Zakopane chapter. Our stay there was very pleasant and highly enjoyable holidays for both of us. I enjoyed the familiar views. I looked at them as if I'd found a lost treasure. Tomek began hiking in the mountains on his own. Arising at dawn, he would set off with a map. He climbed the highest peaks, and it was then that he really fell in love with the Tatra Mountains. Tomek passed through the *Chochołowska* valley to the Grześ peak, another day he climbed Zawrat and Świnica, and later *Giewont*. Once we both went by car to the village of *Małe Ciche* and went on foot to *Rusinowa Polana* and *Wiktorówki*, where we prayed in the chapel of Our Lady Queen of the Tatras. But perhaps the most important day for Tomek was climbing to the highest peak in the Tatras: *Rysy*. Before dinner, we both went to *Antałówka* to swim in the pool.

That summer, as usual, *Halama* brought together many interesting people: Jonasz Kofta, Wojciech Młynarski, Jerzy Przeździecki, Camilla Mondral, and Staszek Brejdygant[3] with Nela Obarska, a popular actress from the Warsaw Operetta. A popular music group *Pod Budą*, with Ania Tetler, was staying next door and sitting at our table. They gave us one of their records. Staszek Brejdygant anticipated a trip to Canada and asked a lot of questions about it. In *Halama*, we listened to tapes with the "spoken" diary of Stefan Bratkowski, lawyer and writer, and had many discussions and conversations until late at night. Barbara (Basia) Wachowicz, who was also staying in *Halama*, invited us for her lecture on *Polskie malwy (Polish mallows)*. Literature fragments were read by the actor Marek Perepeczko, and the audience included Stanisław Marusarz, the brother of Helena Marusarzówna, who had been a famous ski jumper and Tatra courier. I experienced so many patriotic feelings, as always happened during Basia's speeches. Tomek said that he too was also always touched by her readings. "That's an interesting group and they stick to each other," he said about the people whom Basia presented.

The mountains continue to stay in Tomek's memory often speaks about them, and always missed being amongst them. When ten years later Norman and I visited him on his graduation day in the beautiful University of Arkansas campus of Fayetteville, Arkansas located at the foot of the scenic Ozarks, Tomek observed that they were not as beautiful as the Tatra Mountains.

The Tatras stay in the soul of every Pole all life long. Years later, in Park City, Utah, I looked at the bare slopes in the winter and I told Norman of the Tatras. When we came to Colorado and walked around Colorado Springs, I compared it to Zakopane. "It might be just as beautiful, only bigger," I told him.

Tomek spent a few days with Henio's family on vacation in Soczewka, then we both visited a former Major Hubal's soldier, Józek Alicki, in Kamień near Iława. Later Tomek stayed with his grandparents in Łódź. He returned pleased, intent on buying a gift for his grandfather, saying that it should be a book, because Granfather, as he put it, "deserves a gift."

That first summer spent in Poland after our return was so wonderful, and we really enjoyed it. Poland always comes to life and grows lovely in the spring and summer. And people seem to be nicer, less pessimistic and less complaining. I spent a lot of time with Marek Nowakowski, among others, with whom I went for long walks in Warsaw. He lent me "second circulation" (i.e. underground) books. I complained that my eyes hurt after reading the tiny font. He advised me to get used to it, because "only the books printed in that way were worth reading," as he put it. Marek liked to read aloud passages of books, as well as his own stories, which he was working on at the moment. I remember he presented to me some excerpts from Henryk Elzenberg's book *Kłopot z istnieniem* (*The Trouble With Existence*).

At that time, I was also reading an interesting book by Jerzy Holzer *Solidarność 1980–1981* (*Solidarity 1980–1981*). Written in a dispassionate and knowledgeable way, I thought it was perfect. Holzer wrote that it was a historian's duty to exercise self-restraint in judging the actions of people who could not defend themselves, because many Solidarity activists were in prison, and many others could still be imprisoned. The mistakes Solidarity had made (which were of secondary importance for the development of the situation) included in his opinion overestimating its own strength, underestimating the enemy forces, a tendency for internal disputes, which was particularly visible in the last months before December, as if they didn't remember the danger, very weak democratic habits, tendency towards demagogy, and signs of xenophobia. He wrote that many external and internal factors influenced Poles. Sooner or later, however, the state of social awareness would decide. In that sense, the fate of the Polish nation still depends, like it did in the sixteen months of Solidarity, on the nation itself.

Everyone wanted to tell me their opinion about Solidarity. Whether or not it had gone too far, whether or not it had used its chance well...Sometimes I wanted to talk to someone about the phenomena which I had observed in the West. But it turned out that people I talked to knew everything, they had their opinions established, there was almost nothing to discuss. I did not question that. However, I remembered that my friend from Gainesville, Florida, said that although she had been living with her husband, an architect, in the States since the end of the war, and they were interested in the politics and phenomena of the country, they were never able to talk to anyone in Poland about America, because "everybody knows everything, anyway, and they have their strong opinions, and they aren't going to change them."

I reread some of the books that I had at home. Aldous Huxley in *Brave New World Revisited* (Paris 1960) wrote: "In the totalitarian East there is political censorship, and the media of mass communication are controlled by the State. In the democratic West there is economic censorship and the media of mass communication are controlled by members of the Power Elite."

Reading underground books and realizing how difficult it was to publish them, I decided to offer the publishers a gift—a copy machine. I became its owner per the will of Melchior Wańkowicz, who also told me that it was registered in the censorship office. Having observed Polish TV reports of confiscation of copiers brought to Poland from abroad, I decided to immediately give mine to the underground publishers in need. I told Marek Nowakowski about my decision, and he was to inform competent people that "there is a copier to take." During one of our walks, he told me that he found a publisher, and the man was happy with the opportunity to be given the equipment.

"Don't come with the man to my house, the three of us will meet in some other place, I'll give him a big box, but I'd prefer it if he didn't know the source it came from. It would be best not to tell him anything about me, not even my name. Why should he need it?"

Thus we agreed with Marek that he would call me and tell me that we would meet on Wednesday in the *Nowy Świat* café. Using our personal code, that would mean we should meet on Monday in the *Wilanowska* café.

As we met, a young bearded man was standing next to Marek. When we were having coffee, he immediately said that he knew my book *Blisko Wańkowicza*.

We went to the car, I took a large box out of the trunk, the young man packed it in his backpack and we said goodbye to each other. I was very excited before the whole action, but thinking about it later, I realized that we'd acted like boy scouts, we'd planned the whole action carelessly and recklessly...

Marek visited Lech Wałęsa in Gdańsk. I asked him later about his thoughts of Wałęsa, his family and his flat. Wałęsa was a true hero to me. Marek told me a few anecdotes: Once in the morning Wałęsa's car wouldn't start, so he said to the agents who were following him: "Gentlemen, could you help..." And they helped him to start the car. "I start work in six minutes, could one of you turn your siren on and start going, I'll follow..." They did so.

Marek said that Wałęsa had a walkie-talkie on which he listened to the calls of "his" agents. He also stressed that he didn't think the man got bigheaded because of the interest in him and his popularity in the world.

"Imagine an intellectual in a similar situation, he would soon develop a swelled head..."

Marek asked me from time to time to check the train timetable for him. I called him and gave him the message according to the code that we'd previously agreed upon. He tried to be cautious, knowing that his phone was tapped. He wanted as few people as possible to know about his plans. He went to author's meetings organized in private homes, but did not speak much about them. Once, when he travelled to Kutno, two militiamen made him get off the train at one of the stations. They confiscated the books he had with him.

In early March, the TV news informed about "the arrest of Marek N., a writer from Warsaw, who is accused of contacts with Western organizations opposing the People's Republic of Poland" (as I remember these were words or something of the sort). When I phoned Jola, she said that Marek had been arrested the previous night at home. I visited her a few days later. Calm and under control, as always, she created an atmosphere of coziness and was happy to offer supper to me. Jola told me the details: since Marek was in bed with a heavy cold, the agents who came to arrest him called an ambulance before they took him away. The doctor examined him and said that he "could be interrogated." When the agents came into the flat, Marek Edelman[4] was one of Marek's guests. He became so upset, protested to the agents, so they decided to arrest him as well, but Jola told them who Edelman was and that they "shouldn't cause trouble." They only took Marek.

I sent Marek a birthday card to the address which Jola gave me: "Marek Nowakowski, son of Anthony, Detention Centre, Rakowiecka Street, Warsaw."

I spent many evenings with Dagmara and Andrzej Roman. Andrzej worked on a book about a boycott of actors, entitled *Komedianci (Comedians)*. He was well aware of what was happening in Poland and was familiar with current news. I told him about my impressions after meeting his cousin, Zbigniew Brzeziński, in Washington, and about admiring his good Polish.

Dagmara, a strikingly beautiful woman, who was in Naples where she taught dancing at the time when martial law was declared in Poland, saw the writer Gustaw Herling-Grudziński several times. I met in the Romans' house another cousin of Andrzej, a set designer from Polish TV, Teresa Zygadlewicz, and a film director, Andrzej Trzos-Rastawiecki. We started talking about the international situation. Trzos-Rastawiecki said that if in the next two years, Russia didn't declare a war or make any aggressive moves, it would soon lose the arms race with the United States where so much money was spent on modern weapons that within two years the USA would be ahead of the whole world. I drove Teresa Zygadlewicz back to Wspólna Street near Marszałkowska Street. She told me about her home, where the opposition members often gathered in one of the flats. I waited until she went upstairs. Soon after, I was stopped by a car full of men in civilian clothes who checked my ID and then returned my documents with nary a word.

One writer I knew described the situation in Poland like this: for as long as there was a period of tense East-West relations, in Poland there would be conflicts, difficulties, suffocation. The situation was very difficult, people did not tolerate each other socially, in many cases they couldn't stand each other. There were three choices: 1. leave Poland, 2. continue writing, work somewhere, 3. join the government line.

He didn't judge anybody, he said that it was not his habit. "The opposition is being destroyed with ridicule now," he said. "False news is spread that someone has an illegitimate child, or robbed someone else, etc."

Since our return Tomek and I participated a few times in Masses celebrated for our country in a church in Żoliborz. During these services, I heard for the first time of the charismatic Father Jerzy Popiełuszko. I felt somehow the need for that type of emotion, I was hungry for such feelings. At that time, we watched Wojciech Marczewski's movie *Dreszcze (Shivers)*, which made a great impression on us.

My "historical absence" caused by various incidents in my life made itself felt. I was having an accelerated course of modern history. In the fifties I was a child, I did not experience the events of October 1956. I was absent from the stories of my elder friends, neither was I persecuted. I know the sixties, *Letter 34*, Wańkowicz's trial from what others said and from studying the writer's materials. Also about 1968, I learned from stories others told me, so I didn't experience a "clash" with history in March 1968.[5] The seventies were the years of my early youth. This was the period of Wańkowicz's influence: in his environment everything was said explicitly. For the writer the period of transparent prosperity, living on credit, was a cause for concern. The Polish Communist political head of the country, Edward Gierek promised that he wouldn't use force against the people and he kept his word until the end of his rule in 1980. Gierek became famous for his slogan "Will you help?", his propaganda of success, and also for taking huge loans from the West. Wańkowicz feared that people stopped seeing clearly the devastation of the system, pauperization of culture, sociological changes. Working with the writer made me sensitive to the phenomena, and after his death, I knew intellectuals with open minds, who spoke openly about everything. To me it seemed that the whole society was just as conscious...I lived in a kind of glass sphere. People around me were trying to find a way to protest. Those were small gestures, often noble attitudes, but none of them worked on a large scale in the resistance movement. I didn't judge the attitudes of my friends, whether they were brave or just cautious. My foreign scholarships (including the ones from the Polish community abroad; I'd never received a Polish scholarship) definitely made me drift away from Polish reality. My financial status allowed me to lead a fairly comfortable life, even if not luxurious, since I was a person with not too many extraordinary needs. My family, on the other hand, was a good example of the struggle with reality: they had financial problems, problems with work, my younger brother and his wife for many years didn't have their own apartment.

And finally, my absence during the martial law period in 1981 made me now, on my return, isolated in a sense. I felt almost alienated, with a sense of guilt that it was so, and being quite emotional, I even magnified attitudes which I called "heroic." I looked at some people coolly, listening with reason and logic to their stories of great deeds and acts of courage. They seemed to exaggerate, but I also saw that everyone had different degrees of personal courage, and it wasn't my business to judge and evaluate them. Others I saw as irreproachable people worthy of all my support, I exaggerated all they did, and gave it additional meanings. I remember sitting with tears in my eyes in Krzysztof Kąkolewski's apartment and listening to Marek Zieliński, who was talking about his 11-month internment in simple words. He made a big impression on me. Marek was my age, he rented one simple room sharing the washroom and kitchen, and at the same time he was independent, uncompromising, and published bravely in many papers. Militiamen constantly harassed and followed him. During his internment he did not agree to sign any statement to facilitate his release.

I started intensive work. My two books, which I'd published in Toronto, were accepted for publication in Poland: *Kanadyjski senator* (*Canadian Senator*) and the Polish version of *Dreams and Reality* entitled *Kanada, Kanada*. I was invited to Katowice to hold a lecture titled: *Kanada pachnąca Polską* (*Canada With a Polish Fragrance*). I stayed with my dear friend Xenia Popowicz and we talked until late at night. I liked listening to her stories, even if I didn't always agree with her opinions on Polish reality. We were surrounded by different people and we had different experiences.

I looked at the archives of Melchior Wańkowicz and decided to continue my work on it. I published an essay about Wańkowicz's trial in 1964 in *Zeszyty Historyczne (Historical Papers)* in Paris. I started to work on Melchior and Zofia Wańkowicz's extensive and highly interesting correspondence that covered fifty-three years. Their correspondence, including footnotes, an attached calendar and genealogical tree, was to be issued by *Instytut Wydawniczy PAX*, the editor of Wańkowicz's selected works, which together with *Instytut Literacki* in Kraków was preparing a series of Wańkowicz's books.

Editing the Wańkowiczs' letters was not an easy task. For many weeks, I copied the handwritten letters and postcards on my typewriter. The correspondence was preserved in its entirety. The typescript had twelve hundred pages. Some letters were particularly interesting, such as reports of conversations with Jerzy Giedroyc, or with General Kazimierz Sosnkowski. Wańkowicz wrote to his wife about all the issues that worried him, and the whole correspondence formed a kind of biography of the writer. Sometimes I encountered difficulties, some plain anecdotal. For example, the writer used the names with which Giedroyc referred to some writers and journalists. All of them had an epithet assigned: coward, collaborator, traitor...For one name I couldn't decipher the term. And that man had returned to Poland and was quite well-known. Writing "illegible" next to his name was unthinkable; no one would believe that. After two weeks of struggling with the word, I managed to enlarge the letter on the photocopier and managed to decipher it. In another letter, in which the writer wrote of his visit to General Sosnkowski, at some point he wrote: "General Kuka came in and gave us some morn..." I couldn't understand. What General Kuka?...Kukiel, perhaps?, suggested friends...No, no. The word plagued and tormented me. About that time, General Sosnkowski's wife was appearing on television, talking with a historian named Kowalski. One day Aldona Kubikowska phoned me and asked:

"Have you heard what that Kuka had to say to the nation yesterday?"

"What Kuka? What are you talking about?"

"Ah, you know, her family used to call her that."

And thus it turned out that it was the General's wife that offered the guests a morning meal.

Jur Wańkowicz, the son of Marieta and Tolo (Melchior's brother), verified my footnotes on the Wańkowicz family. Karol Wańkowicz and Stanisław Gliwa helped me through their letters from London.

I also started working on the letters of Krystyna (Krysia) Wańkowicz, the elder daughter of the writer, killed in the Warsaw Uprising. While typing the letters and working on them, I was overcome by my own emotions, as they were so beautiful and they moved my imagination and triggered so many feelings. I had an interesting meeting concerning Krysia with one of her peers, Professor Jan Strzelecki. I quoted him in the introduction to the letters and showed him the whole text. The professor honoured me by commenting that I wrote about difficult family matters with tact and proper restraint.

Unfortunately, the correspondence and PAX Publishing Company didn't seem to go together. The editors who were in favour of the publication died. Finally, the job was given to Danuta Oleksowicz, known for editing other books with Wańkowicz himself, and a great expert on his work. The only problem was that she had many other things to work on. In essence, Danuta was doing everything simultaneously. Later she went on partial retirement and as a result didn't work on the typescript every day, but only some two days a week. However, our work did go forward, slowly but thoroughly. I was happy we joined together for the project, I had an experienced, careful editor, which fact was very important with the huge amount of the material, technical difficulties, and footnotes. However, after a few years, when the books were ready for release, IW PAX found itself in a difficult financial situation and started returning books to their authors. I began to look for a new publisher.

There was a lot of confusion around the author of *Monte Cassino*, which sometimes particularly surprised me. Józef Hen wrote in *Polityka* that in 1968 Wańkowicz wrote an "anti-Semitic" book *De Profundis. De Profundis* was written and published in 1943 in Tel Aviv (where Wańkowicz stayed with General Anders's army during the war) and it was not "anti-Semitic."

I once loaned a small Hermes typewriter to Ryszard Kapuściński, who was going on another long journey, and his own typewriter was damaged. The Hermes used to belong to Wańkowicz, who wrote that in 1939 when the war started, he had crossed the Dniester River holding it high over his head. The latest Kapuściński's books were a remarkable success not only in Poland. *The Emperor* was translated by William R. Brand and Katarzyna Mroczkowska-Brand. With that translation in hand, the author traveled to the United States and received a scholarship there, during which he asked for help in contacting important publishers and editors. Kapuścinski became familiar with the market and everything went perfectly. The book was published by New York Harcourt Brace Jovanovich as part of the series Helen & Kurt Wolff Books. The reviews for *The Emperor* were printed among others in *Time, The New Yorker, The New York Review of Books*. Also European publishers were interested in it: English, Italian, Hungarian, French, etc. The book was translated into at least 21 languages. After returning from England, where the book was promoted, he visited me on Kmicica Street. He was really successful, he was talked of on BBC, newspapers quoted him on their front pages. He told me: "Poland is an enclave, it's only here that people still read books. In the West, every hour one hundred eighty titles are released, but the most popular entertainment is films, video tapes...(...) You have to consider—what subject has a "worldwide" import, and only then write. Another novel gets written, so what?"

Polish writers and artists who didn't work full time could receive special certificates from district offices, which allowed them to receive medical care. In the Mokotów district, Wanda Rogowiczowa worked. The widow of a translator and a lovely grey-haired lady, she possessed an impressive war history. Kapuściński and I visited her in the Mokotów district office, and Ryszard lived in the Wola district. She promised to phone there and arrange for such a certificate for him. During our meeting, Wanda asked Ryszard: "Why aren't you living in Mokotów? We care about people here..." She then asked where he'd been born. When she heard he'd been born in Pińsk (she was born near Nowogródek), that he was a fellow Poleshuk,[6] Wanda stood up and kissed him. Stroking his shirt sleeve, the two Poleshuks started exchanging their memories in excitement. It was a wonderful scene. She gave him the certificate. "It doesn't matter that it's from Mokotów, I'm taking you under my care," she stated.

When we left, I was very moved and said to Ryszard:

"Just look, the regulations are the same all over the country, now see what a difference there can be, a person can be treated kindly, helpfully..."

"Of course, here we still have that warmth which you won't find in the West," he said.

Poland and life in it absorbed me more and more. I planted woodbine on the balcony, which formed a green wall, and a miniature spruce. I felt at home, among my people, with my native language. Sometimes I was also alienated and distant. I was preoccupied with the events.

My father often visited Tomek and me during that period in Warsaw and, on one occasion, he also met with a lawyer, Napoleon Siemaszko. He was the last member of the Board of the pre-war National Party and one of the last political prisoners in the Bereza Kartuska prison. As a student, he was involved with the national movement. In the 1970's, Siemaszko became one of the trustees of the National Party in Poland, and later he took an active part in reviving the national movement in Poland.

When Marek Nowakowski was released from a Communist prison for his underground activities, he invited me for a walk in Łazienki Park. Not telling me his feelings while in prison, he behaved as if nothing had happened. I valued that. He once said: "I wouldn't want to leave Poland, go abroad where I would get complexes, be a pariah. In Poland life is "more humane.""

The repairman who fixed my TV asked if I knew that breeding rabbits had been prohibited in Poland. "Why?" I asked.—"Because they keep their ears up in a V-shape" (he showed the Solidarity symbol with his fingers).

Phones worked terribly, and mine was constantly blocked. I often wondered if those weren't deliberate actions. I remember when writer Robert Jarocki called. He said at one point:

"Talk to Bujak[7]. After all, you've already talked to him..."

"No, I haven't talked to Bujak," I replied, surprised.

"What?...Oh, I wanted to say: Bijak, the editor-in-chief of "Polityka"...If you'd talked to Bujak, you would have a press conference invitation..."

Click, the phone switched off.

Another time, after returning from the 3rd May Mass at the cathedral, I talked on the phone about my impressions with Wojciech Krajewski who'd come from Canada. Immediately on finishing the call, my phone was switched off. Over the next days, I had to deal with the telephone company to have the "damage" fixed.

My friends from Canada contacted me often. They brought the English-language edition of *Dreams and Reality*, which was released after my departure. They asked why I hadn't returned, why I wasn't coming back to Canada. They visited me. Janusz Dukszta came with his friend, Frank Haynes, a lawyer from New York. Almost every day we went to various plays at the theatre: *I, Michel de Montaigne* in *Teatr Polski* (*Polish Theatre*), *Ludus Danielis* on the small stage of *Teatr Wielki* (*Grand Theatre*), *Umarli ze Spoon River* (*The Dead From Spoon River*) and *Stachuriada* in Stara Prochownia, *Rain Snakes* in *Teatr Powszechny* (*Common Theatre*), a concert in the Philharmonic...Cultural life flourished and you could boast of it, be proud of it, and delight in it.

I particularly liked the play *Umarli ze Spoon River* (*Spoon River Anthology*), based on the book by Edgar Lee Masters. I later borrowed the book from a library. I wrote in my notebook some of the "epitaphs:"

Alexander Throckmorton
In youth my wings were strong and tireless,
But I did not know the mountains.
In age I knew the mountains
But my weary wings could not follow my vision—
Genius is wisdom and youth.

Representatives of organisations helping the Catholic University of Lublin came to Poland, and with the help of friends from Canada, a dormitory was built. The visitors included some friends of mine: George Jason, representing the Reymont Foundation, Walter Bielaska, an architect and organizer of funds for that purpose, Henry Slaby, who later received an honorary doctorate from the University.

In September 1984, Senator Stanley Haidasz came to Poland with his wife Natalia and a group of Canadian doctors. He had visited Poland many times as a senator, but this time he came as a doctor. The reason for this visit was to take part in treatment of children. In the Polish Stanisław Kostka's Church in Toronto, the Pope John Paul II Fund was established, aimed at assisting abandoned children and orphans in Poland. The fund was managed by a charitable organization recognized by the federal government of Canada. Soon after its creation, a decision was made to help a twelve-year-old girl from Lublin who was suffering from curvature of the spine. The collected money made it possible for the child to come to a hospital in Toronto. After a surgery performed by Dr. Walter Bobechko, the girl arose from bed a week later twelve centimetres (some five inches) taller. After that surgery, many letters were sent to Canada, in which people asked to have similar operations performed. However, the surgery was very expensive. Senator Haidasz persuaded Dr. Bobechko to come to Poland to help children affected by the disease. The surgery was done in a specialist hospital in Zakopane, and Polish doctors familiarized themselves with the new method of treatment. During his stay in Poland, Senator Haidasz received the highest distinction of the Lublin University: "For contributions to the Catholic University of Lublin."

Tomek and I, the Haidaszs and Ryszard Kapuściński all went for dinner at the "Baszta" restaurant in the outskirts of Warsaw. Rysio (Ryszard) changed the table at the last minute (as a precaution). He said that Poland didn't need such aid as African countries: porridge, milk, cheese, etc., because people weren't dying of hunger here. Ryszard proclaimed that we had to realize how to save education, retain access to literature, to the achievements of the West. The subscriptions to specialist magazines ended for lack of foreign currency. What would happen with the technical thought, science, medicine, if we didn't know what was going on in other countries, if we were cut off from scientific literature?

Senator Haidasz said that he'd learned more from him than from all the people he had met before.

Twenty-three year old Greg Glista, Marina's son, came to Poland for several months to study Polish language and culture at the Catholic University of Lublin. Poland made Greg go all wide-eyed. Well-travelled, from a wealthy family, a pleasant man, he was brought up to almost worship the country of his ancestors. He imagined that it would be a bit like...in Zakopane, people in traditional folk costumes, etc. He was amazed to see Mercedes and other Western cars on the streets. We went to Teatr Wielki to see Moniuszko's *Halka*. He was fully focused and absorbed in the opera with all his heart. He'd never seen such beautiful dances, Canada only had amateur Polish-American dancing groups. Later he bought another ticket and went to see the opera again. We met with Marek Nowakowski, whom Greg treated as a hero, influencing him to read at night the English-language edition of his *Opowiadania ze stanu wojennego* (*Stories from Martial Law Time*). We saw the now newly reconstructed Royal Castle in Warsaw that had been completely destroyed by the Germans during the 1944 Warsaw Uprising. After leaving to Lublin, Greg often came back to Warsaw, stayed with me and told me about his difficulties with the Polish language. He returned to Canada with little knowledge of Polish, but with unique experiences. Greg's mother, Marina, and his sister Joann also came to Poland. While driving them all to the Okęcie airport, I realized how much I missed...beautiful Canada.

The Easter of 1984 was spent with my parents. During my stay in Łódź, Bishop Jan Kulik asked me to write a historical book about the Diocese of Łódź. I accepted the offer with some reluctance. I was a bit afraid of an unfamiliar subject, where even the language and vocabulary were sometimes difficult for me to decipher. However, as a Catholic in our family, we always treated the Catholic Church with respect, being aware that throughout our Polish history it had always helped to retain the national consciousness. The church opposed totalitarianism, it being one of the fundamental determinants of our history and our culture. I was also aware that I was living in a time of trivial atheism and common opportunism, although in the last years a new tide of faith was visible, with a growing interest in the Church. In my new book, my challenge was in wanting to present the image of the clergy to all those who appreciated its efforts, courses of action and intentions of the Catholic Church in Poland. Therefore, I agreed to write a monograph about my home diocese, which was a young one, established by a "bulla papieska" (*papal edict)* in December 1920.

Bishop Kulik gave me a certain amount of money each month for expenses. I considered it the final payment, and when the book was sent to the *Pallotinum* publishing house in Poznań, I renounced my fee. An interesting phenomenon was related to the first payment I received from the bishop. Before my trip to Łódź for Easter, I deliberated about asking one of my friends to lend me some money. Waiting for some contracts to be completed, I found myself temporarily in a difficult situation. When bishop Kulik gave me his first envelope with money, he remonstrated that his intention was to have me concentrate only on the subject he'd asked me for and put off any other work. After my return to Warsaw, I opened the envelope and counted the money—it was the same amount that I had intended to borrow. I didn't have to borrow anymore. "Godsend money," I joked.

In October 1984, while celebrating the anniversary of taking his Holy Orders, in the presence of all the assembled bishops and numerous congregations, during the Mass, Bishop Kulik spoke in his sermon about his life and of how much he owed to God. He thanked many people, including..."Dr. Ziółkowska for writing a monograph on our diocese."

I was lucky to meet such representatives of the Church as they were open-minded and also understanding of human affairs.

The painful news of the death my friend Zbigniew (Zbyszek) Kubikowski reached me in August 1984. The funeral was attended by many luminaries of Polish science and culture. Zbyszek was extremely active, wrote books, film scripts, he was an active member of the Writer's Union, and in the Agreement Committee.

In autumn, all Poland was shocked by the brutal murder of Father Jerzy Popiełuszko. Tomek and I took part in his funeral on 3rd November 1984. I had never seen such crowds in Warsaw, nor such disciplined ones.

In winter 1984, Tomek and I again went to Nieborów for winter holidays. I brought the radio with me to follow the trial of Father Popiełuszko's murderers. The reports had a poisonous effect. There was something terrifying in how the Communist government attempted to turn the whole thing upside down with the greatest propaganda perfidy and present the murderers as victims. The prosecutor even said that "the extreme attitude of the priest gave birth to no less harmful extremes, which are the cause of heinous crimes." The words of Lieutenant Colonel Adam Pietruszka sounded evasive, and I didn't believe that he was the last link in the conspiracy chain. Jan Olszewski, the lawyer of the priest's parents, made an excellent speech. The Polish Episcopate lodged a protest against the Communist authorities concerning the way in which they portrayed the trial: as an attack on the Church. Most Catholics were shocked. But there were other opinions, too. At a beauticians shop, I once heard the following words by a woman in expensive clothes: "He should have been shot or expelled from the country."

It was a long winter, and the world grew grim.

One day Ryszard Kapuściński called me.

"You know, I have no water in the house," I said.

"It's normal, don't worry. My friend doesn't have heating and he stays all day in the bath."

"He could warm his hands over the stove, I heard that people did so..."

"But it's better when they turn off hot water rather than cold, because you don't wash yourself in boiling water..."

"But I don't have any water at all, they cut it off because of some failure. Tomek and I haul the water in buckets from the tank truck they provided.

There's a puddle in front of our block, the water's pouring out and freezing..."

"People will fall and break their legs, they'll need plaster casts, but there's no plaster as there's no foreign currency..."

Friends told me that Mieczysław Rakowski[8] reportedly said to someone, rubbing his hands together: "If you only knew what people work for us." The remark made me shiver. So much uncertainty. Artists became neurotic. It wasn't until the nineties that we learned some answers.

Małgosia Holender, whom I knew from working for the TV Theatre, and who now worked as a researcher for a French writer, was visited one day at home by Security Service agents. She told me the details. At 9:00 am someone knocked at the door. Opening the door slightly, "We're here to see you," she heard. Malgosia closed the door and went back to bed, as if nothing had happened, as if she wanted to erase that moment. Ten minutes later the doorbell rang again. After opening the door attired in her dressing gown, the agents showed her their ID cards. Małgosia then asked for a warrant. The agents departed, but returned in half an hour with the warrant, telling her she was to be taken to the Bureau of Investigation on Rakowiecka Street.

There they questioned her about contacts with foreigners. The agents knew that she was preparing excerpts from Paris *Kultura* for the French readers. They said that she either give up that work, or agree to inform them. Małgosia refused to sign a prepared document stating she wouldn't tell anyone about that meeting. While seeing her off, one of the agents told her that in France, everyone who met a foreigner wrote a report.

When later meeting with the French writer, she experienced extreme disappointment with his attitude, for she had expected something else. He agreed that...Małgosia could report on him, provided her work for him did not cease, because he wanted to finish the book. She wanted me to give her some advice on what to do, if to continue to work for him or not. "Think about how you want to continue this. If you see your work for him as important and worthy, and you're not afraid of the consequences, then continue doing it. If not, just give up."

Seven days later, at 10.30 in the morning, I had a phone call.

"Ms. Aleksandra Ziółkowska?"

"Yes."

"We're calling because we don't want to bother you at home. Please come to the Internal Affair Office on Rakowiecka Street at 11.30 am. Someone will be waiting for you in the pass office."

"Regarding?..." I asked.

"We'll talk about it..."

"I'll be there at 12.00," I said.

This was my first time in those buildings. A young man was waiting for me; he had a pass in his hand. "Please come with me..." We went to block H, second floor, room 512 or 514. The doors didn't have name plates. A thirty or so years old man was sitting behind the desk. There was a thin file in front of him, and he was looking at something in it. He checked aloud my data, then my parents.' Finally, he asked a question:

"Are you going abroad?"

"Yes, to England."

"So you go to England to write?"

"No," I replied.

"And do you know any American diplomats?"

"No, I don't."

"And Douglas B.?" He gave the whole name.

"I'm trying to obtain a scholarship, and he is the man with whom I've talked on the subject, but I don't know him."

"And do you know Mary?"

"What Mary?"

"Douglas's wife."

"No, I've never met her."

"And wouldn't you like to make friends with them?"

"No, my circle of friends is big enough."

"Who's coming to visit you?"

"I don't know who's going to visit me in the near future."

"And who is Ted?"

"I don't know," I answered honestly.

"It might be Ned or something like that..."

"Have you perhaps intercepted a letter for me and cannot read it?"

"Not at all! You need a special permit of the prosecutor to do that..."

I said nothing. He took a deep breath and gave me a short lecture about how everybody reported from the American universities, that their schools gave scholarships to people whose opinions they wanted to shape...

"They have a good opinion about you, but they can also be cruel and send you back from the airport...America is a cruel country...I'm sorry that we've taken so much of your time. Now, please write a statement that you won't talk to anyone about this conversation."

"I won't write such a statement," I replied.

"Why are you refusing?" he asked icily.

"Because...because...I won't keep such a promise anyway. I can't keep any secrets...All my life I've had trouble doing that..."

He looked at me carefully, not knowing whether I was joking or not. He said nothing to my response, and the visit ended.

Tomek told me at home: "Don't worry, I'll take care of you." ("Where?", I thought grimly.) Krysia Radgowska said: "It's good you reacted that way..." Krzysztof Kąkolewski said that the visit wasn't that important if they didn't insist on my signature.

I told Douglas B. about the meeting. He turned up the volume on his radio and listened to what I had to say.

"Do you still want to go to the States?"

"Yes, I do."

"So, we'll help you get a private invitation, which will allow you to leave with your son, and then you have a chance of getting a passport. An official invitation from the Secretary of State won't get you a passport."

Meanwhile, Canadian journalist Barbara Frum phoned me from Vienna to say she was coming with her husband Murray to Warsaw. We agreed to meet in the Victoria Hotel. First we went to the grave of Father Popiełuszko. She didn't say anything. Then I drove her to the centre of Warsaw, because she wanted to see what "ordinary people" looked like. Along the way she looked in horror at the dirty, smoky buses. Walking through the centre, Barbara erupted in spontaneous delight in things that surprised her, for instance hot dogs sold in booths, or a young girl selling jewelry. "Private enterprise, that's great!" Barbara was delighted.

Having returned from Prague, there she hadn't seen such scenes. She also mentioned that women as nicely made-up as in Warsaw were not evident. To make her retain that impression, we went with Murray to the vegetable market on Polna Street. "So here you can find citrus fruit, kiwis, pineapples, everything!" she exclaimed. She wasn't interested in the prices. The Frums were both impressed by the interior design and old mirrors in *Petit Trianon* (my favourite café on Piwna Street). "You mean, they didn't confiscate everything during the war?" she wondered.

Later I learned that Barbara Frum devoted the next edition of Toronto based TV *Journal* to Poland, and that it was really interesting.

The following days were taken up by friends coming from Canada, the first visitor being Marianne Ackerman—a journalist from Montreal. She confided her personal issues to me, and we laughed a lot; she reminded me a little of my friend Przema.

In that period, I was also looking forward to my visit to London. I expected similar experiences as in Canada. However, England seemed to me...small and overcrowded, cold, the people cool strangers. I missed the Canadian space, North American warmth and friendliness. I missed a certain familiarity of the American continent, to which I'd become accustomed to.

I spent a couple of the next weekends in Łódź. I helped Krzysio transport his books to his own apartment he was moving into. The apartment was spacious with four rooms, located in the distant Retkinia district. I was happy for him and Ania that finally, after so many years, they and their two children would live comfortably.

I wished for something to keep me from leaving Poland.

When I received a message from the U.S. Embassy that I had been granted the prestigious scholarship of the Secretary of State (my first Fulbright) and was to go to the United States, I didn't know how to tell my parents. How was I not to make them upset again? They were so happy Tomek and I came back to Poland, and now we were going overseas again. Together, we were going abroad; I also knew how important those trips together were for both of us, how they brought us closer to each other, and how his presence helped me. I bought a ticket for my son on LOT, as its fare was a lot cheaper than PANAM's (that was given to me by Fulbright). We flew to New York on the same day on separate planes. Arriving two hours ahead of Tomek, I was to await his arrival at John F. Kennedy Airport.

Chapter Twenty-Three

Visiting the United States

In the summer of 1985, I flew with Tomek to New York. We stayed for a few days with Isabelle and Pierre, then flew for a week to Toronto, where I arranged some publication issues and visited friends. Later on, we went to Florida. Here Tomek started a semester of high school in Okaloosa, Niceville County, and I flew to Washington to meet my Fulbright representatives, Alan Warne and Wright Baker, who with their assistant Donna Hines, set the route of my tour of America.

The route covered thirteen locations in thirteen states: Washington, D.C.;—Baltimore, Maryland;—Philadelphia, Pennsylvania;—New York, New York;—Boston, Massachusetts;—Rapid City, South Dakota;—Yellowstone, Wyoming;—San Francisco, California;—Las Vegas, Nevada;—Grand Canyon, Arizona;—Albuquerque, New Mexico;—New Orleans, Louisiana;—Pensacola, Florida;—New York, New York.

Later, I met many Americans who envied me visiting so many places. Most of the inhabitants of the United States spend their summer vacations sightseeing their huge country, but they don't go everywhere (most often they go to Florida). A few years later I was with my husband Norman in the following other states: Utah, Colorado, Texas, Illinois, Washington, New Jersey, Hawaii, Arkansas, Virginia and later on many more. We made several trips by car, passing the states of Mississippi, Oklahoma, Alabama, South Carolina, North Carolina, West Virginia, Georgia, Tennessee. We have a house in Delaware, and lived for almost nine years in Texas.

My scholarship trip was outstanding, a dream journey. In each place, I had a local sponsor, who took care of me, showed me interesting places, and selected events to attend. I had hotels already booked, plane tickets pre-paid, and a generous allowance. Everything was carefully planned, and proceeded like clockwork. I was introduced to extraordinary people, and also visited friends.

Zbigniew Brzeziński welcomed me in his office at the Center for Strategic and International Studies in North-West K Street in Washington D.C. Again at this meeting, I was left with somewhat of an impression of his being reserved and having a superior intelligence. Having read *Power and Principle,* I asked him about his loyalty towards President Carter, which he indicated in the book and in his public addresses. He answered that he believed personal loyalty to be an important feature of character and that he should show such loyalty towards the President, although he did occasionally criticize a policy.

In Washington D.C., I had an interesting conversation with Jan Nowak-Jeziorański whom I'd met earlier during his visit in Toronto. Our discussion focused on the United States, the role of America, its dangers and its values.

He stressed the contribution of President Woodrow Wilson to Poland regaining independence. The President's famous address and subsequent support for the principle of self-determination of the nations of Central and Eastern Europe resulted from idealistic reasons, and not political interest—our region was at that time farther from Washington's interest than it is now. After the First War, Herbert Hoover's humanitarian help saved Polish children from hunger. (Nowak told me he remembered eating American canned meat as a boy of only a few years.) He reminded me that the United States saved Europe and the world twice from German hegemony, and it paid a high price for that. After the Second War, the States offered the Radio Free Europe station, which broadcast news for nations subjugated by Stalin. He stressed the U.S. commitment to Polish issues after the events of 1981 (the martial law). The only stain on the page of American-Polish relations was Yalta, when the United States accepted the annexation of the eastern territories to the USSR, and Soviet Russia reign over Poland and the whole region.

Nowak believed that it was only in the USA that he didn't feel a foreigner or an immigrant, because it was a society that consisted of immigrants. But he admitted that he couldn't get used to the American culture, its mass character and standardization. He was more European than American and was in his element only in Europe. He saw the symptoms of America's civilization disintegration, the spreading plague of drugs, unlimited sexual debauchery, lowering of educational level, growing crime in large cities, demise of work ethics. He was afraid that a weakening of the United States would not bode well in the long term to the world or to Poland.

In the Washington American Institute, I had an appointment settled by my sponsors with Michael Novak, a sociologist and journalist of Slovak descent, and author of many books. In our brief conversation, he spoke mainly of his fascination with the Pope. A few years later Michael Novak was awarded the prestigious and generous Templeton Prize for activity that helped spread religious ideas in the world. In his last book *The Catholic Ethic and the Spirit of Capitalism,* he proved that Catholic ethics preached by John Paul II answered the modern times and the challenge of the future. Novak referred to the Pope's encyclical of 1991, *Centesimus annus,* which contains criticism of systems that bring destruction of the greatest treasure of societies—human capital. Michael Novak wrote that the Catholic Church used to criticise capitalism for excessive materialism, for its pursuit of profit, and for turning away from the problems of the sick and the poor. The Church of the Popes Leon XII, John XXIII and Paul VI were also critical towards capitalism. But John Paul II believed that backward systems were those that weren't able to trigger the energy of human initiative. From the Christian point of view, a social system which activated those resources was worthy of support. The papal encyclical, according to the ethical principles of the Church, imposed some restrictions. Mainly, even the richest market did not satisfy human goals, because their roots were beyond it, in the non-material sphere. There were also groups of people who for various reasons could not participate in the market production and exchange, and they needed care and attention.

In a Washington coffee shop, I met Ania Erdman-Walendowska, Wańkowicz's granddaughter. She had a smooth, calm face, and a tall, slim, graceful figure. Ania was employed as a pediatrician in a private hospital, was preoccupied with her work and found much joy in it. She explained not writing letters because of being very busy; one activity of concentration included working on creating a family archives. Several times during our conversation, she went to the phone to see if her patients were looking for her. Ania's sons, born in Warsaw, Dawid and Eliasz, were growing up nicely. Her husband Tadeusz Walendowski (whom I'd met a few days earlier) was preoccupied with Polish issues. Listeners of the Radio *Voice of America* were well acquainted with his programms. Ewa Erdman-Lazarewicz, Ania's sister, who lived with her husband near Boston, was raising a daughter. Ania spoke with a certain pride about everyone, also about her friends Ewa and Witek Sułkowski, who'd come to the States recently. She was pleasant and full of warmth. I remember Jan Strzelecki telling me after his return from the States that Ania was an exceptionally "warm-hearted person," and Aleksander Małachowski, could not praise her enough for "exceptional hospitality."

From Washington D.C., I took a train to nearby Baltimore. In the car I occupied, near a window, stood a middle-aged man. A woman came in with a heavy suitcase, and he helped her put it on the shelf. She asked:

"Does this train go to Baltimore?"

"Yes," he replied.

"Are we going to Baltimore?" asked a young man who was passing by.

"Do I look like a conductor?" the man asked me.

In Baltimore, by Nina I. Iwry, my local sponsor, I was shown Johns Hopkins University, introduced to a journalist from the *Baltimore Sun,* and also to a writer of the young generation Madison Smartt Bell. Offering me his books, I was asked to recommend them in Poland.

I also visited Danuta Mostwin (born Pietruszewska) in Washington D.C. at her house, beautifully located amidst rich greenery—she was an author of many books depicting immigration problems of Poles. Her husband, Stanisław Niedbał, after the war adopted the name he used in the times of the German occupation: Mostwin. He was one of the *Silent Unseen—Cichociem-ni,* [1] and as a parachutist used the nom de guerre of *Bask (Basque)*. Before the war he studied law, and after the war ended, he settled in the United States, where he worked in a tailor's shop and learned to use patterns. Able to cut dresses and coats by using her husband's patterns, Danuta showed me dress-es she'd made by herself. On retiring, Stanisław *Bask* Mostwin engaged in social work and held many important positions in Polish organisations in America.

Their two beloved German Shepherds were locked by the hosts in a remote part of the house. The house was very neat and trim, particularly the big library upstairs and the carefully furnished office of the writer. The hostess, a petite lady, read to me a fragment of the most recent book she'd been working on—*Cień księdza Piotra* (*The Shadow of Father Peter*), which was a historical monograph on her family. I knew and valued her other books: *Odchodzą moi synowie* (*My Sons Are Leaving*), *Olivia, Ameryko, Ameryko* (*America, America*).

Knowing my plans, Danuta Mostwin strongly encouraged me to visit Singer.

I visited Isaac B. Singer in his apartment in New York at 86 West Street. For years he divided his time between New York and Miami Beach in Flori-da. Of medium height and slim, he moved quickly and had inquisitive, searching eyes. He immediately dictated the pace of the conversation and a pleasant atmosphere. I passed through a stylish living room to a spacious office. Bookshelves covered two walls. During our conversation, Singer reached for a step ladder, climbed it and searched on the higher shelves for the titles we were discussing.

As we talked, he checked my knowledge of his books seemingly in pass-ing. He was glad I knew *Shosha* and *The Penitent*, and that I'd seen *Yentl*, a film starring Barbra Streisand and based on one of his stories. He gave me a collection of short stories *Short Friday* and also a book—Richard Burgin's interviews with him. The latter book is a valuable memento, as it is the first bibliophilic edition and is full of the writer's hand-written notes, implement-ed in the next edition.

I asked if we could speak Polish. "I know Polish, but it's easier for me to speak in English. I'd rather we kept to that language during our meeting."

The conversation was long. Singer spoke more readily about writing tech-nique and the very process of creation than about himself. "When people are less interested in art, they start to take more interest in artists, and vice versa," he said, as if justifying it. The notes from my meeting with Singer are a valuable source of the writer's opinions on choosing the topics for stories and the whole philosophy of writing..." The writer should not interpret or explain facts. He should describe them and make them lifelike as well as he can...It is important to write about the people and places you know best. You cannot renounce the roots of your mother or father...The writer never should abandon his native tongue and its richness of idioms. A writer, more than other artists, belongs to his nation, to his language, to his history and culture. A true artist belongs to his people, to his surroundings regardless of whether he likes it or not. A cosmopolitan will never write anything outstanding. His work will be a generalization. Literature is strictly connected with one's origin..."

I remember reading the words of John Paul II: "When I must write, I write in Polish. That is my native tongue, which is irreplaceable."

Phil Bella, secretary of the PEN-Club in New York, spoke to me with some regret about a fund established for persecuted Polish writers who were not published officially. American writers agreed to translation into Polish, allotting the fees due them to that fund. But it was expected of the writers in Poland, who managed that fund, to prepare regular reports on how much money was given to whom. The American authors wanted to be aware of the need for and significance of their action.

I came to New York City a few times. Being there always triggers focus, tension, observation. And it is so different from other American cities. It lives in its own rhythm and according to its own principles. New Yorkers move resolutely and confidently. They will excuse themselves when they jostle someone, but they don't look in his eyes and don't want anything to do with anyone. The popular American ease seems a myth in New York City. I looked at the tense faces in the queue, which seem outwardly calm, as if expecting a sudden attack and unwilling to be surprised. Poles on the streets look around, look at each other, they are sometimes tired, impolite, but there is no aggression in them that you can find in a New Yorker's face under a mask of calm.

I went to the Metropolitan Museum. I sat in the gigantic glass-covered room where the Egyptian temple in Dendur stood recreated, and took a walk along the Spanish galleries of the palace in Velez Blanco. Recently a new permanent exhibition was opened in the section concerning 20th-century art. The exhibits included a work by Magdalena Abakanowicz: Androgyne 3. Another work presented irregular pyramids carved in wood, which reminded me of the Tatra Mountains. The sculptor, Ursula von Rydingsvard, was of Polish descent.

During our visit to New York City when Tomek and I stayed with Isabelle and Pierre, for the first time I realized the convenience of having an answering machine, or *automatic secretary*, as we would say in Polish. Isabelle (Iziula) suggested spending the whole day together—she, Tomek and I. After long days and often nightshifts in the hospital, from time to time she had a day-off. We went to the Chase Manhattan Bank, where I planned to cash the scholarship check. They couldn't wait for me in the car, so she said: "We'll meet you in half an hour at the street's corner." I did my business and went outside. There was a colourful crowd. I went to the street's corner. Yet it seemed to me that it was not the corner where we were all supposed to meet, so I went in the opposite direction. All corners started to look the same to me, I roamed and roamed, and got lost. "What am I to do now, before I have to return to Brooklyn with the subway, the whole day, scheduled for just the three of us, will fall through," I thought in desperation. I remembered Iziula saying how she communicated with Pierre: they left each other messages on the answering machine. They could check those messages wherever they were. I decided to try that way. I called her apartment and left a message on the tape, saying where I was and where I was going to be for the next forty-five minutes. I gave the exact address and street number. I waited for forty-five minutes, then another fifteen. Resignedly, I decided to return home when I saw Tomek running towards me. He brightened up on seeing me. I brightened up on seeing him.

"Mom, we found you! It was such a good idea to leave a message on the tape and so good that Iziula thought to check it..."

In Chicago (it was an unscheduled trip, with a recommendation from Jan Nowak-Jeziorański), I met Feliks Konarski, Ref-Ren, author of the lyrics of many popular songs, including *Czerwone maki pod Monte Cassino* (*Red Poppies in Monte Cassino*).

His house, standing on the west side of Waveland, was full of posters, pictures, and paintings; among them and standing out the most was the portrait of the late wife of Ref-Ren, Nina Oleńska (*Volunteer Helenka* from the *Polska Parada (Polish Parade theatre)*. We talked of his memories from Lviv, the places he'd wandered with the 2nd Corps, the *Czołówka (Lead)* band and *Polska Parada*. We talked of General Władysław Anders, artists: Marian Hemar, Ordonka, Renata Bogdańska, Włada Majewska, Wańkowicz..." Poland is still present in my life, in every poem I've written. We are such a tragic nation, there is no family that had not suffered, that had not lost someone close in the last war," he said by the end of our conversation.

On my return to Warsaw, I wrote a script for a two-part musical performance 2nd *Korpus w piosenkach Ref-Rena* (*2nd Corps in Ref-Ren's songs*), which was then directed by Barbara Borys-Damięcka and shown on TV. Feliks Konarski was to come to Poland for the first time after the war. Wojciech Młynarski prepared a special celebration event. Dates were set, and it was at the very last moment that we received news of the death of the author of *Czerwone maki.*

One of my favourite poems by Konarski is *Są ludzie* (*There are people*) from the cycle *Wiersze dla żywych i poległych* (*Poems for the Living and for the Killed*; Italy 1943–1946):

> There are people so happy they need nothing more...
> There are cloudless skies, all blue and aglow...
> There are lands that know no winter or fall...
> There are rivers in whose waters pure emeralds flow...
> There are trees so green it's a cruel sight...
> There are birds of wild colour like from Titian's brush...
> There are cities forever golden or forever white,
> Since rising doomed to the sun's heated flush!...
>
> Yet I'd like to look this once to the skies
> And see grey heavens with a grey clouds' fleet,
> And each cloud shed grey rain as it cries,
> And grey waves of Vistula at my weary feet...
> Go down Marszałkowska on a grey morning in grey fall,
> Sit under grey skies with grey troubles unsaid...
> And be again amongst sparrows countless, grey and small,
> I, a plain grey man...
> And the world does not understand.

I was shown the elegant Boston by Richard Nobbe, deputy director of UNESCO. When in Kennedy's Museum, we saw a film about the President, and Richard had tears in his eyes. Later, I often met people who believed in the great myth of Kennedy, but also others who couldn't stand him and saw him as a weak president of Hollywood fame.

At Harvard University, I met Stanisław Barańczak.[2] I remembered a meeting with him years ago in Toronto, when he seemed abashed as he read his poems. The meeting had been hosted by Miłosz's translator, Louis Iribarne. My impression of the poet from years ago had faded away, and now Barańczak looked content and self-confident. He was my senior by a few years, and asked about my issues in a friendly manner. Miłosz said to me about Barańczak that he was "a benefit to Polish immigration and for America."

San Francisco...Nothing links this city with New York City. Even the homeless seem colorful here and add a certain color to the city. I went to Berkeley for a meeting with Czesław Miłosz. My sponsors had earlier called him from Washington, asking if he would agree to meet me. Miłosz consented. He was in-between trips to Yugoslavia (where his poems were being translated). A date was set. On arriving in San Francisco, I telephoned him to confirm the appointment, and he gave me directions to the university campus. He sounded pleasant and approachable.

I saw a gentleman with a nice smile, dressed in corduroys. He was wearing a cap—it was a windy day. His captivating smile amazed me, it was friendly and contagious. Miłosz actually looked young. We went to a café, where he suggested hot chocolate and a cake. I chose a nut one, and he decided to have one, too. The atmosphere was pleasant. Surprised by that impression, I said my memories of the meeting in Warsaw student *Stodoła* club were completely different, when I was struck by his coldness and dryness. Also, in London, I heard from friends that he was rather haughty towards people, and certainly didn't win them over.

"I was received very warmly in Warsaw, but that was caused by the demand for a more political speech. And I didn't want to respond to such a demand. In Kraków, where I went later, I didn't feel such an atmosphere anymore. The atmosphere of that Warsaw room reminded me of an uprising. The young people made the impression of being very politically minded, and I didn't want to meet such needs. I think that is Poland's undoing..."

"Polish nationalism disturbs us, although I agree with you that it helps us to survive," he said later.

I asked if he believed he'd paid a price for the years of immigration (he was quoted to have once said that the word "immigrant" itself had something contemptuous in it).

"No, I don't think that. In Paris I wrote, I was translated, I was awarded, and stayed there for a few years. In France, I wrote books to be translated."

"And *Dolina Issy*, too?," I asked.

"No, I wrote *Dolina Issy* because my heart dictated so.

"I received a scholarship at the university and came for a year to Berkeley, but I didn't sell my apartment in Paris, thinking I would be back. After three months, I was offered a professorship, so I jumped over all the ranks in a university ladder.

"...What would have happened if I hadn't become a university professor?...I don't know, but I would have managed. If I'd been living in Poland, I would likely write with shades of obliqueness, I wouldn't have been able to avoid that. Although Różewicz and Herbert did. So maybe I would behave similarly, too...who knows?

"...Is it pleasant to see the interest of critics I evoke?...It was pleasant when "The New Yorker" published my poems on a few pages, which they usually don't do. That was very nice.

"...Would I want to be a popular poet?...That's dangerous.

"...What else would I wish for?...A very personal question...Privately, I'd wish for a lot, but I don't want to talk about it. And in general?...*Enlightenment*," that last word he said in English.

"...I'd like to look thirty years younger," he added with a laugh.

"Then medics would take an interest in you as an object for examination. Besides, you look very well," I said.

"I can't complain, women loved me..."

"They loved you, or love you?"

"They love me..."

Later Miłosz asked if it was true that morals had changed in Poland, i.e. a different morality in a way. I answered in a slightly jocular manner, because such was the atmosphere.

"I spoke much about me, too much," I said finally.

"I like listening, it's pleasant," he replied. He drove me to the subway station by car. I took a picture of him then. In the photo, he has that pleasant, cheerful face I had observed earlier.

Before I left for Poland, Miłosz sent me his new book *Zaczynając od moich ulic (Beginning With My Streets)*. He asked me to send another copy to a friend of his in the Suwalskie region.

I started reading it later in Warsaw. I found fragments which seemed to harmonize with his correspondence to Melchior Wańkowicz of thirty years earlier. At that time, I was reading Roman Polański's memoir (*Roman*). It contained many Polish names, those I knew and new, unfamiliar ones. Twice I found Miłosz's name. He and his wife were guests in Polański's residence in Santa Monica, California. A situation was described when Sharon Tate, Roman's wife, was leaving for weekends with her friend Judy, and Roman was visited by a model he knew. He was counting on everyone's discretion, but Miłosz warned him that he'd heard Judy say to Sharon that the latter's husband was having an affair while she was absent. "If I were you," Polański quoted the words Miłosz told him, "I would get rid of both of them, the model and Judy. They want to turn Sharon against you."

Nowhere in the poet's texts did I find a mention of his visit with Polański.

I later met Miłosz in Houston. It was 1992 and he came to his author's evening, hosted by poet Adam Zagajewski (in very good English). Miłosz looked like a huge bear, he'd grown larger and older. He read his poems in Polish and in English (the latter with a strong foreign accent). After the meeting Norman and I approached him. He didn't seem in the best of moods. He reminded me of the Miłosz from the meeting with Warsaw students. I spoke in English, he gave me a curious look, I gave him my name. "Ziółkowska? Aleksandra Ziółkowska? In Houston?" he looked at Norman and me in surprise. But I didn't ask about the cause of his surprise. And didn't explain anything, just shook hands and stepped away. People were waiting in a line to get the poet's autograph.

Philadelphia was shown to me in 1985 by Edward Piszek, a well-known philanthropist and a very rich man, who'd done much for the Polish cause in America, and for Poland. I often admired his persistence in promoting what was Polish and I had a good opinion about him, despite many people criticizing him. As I have written, I'd met him earlier in Warsaw, when he wanted to buy the house on Studencka Street from Marta Erdman. He withdrew at the last minute, when his residence in Fort Washington near Philadelphia burned down and he had to devote his time and effort to rebuilding it. The house on Studencka Street was bought by his secretary, Stanisław Moszuk, a film-maker by education. I was told by a journalist in Warsaw how surprised he was at Piszek's Polish. The American businessman spoke in a peasant di-alect. With me he spoke in English, and it was a language of an educated man. His Polish he'd learned at home, where his parents spoke it daily, and he'd been taught a dialect from their village. Talking in Polish he sounded like a simple man. I wondered if he was ever told of the differences between his Polish and his English.

Piszek came to collect me at the 30th Street Station in Philadelphia in the company of Wiesław Kuniczak, author of many books and translator of Sienkiewicz's *Trilogy*. They showed me the historic part of Philadelphia, among other Kościuszko's house, which Piszek bought and gave to the city. The patriot's house holds the Kościuszko Museum, which is taken care of by the city.

Piszek's residence in Fort Washington is a historic building located among parks and calming greenery. I was given an elegant apartment at my disposal and spent two days with Piszek. I was surprised by his activity and organizational abilities. He took me to the American Częstochowa near Doylestown, where many outstanding representatives of the Polish commu-nity are at rest in the cemetery. I didn't manage to find Marta Erdman's grave by myself, and there was too little time to seek some more information to help me.

Piszek told me of his contribution to the publication of the book *Poland*, written by James Michener, an author very popular in the States. Piszek sponsored his visits in Poland, paid researchers for translating historical ma-terials, and financially supported the whole project from beginning to end. When the book was published, it enjoyed immense popularity and was ranked as a bestseller for several months. I remember much criticism in Poland concerning the book (that it didn't consider certain historic facts, that it didn't sufficiently stress the significance of other ones, etc.), but I support it. It's a popular book and thanks to that it reached millions of readers. Thanks to the book Americans learned that Poland had a history of over a thousand years ("You had some great kings," a friend told me. "My knowl-edge of Poland was limited to the recent years, I knew that your country had Communism imposed on it by Russia, and it was overthrown by Wałęsa...And there's a Polish Pope," she added).

The works of another writer Norman Davies are great historical books popular among the intelligentsia of practically the whole world including those who are interested in Polish history. I think Norman Davies is a special gift for Poland.

A journey following the steps of Margaret Mitchell, author of the book *Gone with the Wind*, and the protagonists of the book and film, reminded me of my search for Clark Gable's pictures with Ala Lasoń in the library as a student. The Southern states had always been of great interest and attraction to me, just like the Western states. They reminded me of the films and books I'd seen and read as a young girl. Now, years later, in Atlanta I saw an exhibition on Margaret Mitchell, at the Loew's Grand Theatre building, or more precisely its ruins, where the film premiered in 1939, and now on Nassau Street there was an exhibition of mementoes from the film. Inside you could hear quiet music from the film, you could buy dolls resembling the protagonists, pictures of the actors, a cameo brooch resembling the one worn by Scarlett. A large part of the collection concerned the production and promotion of David Selznick's film. There was a window from Tara, drawings depicting the interior design and clothing of the protagonists, pictures designed for film promotion and a rich collection of posters. Just after the wedding, Rhett Butler took Scarlett O'Hara to New Orleans for a honeymoon.

New Orleans is a unique city, a city of artists, fascinating visitors with its jazz bands, Creole and Cajun cuisine (countless restaurants, among them the famous *Antoines* and *Two Sisters)* and with the unforgettable atmosphere of the old Vieux Carré—French Quarter. New Orleans, located on the picturesque Mississippi River, is a Mecca of old, traditional jazz, born on the famous Bourbon Street. Each evening you could listen to old jazz on 726 St. Peter Street, in the famous Preservation Hall. The bands of Kid Thomas, Sweet Emmy or Billie Pierce were playing. At the entrance you threw two dollars in a wicker basket, then went into a small room and sat on a bench or on the floor. During those special visits, when I was staying in the old Bourbon Orleans Hotel (I had a four-poster bed) I listened to the Olympic Brass Band with Walter Nelson (named Black Walter, gone by now), Duke Dejon and Allan Jaffe. Jaffe, born and raised in Pennsylvania, moved to New Orleans and was now running Preservation Hall. A professor, teacher of American literature and my local sponsor, showed me around the district, including the house where Tennessee Williams, Hemingway, and Faulkner lived, and the hotel where Agatha Christie used to stay. I cruised with the paddle wheeler *Creole Queen* down the Mississippi River. On leaving, I knew that I would very much like to return to that exceptional place.

Since living in the States, several times, Norman and I have been fortunate to visit New Orleans.

I visited Professor Andrew Schally, son of a Polish general, and a Nobel laureate of 1977 in medicine, in a laboratory on the seventh floor of the Medical Center Hospital in New Orleans. His office was hung with framed awards. He talked of his academic struggle with analogs. He spent his childhood in Poland, growing up mainly in the palace *Pod Blachą* (*The Copper-Roof Palace*), where his father, General Kazimierz Piotr Schally, held the function of the Chief of the Cabinet of the President of Poland. His mother, Maria Łącka, was the daughter of Helena and Karol Łącki. The last Warsaw memory of the then thirteen Andrzej Schally (he changed his name to Andrew in England) was the bombing of 1939. He left Poland with his parents, living in Romania, Italy, France and then Scotland.

When I asked him about Poland (he preferred to speak with me in English, which he spoke with a heavy accent), he replied: "You're asking me about Poland. I don't speak Polish, although I grew up in Poland. I haven't used Polish for many years now. My father was engaged in the anticommunist movement, but I don't do politics. I didn't want to go to Poland for a long time, I was afraid that I would be entangled in some crime—black market money exchange or the like. Later, on receiving the Nobel award, I went there with my wife, my sister and her husband. I saw Warsaw, Kraków, Zakopane, Morskie Oko and Wieliczka...It's difficult for me to talk about Poland...The West never understood it. Maybe there should be more people of Brzeziński's calibre abroad...I highly value the Polish Pope. He's the best Pope in the last five hundred years. I'd like to meet him personally."

By the end of our conversation he added:

"I am a blend of nationalities and professional experiences from various parts of the world. After German occupation, when I was living in England, it seemed a paradise to me. But after five years of bad climate and high taxes I left England. Partly to get more sun, I spent some time in Romania, it has warm summers. Then came my Canadian period. But it's America that is a really important country for me. I like it and value it extremely. America made my work possible..."

Las Vegas...a city with no apparent soul... The heat kept me indoors. The hotel was beautiful, spacious, provided a lot of attractions. I won't forget the sight of elderly people with their eyes fixed on the machines into which they threw one dollar or twenty-five cent coins, pulled the handle and fixed their eyes on the machine in nervous anticipation. That was how they lost the last of their money. From Las Vegas, I made a one-day trip to the Grand Canyon and flew farther.

When I came to South Dakota, it was a clear morning. The air was oppressive, and dust rose with each step. I missed trees which could give some relief from the sun. From far I could see the peaks of the Black Hills, which towered over the prairie. In the west, clouds were gathering, darkening the area. There was a sudden downpour and soon after the sun came out. The only trace left of rain was the smell of ozone in the air.

In the evening, I was surprised with the sounds of the wind—in those areas the wind made uncanny sounds: it sobbed, whined, then whimpered like a child. South Dakota is a true wilderness, where you won't find traces of civilization for miles. There is a subtle beauty in that land, in the non-ending space. I like open spaces. They give me a sense of freedom. Prairies are a rich expanse of grass and wild flowers. But there is mostly grass (it has a deep root system, allowing it to survive the dry periods). The prairies of Dakota used to be the land of Native Americans. Currently, reservations are scattered there.

In South Dakota, I visited Ruth Ziolkowski, the widow of Korczak, my great uncle. The monument of Crazy Horse is to be ten times bigger than the heads of the presidents in Mount Rushmore, and bigger than the pyramids in Giza. Korczak Ziółkowski's idea was not limited just to the sculpture—he wanted to create the biggest Native American centre: a medical centre, a university for Native Americans, a museum of their culture. An Alley of Chiefs is to lead to the foot of the giant monument.

Ruth played a tape with Korczak's speech:

"The world asks you one question, only one: 'Did you do the job?' And there is only one answer: 'Yes.'

"You don't say, 'I would have done it if there had been any money in it.'

"You don't say, 'I would have done it if people had been more sympathetic and understood what I was trying to do.'

"You don't say, 'I would have done it if I hadn't gotten hurt or crippled'—and, God knows, I've been crippled.

"You don't even say 'I would have done the job if I hadn't died.' I don't buy that.

There is only one answer: 'Yes.'"

I saw the Crazy Horse centre, the continued work, the Native American museum, and felt immense pride in my ancestor's work. The local *The Rapid City Journal* conducted an interview with me. It was then, while in the Crazy Horse centre, that I decided to take up the topic of Native Americans in the future, too.[3]

A Cheyenne working in the local hospital in Rapid City shared her bitter memories from Indian schools with me. She showed me her poems, which—as she put it—helped express her pain. "I will never forget the nuns, who threatened us with the devil, and punished us for the slightest offense, and of whom I was terrified." A story like from a novel by Dickens, but that was not fiction but part of American history. Madonna Beard went with me and Karen Arrichoker, a Sioux, to see rings of three-coloured gold, characteristic of the local mine, then we went for a walk. "I'll never forget my fear and my suffering...I can tell you about it freely, because you're not from here, you come from distant Europe..."

Steve Carr and Thom Thorson took me to Deadwood, Spearfish Canyon in the Black Hills and to Mt. Rushmore with the heads of the presidents carved in stone: Lincoln, Washington, Jefferson and Roosevelt (Theodore, not Franklin), at which young Korczak Ziolkowski worked, gaining experience for his future ambitious venture.

In Albuquerque, the biggest city in New Mexico, the 85-year-old Bill Cramp, a known local storyteller and my current guide, was waiting for me at the airport. He told me at the start that he was glad I was Polish, because he had a special sentiment for Poland. In 1939 he was working in the American consulate in Warsaw and living with his wife in the Old Town, but after a few weeks they had to leave Poland because war broke out, and they returned to the States. Now he was excited to welcome a Pole as a local sponsor. He took me to Coronado Ruins, the Santo Domingo and Isleta pueblos. Santo Domingo is famous for the turquoise mined there, and Isleta is located near the Rio Grande River. He introduced me to Agnes Dill, a Native American, a woman with a beautiful face. She told me of the efforts, often ineffective, made by the American government to help Native Americans to live in better conditions and improve their quality of life. She told me that Native Americans believed that they were inhabitants of New Mexico since time immemorial. Their legends say they had lived there forever (while archaeologists say they had come from Asia through the Bering Strait). On the way from the pueblos to the city, my guide stopped a few times in ghost towns remaining after the closed silver mines. He stood by one of the ruined house skeletons and told me to make a picture of him: "You can tell your friends in Poland that it's your rich American friend in front of his residence," he joked.

In Albuquerque, where the past and the present blend at each step, I saw old *adobe* buildings, modern galleries, and restaurants in historic buildings. Native American women sat on the streets selling their products including turquoise jewelery.

With Esther and Bob Parnell, recommended to me by Gene Simmons, a friend from Florida, we went to a *fiesta balloon*—a balloon competition, and to the charming artistic town of Santa Fe. Esther told me she wanted to write a book with interviews with betrayed wives..." I was in such a situation myself," she said without hesitation. I listened to her attentively, not commenting.

The light of New Mexico is exceptional—the daylight clear and bright, from high deserts, creating unusual rays in the sun, rays that reached everything—fields, plains, the desert and forests.

The pink and blue colours of the geysers in Yellowstone, the rusty red of the Grand Canyon, the charm of Fisherman's Wharf and the white buildings of San Francisco, which I also saw from a helicopter, are forever a picture in my mind. I could list the marvels endlessly. How far can you contemplate beauty?

At the end of my stay, I returned to New York again and planned to go straight from the airport to Isabelle and Pierre's apartment. I had a suitcase and hand luggage and, tired with the heat, I gratefully got into a taxi. A black driver with greying hair gave me curious looks.

"Please take me to Brooklyn Avenue H," I said.

"Brooklyn? I don't know where that is," he replied.

"Take a map and look it up, then."

"I don't have a map," he said.

"You don't have a map? Do you have a driving license? I wonder how you got it," I replied cuttingly.

"I only drive people within Manhattan," he started.

"That's not legal, I've read of drivers who didn't want to drive people beyond Manhattan and had trouble..."

I won't give in, I thought. *I won't look for another taxi...*

"Please stop at the President Hotel in Manhattan, I have to collect my itinerary information from there." He stopped the car without a comment.

"Just don't leave, I'm leaving my suitcase and I have your number," I said, putting on a brave face, because I was actually scared he would leave. I returned in a few minutes, and he was waiting. I sighed with relief.

"You must be one of those 'libs'," he continued our conversation (LIB— liberated woman).

"Just imagine, I'm not. I have a husband and three children," I bluffed.

He gave me a look of appreciation. He reached the indicated address without any problems, took the suitcase and brought it up to the steps. I gave him a tip, and he thanked me with a broad smile.

When I told Iziula of the event, she laughed. "Blacks like strong women and you impressed him with your persistence." We both went to the bus station and waited for Tomek, who had been travelling from Florida by bus for three days. He looked as if the world was collapsing around him, and as if he would gladly walk to Brooklyn. He proudly showed us his certificate of completing a semester of high school in the Okaloosa Walton Junior College. We had the last two weeks for New York City, which we roamed by subway and on foot.

In the Polish Institute of Arts and Sciences I had a lecture organized on Wańkowicz as a controversial writer (*Wańkowicz pisarz kontrowersyjny*). Guests included Mr. and Mrs. Seidenman, the last guests in the house on Studencka Street, and Jan Erdman. I was glad to see him again. He came with several friends, content, cheerful, and looked much better than he did when I visited Middlefield.

In a way, both Tomek and I were fascinated by the States. There are people who can't stand America. I belong to those who like it and feel good there. It was nice to talk to a person proud to be a citizen of a world power which would take care of them wherever they were. Americans didn't have the Canadian apprehensiveness and uncertainty. Many could be irritating *(We, Americans!)*, but most were nice and had a positive attitude towards Europeans. They seemed aware of their roots, and their weaknesses, but proud of the space and their position in the world.

One of my Canadian acquaintances told me with indignation of how a certain American said you could feel life vibrate in America..." So much is happening there, it's almost as if the fate of the world was being decided..." My Canadian friend definitely preferred the peace and a particular provincialism of Canada.

Another return to Poland. It was the end of 1985. Tomek had to make up the semester and successfully pass the outstanding material. His returns to Poland were always connected with learning Polish curricula materials that he had not studied while elsewhere. The Warsaw Reytan School on Wiktorska Street accepted him kindly and without a comment. He also started learning to play the flute, he went to afternoon classes in the Musical School on Profesorska Street. All his evenings were busy: beside the flute, there was French, Spanish, religion, then drawing classes were added. He learned German in the Reytan School, and we both enrolled in the French Institute for French classes. I was excited to be able to learn together with my son. My idea, however, turned out to be a failure. Tomek already knew French quite well and was always prepared for classes, as opposed to me, who was falling farther and farther behind. The situation started to make me feel awkward, so I dropped out from the next semester, not wishing to lose my authority altogether with my son.

On some Saturdays he rode horseback at a riding stable near Warsaw. In winter, he bought cross-country skis and sought out nearby routes. I was busy with my literary and publication work, and in the evenings attended various events. In Warsaw, you can always spend your time in an interesting manner by going to a theatre, a lecture, a concert, a discussion meeting. At that time, I frequently went to the KIK[4] club (I was a member), where meetings concerning sometimes controversial issues were regularly organised. I remember evenings with eminent film director Andrzej Wajda, historians Adolf Juzwenko and Marek Drozdowski, as well as with journalists Ewa Berberyusz and Małgorzata Szejnert. The meeting with the journalists, hosted by Andrzej Wielowieyski, was interesting because both of them had returned from the States and expressed strong negative feelings concerning the level of American Poles. Ewa Berberyusz, who took various jobs there— for instance, she sold tickets to Polish events—even said that "there were moments when I was ashamed to be Polish." A stormy discussion ensued. I also took the floor to say that everyone was entitled to their own opinions, but that opinion depended on one's experiences, and those were variable. Opinions similar to Ewa's had been expressed by others, even Czesław Miłosz himself, who wrote about a "primitivism of [American] Poles." Jan Nowak opposed that opinion, rightly emphasising the diversity of the community. He said that beside the "old Polish immigrants," who came from the poor areas of Galicia or Silesia, there was the post-war wave, which included people of the calibre of Lechoń, Wittlin and Wierzyński. I have many friends among the post-war immigration wave, and those people often lead in their professions. I returned to the immigration topic in the book *Korzenie są polskie* (*The Roots Are Polish*).

In that period great activity in culture was generated by the Church. They organized meetings with actors, lectures, speeches, discussions. I was also invited to my parish of St. Dominic to give a lecture on Wańkowicz. Never before and never since have I had such a huge poster advertising my lecture. But I was not among the big group which admired the priest, Father Wiesław Niewęgłowski, so very popular at that time. Perhaps it was my spirit of contrariness, perhaps my surprise with the attitude of some people (they were more Catholic than the Pope), perhaps I just dislike crowds. Who do I like?—I like my friends.

I was invited by Professor Marcin Kula, author of many excellent treatises and books on history (Tomek valued his history of Brazil), to the Warsaw Archdiocesan Museum to take part in the panel "Czy straceni dla Polski?" (Are they lost for Poland?). Professors Marcin Kula, Marek Drozdowski (son of a cavalryman, author of many books on history and radio and TV programs), Andrzej Paczkowski, Jerzy Holzer and Bronisław Geremek, among others, gave their opinions on Polish immigration. We discussed the value that Poles living abroad attributed to Poland. When I think of that meeting years later, I mostly remember my own nerves on seeing the honourable circle of the professors. Earlier, in the Institute of History, Professor Marek Drozdowski organized meetings concerning my two Canadian books. They also included famous historians, members of the institute, but somehow the atmosphere was more casual.

I remember many interesting cultural events. Television showed Andrzej Wajda's play "Z biegiem lat, z biegiem dni" (*Over the Years, Over the Days*) in episodes, cinemas played *Cudzoziemka (The Stranger)*[5] with a brilliant role of Ewa Wiśniewska. Theatres always had much to offer. Theatre Royal came from England with a play based on Kapuściński's book *Cesarz* (*The Emperor: Downfall of an Autocrat*), which was staged in the Studio Theatre and Ryszard invited us. Also Marek Walczewski and Małgorzata Niemirska invited us to see *Jacques the Fatalist*. I remember an evening dedicated to Jerzy Wasowski, a known composer and actor, with brilliant actors: Wiesław

Michnikowski who sang *Addio pomidory (Farewell, Tomatoes)*. Many notable intellectuals and artists attended. *Polska Madonna*, with lyrics by Agnieszka Osiecka, was sung by Maryla Rodowicz. I liked the beautiful songs of Alicja Majewska and Edyta Geppert.

I told my American friends that when a new book was published in Poland, everyone read it and later everyone discussed it. *Wojna w eterze (War on the Radio)* by Jan Nowak, *Sublokatorka (Lodger)* by Hanna Krall, *Oni (They)* by Teresa Torańska, Krzysztof Kąkolewski's *Dziennik tematów (A Journal of Topics)*, Lech Wałęsa's *Droga nadziei (The Road of Hope)*, *Hańba domowa (Civil Dishonour)* by Jacek Trznadel. The latter one I read with mixed feelings. Due to my age, I hadn't experienced those years and those trials of the people who were included in it. I was afraid to blame or accuse anyone, I was afraid of generalizations and great words. I read that many people learned about the executions of officers and murders of Home Army[6] soldiers only in 1956. I asked my father about that period. I had never asked him about those things before.

"The families knew, friends did, so others knew, too. Maybe there were people who didn't know, such thickheads, just like now, who don't know anything and are not interested in anything," Father responded sharply.

"Was it difficult to be a non-Communist Party person?" I asked.

"It was difficult to have a career," he said. "But it didn't make it that difficult to live and work...They locked you up for speaking out the truth, even for telling political jokes if someone informed on you..."

In the opinion of Zbigniew Kubikowski, people didn't have the "Russian experience." Those who had gone through Soviet camps, were now mainly in the West. The Poles in the country had experiences from the Nazi occupation.

In *Budowanie Niepodległej (Building the Independent One)*, Wojciech Giełżyński wrote about the period before the First War that it was the "youngsters who fought and won Independent Poland." The mitigation of their fathers was in vain, the stigma of the January defeat,[7] the advice to look to the East, to Russia's vast stretches of land inviting researchers, traders, engineers, tempting all with gold and rubles...Giełżyński gave examples of how extremely close national awareness of that period was to Russification. The fragment of the book about the defense of Lviv of 1st–22nd November, 1918 by the *Orlęta (Eaglets[8])* was shocking...those who freed the city were almost children, adults drank, escaped, there was chaos. I later found a similar tone in a book by Agata Tuszyńska, *Rosjanie w Warszawie (Russians in Warsaw)*. Maria Śniadowska-Komornicka, who'd seen the defense of Lviv as a seven-year-old, currently living in Wisconsin, USA, sent me a beautiful description of the atmosphere of those days and recalled eminent names of generals: Rozwadowski, Sikorski, Haller, Jędrzejewski, Iwaszkiewicz, Boruta Spiechowicz. The uneven fight with a well-armed enemy united students and professors, Lviv *batiars* (street vendors and mucisians) from city out-skirts, townspeople and professional soldiers, girls as nurses or with rifles in their hands next to labourers, and all of them well-coordinated, like one family, each at his or her post.

Another book which made an impression on me at that time and reminded me of Herling-Grudziński's *Inny świat* (*A World Apart: a Memoir of the Gulag*), was a memoir of Wiktoria Kraśniewska from 1944–1956, titled *Po wyzwoleniu* (*After Liberation*). The book described her stay in a Soviet forced-labour camp, then working in a *kolkhoz*, a collective farm, until her repatriation to Poland. She wrote that Sovietness was a chance for medio-crities, and so mediocrities tormented anyone who knew them. The more talented and more honest persons were always looked upon with suspicion. Each Russian, wrote the author, was a barbarian who'd just been freed from the Mongolian yoke, so they were filled with a lust for reprisal, an imperialist drive: to conquer the world just as the Mongolians had. I found interesting thoughts about Russia and our attitude towards it in Andrzej Walicki's *Spot-kania z Miłoszem* (*Meetings with Miłosz*).

I was also immersing myself in the memoir of Katherine Mansfield, au-thor of *Garden Party* and *Bliss*. Her journal was depressing at times, perhaps because she wrote it when she was very ill, and in a tone of somewhat cruel truth, her view of her life appeared. Mansfield wrote of relishing in petty derision the posture which overcame women when they suffered. She be-lieved it was a deeply buried feeling, but also deeply rooted. At such a time, women didn't spare the ones they loved, as if tormenting the men who loved them brought them relief. The author also wrote that although preferring to stay in hot rather than cold climates, she also preferred to stay among people who loved her too little than those who loved her too much.

Ryszard Kapuściński gave me the typescript of *Lapidaria* to read. He wrote down thoughts, associations, generalizations, some clearly journal-like notes, in the form of a journal. He wrote that the condition to subjugate a community was to downgrade it to a low level of existence. Decrease of comfort and increase of threat was a result of the policy of those who wanted to strengthen their rule. They knew that someone exhausted with the struggle against a thousand adversities was an easy object for manipulation. The struggle for the person was to survive, and that was an absorbing, time-consuming and exhausting activity. Ryszard wrote that both the poverty of needs and the material poverty were convenient for the authorities. Poverty weakened and crushed the man, and someone whose needs were poor didn't even know that there were things for which he could fight, which he could demand. Our survival?—ever striving for things impossible to achieve.

In March 1986, I received a message from Jan Erdman (husband of the late Marta) with the news of his marriage. Actually, two messages came. I suppose he didn't make a list of the people he'd sent it to. He added by hand: *"Oleńka, I think it's the «last great adventure» in my life."*

I was a little surprised. I also thought that I wouldn't call a marriage a "great adventure" and that it was a very American thing, marrying at that age... (Erdman was 86 years old). I was told that he called the Museum of Literature in Warsaw to have the message of his new marriage framed and hung in the room with mementoes of Wańkowicz. Allegedly, it was thought to be highly inappropriate...But I don't know how far the story was true. Actually, many stories appeared concerning his marriage. His new wife was a Pole, a widow from Quebec, Krystyna born Niemcewiczówna. After the wedding, she moved to Middlefield and they both lived near Albany, a place I had visited. I wondered how she would feel there. I remembered the house was practically filled with mementoes of Marta Erdman and Melchior Wańkowicz. Małachowski told me that earlier Jan refused to stay with his older daughter near Washington, where she offered him a flat in the same house, but with a separate entrance. He chose a different way of spending the last period of his life. I also remembered he had cancer.

Six months later, I received a message that Jan Erdman was dead. The community of journalists and writers was shaken with the news. Actually, Jan Erdman had committed suicide. He left a note in the kitchen saying where to look for his body, went to the nearby forest and shot a gun into his mouth. His new wife was in a wheelchair after a hip surgery and couldn't move freely. The fire brigade looked for him. Danuta Mostwin told me that at the funeral there were two groups. One of them was Erdman's widow, in a wheelchair, almost completely alone, and the second was all other attendees. Numerous rumours circulated about her. Ludwik Seidenman, a long-time friend of Marta and Jan, told me later that after the second marriage Jan told him that "Krystyna is not of Marta's ilk and eloquence." Stories about them related that they had many problems in their marriage.

"Marta came and took him," claimed Danuta Mostwin. "He shouldn't have married..."

"Why did he marry?" people wondered. "Why did he publicize that marriage so much? Even very young people have conflicts, not to mention older ones, with experiences of life spent together with someone else. It would have been better for them to sell the house in Middlefield and live in a big city, to have a social life, and not live in the wilds with their past and memories, in a house full of mementoes of Marta's presence...That new wife, a poor woman, what an odium to be subjected to..."

Krystyna Jaroszewicz, a peer of Wańkowicz's daughters and wife of Marek, a respected architect, living in Florida, told me a moving story. Krystyna Erdman, born Niemcewicz, was her friend from their school years. She wrote her earlier, being happy by the marriage, which was to change her lonely life. After the death of Jan Erdman, Krystyna Jaroszewicz sent her a letter with condolences. Krystyna Erdman was reportedly very grateful for the friendly words, so rare, because almost everyone turned away from her as the "cause of the evil."

An American acquaintance told me that if Erdman didn't want to live, he could have taken his life in a less dramatic manner. He could have chosen such death that no one would be certain it was a suicide. Jan Erdman, with a partially cured cancer, was likely suffering from deep depression. He made many people miserable with his act. Alina Żerańska, a Polish immigrant journalist who knew the Erdman family, indicated strong depressive states were often observed particularly with older people.

I remember that Wańkowicz wasn't very fond of his son-in-law. On receiving the news that Marta's wedding was to take place soon, he sent a telegram asking them to wait with it. Jan Erdman was Marta's senior by fifteen years. In a letter to Erdman (of 23rd September 1944), Wańkowicz explained he had been afraid that the man had been "too far formed in spirit not to affect Marta, who was just developing to life." The certain regret he felt on learning about Marta marrying Jan Erdman, stayed with him for the rest of his life. Erdman was not the husband he'd imagined for his child, and surprised with Marta's sudden decision, he regretted having been omitted when the decision was made. Earlier, his daughter sent him letters which described her friendship and then engagement to a young boy, her age, by the name of Paweł, and Wańkowicz actually had no reservations about him. Working on Wańkowicz's archives, I found Marta's letter to her father which seemed particularly interesting to me both as a general truth and as a truth stated by her, a young person in the time of war who was then in love with a young man named Paweł.

> I think that when you start your life, you can be happy with more than one person, so I don't believe in hearts broken beyond repair. It's only later that people start being indispensable to each other. You only have to find someone who meets two conditions of a good start: honesty and good manners (in a deeper sense than choosing the right fork). And if being with someone like that you feel cheerful and "comfortable", if you trust him, if you feel his tenderness and goodness, and you admire his fortitude, and if you feel a growing certainty that 12 children are more important than fame and glory...then...what are you waiting for?

The writer still controlled the situation, advising his daughter a very practical approach to the matter, and also approving of her choice. Zofia Wańkowicz was also acquainted with the issue—so far that when she learned of her daughter being married, she wrote to ask, "How is Tili's husband, Paweł?"

Wańkowicz had known his son-in-law, Jan Erdman, earlier as a good sports reporter, but certainly he wasn't thinking of him in terms of a husband for his beloved younger daughter. Years later, he spoke with reluctance about Erdman's "doctrinarism," saying he had imposed his vision of the world on Marta, and she, being a "conjugal" type—in the words of Wańkowicz—adapted quite obediently to her role as a wife.

Also Erdman showed no great liking for Wańkowicz either. He had to know about his father-in-law being rather unfriendly to him. In the introduction to Marta's book, he writes openly about Tili's father's reaction to her letter in which she informed him of her decision to marry:

> When we set up the date, the little daughter informed Melchior Wańkowicz of the joyous event, who was then fighting with the 2nd Corps somewhere on the Italian shoe. Meanwhile, instead of a blessing there came a telegram suggesting that we postpone the wedding until peace is restored, or in other words, without the diplomatic dodging—to break off our relationship. Fortunately, the telegram came 14 days after the unbreakable oath was taken. It had been delayed in the army censorship.

Lack of any greater enthusiasm in the relations of Erdman and Wańkowicz can be seen in later, enigmatic and sometimes scathing comments made by the author of *Battle of Monte Cassino*. His son-in-law returned the favour with similar ones. In his only book *Droga do Ostrej Bramy* (*The Road to the Gate of Dawn*[9]), when writing about Major Hubal's unit, Jan Erdman quoted Wańkowicz many times, and at the same time did not fail to quote—with a certain satisfaction and spite—a misprint which had crept into the first issue of the book on Hubal soldiers. As if publishing the book in exile soon after the war's end didn't envision sloppy revision.

In Poland, we learned suddenly of the tragedy of Chernobyl. The circumstances of the explosion, the fact that the information was delayed and awareness of the threat made everyone greatly depressed. Many people drank iodine, which was said to help. I was given a whole bottle of iodine from a friend, George Dembiński, and we both went to share it with Marek and Jola Nowakowski, and to Suchedniów, to Joasia and Krzysztof Kąkolewski. Warsaw was full of rumours. Reportedly, some foreigner locked herself up in her hotel room, drew the curtains closed and didn't want to leave, she was in shock. A friend from Florida, Gene Simmons, called to advise me to drink wine rather than water...My friends from abroad who visited Poland at that time brought odd gifts: Bumek Heydenkorn brought milk powder, and Senator Haidasz and his wife brought bags of sugar and pepper. When they saw my surprised looks, they said they'd read in the papers that now we had "absolutely nothing" in Poland.

As usual in each situation, jokes about that occasion started to appear in Poland. Tomek brought a grisly one from school: An old man walked with his grandson in the desert. "Grandpa, how is this place called?"—"Chernobyl," said the grandpa and stroked the boy's head.—"And what was here earlier?"—"A nuclear power plant," said the man and stroked the boy's...other head. (Years later I saw a program on American TV about Chernobyl and the consequences of the explosion. I was then reminded of that sad joke).

Both Tomek and I, however, knew that Poland was our place, that we would visit Canada—if possible—and we would always have affection for it, but we would stay "home." At that time, Tomek went for school trips to the *Bieszczady* Mountains, to the *Świętokrzyskie* Mountains, to canoeing competitions, and he also took a trip alone to Łeba, to the seaside, for a few days. I liked taking short trips to *Kazimierz Dolny*, and once I had the opportunity to go by yacht to *Ruciane*. Both Tomek and I were invited for a several-day trip in a huge trailer to the beautiful Suwalskie region, which I hadn't seen before. I was invited to have lectures in Opole and twice in Stalowa Wola, which I remember with particular fondness. The City Library there adopted the name of the author of *Sztafeta*, a book that praised the pre-war Central Industrial District. [10] I had the opportunity to meet Bishop Edward Frankowski, known for his unyielding attitude. Tomek still spent all holidays together with me: in winter in Nieborów, and in July in Zakopane. I liked walking along *Kasprusie* Street to *Strążyska* Valley and returning to *Halama* with the route Pod Reglami. Together we went to the valleys—*Dolina Małej Łąki, Dolina Lejowa*. I remember I needed a band-aid and I could find none in the whole of Zakopane. They didn't even have hydrogen peroxide. When I was in a pharmacy, a man with a bandaged hand came in asking for a dressing, because he wanted to change it. "We don't have bandages," was the reply.

On the other hand, social life thrived as always. Conversations after supper in *Halama* gathered groups of people at the tables. Alicja Sternowa spun tales about the poet Broniewski coming to the meals in Obory naked. Andrzej Szmidt, a poet, told us a story which made a great impression on us. He was studying at the Catholic University of Lublin in the 1950's. *Radio Free Europe* broadcasted the news that both he and his father were "stoolies," and they ought to be avoided. "It was hurtful, untrue, but I didn't know how to appeal against it, how to prove...What was I to do?" he said even now, years later, with pain and anxiety. "People turned away from me..."

He suffered greatly. Then additional, personal problems appeared. He fell ill. When years later I read in New York *Nowy Dziennik* that Andrzej Szmidt had been granted the Czesław Miłosz Award for his poems, I was greatly pleased.

I had another invitation to hold lectures in Zaolzie, and I went there again with pleasure. Kazimierz Kaszper, a poet friend of mine, was living in Polish Cieszyn. When asked why he'd moved to Poland if there were such empty shops, he repeated an anecdote about two dogs:

Two dogs met on the bridge over the Olza River. One was returning to Poland, the other to Czechoslovakia. "Why do you go to Czechoslovakia?" asked one of the dogs. "To eat my fill. And why do you go to Poland?"—"To bark my fill."

Janusz Dukszta from Toronto visited Warsaw again, bringing a friend, a New York lawyer Frank Haynes. Frank was black. I'd met his family earlier, and it was a very interesting one. His mother was a nurse, and his father a clerk. They had seven children, all thoroughly educated. I was friends with Frank's sister, Patricia, who worked as a journalist of NBC in Rockefeller Plaza. One of his brothers acted on Broadway, another was completing architectural studies at the prestigious University of Pennsylvania. Frank loved opera and ballet, regularly went to Germany to theatre meetings, and liked travelling all over the world. He particularly liked Warsaw and its theatres. I took Janusz and Frank to a name's day party in Andrzej Roman's home. Each year, people gathered in the apartment on Świętojerska Street. Many of them were well-travelled. Frank was amazed that most of them, including Andrzej and Dagmara's young son, Zbysio, spoke good English. Janusz, who always followed fashion trends, admired Teresa Zygadlewicz's dress, and said it looked like straight out of the newest magazine of the Montana house. "Take a look here," said Teresa and showed him Montana's label. Reportedly, on his return he told his friends, amazing them, that Poland was a much more complex country than American press presented it.

Another visitor to Poland was Jack Weissman, a New York doctor with a recommendation from Janusz Dukszta. Janusz sent his friends to me, knowing I would carry out the set task and show them Warsaw. Jack loved Chopin's music and wanted to see Żelazowa Wola, where the composer had been born. When I showed him the place in Saint Cross's church where Chopin's heart was buried, he looked at me wide-eyed. He knew that the grave of that great composer was in the Paris Pere Lachaise, so he was amazed on hearing it... "Back home, we bury even great personages whole," he commented, affected.

I brought him to the Museum of History in the Jewish Historical Institute. He was bothered by the modest collections, the modest building. I didn't know at that time that he was toying with the idea of donating a large part of his fortune to the museum. Neither did I know he was nearing death.

Roman Rodziewicz from England made regular visits to Poland. A handsome captain, Mieczysław Maksymowicz, came from Malta. An ex-pilot of the 303 Polish Fighter Squadron,[11] he was also a pilot of many European airlines after the war. Thanks to him I met Stanisław Skalski, a legend-pilot living in Warsaw.

Poland fascinated, amazed, awoke various opinions. I remember a comment made by Aleksander Jordan Lutosławski from Miami, who often came to Poland in those days: "After a few days in Poland, I have the impression that in Poland everything is arranged somewhere on the side, on the stairs, the right people are always absent, travelling somewhere. Full grotesque..."

My interview with Zbigniew Brzeziński was printed by *Przegląd Katolicki* (*Catholic Review*). Ania Bernat, talented and personable, thoughtful, was working there and courageously accepted a text for printing, defending it till the end. After that publication, an attack on Brzeziński, on *Przegląd Katolicki* and on me was printed in the Communist *Trybuna Ludu*. Jerzy Lobman wrote that Brzeziński was "no model to follow," that he didn't deserve to have so much attention devoted to him, and in general *Przegląd Katolicki* likely had too much paper if they gave so much space to that interview. I soon received a letter from Dr. Brzeziński. He wrote:

> Thank you so much for the text of the interview with me that appeared in Warsaw. I was delighted to see it, and I think that you have done an excellent job of interrogation and translation. I was also amused (but not surprised) to see the rather negative reaction that this interview immediately produced in another Warsaw newspaper...What was striking about that reaction was its extraordinary stupidity.
>
> I look forward to seeing you if should some this way again (...)

On one occasion in a public library in Koszykowa Steet, I was shown a paper concerning my book *Senator Haidasz*, which was published in Toronto. I copied a fragment from that paper: "Due to certain fragments in the content of the book *Senator Haidasz* is only fit for controlled use...The propagation of the book is banned."

Soon, a Polish edition of the book was published. Time ran ahead fast. Changes were coming both in Poland and at home.

In the middle of high school, at the end of the second year, teachers and parents talked at all meetings about the children's future.

"My Teodorek chose film directing and law," said Mrs. Maria Sobczak. Another mother spoke about the usefulness of organization and management, studies which her son was planning to do.

"And mine hasn't decided yet," I said, dejected.

I returned home with a certain reproach and complained to Tomek:

"Other mothers know what their children want to do in the future, and you keep on thinking and thinking..."

"Then tell them what you want, if you feel better with that. I must think seriously, and not make a quick decision to please you and others," he replied sullenly.

Our friend, Maciek Czaplicki, a medical doctor, took him to the teaching hospital of the Medical Academy to show him surgery. But Tomek was not interested in medicine. At first, he insisted for a long time that he would become a sailor (because he would "sail and see the world"), then he wanted to study shipbuilding at the University of Technology in Szczecin. Of course, I preferred that he choose studies in Warsaw, so I could have him with me. But with Tomek, you had to tread carefully and be delicate in suggesting, otherwise he clammed up and didn't allow another close conversation on the same topic.

"Choose one more field, get acquainted with it, you'll see. In a while you'll think it over again. You have almost two more years to think."

He considered archaeology and architecture. Of the latter field, he spoke more and more often. Krystyna Goldbergowa, a figure among the Polish reporters, whose son Artur and his wife Ina were young architects, asked them to meet us and speak of their profession. They turned out to be very passionate and articulated. They exuded optimism and love of architecture. We knew that Tomek would have to take separate drawing classes for at least a year, because that was an important part of entry examinations. He decided to take the classes. Marcin Słupeczański, a student of the last year of architecture taught Tomek along with a small group. He returned from the classes delighted, and practiced for hours. He told me that it was said that anyone could learn to draw with some exercise. That it was later, at a higher level that talent showed. Tomek liked drawing even as a child and now studied it with enthusiasm. After the year, he didn't stop, he continued the classes and so architecture became his final choice. When we went to Nieborów for the winter break, or later to Zakopane in the summer, he took his drawing board with him and practiced. I asked him to give me one of his drawings, but his own view of them changed. As a small boy, he used to bestow his drawings on me, but now he almost hid them carefully and kept them for himself.

Tomek had a friend whom he taught how to play tennis (he was always borrowing another racket for her somewhere), and for whom he likely once kept a white rose in the bathtub all night. He didn't confide in me, however, and I didn't know his secrets.

In June 1987, the Pope came to Poland for the third time. Tomek and I went to Łódź, which was to be visited by the Pope. Mother, as a church choir singer, had been practicing for many weeks in preparation for the visit. Bishop Kulik handed me an invitation to the meeting in the cathedral. After that, we returned to Warsaw to take part in the farewell Mass in the *Parade Square (Plac Defilad)* on the next day. Poland became empty and sad when John Paul II left. We grew accustomed in a way to the Pope's presence and believed he was almost next to us, vigilant and concerned with our matters. We felt more cheerful with his constant presence; the Pope seemed to be a counter weight to all our national sorrows and doubts.

In October 1987, in the oldest Warsaw church, the Blessed Virgin Mary's in the Nowe Miasto marketplace, Joasia and Krzysztof Kąkolewski had their church wedding. actress Kalina Jędrusik and I were the official witnesses of the sacrament. After many years of civil marriage, our friends decided to have a church wedding. The couple's happy faces were a pleasure to see. They always had great tenderness and affection for each other, and in my opinion were one of the most loving pairs. Krzysztof said touching things about the confession with Father Kazimierz Orzechowski, about Father Wiesław Niewęgłowski, the priest of artistic communities, who attracted many people in that time and bravely fulfilled his mission. The wedding guests included Stefan Bratkowski, Professor Alina Brodzka, Professor Ignacy Wald and Father Wiesław Niewęgłowski. I remember that Wańkowicz told me earlier of the reception organized when Joasia and Krzysztof had their civil wedding, and he was one of the guests (as was, among others, Stanisław Dygat, a writer and Kalina's Jędrusik husband). The author of *Ziele na kraterze* reported, amazed, that Joasia wore short shorts, very fashionable at that time, and only for the reception at home she changed into a beautiful dress. At the ceremony that I was now attending, Joasia wore a stylish, grey costume.

In the seventies and later the eighties, a few hundred dollars could buy many things. I decided to spend the money left from my scholarships on further travels, which were relatively inexpensive with the ticket prices in zlotys. Jan Nowak-Jeziorański wrote after years about himself reliving independence for the second time in his life. He wrote in his article that when he was lying in a Warsaw hospital (with a broken leg) in 1993, he asked a middle-aged doctor when Poland actually regained independence. After some consideration, she replied it had to be in Gierek's time (1970-80), because since then you could freely travel abroad. Nowak wrote that he realized then that some people thought in that manner, and that it had nothing to do with the "division into commies and all the others". He reminded the readers that Gierek's rule was in many spheres more liberal than in the time of his predecessor Gomułka, because in those years the movement of collective protests was born, the Worker's Defense Committee was established, "second circulation" press was published, and finally, Solidarity was born. Social pressure led to a gradual extension of the freedom margin, up until a semi-freedom state, which facilitated assimilation and acceptance of the reality, and blurred sharp distinctions.

My travels took me to new parts of the world. On the way to Bangkok, the plane stopped in Tashkent, where we waited for three hours in a dirty waiting room, without chairs, with no possibility to buy a drink. The employees at the Tashkent airport gave the gathered Poles dark looks. "Nielzya—not allowed" was their response to all our questions. They isolated us and locked us away, annoyed that the people "moved too much." What a different world. Never before had I seen such a place. Michał Radgowski said that after travelling the world I absolutely should see Russia, that it was truly a different world from what I knew, that I needed it for my education and generally to expand my knowledge of the world. I never went there, however. I kept postponing it. Now, living in the States, I would like to see for instance Georgia, the country in the Caucasus that is named the same as one of the American southern states. Mostly, I would like to visit Lviv, Vilnius, the former Polish borderland—Kresy. Maybe it was the feature articles by Teresa Siedlarowa, that I read in the New York *Przegląd Polski*, maybe texts by Ewa Owsiany, the stories of Basia Wachowicz, the impressions of Tomek, who'd seen Vilnius, or maybe the distance and memories of the books of my childhood and youth that evoked the longing in me for those places?

My travels...The cosmopolitan amalgam of the East and the West: Bangkok, where the dynamics and rhythm of a big modern city subdue the ancient style of the East. Disgusting street pissoirs...In *Thon Buri*, I admired the floating market, saw the *Nakhon Pathom-Phra Pathom Chedi* sanctuary, spent a night in a Thai village of *Suan Sam Pran*, which is called the Rose Garden, saw various performances—a colorful presentation of classical dances, kick boxing, cock fights, been on a crocodile farm and snake charmers...

I also went to Egypt, the country where kings were worshipped like living gods...where the temples sparkle with gold and stones so amazing that the thought comes that they are passages between heaven and earth, where pyramids and tombs were built with absolute precision in order to exist for all times...

I saw a papyrus manufacturing company and listened to the story of how papyrus is processed. I bought two paintings on papyrus: both showed the holy family escaping from Egypt. Other, cheaper ones, without durable dyes, could be bought at each stop. I also visited a small company that produced carpets. In a cellar eight children are seated. The company's representative said that they could start working when they were five. For two years, they learned weaving, and then they could work full time. While they learned, they received three Egyptian pounds a day and a meal at noon. He spoke about it with pride. A young woman was weaving a carpet, and a baby lay quietly next to her on a chair staring ahead. The children's appearance was depressing. They were all on piecework, tiny, their backs towards viewers, they were weaving the threads, looking at the pattern on a piece of paper. A seven-year-old boy, with a separate work stand, was weaving so quickly, running his little fingers over the work and bending, that he looked as if he was having an epileptic fit. The children smiled at us. A few asked for candy, they pointed to their mouths, one whispered: "fluce" (money)...Those children had no idea about the childhood of their peers in other parts of the world. It was cool and damp. What diseases awaited those kids? I remembered I'd read that in the time of pharaohs children didn't work...

Another trip...Unusual colours in Palestine. The dominating ones were white, sand-coloured, the red-brown colour of the soil, turning rusty, yellow grass. The desert was a pearly shade of grey, similar to a camel's coat. Such places I knew from Sunday Gospel readings I'd grown up with...

My closer trips over native Europe: West Berlin, Cologne, Brussels. Near Paris, in Maisons Laffitte, I met Jerzy Giedroyc. I'd heard so much about him for many years—from Wańkowicz, from Benedykt Heydenkorn, and from Marek Zieliński. We'd also exchanged a few short letters once, and he published my essay on the trial of Melchior Wańkowicz of 1964 in the quarterly *Zeszyty Historyczne.* I was happy that he agreed to meet me. For a long time, I couldn't find the street where the building of the famous *Kultura* stood. The tall, extremely handsome man of regular features asked among others about the correspondence of Wańkowicz and Miłosz, the writer's archives, my plans.

In Paris, I saw Przema and her daughter Wandzia. I was particularly enraptured with Wandzia's sweetness and maturity. In the evening, I was invited to a performance in *Moulin Rouge.* I walked the streets of Paris and was very happy to be in that marvellous city...Colourful and artistic, I would so love to become better acquainted with it one day. I understand people who love France and Paris. Somehow, fate directed me to other parts of Europe and the world.

Tadeusz Olszański loved Hungary. I visited Basia and Tadeusz in Budapest, and it was a highly fascinating visit. Any contact with them was always a pleasure. He, a fluent speaker of the language (splendid translator), worldly-wise, sociable, gave me a tour of Budapest as his native city (his mother was Hungarian). Both Basia and I scoured the city, took baths in the hot springs on *Gellért Hill,* Tadeusz took us to the beer cellar *Apostolok, Mátyás Pince,* where a Gypsy band played.

Another transatlantic trip: Canada and the States: Florida, Baltimore, Toronto, Georgian Bay, New York. Tomek celebrated his 20th birthday in Florida, where he planted a banana tree in Niceville near Pensacola. Later, we learned from letters that the tree grew well and started to bear fruit.

I remember so many scenes. Here's one from New York. I was sitting on a bench in Washington Square, watching people. An elderly Native American approached me.

"Woman, do you believe in music?"

I was silent as the grave, per Isabelle's instructions.

"Just say—yes or no," he insisted.

I didn't even look at him. He finally left. Three men came to sit nearby. They had powder, lipstick, mascara with them. They carefully did their make-up, glancing in the mirror. They glanced over to see if I was watching. They needed an audience.

Frank Haynes lived on the 20th floor of Lincoln Plaza 30, opposite Lincoln Center, just next to Columbus Circle. He took us to a restaurant where the waiters roller skated, and the food was also delicious. Isabelle showed me the intensive care unit in the world-famous oncological Memorial Hospital, where she had her internship. I saw immobile human bodies attached with tubes to machines, which were working loudly. In Scarsdale, an elegant New York suburb, we visited Mr. and Mrs. Szamborski, who were living in a large residence surrounded by a park. Tomek and I went by subway to the Chinese district and ate supper in one of the small local restaurants. We felt quite at home in the States. Being guests, we didn't have the problems that the locals spoke about: rising taxes, expensive healthcare, downfall of education, spreading wave of drug abuse and crime. Then we returned to Warsaw again.

I did and still do like flying on an airplane. After the sometimes feverish packing, weariness from travel preparation, relaxation on the plane was a pleasant aftermath. The awareness that time on the airplane is entirely at my disposal. I can read, write, dream, be bored, make plans, analyse future days, converse with the person next to me. I can focus while on the plane. Jerzy Korey-Krzeczowski from Toronto told me that he always wrote his poems on the plane, suspended in space.

Journeys are like adventures, they free you from everyday life, change your view of yourself and of others. The shades and sounds of other places remain in me. The colours of the desert in Israel, the noise of horns in Bangkok, the voice of the muezzin in Istanbul calling for prayer in the morning, the emerald waters of the Pacific in Acapulco, the excitement on the streets of New York, bluebonnets flooding Texas fields in the spring, the colour of the lakes in Parry Sound, the red of the Grand Canyon, the incredible palettes of Yellowstone geysers, music streaming out of cafés and beer cellars in New Orleans...I always brought something from my journeys: books, mugs, bathroom accessories, shoes, lingerie. In the white sands of Florida in the Gulf of Mexico I found shells. I took them home to Warsaw, and placed them in a glass jar filled with water together with Baltic shells: I kept it as a decoration in the bathroom. My favourite ones included a round shell with five holes and a delicate pattern. The shell originally drew my attention and I proudly showed it to my American friends. They told me the shell was called the sand dollar or the Holy Ghost shell, as it symbolized Christ's birth, crucifixion and resurrection. If you took a really good look, you might notice many symbolic grooves. The five-pointed star represented the Star of Bethlehem, and five cracks symbolized the five wounds of Christ. The other side of the shell resembled the Christmas poinsettia and a bell. If you broke it, with some imagination you could see birds, doves of peace or, in another interpretation—angels which sang to the shepherds on Christmas morning...

Twice, in the Decembers of 1987 and 1988, I took part in Christmas meetings[12] organized in an apartment on Wilcza Street. Many intellectuals came and even the U.S. ambassador.

I remember that writer Jerzy Konwicki sat with me on a sofa. He said: "I made *Dolina Issy* into a film, because I wanted to please Miłosz, but he was indifferent to it. When writing his book, Miłosz referred to Wańkowicz's *Szczenięce lata*. In particular, one fragment resembles the latter book, where he even named the dogs the same. I would have preferred to film *Szczenięce lata*, it is more fleshy, better..."

Tomek and I were invited to the Christmas meeting of 1987 at Basia Wachowicz apartment. Being there I experienced that people who didn't like Wańkowicz were sure to tell me so, like the widow of writer Paweł Jasienica's did. Many years later, I learned that she was a Communist informer who reported on Wańkowicz and others.

And another meeting, this time in the Blessed Virgin Mary's church, with e.g. Jan Józef Lipski, the Kąkolewskis, Aldona Kubikowska, Aleksander Małachowski, Camilla Mondral, Andrzej Szczypiorski, Andrzej Jarecki, Grażyna and Andrzej Miłosz...

I really miss such Christmas meetings now, the beautiful Polish tradition so carefully nurtured in some communities. Christmas meetings are organized by companies for their employees. Those are often sumptuous receptions, but bear no resemblance to the moving Polish tradition. I heard that there were communities of Poles abroad that celebrated the custom, but I never had an opportunity to take part in such meetings when abroad.

23rd January 1988 was a day marked by Tomek's prom—the traditional formal dance in the last year of high school. The tailor made suit was the first (and at that time the only) suit in his young life. According to my mother's instructions, it was dark blue. Both the material and a white shirt and accessories were given to him by his grandmother. Many years earlier, she similarly had a white suit made for him for his First Holy Communion (thus a correction: it was the second tailor-made suit in his life). My mother sincerely believed it to be a tradition, and in a way her duty to bestow the gifts on her grandson. In the Reytan's High School, the young people were taught the figures of the classical polonaise for several months before the event (as that dance traditionally opens each prom), and Tomek additionally took dancing lessons in our area. Thus, his preparations were very thorough.

In that period so difficult for Poland, when shops often stood empty, buying shoes became a challenging task. We finally managed to buy the only shoes available, which Tomek disliked from the beginning. At the last moment, he left the new shoes at home, and put on his white, comfortable American sneakers. I didn't dare protest, as the thought prevailed that I shouldn't spoil the big day for him. The evening alternated between rain and snow. I drove him to school. He said I could stay a moment, but "I am not going to take care of you" At the school entrance, the list of attendance was checked, then Tomek went to the cloak room, and I went with the mothers, who had been making preparation for the event for some days. I stood to the side and looked at the young people—about 200 of them—in bewilderment. The boys in suits, looking uncertain, serious. The girls stunning, dressed like for a ball, dark skirts, snow-white fashionable blouses, fresh, with delicate make-up, scented, adult, slender, dressy. I was moved. I stood and looked at those beautiful young people. The polonaise started—the pairs came out to the floor. They seemed noble to me; I had so much warmth and kindness and good wishes for them. I saw Tomek. Preoccupied, excited, with a small smile and eyes fixed on his partner, he didn't see me. They were one of the first pairs. The girl wore a dark blue dress with white frills at the bottom and a white collar, looking very youthful.

I soon returned home. I called Teodorek's mother, Mrs. Maria Sobczak, as I wanted to talk about our sons. No, no, she hadn't gone to see it, Teodor firmly forbade her to. She said she was worried about the final exams, entry exams to future studies, and about the first contacts with girls. She hoped for romantic encounters, to give them good memories for the future, other ones could give them complexes.

I called my parents and told them of my impressions. I always digested the emotions and important moments related to Tomek together with them.

Tomek returned just before midnight. He was sweaty, he'd run, there were no busses. Full of impressions, excited, he caught me round the waist and danced, asking if he "did the steps right." He shared his impressions. He spoke of how the dancing elite went to dance with the teachers, how the physicist danced in tiny steps and with eyes downcast, and the boy was tall, and she petite. How the German teacher danced "cavalier style," how the Polish grammar teacher gave others proud looks, as if wishing to say: "I can dance as well"...He returned full of youthful excitement. It was truly his first ball. He said he looked for me when he was dancing the polonaise. The fact that he thought of me in that moment moved me so deeply that I fell asleep filled with tender thoughts...Oh, yes, mothers will be mothers...

After a hundred days,[13] final exams came. Earlier Tomek dislocated his ankle while playing soccer and had to wear a plaster cast. I drove him to school, and he limped to the exams with a cane. His results were exceptionally good, which amazed me and him as well. And of course, the results made his grandparents happy.

Entry exams to the faculty of architecture at the Warsaw Polytechnic Institute were conducted in two parts. First, there was a three-part exam in drawing in May, which usually two thirds of candidates failed. They then had time to submit their papers to other faculties. In that year, in three successive days, the young people had the following tasks: to draw the exhibited items:

a glass vase, a wooden bowl and silk fabric; to draw the map of Europe from memory and mark the characteristic buildings of one European capital; to design a street with low buildings. Results were put up: Tomek was in the group which passed all three exams. After a break of a few weeks, in the beginning of July, he took other exams. After an exam, a list of names was displayed, with the scored points next to each. More people failed and the group gradually grew smaller. I talked to my parents on the phone every day. We were all very excited about Tomek's exams. That atmosphere of excitement is so characteristic of Polish schools...I missed it in the States and Canada, when listening to the stories told by mothers of young people. Those countries have different ways of recruiting students.

On Saturday about noon the final results were to be displayed. Tomek called me to say that he passed the last exam and was admitted. Thus he became a student.

In that time I became friends with Joasia and Wojtek Reszczyński (he was a popular radio journalist). I knew their aunt, an immigrant Polish writer, Danuta Mostwin, whom I visited in Baltimore. She visited Poland (after many years of difficulties she was granted an entry visa) and made contact with publishers. I took her to Lublin, her native city, listening on the way to the story of the dedicated purposeful and ambitious road she'd taken in her life. I heard of an American scholar, Margaret Mead, a famous anthropologist who supervised Danuta Mostwin's doctoral thesis, and of Jacek, her son, my peer, a doctor urologist working in the famous Johns Hopkins Hospital in Baltimore. Joasia's mother, Mrs. Barbara Wendołowska, an erudite woman, told me my fortune with cards. She saw another trip awaiting me. I was to travel and...marry.

The times were good, because I made another friend, Ania Brzozowska, an attractive, talented journalist from the magazine *Kobieta i Życie* (*Woman and Life),* who'd recently lost her husband, a young writer and translator, Marek Wydmuch. Wealth in life occurs when gaining friends.

Chapter Twenty-Four

Norman

Writing about happy love is not easy. I think that all good emotions are and have always been in some ways similar. Only the unhappy ones are material for novels and great dramas.

For some time in my life now, there was Norman. I liked him and was interested in him, but he wasn't most important to me yet. Due to the distance between us, we had contact mainly by mail. At first he wrote to me once, then twice a week, and he telephoned me every Saturday. In his letters, he told me about himself, his life, his dreams. And I thought more and more of him, and wrote to him more and more often.

In the spring of 1989, I received news that I was granted a three-month scholarship by the New York Kosciuszko Foundation. I wanted to finish the publication work I'd started, and postponed a trip to the U.S. until the following spring. Norman didn't want to wait so many months, so he visited me in September, then again in December and February.

When he came to Warsaw for the first time, it was 1989, some places in Poland needed at least renovations. I told him our real airport was under renovation so that he shouldn't be surprised by the makeshift building. I was ashamed of the squalid, very provincial Okęcie. When he came again, he didn't ask why the temporariness remained. He asked little, in general, looked carefully at everything, didn't complain about anything. Norman enjoyed going to the Old Town almost every day. When we saw a documentary about the bombing of Warsaw and its destruction, he said aloud: "Jesus!" He was deeply moved by the film and later told his friends about it. He slowly learned Polish history, starting from the latest times. Slowly he developed a feeling of strong affection for the Old Town where he first told that he was in love with me. During his third visit he proposed, and then wrote about it in each letter.

In Warsaw, wherever we went, we met my friends. At a concert in the Łazienki Park, we met Marysia and Marek Drozdowski, and during a walk in the park some other friends. Norman thought I was such a popular person, and I couldn't explain to him that there were certain places or cultural events where friends met. That is the beauty of living in Warsaw. I think we were both amazed the most when, walking on the streets of West Berlin (the wall still stood back then), we suddenly met a group of elegant gentlemen, and I knew all of them. Andrzej Roman was there for a symposium with a group of journalists. I admit I miss that feeling in America, where I move about a lot, and it would never cross my mind to wonder at an airport whether I know someone there. But when I get into a plane for Warsaw, I usually see familiar faces. And it's a very beautiful feeling, that lack of anonymity.

Krysia Radgowska, who met Norman at the opera (we met unexpectedly at a performance of Wagner), told me: "Be careful not to mess up something important and valuable. He is a very interesting man of high class, not to mention very handsome...Take a good look and consider him carefully. It would be good to see him in his own territory, in America, too."

Marysia Drozdowska said: "Don't wonder too much, always go ahead," and Kaja Szymańska saw only good sides to it. Tomek...

Tomek was uncertain as to the final decision, but very friendly towards Norman. He was the only person who officially knew him, my friends actually met him by chance. But Norman fully occupied my head (and mind, as Father would say), I started to speak of him only in serious terms, surprising those who knew I hadn't been that serious before...

Norman had European connections. He spent many years outside America and that made him sensitive to foreign cultures and at the same time gave him a critical view on the issues of his own country. He spent twenty-two years abroad, only visiting the States every other year. Employed for sixteen years in Saudi Arabia and five years in New York City for the Arabian American Oil Company (*Aramco*), his responsibilities dealt with refinery process technical service and development of refinery process plants and oil production and pipeline facilities. After transfer to Exxon Corporation, he specialized in contracts engineering services for its affiliates including four years in London on the Shell-Esso North Cormorant Project (it was the first successful offshore North Sea oil recovery project) and three years in Stavanger, Norway on the Esso Odin Project. Both offshore oil recovery projects inclusive of design, detailed engineering, facilities fabrication and installation. He travelled almost all the world, and it gave him great love and respect for other cultures, other nationalities.

As a very young man, he was a cadet officer in the Navy. He was interested in aviation since early years, and took flying lessons as a student. He later owned a small single engine aircraft (an Aeronca Chief 1948). As a boy, Norman took classical piano lessons for eight years. Norman's favourite composer is Chopin (of course, we visited Żelazowa Wola, the revered Polish composer's birthplace), and a melody he loves is *Indian Love Call* by Rudolf Friml, from the film *Rose Marie*. And naturally (why "naturally" I am going to write about below), the theme melody *As Times Goes By...(A kiss is just a kiss...)* from *Casablanca*, due to the film's heroine.

Norman is a second-generation American, with grandparents from Germany and from Sweden. His cousin was the famous film star Ingrid Bergman. Ingrid's father, Justus, was brother to Norman's grandmother, Blenda. Blenda Bergman immigrated from Sweden to the States, where she met her future husband, Carl Adalbert Heinrich Boehm. Their only son, Carl Norman, was Norman's father.

He met Ingrid (as her first cousin once removed) when a young boy, in his grandmother's home in Washington, New Jersey. Bergman had come to the States as a 25-year-old novice actress. *Intermezzo*, her sixth Swedish film, caught the attention of a famed movie producer in the United States. Ingrid was invited by the producer David Selznick to come to Los Angeles. At the time, Selznick did not have much to offer her in California, so for the time being, he preferred Ingrid to stay in New York for two or three months. While there, the producer Vinton Freedley had a part for her in a play. She was playing Julie in a play by a Hungarian author, Ferenc Molnár, titled "Liliom." Those were her beginnings on Broadway.

Norman's father brought her home for a weekend. She came with her daughter Pia, who was less than two years old at the time. Petter Lindstrom, her husband, travelled all over the world and Ingrid was in the States alone for the whole summer. Norman told his friends of her. He was proud that his Swedish cousin was an actress written about in papers. She was very beautiful, natural and casual, had a brilliant smile and such a bright face. Norman played the piano for her, and she praised him. He remembered playing Strauss' *On the Beautiful Blue Danuve*, Rimsky—Korsakoff's *Song of India* (among others) and as a climax Chopin's *Minute Waltz*, the famous waltz for solo piano.[1]

Ingrid kept writing to her aunt Blenda, also wrote to Carl Norman, and also exchanged letters with Norman. Most of Ingrid's letters survived and are a valuable memento. Norman also has a picture of her with a dedication, photos of both of them, and a copy of her autobiography signed to him.

Norman saw Ingrid during his travels. In Paris, he met Roberto Rossellini, then her second husband. They spent three days together, including a visit to the *Lido* nightclub.

He saw Ingrid again in London, where she was on location making the film *Anastasia*. Over a bank holiday, Norman was invited by Ingrid and travelled with her by chartered plane for a few days in Deauville, France. The group also included the actor Yul Brynner, the director of the movie Anatole Litvak and his wife and Ingrid's niece Fiorella Marianni. They went to dinner, the casino and nightclubs together. While at a nightclub, Norman met and danced with Rita Hayworth, who was then a wife of Aly Khan, a member of the royal family of Egypt; as Norman remembers, she danced wonderfully. Of course, he danced with his famous cousin. Later he saw Ingrid in New York City, where she went to receive a Look Magazine award for *Anastasia*, accompanied by third husband, Lars Schmidt. While living in London, he visited her there. She had a small apartment in Chelsea, and Norman then was working for Exxon. In 1975, he visited her backstage at the Sam S. Schubert theatre, where she played in W. Somerset Maugham's *The Constant Wife*. The last time Norman and Ingrid met together took place at the Italian restaurant Tratoo in the Chelsea area of London. It was December 1981. She looked ill, pale and tired. From Israel, where she finished making *A Woman Called Golda*, she returned very ill. Her condition was serious. He learned of her death while in Norway.

In spring 1983 Norman returned to the States. He wanted to be closer to his parents, so he took a job with DuPont and settled in Delaware, where his mother was living in Claymont. His father (his parents had long been divorced) died in December 1983. Norman maintained a friendly relationship with his father's second wife, Marien.

When in the beginning of April 1990, I came to the States for the three-month scholarship, Norman was waiting for me at the JFK airport in New York City. He'd already set the date of our wedding: 8th June. I was enchanted with him; I was in love, but I couldn't make the final decision. During the day, I was busy with my own things, preparing the materials for a new book, and at nights I worried and didn't know what decision to make. Once I crossed the street lost in thoughts, and a car stopped with tires squealing. A police officer stood on the sidewalk. "Do you want to be one of the statistics?" he asked with a smile.

During that time I was invited by Stanisław Jordanowski, president of the Pilsudski Institute in New York, to give a lecture in that honourable institution. I had an exceptionally bright and grateful audience. I also had the opportunity to meet Danuta and Andrzej Cisek, who'd funded the Jerzy Łojek Award.[2] I'd heard much of them back in Warsaw. I was also invited to partake in the annual symposium organized by the New York Polish Institute of Arts and Sciences in America, which took place in Georgetown University in Washington. I was shown much friendliness by Erna Hilfstein from New York, who like me was taking part in a session on the role and significance of language. Also, I then met Róża Nowotarska, a painter and journalist known from the Voice of America radio, Paweł Boski, and Alina Surmacka-Szcześniak, an academic granted the outstanding Nicholas Appert Award, with whom I later formed a closer contact. In Alexandria near Washington D.C., I visited Stephanie Garbacz, a great traveller and lover of foreign cultures, and Colonel Joseph Garbacz, who was responsible for the construction of the beautiful Washington underground (both were of Polish origin). Together with Norman, I visited Edward Piszek, who lived near Delaware, and talked to writer Wiesław Kuniczak, who was working on translating Sienkiewicz's *Trilogy.*

It was such a special time. I was a scholarship holder of the respected Kosciuszko Foundation, and I was in love and had a man I cared for in his country.

This American stay was a totally different from all the previous ones. I was constantly wrestling with my thoughts. I knew that marriage would at the same time be a decision to leave Poland, and I was afraid how I would manage it all emotionally...Tomek, Parents, Warsaw, Poland...I thought I'd already had that issue covered on return from Canada...I knew then that Poland was my home and I would return there. And now, again, in another reality, that same problem returned, but in a form so changed. Love is not only looking into each other's eyes, but also being with each other and looking in the same direction. How would I live if the person closest to me was a foreigner who didn't speak Polish, who did not know Polish concerns or past history?...And also I didn't want to be mistletoe on a foreign national tree.

I rebelled, but also surrendered to emotions, and I tried to tell Norman about all that, too. He listened patiently. He had sensitivity and gentleness in him. I always wanted to choose someone towards whom I could have an unswerving wish to be good, and he did evoke such feelings in me. For me, it was so pleasant to forget about everything and simply enjoy the presence of the beloved person. The best time is always now, because that's the only time that we have. You cannot live in regret of what has passed, and wait for what is going to happen in the future.

It was the first time that I didn't take Tomek with me when leaving for the States. But the situation was different: he was studying architecture in his second year, he couldn't interrupt his studies, and right after the exams, he was going to training in Czechoslovakia, and field classes in Toruń and Kazimierz. I called him, asking how he was, how he was managing, wrote letters with advice and recommendations, and also...I asked him what I should do, and shared my doubts with him. He replied:

> ...Not knowing if you are doing exactly the right thing by marrying, is a typical reflection of a diver before he dives. You simply see more sharply what is

going to happen, what you will have to sacrifice, and sometimes you cannot be entirely sure whether you can keep something in the same way. It's only natural. But remember that if anything holds you back from marriage, you must decide to consider it. You are the most important person and matter: this is what counts most.

(...) Remember I am here for you to always rely on! I forward good wishes from Grandmom, Grandad, Henio's and Krzysio's families, the Bishop, Maciek, Mr. Olszański, Michał Radgowski, George Wiel, Janusz Podoski and many, many other friends of yours. Lots of love, Your Tomek.

Warsaw, 13th May 1990
Dearest Mom,
Just yesterday we talked on the phone and you mentioned you were waiting for my letter. I got back from church today and found a second letter from you in the box. It is something else to be able to read some reflections and direct news from someone than just hear each other for a few minutes of often chaotic conversation. I decided to write to you at once!

I'm sure you are very much interested in what the apartment looks like and how I manage. Well, all rooms are tidied in time periods depending on when I realize that "it's messy" and "Mom would surely not allow that." Your room is practically always tidy, and it is an oasis where I go only to watch TV or rest some. As I mentioned in our talk yesterday—we didn't have cold and warm water in the kitchen for two weeks, so I did a big laundry only a few days ago.

I cook dinners myself and often miss your exquisite dishes, which I am frequently unable to reproduce. But in general an hour daily for making dinner gives me the opportunity to add variety to my activities and improve my "culinary technique."

I spent nearly 5 days with Grandparents for Easter. The atmosphere was very nice, everyone in good spirits, joking, and the kids never once asked to turn the TV on during Easter Monday, which we spent together. Everyone misses you awfully and can't wait to see you!

Learning goes nice. But as usual, the ending will be most important, that last-minute effort in which you have to "drag to the end" all courses and projects. I think I will be able to create such working conditions for myself that everything is fine this time as well. My trip to Budapest was very interesting and full of experiences. I stopped in Košice, a day in Miskolc, and then three and a half days in Budapest and finally a day in Bratislava. I bathed in Hungarian bathing resorts, walked some about and got to know the culinary delicacies of Hungary. But mainly I observed life in Hungary (and Slovakia) and admired the great Budapest. I had a very interesting sense of a certain inability to understand, of being lost, which resulted from the fact that wherever I had been, I could communicate in some language, in almost any situation, but in Hungary I had serious "problems," including learning the basic expressions. I must have looked really funny, sometimes forced to explain something by sign language. Hungary is almost entirely Western, at least as concerns living standards, or rather the possibility to gain a standard corresponding to the one in the countries of Western Europe. Hungarians are very polite with one another, make contact very easily, smile a lot, and the atmosphere everywhere is (if I were to describe it with one word) cheerful. Maybe it's excitement resulting from political and cultural hopes coming true. I wondered if Poland looked the same, if it made a similar impression during the times of the hope of Solidarity in 1980–81. I have heard of everyone's enthusiasm, after all, and you can feel that. (...)

I remember the evening when I was introduced to Norman's mother. The petite, white-haired, very neat lady with pretty blue eyes gave me a close, but friendly look. And such she remained to me for all those years.

Norman took me to the town of Wyoming in Pennsylvania, to visit Marien. "Marien was good to me and Father was happy with her," he said to me. "So now, after Father's death, I gladly visit her."

Marien was a retired teacher of fifth and sixth grades of elementary school. I was scared to death about how she would accept my English. By the end of another visit, she said that she would be happy to have me in her family, and that Norman and I had a "similar state of emotion" and hence we felt so good with each other. She told me that Norman was emotional and noble.

I felt good among Norman's friends and relatives. My friends were scattered throughout the States. We drove to Danuta and Stanisław Mostwin's home in Baltimore and I introduced Norman to them. Then in Gainesville, Florida, Krystyna and Marek Jaroszewicz also met Norman and gave me their good opinion of him as the Mostwins had.

Early morning on 8th June I had an appointment with the hairdresser, who talked of her own wedding with excitement. I broke down in tears then, thinking about my life, about the fact that my parents and Tomek were far away, and that everything was so strange. At home, I put a tea compress on my eyes. When Norman came with the flowers for me and posies for our friends to pin on, he didn't guess I'd been crying. He was so happy. And so was I.

During the wedding, he was moved and his voice quivered. I looked at him in admiration.

His mother gave me a hearty hug. "I always wanted to have a daughter," she said. Tomek called from Warsaw with loving words.

Many times later, when seeing people I knew, I heard from them that Norman's mother spoke much good about me and that she was happy that her son married and was in love. I was always moved with that. When Norman and I were departing together to Warsaw for the first time, she gave me (a woman then unknown to her) a hand-made sweater. It was such a friendly and inviting gesture. Later, when I was to be married, she bought me pearls and earrings, a blue garter, and lent me a handbag ("something old, something new, something borrowed, something blue"). On my wedding day, she gave me a delicate, hand-made, golden bracelet, her favourite one, that she now shared with me. She kept knitting new sweaters for me, invited us to dinners, shared her recipes. Like my own mother...

After our wedding, both women, Norman's mother and Marien, competed a little for our affection and our time, and that was very nice. They didn't show much jealousy towards each other, but both wanted to be distinguished, each in her own way. And Norman managed that somehow.

Gradually everything seemed to unclog and all went easier. A new day came, and it was always a beautiful one. Important was not only what I felt towards Norman, but also how I felt in his company, what I was like when I was with him. I felt attractive, young, loved.

We went to New Jersey for a high school reunion. The band was playing *Big Band Music*: Benny Goodman, Glenn Miller, Tommy and Jimmy Dorsey, Woody Herman...I saw my husband among his schoolmates, and heard many warm words about him. I looked through the *Year Book*, a commemorative book issued each year by the school. A slim boy, serious, with a hint of a smile gazed at me from the pictures. His school friends were nice and all wanted to praise him. "A man of the world, a traveller..." In the town of Washington, New Jersey, where he went to grade and high school, most of his schoolmates married their local sweethearts and stayed there. One of such couples were Eve and Art Schaare, who remained close to Norman for all those years. Art went abroad only once in his life when he was in the army, and was sent with the occupation army for a year in Japan. On return, he studied in the East Stroudsburg State Teachers College nearby, then returned to his home town as a teacher and eventually rose to the position of school superintendent. Others were local doctors and lawyers. In popular opinion, Americans move very often. However, there is a large group which never moves at all and lives in their beloved, tidy, small towns. Marien was born in Wyoming, Pennsylvania. Her great-grandparents came from Scotland and lived in that state all their lives. Also her parents and she herself spent all their lives in Wyoming.

A close friend of Norman was Bob Ackerman. They'd worked together for Aramco in New York, and then in Saudi Arabia. We visited Bob and his wife Margaret in their home near New Alexandria, Pennsylvania. A private road led there through a forest. On a small lake, among tall, thickly growing spruce trees there stood a spacious house, modest on the outside, beautifully furnished inside, uniquely located so that one had the impression of living in greenery. We liked going there for a few days in each season; the view was always breathtaking. On our visits, we were always greeted by a German Shepherd as Bob loved the breed, and as long as Norman knew Bob, he always had one. First we knew Fritzie and later it was Frieda, and they observed us in a friendly manner from where they were locked behind the fence. They weren't vicious and didn't prevent access to the house, only their look was threatening. The master of the house was a miniature, white-grey schnauzer named Tess. She was highly intelligent.

I was in love with my husband. He adored me, showered me with dictums, also with poems, which he wrote and then hid in places where I would easily find them. That habit survived until today. These are some of Norman's sayings:

"I love you very much, double much, triple much."

"You know what?" he asked me out of the blue.—"What?"—"I love you."

"I like to be married...I always have a date with a beautiful woman."

Marian Brandys from Warsaw thus replied to my message telling him of my wedding:

"(...) I was very happy to receive your letter. For now, I do not offer congratulations to you, because I don't know your intended, but him I congratulate heartily, because he found the greatest wife he could ever get. Your humble servant. Marian Brandys."

I was missing Tomek, and right upon marriage, Norman and I sent a number of applications to American universities, so that Tomek could transfer to an American university to study.

Tomek passed the TOEFL exam, required by American universities, passed all final exams at the second year of his studies at the Warsaw Polytechnic Institute, completed the training in Czechoslovakia and field classes in urban and rural architecture in Kazimierz and Toruń, and...started his summer break. We were to meet in September in Warsaw and spend over six weeks together. He went for a few days to Henio, to a lake where my older brother was spending all his vacation with his family, camping. He then set off on his dream European journey to Bulgaria, France, Portugal and Spain. He stopped in France, where he picked tobacco on a farm in Alsace. We were in constant contact via phone and mail. He kept his word and called each week on Friday. He left his number, and I could always find him, if needed. After two weeks he left France and set off farther. A card came from Barcelona, in English, to Norman, and a postscript in Polish: "PS. Dear Mom—I'm sending all my love to you. The vacation is really great. I manage well, but I always remember that you are with me. Your Tomek."

The next Friday there was no call. Saturday passed, then Sunday, Monday...I couldn't sleep with worry, I prayed for him, wondering in desperation how to find any news on him. He called on Wednesday. "Mom, I was robbed, but everything's fine, I found the thief myself, don't worry..."

Letters came soon.

Lisbon, Wed 29th August 90
Dearest, beloved Mom!
It's the third day that I'm in Lisbon. It's 9 am right now, I'm sitting on the wharf of the port near Praça do Comércio and looking at the ocean's gentle lines...and beyond the ocean is America and you. Well, enough of that soppi-

ness. Yesterday I bought a ticket to a Lisbon–Paris–Plzeň train. It's valid for two months and I think I will be able to see a lot of interesting cities again on the way back: Bordeaux, Burgos, San Sebastian, Salamanca, Tours, maybe Stuttgart. (...) I'm doing quite well, I eat a good deal, not to say a lot, I'm also well provisioned. However, the cheque that Norman sent me from the Delaware Bank is not accepted by any Portugal bank, because they don't have any relations with it. Besides, I'd have to pay the commission, and it would deplete the money considerably with that amount. But I'm not badly off, although I will try to find a job picking grapes near Bordeaux. Now the situation has changed: that feeling that I am farther and farther away from home, that it's increasingly difficult and expensive, is passing. Now I will be nearing home each day. I know how important letters are, they give a completely different kind of contact than phone. You can't imagine how happy I was when right on leaving the station I went to the main post office—Lisboa, to poste restante, and I could read the two letters from you.

I called Norman "Collect", because I thought you might try to reach me by phone in Alsace, and there's no more than a memory of me there by now. It was very nice talking to Norman. I'm embarrassed I'd sent my TOEFL to the wrong university. You are both trying so hard to manage my matters in America, and I'm doing nothing for now, just travelling around.

You are really very brave, you manage wonderfully and take care of our business. You keep a wonderful atmosphere with Norman. Keep it up.

I think Grandma has by now returned from the pilgrimage. I believe we can both explain everything and that Grandma needs someone who would be able to present the matter from a different point of view—ours. It's always the absence of both of us that puts her in such a mood. Stay optimistic and fill your time to be as happy as possible. I expect I'll see you about 27th–28th September in Warsaw. I'll try to return (depending on the grape harvesting) on 24th September. I'm listening to the radio and trying to follow what is going on in the gulf, and in Poland. I even get BBC now—only Spanish stations. I hope everything turns out fine...Please give my regards to Norman and his mom, and tell him that it was really nice talking to him. I hope your home is one of your (and my) dreams. Bear up! I love you so much! Take care of yourself and Norman!
Kisses, Your Tomek

6th September 90 Lisbon
Dear Mom—I wrote this letter on that ill-fated day when I was robbed. I didn't manage to send it. I can only do so now, when I'm leaving, and when so many things have cleared up. But everything is fine. I think I will stop in Salamanca, then in the French and Spanish Basque country. Please take care of yourself! I'll see you soon. I'll be waiting for you at the airport! I love you so much! Take care of Norman and give him my regards. Give my best to Grandmom and Grandad, Tomek

7th September 1990
Dearest Mom, just yesterday we were talking on the phone. So much to tell you, so much has happened. I hope we'll be together in 3 weeks. I am in a

good mood, that week in Lisbon and the days with the Pallotine Fathers gave me the desire to rejoice. Such things, events and reflections cannot be experienced other than personally. The atmosphere of the last days was very, very nice, and it is with regret that I'm leaving. But I learned something new about myself and the world, about people, each day and in various situations. I'm heading home, and will stop in a few more cities, including Paris. I will try to find a job picking grapes in France. Everything is fine. Regards for Norman— Your Tomek.

I didn't understand much of what had happened. Only later, in Warsaw, he told me the details—as repeated below.

Tomek was hiking across Europe with a huge backpack. One morning he was looking at paintings in the Lisbon cathedral. He rested the backpack against a bench and studied the painting details, while keeping his backpack in eyesight. He lost sight of it for a few minutes...He returned there and saw it was gone. Such a huge backpack, heavy like a huge weight...Tomek ran out of the cathedral, and asked pedestrians nearby for someone with a large backpack...Valuable minutes trickled away, and he found no one. With everything in the backpack: his passport, money, train ticket home... the world seemed to be collapsing around him...He only had the shorts and shirt he was wearing...Thinking intensively, Tomek decided to go to the police station and report the theft. He had more long hours for thinking. What should he do?...He went to the port to ask if there was any ship returning to Poland; maybe they'd take him...There was none, and none was expected. He wanted to call me, but he hadn't memorized our number, that was in his telephone book (stolen). Being a weekend, the American Embassy was closed. He had to spend the night somewhere. Tomek proceeded to the gate of the Pallotine Fathers and knocked, after recalling that I once wrote a book published by the Pallotines, but in Poznań. He was accepted heartily, and taken in. Subsequently, he reported the theft of his passport to the Polish consulate. A new one was to be issued in about two weeks. A day passed, then another...He visited the consulate, waiting for the passport. The clerks were very pleasant towards him. So much was happening in Poland. They waited for news from Warsaw, wondering if they would be recalled. Tomek thought intensively about what had happened, and seemingly recalled the face of a Portuguese, a middle-aged man who had been observing him in the cathedral. But he was not sure if his recollection was true, or if his imagination was playing tricks on him...Each morning Tomek attended Mass in the Lisbon cathedral. There weren't many people. He recalled the thief had also taken the figurine of Saint Anthony and the rosary from his grandmother...Saint Anthony was a patron saint of the robbed...On the fourth day, by the end of the Mass he noticed a man's silhouette in the cathedral's side aisle...He had a hunch and moved closer, but the man slipped out through a side door. By then, Tomek knew well every nook and cranny and quickly found him. He barred his way on the stairs in front of the cathedral.

"The only thing I want from you," he said in Portuguese, "is to get back my passport and ticket home..."

"I don't know what you're talking about," replied the man.

Tomek didn't know if the man was bluffing or not, but he repeated:

"The only thing I want from you, is my passport and ticket home..."

"I don't know what you're talking about," repeated the man and put dark sunglasses on.

Tomek looked at him in amazement...those were his sunglasses. He looked at the jeans and jacket the man was wearing...that was his jacket. He grabbed the man's arm.

"He could have stabbed you," I said in terror.

"But I was stronger than him..."

"What happened next?" I asked.

"I held him and asked a Swedish couple that was watching the whole scene to call the police. I waited for them to come, and we all went to the police station. I had to watch him there, because we were left alone, and an exit door was open. The thief, the police, and I all went to his flat. He was renting a room in the attic from some poor family. When we all arrived, the family was eating my tinned meat...In his room, under the bed, I found the backpack, the sleeping bag, some of my clothes, the passport, the ticket...The money was gone, and he didn't want to say where he'd hidden it. In the bathroom I saw my toiletries. I also saw the figurine of Saint Anthony with the rosary from Grandmom...The officers carefully noted his personal data, and I knew he was going to be arrested. I looked at him and felt sorry for him. I went over and took his hand. "*Con Dio*," I said...The Portuguese looked at me, his eyes glazed with tears, he threw his arms around me and sank his head. We stood like that for a moment."

After finding most of his things, he was loaned some money by the consulate. He called me in the States to say he wouldn't be returning straight to Warsaw, as we'd agreed, but going to France to work. He wanted to return the loaned money. Finding a job in a vineyard near Bordeaux, Tomek liked it very much and has many good memories from the time. When he earned enough money, he returned the loan to the consulate in Lisbon, visited Paris (where my friend Przema gave him a very warm welcome) and returned to Warsaw.

The story told to me by Tomek came back to me later like an echo. Two years after the event, I saw a reprint in the New York *Nowy Dziennik* (of 25th July 1992) of an article by a Pallotine Father, Adam Gładysz, first published in Paris *Nasza Rodzina* (*Our Family*). The article was titled *Polacy w Portugalii* (*Poles in Portugal*). Father Gładysz wrote how often Poles had problems, how often they felt lost and unhappy. At the end of the article I found the following fragment:

> As the last one, I shall mention a student of architecture, very pleasant and well-mannered, who was completely robbed in Lisbon (not a rare occurrence) when travelling as a tourist last summer. He stayed with us for a few days, until our Consulate could issue documents for him. Within a few days the boy tracked the robber down, regained most of his things, and handed the culprit over to the police. The last act of the drama played out in my presence in the police station: Tomek and the thief, already handcuffed, fell into each other's arms and embraced each other with tears in their eyes.

On reading, there were tears in my eyes, too...In Warsaw, I obtained the Portuguese address of Father Gładysz and sent him a letter, thanking him for giving shelter and care to my son. He replied:

> ...Your son, Tomek, I often remember with warm feelings, as a cultural, bright, resourceful and talented person. His drawing of our house as seen from the garden has been framed and hanged in our living room.

A visit, the first after my marriage. After five-months' absence I came to Poland and stayed for a month and a half. Almost all that time I felt like it was my own funeral. My parents were obviously aware that I would now be only a guest in Poland, and they took this very badly. There were tears, nerves, mutual irritation, reproaches. I was leaving, and Tomek was to join me soon. I was taking the grandson away from my parents, who'd helped to raise him and who loved him above everything...

Norman joined me for two weeks. The impression he made on my parents was nice and gave them a sense of relief. He didn't seem a "thick-skinned American". He said that in the new Polish reality the world was open, that we would be visiting, that I certainly would, that I wasn't severing any ties, that he understood it all. After our marriage, Norman reminded me that it was most important that I plan to visit Poland and my family at least once per year, and I have done so and even more frequently.

In the fall of 1990, the Poland I visited after six-months' absence was filled with meetings and talking with friends and acquaintances. The comments I heard amazed me: "stupid nation," "Wałęsa will be carted away, and Urban[3] as well, "Some people are angry with you for leaving," "Your West"..."Everyone would like to immigrate," "In a new life I wouldn't want to be born in Poland, I'd rather be born in the English countryside, for instance."

They told me that in Poznań people wrote on the city walls: "I live to have more, more and then a Mercedes" or "The better tomorrow was yesterday."

I went to Zakopane with Norman and we saw the valleys. He was awed with *Chochołowska, Dolina Białego, Kasprowy Wierch.*[4] Basia Wachowicz was staying with her husband Ziuk in *Halama*, Zbigniew K. Rogowski was there, freshly after his return from Rio de Janeiro, where *Halka*[5] was staged with his stage design, and Bogusław Kaczyński was there, too. All were friendly and spoke English. Norman felt wonderful, took pictures of the houses and decorative fences of the Highlanders and wrote to his friends in America that houses in the Polish mountains were as beautiful as you'd find in Switzerland.

We went to London, all three of us, then Norman returned to the States, and I went with Tomek for two more weeks to Warsaw. We felt harmonious and somehow mature with each other. For me to leave him was, as always depressing. At the beginning of the New Year, he was to travel to the States, where everything was ready for his coming. We were again leaving our family, friends, Warsaw, Poland. I followed Norman—like to my own funeral—in tears.

Before leaving for the States, Tomek took a trip to Vilnius and to Berlin. He said he couldn't part with Europe.

At the end of November 1990, Norman and I moved to a new house in Servan Court. The complex of about thirty buildings was surrounded by a prominent stone wall. Within the stone enclosure, a home for Catholic nuns had been maintained, however, the church sold the site to the city. Right opposite the entrance to Servan Court stood a large Catholic church of Saint Thomas, made of white brick and stone. The outside of our house itself seemed rather...European to me. The house Number 11 was exceptionally functional: three and a half bathrooms, a fireplace, three bedrooms, a living room and kitchen, and a patio, enclosed by a small garden. From the back, the patio was surrounded with a decorative, tall, wooden fence dividing us from the neighbours. Coupled by the perimeter outer stone wall and the wooden fences, the house was very sheltered. The wall was covered by the evergreen pachysandra, violet clematis was climbing the fence. In the garden, a holly tree grew, a spruce, and flowers. We planted a white birch (in front of the house), azaleas, roses, a miniature silver fir, a juniper and small flowers. We erected a bird feeder for which we bought seeds that attracted various birds. A grey squirrel (in Poland, we have beautiful red ones) came to the garden. The visitor named "Squeaky" wasn't afraid of us, gladly ventured into the house and ate from the hand. He or she also ate sunflower seeds. Becoming domesticated, "Squeaky" waited for me to bring it nuts. He or she took them in its paws, took a bite, but didn't eat them. There were buried in the garden. However, the squirrel's favourite were the sunflower seeds.

The garden soon had its own history. The feeder was visited by red cardinals, blue jays, mourning doves, red finches, starlings and sparrows.

Sparrows are the same all over the world and make you feel at home. One day I took out what remained of a seafood salad and gave it to the birds. Twenty minutes later a white seagull came. One had never appeared before. How did it get to know that there was some seafood available?—I wondered. I watched it, and seeing me through the door, the bird panicked and started to take off. Each time it hit the fence and fell down. There was not enough "runway" for a "takeoff," and the small patio had a high fence. I saw the bird vomit the food it had eaten, thus it lost the ballast and, being lighter, was able to takeoff almost straight up, without running.

On another day, in winter, I saw a big, sturdy bird in the middle of the patio. What a strange new bird, I thought, came closer and saw a hawk...eating a sparrow.

The hawk gave me a cocky look. When I opened the door to the patio, it grab its prey and flew away. From that day on, the birds were scared. They sat immobile in the holly tree, and ate furtively. I saw the hawk circle above the garden a few times a day and saw it eating sparrows at least four times. In my small patio a murderer had become audacious! I stopped feeding the birds, as I felt as if I was an accomplice to the crime by attracting them to the feeder.

"How can it just grab birds from my garden like that, they're nearly domesticated!"

"A hawk also has to live," said Bob, Norman's friend.

"Let it hunt in the fields, not in my garden," I protested.

I soon read an article in the newspaper that many homeowners complained about hawks grabbing birds from the feeders, but that it was a rare occurrence, as hawks only came to the city if very hungry. They left in the spring.

While waiting for my son, I was furnishing his room on the upper floor. Tomek's first room, in Wańkowicz's house on Studencka Street, was tiny. Included were a bed, a built-in wardrobe, a folk-style shelf for books and toys, and a small children's table with chairs by the window. An aquarium with fish stood on one of the shelves.

Another room was in our apartment on Kmicica Street. Next to his bed and two bookshelves, by the window there stood a large desk, made by Henio and fitted to the wall, a chair with painted decorations and a swivel chair that squeaked whenever it was turned at the desk. He kept his bike under the window. The bookshelves were at first filled with books he was given by his grandfather: fairy tales, adventure stories. Later he bought books for himself: albums, monographs on particular countries, histories of various nations. (His grandfather took meticulous care to give Tomek titles on Polish history.) He also brought books from the States and Canada. On a shelf by his bed an old Philips box radio was located, which he listened to in the evenings. He later added a tape player and listened to music as he did his homework.

One day, when he knew he'd be alone for the day, Tomek packed the toys and books of his childhood and took them to a basement storage locker. He then anxiously waited for my reaction. He distressed me with that gesture, I missed the things from his childhood that he said goodbye to in such a way, but at the same time I understood that he wanted to have more place for new treasures of adolescence. I regretted we didn't live in a large house, where I would keep his toys and childhood clothes in trunks in the attic. I am generally a hoarder and hate parting with things which have served me well for years. I tame them and would gladly keep them forever. They include Tomek's things.

Tomek's room on Kmicica Street reminds me of his late childhood and adolescence. Here Tomek would put his blocks, his toy soldier armies, and fight battles, carefully prepared with plans drawn. He invited me to his room for their final battle. Here at the desk he made his first drawings, and did homework.

From the very beginning, I was preparing my child to be self-reliant, but when he started showing his independence, he often irritated or distressed me. As a baby and a small boy, he didn't want the door to be closed. He wanted everyone to sleep in one large room and talk in the evenings ("Like some Latino," commented Marysia, Henio's wife). As he grew, he gradually protected his privacy more, and required it be abided by and respected. In his life, there appeared areas about which I knew little. Some names of school friends appeared, but actually this sphere, like many others, was only his. We met on neutral ground, meaning the kitchen table, and sometimes in my room, where I had my desk and where he came to watch TV (he had a small TV set in his room for a time, but it broke down and we didn't buy a new one). He came to the living room to talk when my friends came. When he was a little boy, he avoided them and closed the door to his room, but then be started to like being with some of them. He always eagerly listened to Rysio Kapuściński, played chess with Michał Radgowski, joked with Maciek Czaplicki. He saw my friendships with women from yet a different angle. He liked for instance the hair-do of Krysia Radgowska ("You should wear your hair like that, Mom") and the long hair of Joasia Kąkolewska, who—like Przema—was seen as attractive by likely most of the men in my family.

We accept the maturity, adulthood and independence of our children, or at least this is what we say to others and to them. We are glad the child learned to walk and can roam the various confines himself, that he later cycles and hikes, that he then drives a car and is self-reliant. But no day passed when I wouldn't be waiting anxiously for Tomek to return home at a late hour. When later, in the States, I knew he was coming to us from faraway Arkansas, I kept glancing at my watch and no more than napped at night, ready to wake at the first sound of the door being opened.

"Why aren't you sleeping?" he asked with near-reproach on seeing my figure appear at the moment of his return. I later learned to distinguish the sounds of his return. Then I breathed easy and went to sleep. I didn't trouble him with the sight of me awake anymore. Norman knew I wasn't sleeping and comforted me, saying that Tomek came from far and that there was no reason to worry. But I still lay there in the darkness and thought of him.

In the house in Wilmington, Tomek had a spacious room upstairs, with a separate bathroom. The room had a high ceiling and an additional exit to the attic, where were installed shelves. Here I kept a cedar wardrobe for winter clothing, Norman kept his sports equipment, and my son kept the trophies he'd collected, like sports diplomas or models of buildings, tubes with drawings, and climbing boots.

In mid-November 1990, when I returned to the States, I read of the elections in Poland, about the changes that were occurring.

"I wish I was there, so much is happening and I'm not taking part in it," I complained to Norman.

"But you're organizing the house here, you're needed, too," he defended himself.

I went to Toronto, where I was to collect materials in the library of Professor Marek Drozdowski for a publication concerning Canada's reaction to the Warsaw Uprising. This was an occasion for me to meet some friends, and I visited Hanka and Bumek Heydenkorn, Janusz Dukszta organised a party and invited our common friends.

I was staying with Grace, which gave me the opportunity to get to know the new occupant of her apartment: an Abyssinian cat, which she'd named John Henry. He was very beautiful and exceptionally emotional for a cat. Following her like a dog, he moved from place to place, jumped on her shoulder and wanted to stay like that, cuddling up to her. Grace's daughter Isabelle had found the cat somewhere and gave him to her mother. The poor animal had been kept in a cellar, and the owners gladly got rid of him, and now John Henry was paying Grace back for her care with all its feline love. And love it had...loads of it. When Grace was leaving for work in the morning, the cat saw her off to the door. Staying with me, he received my invitation to play with cold indifference. Like most felines, John Henry preferred to catch up on sleep to be in a good shape when his mistress returned. An hour before her return, he moved to the hall, sat opposite the door and stared at it, immobile. When Grace unlocked the door, John Henry jumped up and welcomed her in wild leaps and jumps. I have never seen such an emotional cat before, and I was really amazed. Isabelle told me later that when she told her mother about her daughter Danielle, Grace immediately offered stories about John Henry. And so they exchanged praise of their loved ones over the phone.

For the New Year, on 31st December 1990 Tomek came. He welcomed me at the airport in Philadelphia with the words: "Mom, I've forgotten how nice people are in America."

A week later, he flew to Fayetteville to the university.

We saw him off at the airport, where he had a flight with a change in Dallas. The time was 6:00 am. In the last twenty-five minutes, Tomek wanted to talk with us some more. "No, it's better you go..." I said. We hastily said our goodbyes. Then his silhouette disappeared in the jet bridge leading to the plane.

Returning with Norman to Wilmington on the I-95 highway, it was sleeting. I suddenly started to cry, feeling sorry for myself, for Tomek, I cried and cried...

Norman went to work deeply moved, and returned with a pot flower and a little card saying he loved me and Tomek...

My son called each day after his departure. He was worried that they wouldn't recognize all the courses he completed at the Warsaw Polytechnic Institute (eventually they did recognize them all). He liked the dormitory, the view from the window of the Ozark Mountains, the fact that in the indoctrination party he spoke French and German. Like all American students, he had to take classes in English (this is how possible deficiencies from high school are levelled out).

"Should I worry about you?" I asked.

"Not so much, although I worry, too—about you and about myself, but trust me. I consult about everything with you, so that you know what is going on with me, but I do what I believe to be practical and right."

To have some additional money, he started working in the student canteen each day from 7:00 am to 9:00 am ("because money flows out so quickly," he said). Fifteen past nine he started classes. Later he had other jobs, among them night duty in the dorm. He sent us a letter with a drawing depicting his dorm room and the view from the window.

01/18/ 91
(...) I'm writing after a week of my first impressions of my studies. It's Friday afternoon and I just got back from design classes. The weather is beautiful and warm, the sky limpid. The seventh floor gives me an amazing view of the campus and Fayetteville.

The people are really—as Norman says—very friendly and outgoing. Everywhere you can see young people, smiling faces, passers-by greeting each other. I don't know the area yet, but maybe I will set out somewhere to explore the local mountains, forests and waters.

I was finishing two books at the same time: *Nie tylko Ameryka* (*Not Only America*) and *Korzenie są polskie* (*The Roots Are Polish*). They contained impressions from my travels, meetings with Singer, Miłosz and others. I started cooperation with the New York *Nowy Dziennik* (and its literary supplement *Przegląd Polski*), a paper that enjoyed the opinion as the best immigration daily, and embraced the good writing of columnists and historians from all over the world. The editor-in-chief was Bolesław Wierzbiański, and the literary supplement was managed by Julita Karkowska. The cycle *Z soboty na niedzielę (From Saturday to Sunday)* had a regular feature by Jan Latus (who later became the editor of a separate supplement titled *Weekend*), and also texts by a music expert, Daniel Wyszogrodzki. *Nowy Dziennik* published translations of Zbigniew Brzeziński's texts, articles by Jan Nowak-Jeziorański, Andrzej Pomian, and linguistic reviews by Krystyna S. Olszer. Zbigniew Racięski wrote texts for them from London. The publication regularly offered features from Poland, among others by Jacek Fedorowicz, Szymon Kobyliński, Zbigniew Sierpiński. *Nowy Dziennik* reprinted translations or reviews of articles concerning Polish issues not only from American, but also from the European press. *Nowy Dziennik* became my link to Poland and the main source of regular news. Letters were yet another and the dearest link to Poland. Letters from family, from friends, and those also related to professional issues. They were my cure for my yearnings and sorrows, my curiosity, my need of contact.

In February 1991, I welcomed letters from the Radgowskis:

Dear Oleńka
I've been thinking for some time now about you, your name's day parties, gathering the people, meeting almost ritually and about how the landscape around us has changed—the human one, the political one, and the natural one against which the other two were cast.

We wish you to save the best from it and to gather the greatest of the new.

We shall see how we manage with ours. We are living here somewhere within the budget, Lithuania, Gorbachov, Bush and his electronic toys (ugh, but still we're lucky!) and the everyday which is dirty, messy in each plan, not logical, but incomparable.

Let us wish for no more turbulence, and for our years to flow slower. Beside that, it's pretty much spring. And today, on your namesday, we're having a warm rain that washes away the remaining snow. The streets are full of traders with oranges, bananas, mandarins and a whole lot of colorful and oh-so-noisy things. Some enjoy that, some frown upon it. I hope the former will win, and in general, those with some imagination.

Have you already lined your nest in the new house and become used to rising early? How well is Tomek managing? My love for your dear husband. And once again kisses for your namesday,
Krysia

Oleńka, a February without your name's day party on Kmicica Street is an utterly nonsensical month. The state of Delaware is only to be envied. And on a more serious note, I'm missing you and remembering you fondly, and sending kisses for your name's day,
Michał

The News Journal, a daily issued in three states: Delaware, Maryland and Pennsylvania, published an extensive article about me, with a color picture. That helped boost my spirits in a way; I was pleasantly given to understand that I was remembered and recognized by the clerks in my bank, my post office, and so on. Also many people approached me directly and I made new contacts. I was shown the University of Delaware in Newark by Ed Okonowicz, a journalist, and also by a physicist, Donald Crossan. His wife Ruth had written the history of the state, founded by Swedes, and belonged to the honourable Swedish American Society. I liked the small state, known as the first state for its signing of the Constitution. Delaware was strategically located in a good place—on the axis between New York and Washington, near Philadelphia and Baltimore. I also started to "domesticate" Delaware. The American University of Women and the local public library invited me to present a lecture. I spoke of Poland, of Korczak Ziolkowski, presented a film about the sculptor and his work: the Indian chief Crazy Horse.

Already back in the 1980's, when coming to visit me and Tomek in Warsaw, Father would also visit his friend, a lawyer, Napoleon Siemaszko. In Łódź, he was friends with another lawyer, Jerzy Zielak, Kinga Wiśniewska and a whole group of barristers. My father was instrumental in organizing talks about a national movement for young people. Out of that, the Roman Dmowski Institute was born in 1989, and a year later the National Democratic Party was established as a regular political party. They worked together with rightist scouting organizations, and the developing *Sokół (Falcon)* sports organisation that had its roots back before the First World War. A few years after the party was established, it had grown to two thousand people, active in eight districts. As Jan Zamoyski put it:

> We are not in an embryonic state, but neither do we have great strength. Before the war, although National Democrats were not exactly welcome by the Sanation, the party had over two hundred thousand members. The National Democratic Party is different from the National Party, founded earlier by Maciej Giertych. Members of the National Democratic Party stress their different ideology. In its program there is no place for nationalism, but we focus on the idea to match Europe economically, culturally, and in every sphere of life.

Father sent me a letter; little did I know it would be his last:

Łódź, 26th June 1991
Dearest Oleńka,
I can add but little to what your mother has already described to you in much detail.

I feel reasonably well, whereas Mommy's state of health gives cause for some anxiety, although she tries to remain lively, and buy things where she can get them cheaper.

After all these years, I may finally officially take part in life in accordance with my convictions.

I am one of the founders of the "Sokół" Society in Łódź, founding member of the Roman Dmowski Historical Institute, and a member of the Organisational Committee of the National Democratic Party.

On 22nd–23rd June this year, I took part as a representative in the Convention of the ND Party in Warsaw, in the building of the Warsaw Polytechnic Institute. Jan Zamoyski is president of the RD Institute and the ND Part; he is the son of a man who was a friend to me and long time associate of R. Dmowski.

I also took part in the celebration of the 200th anniversary of passing the 3rd May Constitution, which took place in the Castle in Warsaw. The said Convention gathered delegates from the whole world.

I actively participated in the Publishing Committee that issued the memoirs of a commander of a Partisan Unit, *Między młotem a swastyką (Between the Hammer and the Swastika)*. The author has donated all the money from the sale of the books to invalid children in Poland.

I read a lot of tiny print that is hardly legible. I use a large magnifying glass, it magnifies about 2x. However, it is with some difficulty that I read barely legible print, because it does not magnify the print sufficiently.

(...) I am sending warm, sincere wishes of health to you, Tomek and Norman, Love...

During his mid-year break in May, Tomek set off for a trip to Mexico. I was glad that Father had his joys, that Tomek was managing well with his studies, and that I had a loving husband. Seemingly, the 90's brought the regulation of many issues, and some relief. Norman and I travelled extensively across the States: skiing in Utah at Snowbird and Park City, and visiting Salt Lake City. After a long flight across the States and the Pacific Ocean to Honolulu, Hawaii on the island of Oahu, we strolled down the Waikiki Beach, and in the evening along the Kalakaua Alley, we drank coffee with macadamia nuts, and admired the small Catholic Church of St. Augustine with beautiful stained-glass windows showing scenes from the New Testament. We saw Pearl Harbor and stood above the sunken USS Arizona, the battleship destroyed by the Japanese. In haste, I sent a few postcards without stamps from a post office. I realized my mistake only after I'd thrown them in the mailbox. We reported this to the postal clerk, he asked in which box the cards were deposited, then he pulled out all the mail from within, found all my letters and stamped them himself. For a long time I was amazed by such kind behaviour in the States, then after a while I became accustomed to it and treated it as a normal occurrence.

Our trips took us across Europe: Cologne, Düsseldorf (we went to a Christmas meeting of the Union of Poles, invited by Ms. Paulina Lemke), West Berlin (we saw the wall, still standing, and someone said it would stand at least another 10 years), we flew to Frankfurt, then took a train through Switzerland to Genoa. There we rented a car and drove over the "sun high-way" to San Remo for a week. Then we saw Rome. From there, Norman flew to the States, and I returned to Warsaw. I visited Poland again. Norman called me and wrote letters every other day.

A happy person thinks that he or she will never be unhappy again, and that's the most pleasant feeling.

The New Year 1992 was approaching. At the end of 1991, I left with Norman for a journey to South America, visiting Rio de Janeiro and the Iguassu waterfalls. In Buenos Aires, while listening to CNN news in the hotel, we learned of the bankruptcy of Pan American, the airline we were flying with whose tickets became invalid. There followed great confusion, and many other airlines didn't want to take care of the excess travellers. As it turned out, we also faced a wait in a long queue for seats on return flights, a forced prolonged stay in Argentina, additional expenses, etc. Desperate, I thought about a different way out, that Norman jokingly calls "via the Polish mafia," who find each other and help each other, etc. I found representatives of the Polish LOT airlines in the phone book, called the *Agatur* office, explained our situation to a lady with a pleasant voice, and asked for help. My actions brought results. Poles support each other! Happy to have this "Good Samaritan" travel agency successfully make all arrangements, we thanked the owner of Agatur, Mr. Andrzej Grabia-Jałbrzykowski. He turned out to be an exceptional person. He amazed Norman and me with his fluent knowledge of several languages, delightful personality and refinement. During our meeting in the travel office, the owner conversed in Polish with me, in English with Norman, in German with two priests, and in Spanish with a Puerto Rican couple we had met in the same straits as we ongoing at the same time....an amazing performance! He gave me his memoir that was published both in Polish and in Spanish, *O tym i owym* (*About This and That*). The book was a collection of stories and reflections from travels nearly all over the world, and also from his childhood in an estate in Ujazd near Kraków, and from the Kraków school. His uncle was a Vilnius archbishop, Romuald Jałbrzykowski, a name known in the history of the Church. The main passion of Andrzej Jałbrzykowski was heraldry. He was a co-publisher of *Materiały do biografii, genealogii i heraldyki polskiej* (*Materials to Polish Biographies, Genealogy and Heraldry*). We arranged to meet on the following day.

Andrzej told me of Domeyko's library, Andrzej Munk, Gombrowicz, and the painter Zygmunt Grocholski.[6] Thanks to this new acquaintance, our last two days in Buenos Aires were pleasant. In the evening we attended a music and tango dance performance at *La Ventana* and had the opportunity to admire the classical figures of the dance, which had been born in that very city.

Incidentally, Norman and I were most appreciative of the travel arrangements that were made as were our Puerto Rican friends. Together, our circuitous routing home took us from Buenos Aires, with stops in Sao Paulo, in Chicago, in Toronto and to Philadelphia, with a stop there for our friends continuing on to Puerto Rico. Our travel consumed thirty hours and our friends a longer time. We epitomized the weary travellers.

In the fourth year of architectural studies in Fayetteville, students were sent for a semester of studies in Rome. For Christmas 1991, Tomek came to Poland, spent Christmas with his grandparents and right after set off by train through Vienna to Rome, where he was to spend the following five months. My parents were happy to have him home, and to know he'd be closer to them—in Europe, and more than that, he would be in Rome, which was in a way familiar to Poles.

> Roma, 25th January 1992
> Dearest, beloved Mom,
> I haven't written to you for so long, I can't remember when the last time was. I know that in a few days I will get a letter from you, and I am already looking forward to it. Thank you for always thinking about me like that. I will call you tomorrow. The semester is almost in full swing (considering regularity of the work) and I'm trying hard to make the project the best possible. From what I've seen so far, our Professor has a more "European" approach to architecture and teaching. I like that. But we shall see more as I talk to him further. (...)
> I am living in a 19th-century building in a very old and historic part of the city, Trastevere (i.e. at the other side of the Tiber River) and the conditions are often quite Spartan (literally). (...).

Right after the New Year 1992, Norman accepted an assignment to prepare contracts for Exxon affiliate and we both went to Houston. For the first month, the company booked an apartment for us in the Stouffer Presidente Hotel. In early February, we rented a flat in the City Scape centre. I liked Texas, loved reading about its history, we continued to enjoy visiting new places. In mid-February, we went for three weekend days to San Antonio, one of the most beautiful cities of America, with the famous, historic Alamo. We stayed in the Hilton Palacio Del Rio on the San Antonio River, which meanders through the city, thanks to which the city has been named the *American Venice.* In the park on River Walk, I took pictures of Saint Anthony's figure, meaning to send them later to my mother.

We returned to Houston Sunday evening, tired with the drive and fell asleep quickly. At 3:00 am in the morning I woke up suddenly. I lay in the darkness for a few minutes, then said to Norman:

"I'll call home..."

"But you call them Saturdays," he said sleepily.

"Doesn't matter, I won't wait until Saturday."

Not to wake him fully, I went to the living room, closed the door and dialed the number. It was 10:00 am in Poland. Mom answered the phone.

"Oh, Oleńka, it is so good to hear from you. Daddy has gone out a short time ago, he's not here, so you can't talk to him..."

Suddenly during our talk, I heard knocking at the door. "Mom, I'll hold on, I'll wait, go check who's banging the door," I said. I waited a moment. Mom returned to the phone.

"The neighbour came to say that Daddy collapsed in front of the block, they're calling an ambulance..."

"Oh Lord, go there, I'll call in half an hour," I said quickly.

I returned to the bedroom. I said to Norman that while I talked to Mom, she got news of Dad collapsing. We were very worried over the news.

After half an hour I called again. Mom said briefly:

"I ran downstairs, because the ambulance was already there and he was inside it. I told him you'd called, he looked at me but didn't say anything. He was sitting, breathing hard, but he was conscious. I brought his briefcase home."

Norman went to work in the morning. I booked tickets to Utah, where we were supposed to go skiing in three weeks. I stared at the clock and finally telephoned Łódź.

"Mommy, how's Daddy?"

"Daddy...Daddy is gone," her voice sounded strange.

On the next day, the morning of 18th February, I was on a plane to Warsaw. Norman sent a fax to Tomek to the faculty of architecture to contact us immediately. When Tomek called, Norman told him of what happened, and to take a plane to Warsaw. Reportedly, Tomek didn't understand for a long time what Norman had said to him...

Eight hours of flight to Amsterdam. Then change for Warsaw. I was slowly nearing Poland. Many thoughts kept rushing to me, one after the other. To me, my world had collapsed around me. I lost my father, I kept saying to myself, sitting frozen to the spot.

I stayed with Mother five weeks. Tomek came for the funeral, and returned to Rome after a few days. After he left, two letters came addressed to my parents. One from me, with pictures from South America, and the address and phone number in Houston. The other was from Tomek to his grandparents. He wrote it on the train from Venice to Rome, apologizing for not keeping in touch for so long. The letter was dated 17ᵗʰ February. His grandfather was dying on that day....

...When Father was dying, both Tomek and I were outside of Poland. We both thought about him, we both had the impulse to keep in touch. His grandson wrote a letter, and I called...If I hadn't called that night, but only in a few days, on Saturday, it would have been already after the funeral. Nobody had my new Texas number yet and they wouldn't have been able to notify me. "Your father came to you to let you know what was happening with him," said Marysia.

With the ID tag that was returned from the hospital, together with personal things, there was my picture. I didn't know he'd carried it with him.

When I returned to Norman, it was Friday. "I will be with you all weekend, you'll get some sleep and some rest," he said, looking at my warm black clothes in which I'd travelled from Warsaw. Houston was already having a heat wave. On Monday morning, just two days later, on 16th March, we received a message that Norman's mother had died. We flew to Delaware to organize her funeral. On the plane, Norman told me that when he called her to say that I'd gone to Poland and that my father had died, she broke down in tears.

Delaware was rainy and cold. In Norman's mother's apartment, we chose the dress, then went to the undertaker's where they "arranged everything"— from flowers and a note in the press to the funeral itself. On the morning of the funeral, we went to the Funeral Home.

The lights were on. She was lying in a room that didn't have a cross or any other emblems, with her hair and make-up carefully done. There were flowers with cards. The head of the funeral home asked about the last months of her life, and listened attentively.

The minister said she was now standing before Christ. That she'd had a dry wit. When he visited her in the hospital, he tried to comfort her by saying that she would soon see George (her late second husband)..."That's all I need," she said sarcastically. Having been baptized Lutheran at birth, she was a believer and professed her faith in Christ.

There were no prayers, no funeral ritual like I'd only just gone through in Poland. It was sleeting. The limousines set off. In the cemetery that had no tombstones, only bronze plaques were laid on the ground, a covered hole was waiting under a tent. The coffin was placed on a stand. It started raining. When carrying the coffin from the limousine, it was covered with plastic tarp...*Why do they take such pains with a coffin that will be buried in a moment, anyway,* I thought. The minister said a few words of comfort, the director of the funeral home provided each of us with a carnation to place on the coffin. Then everyone went to their cars.

"Wait, will they not bury the coffin?" I asked Norman.

"No, that's a very painful issue, workers do that after the people leave."

"But following the coffin to the cemetery is exactly about accompanying the deceased in their last journey," I said.

Poland and America are worlds apart. For the next weeks and months we heard a call from the funeral home each week. They asked how Norman was feeling, how he was managing after his mother's death. At first, we took it kindly, but we were soon annoyed with the frequent contacts. Then they chose to contact us via mail. In one of the letters, the funeral home proposed that we reserve through them a place in the cemetery for Norman (and people close to him), submit suitable documentation to them and they would take care of the funeral. They sent us the documentation with a pre-paid return envelope two more times, until they tired from our lack of response.

While I was in Poland in February, Krysia Radgowska was one of the few people whom I saw. She sent me a card on learning of my father's death. Michał said Krysia was in a hospital and was having some examinations done. We visited her together in the hospital in the Mokotów district. She looked gaunt, thinner, but she was all smiles and tried to be particularly nice to me. I couldn't bear the emotions I felt anymore, and I started crying and talking of the circumstances in which I'd learned of my father's death. Instead of lifting her spirits, as she was waiting for the results of further tests, I wanted words of comfort from her. "Poor Oleńka," she said to me sympathetically.

Now, in June, soon after my arrival, Michał called to say that Krysia was gone.

The funeral took place at 11:00am in the morning. Norman was coming on that day. I didn't go to my friend's funeral, failing to make it in time. I went with Norman on the next day. To find her grave in the old Cemetery took us a long time. Michał gave us directions, but I still was confused in the alleys. Searching for the grave, we saw partridges fighting. I approached a few fresh graves covered with flowers and read the words on the ribbons of the bouquets. The fourth one was her grave. I saw the name of one of the most cordial and loyal women I'd known.

I'd read somewhere that only a loss remained ours forever. And that when a person was unhappy for too long, their heart shrank and there was no place left for feelings.

I wouldn't be able to say how long I remained unhappy. So far, not a day has gone by without me thinking of my father. And I'm constantly worried about my mother.

I understand that an era of my life has come to an end. I stopped being a child to someone, a child that can allow herself many extravagances because she knows she'll always be forgiven. I dedicated one of my Canadian books to my parents (*with unceasing love and thanks for ceaseless understanding*).

So many changes have occurred, both in my personal life and in the world. Poland is a free country that has struggled to have a new place in history. The fact that I am living in the States, makes my home country grow more distant in one manner, but at the same time grows closer in another way. This dual feeling brings closer all the past years, dear people, special places. I sometimes think that distance strengthens feelings. Distance or loss may sometimes help one analyze and understand. Distance can break us, too, but it can also strengthen us and add new values. You may experience a third value, as Danuta Mostwin would say.

I dream of returns. I plan them in details. When I return to Poland, I visit my family, my friends, stay some with Mom and in my apartment in Warsaw. I wish to somehow return to the past or at least bring it closer. But not keep it still. Time does not stand still. The people close to me are changing, and I am different, changing. By living away from one another, our minds are filled with different issues. We don't discuss them together, so we arrive at very individual conclusions. That doesn't mean we stop loving or grow indifferent to one another. But when meeting, we are as close as we used to be and that no time has passed. We remember such people later with particular fondness, and think of others with pain, regrets or a sense of guilt.

Distance nurtures sorrows. How do you get rid of the cold, ever present voice of your conscience? Father Sadzik wrote that only supernatural intervention could save us from ourselves.

We feel longing and suffer because time flows and takes people, parts of our own selves, our dreams and illusions away from us. My yearnings are often related to childhood and early youth, because that period is gone never to return. I may miss it and idealize it, but I know it will never return. Just like the childhood of my son. My mother also has such yearning. She's never left her place, closely related to people in her circle, and remains attached to the graves of the people closest to her.

In the last days of October 1992, I came to Poland again and on 1st November, All Saints' Day, I was at my father's grave with my family.

Chapter Twenty-Five

Notes and Thoughts

3 ʳᵈ January, Wilmington, Delaware

Norman says that at work, when he has a moment free, he writes down phrases from Berlitz on a piece of paper, puts it on the desk and glances at them every now and again during the day. He has trouble pronouncing them. I remember teaching one of my friends to count in Polish from one to ten...*Jeden, va, shee, tshteree, piench*[1] ...It was harder and harder to pronounce them. When I said "*sześć*" (sheshch), he asked, "Are you sure this is a different word?" Polish sounds very "rusty" to foreigners.

Each language has its own set of tongue twisters—*stół z powyłamywanymi nogami, chrząszcz brzmi w trzcinie*[2] etc. Norman reminds me of the English ones which the locals have problems with: *she sells sea shells by the sea shore* or *she sifted thistles through her thistle-sifter"*...or: *How much wood...Could a woodchuck cut...If a woodchuck...Could cut wood...* or: *Bugs black blood...A big black bug bit a big black bear...Made a big black bear bleed blood.*

Norman calls me to say triumphantly he's learned a phrase which is very important when talking to people:

"How are you—*Jak się pani miewa*...(*yuck sheh panee myevah*, he says it)...And then," he says, "the person should answer: Fine—*Doskonale!* (*dosh-koh-nah-le*).

"Don't learn that, this is not going to be useful in Poland! You don't ask like in the States: 'How are you?' You wouldn't greet my mother or brothers, or friends by saying: '*Jak się pani miewa.*' We have different forms. Nobody asks how you are, and definitely no one will answer to that with 'fine.'"

"Nobody's feeling fine?" he wondered.

"It doesn't matter if they feel good or bad, no one will tell you they feel fine."

For me, it was difficult to explain that we Poles like complaining about our lives, about everyone, about the others. If you ask how we were, we would usually list all vexations or failures in answering...Perhaps this is so because—despite the saying that a friend in need is a friend indeed—we know it is also in joy and in success. Hearing about the successes of their friends and rejoicing with them does not come easy to all people. A success can be a small one, it doesn't have to be staggering, but we like sharing it with the people closest to us. Yet there are people who really like us only when something bad is happening in our lives. Then they show us their attention, sympathy and support. When everything goes fine, they grind their teeth and can gossip and betray us to others. As if it was more difficult to enjoy someone else's success than to show them sympathy in misery. As if it required more character.

Tomek and I went for one day to New York City. It took two hours by car to get there. Whenever I am there, the city gives me much excitement. Tomek loves the city and likes going there. I like going there, too, but Norman does not like the city. He knows New York City, having worked there for five years for Aramco at their 505 Park Avenue offices, before leaving for Saudi Arabia and after his first two years there. During the weekends and week nights, he ice skated in the Rockefeller Center and Wohlman Memorial Rink in Central Park. We spent our first wedding anniversary in New York City. We stayed in the Waldorf Astoria Hotel. It was June. At high noon, we saw rats running about in Central Park. Dirt, drug dealers, aggressive beggars and various human wrecks were evident everywhere. Next to them, we saw elegant, expensively dressed passer-bys. Similar feelings now result: freaks scare me, elegant ladies thrill me. It's easy enough to go down a few streets to get from pretty clean neighbourhoods to squalid ones. New York City is a peculiar city: a Paris and a Calcutta. Next to elegant shops, like Lord & Taylor, or Saks Fifth Avenue, street trade goes on. The rich and the famous, elegant displays: Gucci, Dior, just next to poverty and dirt, human degeneration. Street vendors, like in the bazaars of the East, lay out their stands on the sidewalk and noisily tout the sometimes miserable goods. Poland seems to me so normal and pleasant with its norms set by the society, by the public opinion, that I miss it now with a nearly aching heart. For me, Poland radiates a sense of security and order. But you can think that only when you leave, because the whole view changes. Probably this is the reason why Janusz Głowacki's play *Antygona w Nowym Jorku* (*Antigone in New York*) is received differently by dwellers of Warsaw or Prague than by New Yorkers or visitors to the city. And each person is true in their reaction, and each has a right to their opinion.

But at the same time, only in New York City do you feel it's the very city where the most goes on in the area of international finance, business, culture, literature, theatre, film. New York City is the capital of the world, even though lovers of Paris or London would vehemently disagree. That is also the phenomenon of twenty-eight ethnic groups with over forty languages blending. Buzzing cafés, so many cultures, so many nationalities...

How often we talk of what place is most pleasant to live. Our friend likes Delaware, because he grew up here and works here. He also sees the benefits of that thriving state, one of few which does not have a sales tax. And we are still considering whether to move to a different place. I am particularly excited about whether to stay in the green Delaware, settle in my likeable South, or maybe in Colorado, which Norman admires so. And I'd like to spend many months in Poland, not just visit it. My friend in Houston, whose husband has a violin-making workshop, has played for many years as the first violinist in the Philharmonic Orchestra there. They have dozens of friends and are very likeable. She told me once, "If you leave your country and stay in exile, you will always be looking for new places, nicer and better, because you'll never feel at home again. You'll feel the pull to go somewhere all the time."

I tame new places where I come to live, and I am sorry to leave them. I sometimes think I could live just about anywhere: in Mexico, in California and in Florida, Colorado and Texas, and God knows where else. At first I thought it was a healthy sense of freedom and adaptation abilities. Sometimes, when I have a bad day, I think it proves my uprooting, as my father would have sternly put it. But those thoughts about moving come to me outside of Poland. In Poland, I keep thinking how to do it so that I could come and stay not for a month, but for several, for instance six. In Poland I am at home. For vacation you can choose new places again and again. And those trips and moving are a like long, continuous vacation.

10 th January, Wilmington, Delaware

We've come to Longwood Gardens. They're located in the Brandywine Valley in Pennsylvania. It is one of the most beautiful and largest botanical gardens in the United States. The trip from our house to those gardens takes about half an hour. You can admire them at any time of the year. They have true flower jewels: marvellous orchids, thematically arranged, round-bellied and winding cactuses in hothouses, avenues of azaleas, a palm grove, Japanese gardens with bonsai trees.

I am sometimes troubled by certain thoughts about my life—that I had traded my most ardent wishes to countless small desires. That I didn't settle my life the way I wanted, although I lived the way I wanted.

Another day I read *Nieobjęta ziemia* (*The Unencompassed Earth*) by Czesław Miłosz. He writes about his fight with *delectatio morosa*, to which he was always prone. That term was once fashionable in monasteries. Monks suffering from *delectatio morosa* lost themselves in dwelling upon their sins, which was a way to put aside the most urgent, current duties. Miłosz writes that it is a philosophy of freedom which consists in our choice now, today, having a backwards effect, changing our actions. The philosophy of freedom professed by existentialists borrowed the methods of confessors, and it advises us to always look ahead, and never back.

In the mail, I find a letter from Warsaw, from Szymon Kobyliński. A fragment of it struck me and won't leave me:

> …God bless you also for the good word about my text, resulting amongst others from a constant awe—verging on stupefaction—that our fellow men (particularly fellow artistic men) are at all able to live in that country where they do not pick up the scrap of bread from the ground out of reverence,[3] but they throw pies in the faces and a barely bitten hot-dog in the trash. It is not about affluence, clearly, but about what I'd call habits of respect. And if we repeat to our grandchildren with good effect that food is not to be played with, then in such talk there are held some of those roots that you have written a book about, and I, an article…

2nd February, Wilmington, Delaware

I keep thinking about Szymon's words. I remember his feature in which he expressed his astonishment at the lack of taste and style in the construction of American houses, which he saw on watching some TV series. I can talk about architecture, if not with Tomek who's studying, then certainly with Marek Jaroszewicz, the highly regarded University of Florida dean of architecture in Gainesville, Florida. First of all, he stresses the difference of attitude of life between the American society and Europeans. Americans are a nation in constant, almost hectic movement. Statistics show that an average American family moves every five years, and it is often to the other end of the continent. Due to this, a typical house is not built and treated as a family home to serve successive generations, but as a utilitarian object. People move from place to place, from work to work, seeking a better job, with higher income, and all that impacts the attitude to the place of living. A house is bought as needed, as required by changes in life. In Europe, building a house is rare. You mainly buy, or rent a flat. An average person in Poland lives in an apartment building, whereas an average American lives in their own house. Hence the houses here, in order to be accessible for most people, are built quickly and from the cheapest materials, among them e.g. wood. As to the taste and style of the particular houses, those are the result of fashion, and also the taste of their owners. I've seen wonderful residences and nice, small houses, but also hideous ones.

7th February, Wilmington, Delaware

We're going to Wyoming, Pennsylvania, to visit Marien, the second wife of Norman's father. She's 84. Marien likes recalling the times when she was full of life and travelled far. Most of her friends and her whole family are gone now.

I'm wondering how cruel fate would have been to us by giving us exceptional longevity, even if we were given eternal youth. We would see others, people close to us age, get sick, and die. We would have to constantly grieve for others, and how lonely would we be, unable to share the pain and mystery of existence with anyone.

The eighty-year-old Miłosz writes in (mentioned earlier) *Nieobjęta ziemia (The Unecompassed Earth)* that although you feel love and the passion of life in your youth, you need a certain liberation from complications, even to a small extent, from the concern of your own fate, in order to just enjoy being alive among the living.

The eighty-year-old Wańkowicz complained, in turn, that many friends among his peers had died, that he was feeling more and more lonely, living among a different generation which did not have the same memories and references. He said he sometimes felt as if he was walking in a desert.

10th February, Wilmington, Delaware

I'm reading a biographical book by Ofelia Alayeto, published by "Scripta Humanistica," on a Spanish poet, Sofia Casonova. She was the first wife of the philosopher Wincenty Lutosławski, and mother to Halina Meissner and Manita Niklewicz. She died in Poznań in 1958. A fascinating person, she had such an interesting life. Casonova's book is worth recommending to a Polish publisher. I have a book about Lutosławski, *Jeden krótki żywot* (*One Short Life*), which was recently reissued in Poland. Aleksander Jordan Lutosławski, philosopher's son, called twice from Miami to say he was reading it yet another time, and that he was once again moved by his father's diaries, and affected with his own smallness as compared to his father's industriousness, talent, work, and achievements. Aleksander Jordan Lutosławski, a pre-war Polish diplomat in London, is a highly regarded translator of Paweł Jasienica's books. He has also translated *Malowany ptak (The Painted Bird)* by Kosiński, and has published many of his own texts in leading American periodicals. But he is embittered and regrets the decision to leave for the States that he made right after the war. Aleksander told me: "I was young and wanted to see America. My decision was a big mistake, for had I stayed in England, I would have fared far better financially and culturally. In England, I had access to the elite of the country, and in America there is not really such an elite. And even if there was, I wouldn't be popular with it..."

Wincenty Lutosławski writes in his book that he was influenced by Teichmüller, with whom he'd been friends for thirty years, until the philosopher's death in 1920. Teichmüller was famous for his work on randomness of the laws of nature, in which he fought the widely spread belief in absolute necessity, which people usually want to see in casualty. To put it simpler: he proved that what is, could always be different.

13th–16th February. On the way

After an early breakfast we set off from Wilmington, Delaware, to Texas in a fully loaded car. We pass Pennsylvania, Maryland. As always, we change behind the wheel every two hours. I listen to the radio and music from tapes. I like Louis Armstrong's *What a Wonderful World, The Sunshine of Love, Give Me Your Kisses* and *Chinatown, My Chinatown.* At one of the stops, next to our car an elderly man gave some water to a small cocker-spaniel pup. We stroked the playful animal. "I'm bringing him as a surprise for my wife's birthday. When she was a little girl, she had a cocker-spaniel, and I know she'll be happy. I came up with this plan together with my daughter, and only she knows I went so far to get a dog from a good place. My wife thinks I'm visiting a friend..."

A long ride through Tennessee. At stopovers, we see mementoes of Elvis Presley. In Arkansas, passing the town of Hope, we see a large notice: "President Clinton's Birthplace." Similarly, on crossing the Mississippi River, we read: "Arkansas—the state where President Clinton comes from." Texas, where Presidents Eisenhower and Johnson (Eisenhower was raised in Kansas) came from, don't have such notices when you cross the border at Texarkana. Tomek told me later that when he passed Denison, a town in Texas, he saw a notice: "The Birthplace of President Dwight Eisenhower." We didn't pass through Denison when going from Delaware to Dallas. We're staying for the night in Little Rock, the capital of Arkansas.

In the afternoon we reached Dallas. The apartment we rented is modern, furnished and decorated black and white. The kitchen is white, the carpet, pots, armchairs and sofas black, black bedspread and towels. A decorative bouquet of flowers offers a touch of red. There is an additional desk for my computer. Downstairs is a gym and a pool. The building, surrounded with palms, is located in an artistic district. There are galleries and refined restaurants around. A colorful cable car goes down McKinney Street. In Dallas, together with a local law firm, Norman was researching work related documentation to support a claim process, whereby the Japanese company Kajima Construction will sue the Chinese Formosa Petrochemical company for over 30 million dollars of compensation. It looks like we will stay here at least three months.

Dinner in Pappadeaux: Cajun seafood.

20th February, Dallas, Texas

Weekend. We visited the place where President Kennedy was assassinated. I wanted to see the area immediately on coming here. On coming to the intersection of Elm and Houston, I recognized it at once. I remembered it, like everyone, from pictures and films: a red-brick building, intersection of roads, a bridge. The place itself is called Dealey Plaza. The centre of Dallas has been filled with skyscrapers, but this place remained untouched. We were infected with a certain sense of dread, walking in silence. Just a few tourists walked about, all focused and affected. The guides sold papers, related the course of events, showed where the presidential limousine came from, where the shots came from. That story, told anew, still gives you shivers.

Allegedly, when in 1972 there was a fire in the book depository at Elm Street, city inhabitants said the building should have been left to burn down and be wiped off the surface of the earth. They were afraid it would become "Oswald's temple." The head of public works decided that the building would be renovated, and a small museum of the President would be opened on the sixth floor. There were many who opposed the idea. They were afraid of having the disastrous day constantly recalled. Yet finally, an exhibition was opened in 1989, showing Kennedy's achievements as a president. The exhibition is commendatory of Kennedy and Americans like that.

Each year 3.7 million tourists come to see the assassination place. A one of a kind attraction, a mystical cult surrounds it. People still find it difficult to accept the fact that some lunatic could shoot the president, with a rifle that cost twenty dollars at that time. Americans cannot believe the assassination without seeking conspiracy. An anecdote is told: If God himself were to come to earth and say that Oswald worked alone, people would say: "My God, that conspiracy against the president's life is even further reaching than we suspected..."

24th February, Dallas, Texas

At a distance, many things seem worse, more dangerous, more serious. Hence you have to save yourself in letters. I think about it as I read and write letters.

In the evening, we watch *Cadence* with Charlie Sheen and Martin Sheen. At some point one black man says to another:

"I dreamt I woke up and I was *white*."

"That's no dream, man. That's a nightmare," answers the other.

11th March, Dallas, Texas

In *Time* I read of the III Symphony by Henryk Górecki, about which I've heard so much already. I am glad of his success as a Polish composer. "Time" writes that when it was played on the radio in Santa Monica, California, people stopped in delight to phone and ask about the symphony. The CDs enjoy record sales. What is most curious is that the symphony was composed many years ago. The composer himself is presented as a modest, pleasant man who lives with his wife and daughters in Katowice.

I've always heard it was better to grow up with siblings, and now a book has been published showing a different point of view. Its author, Ari Kiev, a doctor, writes that single children achieve more in life, because they are not compared to their siblings ("Why can't you be like your brother?") and their model is their parents. They identify with adults and pose greater challenges to themselves. It is also a myth, writes Kiev, that single children are selfish.

13th March, Dallas, Texas

We went to Fort Worth to the American Art Museum. I bought a poster with copy of a painting by Remington.

14th March, Dallas, Texas

A gun show, so popular here. The buyers are men in cowboy hats, or another group: shorn heads and tattoos, leather jackets. There are so many strange characters that I'd love to take pictures (but that's forbidden). In Texas, you have a gun show almost each week. Norman is astonished that in *The Dallas Morning News* they continuously advertise discounts for guns. We are in the Wild West, after all.

In a *Western Style* shop, Norman bought a black Stetson cowboy hat (100 dollars!). He says he always wanted to have one like it. When he was a little boy, for a short time, he dreamed of becoming a cowboy. And I'd thought it was only in Poland that boys wanted to become cowboys. I bought a suede jacket with fringes, in Native American style. In the evening, we go for a walk, as usual.

3rd April, Austin, Texas

We're going to Austin. Along the roads and highways in Texas wild flowers are planted. Planting of roadside wild flowers was the inspiration of and efforts by Lady Bird, the wife of President Johnson. I'm driving and admiring bluebonnets...(they remind me of the Polish lupine, only it's blue). I recall the fields and forests in *Lipce Reymontowskie*, the swoosh of ripe corn, the taste of sun-warmed blueberries and blackberries plucked in Radziejow-ice, birds singing in *Las Kabacki*, the quiet and charm of the Wilanów park, white birches in Nieborów, the shape of the trees in the *Łazienki* park, the smell of lilac and jasmine from the garden of my childhood, the smell of air in the *Tatras* right after the rain...

8th April, Dallas, Texas

Norman likes his work in Dallas, because he returns home earlier. Commuting doesn't take as much time as in Delaware (where he endured one hour drives each way on the highways).

Tomek called to say that he was the only one to receive the Larry Obsitnik Award, granted each year by the Fulbright College of Art and Science. He, a student of architecture, received an award of a neighbouring faculty. He studies Photojournalism as an elective. "I have no one to share it with, that's why I called you immediately," he said. He was pleased. There is going to be a ceremony at the university when they give away the awards of all faculties, awards from different disciplines. And they will send information to the press, to the student's home state, and Tomek will be named in Delaware.

11th April, Dallas, Texas

Easter. In a small Polish church, which we found with difficulty, the atmosphere is so different from the one in Poland. I always sang *Te Deum* loud and clear, and here no one stood up, no one knew the words. Norman seems to prefer going to services in English. He doesn't mind Catholic services. He says the most important thing is that we are both Christians and respectful of each other's religion. He belongs to the Presbyterian Church, one of the Protestant churches. He told me he had a colleague at work that was a Buddhist and who told him that Buddhism taught self-improvement. Norman answered that Christianity additionally taught how to spread goodness. The concept of sacrifice is present only in Christianity.

12th April, Dallas, Texas

In Poland, we have the second day of Easter, and here everyone is already back to work. I reflect on how important penitence is in Poland, how significant Easter confession is. God is shown as punishing and just. Children are warned: Watch it, or God will punish you...In America, and similarly in Canada, I've never heard such an expression. Here, God is merciful and forgiving, God loves everyone, loves those suffering from AIDS. In Poland, Bishop Jan Kulik told me: "God is justice appeased by love."

16th April, Dallas, Texas

We are moving to a bigger apartment on Turtle Creek Boulevard, a tree lined boulevard running along a stream and parks. We are to stay in Dallas at least half a year longer, and we decided to move to a bigger place, more so because Tomek will be visiting us. Turtle Creek Boulevard is one of the most elegant streets in Dallas. Not far from our apartment The Mansion on Turtle Creek is located, said to be the most elegant hotel in all of the United States (it wins all polls, right after Windsor Court in New Orleans, the next ones

being: BelAir in Los Angeles, Sherman House in San Francisco and Haleku-
lani in Honolulu).

Arun Gandhi, grandson of Mahatma Gandhi, repeats the teachings of his
grandfather that disasters and harm result from the Seven Social Sins against
the basic truths. These are: * *Wealth without work* * *Pleasure without conscience* * *Knowledge without character* * *Commerce without morality* *
Science without humanity * *Worship without sacrifice* * *Politics without
principles* *

26th April, Dallas, Texas

It's sunny, as usual. Today I met a neighbour living in our elegant building, Leila Wilson. She asks to be called Lee. She offered me some tea, which
she orders from Harrods in London. She was born near New Orleans in
Louisiana, graduated in History of Art and works twice a week in the Art
Museum just for the pleasure of it. Her husband Drew has his own legal
office in the city. Lee speaks with a Southern accent and is an enthusiastic
conversationalist. She asks about Poland, and I appreciate her interest. Lee's
husband travels a lot around the globe, recently he was in China, but he
travels with his mother (Lee talks of her as Mrs. Wilson). Lee doesn't like far
travels, loves her South and knows each and every smallest town in Mississippi and Louisiana, where she has family. She told me of her childhood
friend, Sue: who was so talented, but she married...And on with some secrets
from Sue's life.

I think that the motivation to share the secrets of our lives and those of
other people's lives is our age. When we are in our twenties, we try to
become independent of our parents, be similar to our friends. We share
secrets to be accepted by the people around us. In our thirties, our family and
career make us susceptible to telling secrets in order to obtain affirmation
and support for our decisions and judgements.

When we are in our forties, we focus on our inner life. We share secrets of
our lives to talk about nagging remorse, to rid ourselves of the sense of guilt
which follows us as a result of our choices in life.

Lee tells me that once you're fifty or older, when you're finally at peace
with yourself, your concern for other people who you care about makes you
sometimes...indiscreet. So later sometime, perhaps I will then write a very
indiscreet book about me, my friends and acquaintances?

And when seventy, maybe I will have turned into a nasty old hag who
will write memoirs full of gossip, bitterness, and betrayed secrets of people
close to me, my friends, my own...maybe I'll have become quite acrid and
make my friends into some monsters?

Norman says: "If you can say nothing good about a person, don't talk
about him at all." And I repeat the saying (quoted earlier): *If John speaks
badly of Mary, then something is wrong with John, not with Mary.* And yet, it

is sometimes so sweet to be able to say something wicked about another, the moreso that we know them so well...

You usually write down a story of events which happened in your life, or in someone else's. You want to see life in the story, but it's just an outer cloak. An event affects our life in so far as how much we desired it. Dozens of events pass us by, within our hand's reach, but they are meaningless, we don't have any use for them, we don't meet them halfway. And when what seems like coincidence happens in our life, some kind of shock, it means we've been waiting for it.

3rd May, Dallas, Texas

A telephone call in the morning. Another taped message pestering us..an exceptional offer to buy a plot at the cemetery, and where to go to get it. More and more various solicitations come by phone and, of course, by mail. Addresses are sold, and time and again we receive an ad from a new bank, new laundry, new mail-order shop, a request for donations, etc.

More and more talk-shows concern "child abuse." They also often invite criminals of various kind, who break down in tears as they explain their difficult childhood, and move the audience, who mainly sympathize with them, paying no heed to the crimes they've committed. Later, such people make up the juries in courts and pronounce verdicts which astonish the rest of society. I sometimes have the impression that America has become a society of people who mainly need sympathy, a society of victims.

In a daily CNN program, they speak of what seem almost common traits recently: children blame their parents for their own failed life. I'm reading a book by an author of a popular program, a doctor of psychology, Sonya Friedman: *Smart Cookies Don't Crumble*. The author reminds women of a few principles:

> 1. The only person you will live your entire life with is yourself. Not your husband, not your kids, not your friends. 2. Smart Cookies know that changes are an inevitable part of life and that dreams can fade. Accept changes. People go away, change, you change as well. 3. If you're dreaming of a prince, if you don't like your life—don't wait passively, do something to change it. Only being active will change your life. Have an aim in life.

And I have my own truth: it's not the problems that we face in life, but how we cope with them is what determines the quality of our lives.

7th May, Fayetteville, Arkansas

After breakfast we set out to Fayetteville. It's a seven-hour drive through the green fields of Oklahoma, passing the Eufaula Lake and the Ozark Mountain country. Fayetteville lies at the foot of the Ozarks Mountains, the University of Arkansas has a green and very picturesque academic campus. We are staying in the Mountain Inn, in rooms booked for us by Tomek. We call him, and coming immediately, he was obviously excited and hospitable. He takes us for a tour around the area and shows the university, founded 1821, with its beautiful old buildings. The architecture faculty in Fayetteville won renown when one of its professors, author of many books, Fay Jones, received the highest award in architecture. The architecture building is comprised of laboratories, classrooms including those for computer usage. Tomek's project (of a jail) hangs on a wall, as the awarded one. Everywhere we see young people, as it is in so many of such campuses. We partake of a delicious seafood dinner. It's the end of the academic year, a day before official graduation with diplomas, many parents have come, and now the tables are all taken by the crowd of young people and their guests. I keep glancing at Tomek, who now seems strangely more serious to me. Usually, when he comes to us, brings a flurry of activity and commotion. Now, he is the host here.

8th May, Fayetteville, Arkansas

After breakfast we go to the campus. In the Old Main building, the families of students who graduate this year from the five-year architecture studies slowly gather. We take places in rows reserved for the parents. They give us a printed program of the graduation, and a list of students of the particular faculties (from the faculty of law President Clinton, once a teacher in Fayetteville, is now receiving an honorary doctoral degree). A separate brochure is provided us with information only about architecture and this year's graduates. Half past one, we hear the Coronation March and the procession enters—first professors in gowns, then students in gowns and caps. There are about forty students. I see Tomek—his face shows emotion. They sit neatly in a row. First the welcome is given by the Dean, Daniel D. Benneth. Diplomas are handed out, but not the real ones yet (the official ones will come in a few weeks by mail). Everyone has their name read out. Norman stands to the side and takes a picture of Tomek. The group's tutor Michael Buono speaks first, then one of the students. Everyone wants to say something funny. End of the ceremony. We talk to Michael Buono, he congratulates us on Tomek, we take pictures together.

Tomek shows us his dormitory, his room. He takes us for a drive around the campus. We go for lunch, then to a bookstore. After a break we meet for supper in the Mandarin Restaurant.

Late evening we all go to the film "Indochine" with Catherine Deneuve. Norman and I return to the hotel well after midnight.

9th May 1993, Fayetteville, Arkansas

In the morning Tomek comes with a card (Mother's Day) in which he wrote:

> To my Dear, Dearest Mom on her day,
> Thank you for the two great days of Graduation, for your care, for the help, for
> the last five years of effort, worries and advice. Dearest Mom—I love you, and
> I thank you for everything!

I broke into happy tears. Breakfast with all three of us. Soon Tomek and I switch into Polish. Norman sits there in silence, allowing us this kind of intimacy, and I want to be a "Polish mom" and talk to my son in our language. At noon we leave Fayetteville. Tomek stays for a few more days. Later he's going to work as a journalist and photographer on a newspaper, as a result of his elective—Photojournalism.

It's raining as I drive. I am silent and yield to the mood. In Dallas, right on coming, a call from Tomek. He asks how the trip was, and thanks us for coming and for the two days together.

15th May, Dallas, Texas

Tomek came for a few days. We all went to Fort Worth to the Kimbell Art Museum. It's an interesting building of beautiful proportions, built in 1972 by Louis I. Kahn. He used natural light. Louis Kahn, next to Frank Lloyd Wright and Mies van der Rohe, is the most famous American architect. The Muesum holds among others the works of Titian, El Greco, Rubens, Velazquez, Rembrandt, Goya, David, Delacroix, Cezanne, Picasso, Matisse.

On "20/20," Barbara Walters showed a program about 90-year-old people in one of the East Coast states. One of the women is an aerobics instructor. They talk with a doctor who claims that the most important characteristics which allow us to survive are optimism and the ability to adapt after losing people close to us. A talk with one of the women (she is 92, and looks 80). Her 70-year-old daughter died the previous day. With tears in her eyes, slowly choosing the words, with some kind of dignity, she said: "Yesterday I received a message that I lost my daughter. It is very hard for me...For the whole day, I've been thinking, recalling the time when she was a child. What a great gift from God she was. When she was a little girl, she said as she went to sleep: The Lord and I go to sleep now. I believe that she's also asleep now. And that I'd given back to God his greatest gift to me in my life, that child...

I read once a beautiful book on old age, given to me by my father, by Zofia Starowieyska-Morstinowa: *Patrzę i wspominam* (*Looking and Remembering*). I have it in my Warsaw collection.

The most popular books in the bookstore seem to be how-to books. They concern almost every aspect of life; how to build a house, how to sell it, how to find a fiancé, how to marry, how to divorce, how to get money, how to manage loss of money or loss of a dear person—how to act in the time of mourning. About tax maneuvres, about health and beauty, how to obtain permanent residence in the USA, how to find a job. Americans know the worth of practical knowledge and gladly refer to it. They know they can save money and disappointments if they refer to the right source of information.

28th May, Dallas, Texas

Lee, with whom I've drank her tea from Harrods, told me that when visiting Drew's family after her marriage to him, she was surprised when after the afternoon spent together, they said their goodbyes, got into the car and simply drove back home. Goodbyes with her family when visiting were not that simple. They always give her something to take with her: a melon, roast meat left from dinner, a box of home-made pasta, apple pie, an ivy seedling from the garden...When she visits her sister, the latter daily puts on the sideboard things for her to take: a jar with preserves, hand embroidered cushion, hand cream. When her sister buys two pounds of bacon at a discount, one pound goes to Lee.

"This behaviour of ours astonishes Drew," she tells me. "He is amazed at our practices. I tell him that families who once owned farms, like ours, are taught to share everything with everyone who comes to our house. Our ancestors have long ago sold their farms and started to live in houses with gardens, but we still keep the tradition. We lend one another gardening tools, maternity dresses, garden chairs...When I read in the household section what to do with leftover turkey after a Thanksgiving family dinner, I just can't understand it. There is never anything left over at our home, it's shared among everyone...Recently, when I visited my Mom, she gave me some rice that she bought without her glasses on, so it wasn't her favourite type, and a box of chocolates left over from Halloween. "Wait a moment," Mom told me, "I want to give you a dress that I didn't like since the beginning, it doesn't fit me well, and pink is not my color." "Mom, I bought you that dress," I said. "Really? That's all right, I'll send it to you when your cousin goes to Dallas, and I'll add the apple pie that you like so much," my Mom replied with a smile."

I really like Lee's stories.

29th May, Austin, Texas

I'm going with Norman to Austin. We're staying again in the Stouffer Hotel. We drank some cappuccino, and a group of some Japanese were sitting nearby. "They are usually silent like this," says Norman. "They likely wonder how it happened that we, Americans, won the war..."

31st May, Dallas, Texas

I'm reading Ryszard Kapuscinski's *Imperium (Empire),*[4] and I am truly impressed by the book. Tomek sent Norman a beautiful card. He wrote:

Dear Norman! It was wonderful that I could have you both here during my graduation. It was one of those special moments, when one realizes that part of his life is over. You made it possible that I was able to study, and I will remember it always. Thank you for the three wonderful years! (You will always have a special place in my heart). Thomas

1st June, Dallas, Texas

Tomek is writing an article about a sick young man. The man has had an accident and his memory is slowly returning. The article with Tomek's photos is to be in a cover story, titled "Step by Step." He calls me, excited.

It's Children's Day in Poland, but they don't celebrate it here (children have their day all year round, said Lee). Yesterday in *The Dallas Morning News* in the *Dear Abby* column, a mother's letter was printed in which she promises her children that when she grows old...she will be staying with each of them in turn, will borrow their cars and come back two hours later than she promised, will leave her clothing lying about in the whole house, won't switch off the lights, will drink milk straight from the bottle with the fridge open...When she comes to live with them, she will bring an animal which hasn't been house-trained, will borrow her son's sports jacket and return it with her artificial teeth left accidentally in its pocket, will wear an earring in one ear only and will sometimes dye her hair orange. When they leave for three or four days, she will be having parties, will buy a stereo and listen to Glenn Miller's hits, playing them loudly.

3rd June, Dallas, Texas

In New York's *Przegląd Polski*, Krzysztof Zanussi states that the whole Europe should defend itself from Americanization. He almost prophecies Polish national doom.

In TV a film about President Johnson potrays that he did a lot for the country, signed many important acts, was consistent. The Kennedy family, in particular Robert, humiliated him as a Vice-President and ridiculed his manners. Johnson was chosen as the Vice-President candidate by Kennedy in order to have the support of the huge state of Texas. He inherited the Vietnam issue after Kennedy's death, and it was also difficult to be president after the death of such a popular president as his predecessor was. John Kennedy was involved in the Bay of Pigs, the Berlin Wall, Vietnam...but still he remains for many a mythical and beloved figure. A significant role was played by the press and television, which made him to be an almost Hollywood-style star. His father, Joseph Kennedy, made sure it would be so. Johnson died at 65, alone, in his estate in Texas.

5th June, New Orleans, Louisiana

We are staying in the Hilton Hotel, just next to the French Quarter. We change and go to dinner to *Cajun Creole Olde N'awlins Cookery* on Conti Street and listen to the music long into the night.

Pool in the morning, then a walk along the River. I buy two *Navajo* skirts and two *Chick's Design* blouses. At 7:00 pm, we come to stand in front of the Preservation Hall on St. Peter Street. We're the sixth couple in the line. I look at the street. The garbage truck takes away loads of trash bags, but a dreadful fish stink lingers. The line grows longer. Finally they open the door of the gorgeous, old, shabby building, and we have seats. The concert lasts half an hour, then a 10-minute break, and so on until late at night. When we leave, people stand patiently in line, waiting with the others to listen to the old masters of jazz. You can leave when you want. Delicious jumbo shrimps for supper. As I fall asleep, *The Closer Walk*, the repeating rhythmic melody of the funeral song, still plays in my head. The first part is sad, and the second joyous, then the band returns happily from the cemetery. A man from Massachusetts sitting next to us in the Preservation Hall told us he came there each year to listen to the music in New Orleans.

6th June, New Orleans, Louisiana

New Orleans is also a city notorious for murders. There are over three hundred each year. In Dallas, there are four hundred seventy, but it has twice as much population. Most victims are blacks under thirty, blacks are nine times more at risk of attack and murder than others. I read about it in today's newspaper.

In the morning, a walk along the Mississippi Riverwalk. After lunch we go to the French Quarter. It's hot, muggy, humid. In *Pat O'Brien's* bar (founded 1791!) Norman orders a Guinness, and I order cappuccino. The supper is delicious, as usual in New Orleans: shrimps Creole style.

In the evening, there is a concert of the famous clarinettist Pete Fountain in our hotel. He has published many albums of his own, performed publicly in front of four presidents, and is still a great attraction of New Orleans. Norman likes him very much, and tells me Pete gained his popularity when he played with the *Junior Dixie Band* on Bourbon Street and soon became a member of *The Basin Street Six Band.* Lawrence Welk invited him for two weeks of performances, and he made Pete nation famous. They both performed in Carnegie Hall, playing among others Benny Goodman's *Chinatown.*

In the hotel, I call Tomek on the campus. He says he's climbing rocks, using ropes, etc. I'm anxious for him, but I hope that he'll get over it, that he only wants to give it a try, like with boxing and many other sports.

8th June, Dallas, Texas

Another wedding anniversary. In the morning I was brought an azalea bush with rose-colored flowers and a note *(Sweetheart—Thank you for the happiest years of my life—Norman)*. The weekend trip to New Orleans was our anniversary trip. We have supper in the *Olive Garden*, a nationwide chain.

10th June, Dallas, Texas

A package with Warsaw mail from Adam Ruciński, an issue of monthly *Twój Styl (Your Style.)* An interesting article about Teresa Pągowska, a painter. Her recipe for happiness: "A person should have daily a certain amount of laughter, many hours of solitude, and a friend next door."

Aleksander Solzhenitsyn announced that in May 1994 he would be returning to Russia after thirty years in exile. In 1975, he settled in Cavendish, Vermont, a town of less than fifteen hundred inhabitants, with his wife and three sons. In a sort of a farewell meeting, with two hundred people present, the writer thanked everyone for the peace he was given during his twenty year stay there. His son translated for him. The writer said he didn't imagine any better place or greater people: "You've forgiven me my exceptional lifestyle, and even felt it your responsibility to protect my right to privacy." His sons stay in Vermont.

13th June, Dallas, Texas

Lee returned yesterday after a few days spent with her family in Mississippi, and told me she won't be building a house and moving to her home town, after all. She prefers Dallas. "My sister has for years been telling me how awful her husband is, and now that she's divorced, she exhausts me with her talk of how she misses him...Others also talk to me about their tangled family relationships. I prefer my life here than spending long days only with them..."

Tomek called to say that his reportage with photos has been given a whole page. Norman writes poems to me on small slips of paper some two times a week and "hides" them somewhere, e.g. in the container with vitamins. I now have a large collection of the poems.

20th June, Dallas, Texas

Father's Day. Tomek sent Norman a card with a moving inscription:

> For the last three years, you were my great best friend. Many times I needed you, or only a helpful hand. Every time I could count on you for your understanding and advice. It never happened that you reacted indifferently. I will never forget, I will always remember. It was also time that I made mistakes, but you never made me feel ashamed or embarassed or to be rejected. For all these reasons and for many thousands of things...Thank you. Have a good Father's Day Thomas.

26th June, Tyler, Texas

I remember an exhibition I saw in Houston, of photographs by William Wegman, showing dogs that "resembled people." In *The Dallas Morning News* a few days ago, I read an article that described how a dog knows that another one is dead, and how it accepts that. And about research showing that older people, when they have a dog and take care of it, they become healthier. They start feeling needed, they offer and receive tenderness and attention. I like the following Native American story of the dog:

When God created man and animals, He put them all on the great prairie. He drew a line and put all people on one side, and the animals on another. The line grew thicker and broader. In the last moment, before the line grew so broad that is was impossible to cross, the dog jumped over it to stay on one side with the man.

10th July, Little Rock, Arkansas

Norman and I visit Liza and Michael Blair. They are Native Americans, Michael a Cherokee, and she a Sioux. They want to move to Pine Ridge, a reservation in South Dakota, to be with Indian people, to work for Native Americans. Ruth Ziolkowski, Korczak's—my great uncle's widow, advises me to go there, too, to write about the problems on reservations.

I'm reading Zbigniew Brzeziński's *Out of Control*. I am struck by his analysis of the significant role of the United States. Brzeziński believes that in a case of threat most countries will still seek support and security mainly in the United States, not in Western Europe. At the same time, he sees the crisis of values, loss of idealistic attitude and the atmosphere of unlimited tolerance. He sees the greatest threat to America in their loss of values, but he still believes that despite the materialism, Americans will continue to see their role in the world in Messianic terms. Brzeziński recalls the thoughts of John Paul II, believing that moral and spiritual values are more important than technological and economic achievements.

27th July, Dallas, Texas

I've been exchanging examples of pleasant moments in life with Lee. For instance: when a child falls asleep in your arms; when, as it grows, it laughs at your jokes; when you dive under a feather quilt on a cold evening; when you wake up rested before it's time to rise, and can have a nap yet; when you read a book or watch a film and hug the dog sitting next to you on the couch; when you sit on a bench in the park on a spring day and let sun warm your face; when you walk on the beach at daybreak or at dusk; when you drive and listen to songs from the 60's...Lee never crosses the borderline of privacy in our talks-confidences and I like that very much.

3rd August, Houston, Texas

We go to Houston with Tomek, it's less than four hours by car. The city has such a winding net of highways and streets that I believe you must have a secondary school diploma to be able to master it at once and not turn into one that leads you into a completely different part of the city or even out to Galveston. My driving in Poland and trips to Kraków seem like a picnic trip. Here, driving is a feat in itself.

5th August, Houston, Texas

In the morning, Tomek is at an architectural firm. I talk with Marylka Tittel that Americans admit so easily and willingly that they don't know something, haven't read something, etc. Poles, reportedly all Europeans, would never admit to not knowing something. They prefer to pretend they know and understand everything. Some professors from Europe are particularly irritated by that difference. I once read an article by a British professor who could not bear the fact that students asked questions openly, rather than e.g. surreptitiously supplement their knowledge in the library and be ashamed of their lack of knowledge. He broke off the contract and returned to Oxford.

9th August, Dallas, Texas

Tomek's birthday. Gifts. I recall with Tomek his other birthdays: the first, which I remember, on Franciszkańska Street (as tradition tells us, we put a tray with various items in front of the child for him to choose as a prediction of his future; he chose a pen), the fifth on Studencka Street, when Wańkowicz composed a rhyme for him; the tenth with his grandparents in Bukowina; the nineteenth in Florida (he planted a banana tree); the twentieth (which he spent alone) in Bordeaux, etc.

10th August, Dallas, Texas

Enormous heat. How did Americans manage before air-conditioning was invented?

31st August, Wilmington, Delaware

I've read the words of Mother Theresa, very beautiful: *It's not how much we give but how much love we put into giving.*

I like the Polish distinction: acquaintance, good acquaintance, friend. It's a hierarchy of promotion. Americans overuse the word 'friend' so much. But I also know Poles who do that (as I do sometimes). Talking of friendship is often projecting our dreams, an illusion.

1st September, Wilmington, Delaware

It's an important date in Poland.[5] I think that the war and concentration camp experiences of Eastern Europe enrich its inhabitants with a scale of emotions unavailable to Americans. Vietnam changed their view of themselves, but not completely. American "normality" somehow crashes against the near-pathology of humans. People coming from Europe are often "richer" in that. Not having such experiences, Americans have retained some primary innocence, which is not an asset of the spirit, but gives life energy instead, a faith in the sense of your actions.

10th September, Warsaw

No one was waiting in the early morning at the airport. Mr. Adam Ruciński, my good spirit in Poland, mistook the dates. I took a taxi—a very unpleasant experience. The driver looked at me for a long moment. "Where d'you live?" "In Warsaw." He kept on questioning where I had been and for how long. "A week in Copenhagen," I lied. He looked at my luggage. He didn't help carrying it, clearly displeased. I think he thought at first I was an "ignorant American," whom he could touch for more money.

The phone isn't working. The bank pays the bills each month, but often when I come, the phone isn't working. I go to the Rucińskis. They're surprised I'm here already. From them I call Mom and the phone repair office. Elżbieta offers coffee, etc., but I go back to tidy the apartment. They soon bring me the keys to my old *Polonez* auto. I change into jeans and methodically scrub the balcony, take out the white furniture, then wash the windows, the floors. I take off the sheets covering furniture and polish them. Finally I bathe. I am so tired, but slowly I calm down and can enjoy my stay. I am home, I have my books, my treasured china around me, everything is waiting for my return, and now, after those few hours of cleaning my apartment, I feel calm and I feel at home. Then I call my friends.

12th September, Warsaw-Łódź

I lay awake long into the night. Jet lag lasts about a week with me. Seven hours of difference betweenTexas and Poland makes me yawn at noon, and sleep best in the morning. I go to Łódź. At some point I stop on Puławska Street to let a car from the right join the traffic. A Volkswagen overtakes me at full speed, the driver opens the window and yells: "Learn to drive, you idiot!" *I'm home*, I think.

I like the greenery along the road and the fields. In two hours I'm at Mom's. Almost immediately on greeting each other, we go to the cemetery, to visit Father. I call Krzysio and his wife. The evening with Henio and his family is spent talking till late at night. Michał and Łukasz have grown. They have additional English classes. Michał has entrance exams for university studies next year. I remember how anxious I was when Tomek took his.

14th September, Łódź

In the morning I cried about some little thing. I seem so "weepy," what is the matter with me?

A visit with Bishop Jan Kulik. He tells me how the parish helps old people. Old age is an almost awkward issue in Poland. When you complete your life duties defined by social conventions, you can only "enjoy the life of others," meaning mainly your grandchildren. Your own happiness is fulfilled in others. I remember a town in Florida where old people live in comfortable homes, go to restaurants, go dancing, flirt with each other, remarry. The elderly people in my country have other paths defined for them. Phone calls are so dreadfully expensive that they are not even free to talk to their beloved grandchildren or friends when they wish. You make rare, short calls; it's outrageous and ludicrous.

In the afternoon, I take Mom to Warsaw. I stop near Rawa, I become sleepy, so I take a fifteen minute nap. Mom sits quietly beside me. In the evening a visit from Michał Radgowski. He's in good shape, energetic as always, brings a lot of stories and laughter. He helps me to start the record player.

21st September 1993, Warsaw

In the evening, I visited Andrzej and Dagmara Roman. We talk among others about the fact that in Poland there occurs a singular phenomenon of being bored with immigration. The attitude towards the London immigrants is indifferent. People are bored with their "ashes," heroes and government. Attitude towards American Poles is various: there is some jealousy and admiration, but also some boredom and nonchalance. A popular topic seems to be a "growing boorishness and brutal Americanization of Polish cultural life." I noticed this from interviews, not only with filmmaker Krzysztof Zanussi, but also painter Jerzy Duda-Gracz and others, done by *Przegląd Polski*. Journalist and author Ludwik Stomma wrote in *Polityka*—the topic picked up in New York's *Nowy Dziennik*—that many people say they are bored with journalist and politician Jan Nowak-Jeziorański, with him calling upon his fellow countrymen to give collective effort and tighten their belts in the name of capitalism or general harmony. I wonder how sometimes Poles go from great love to near-condescension. Nothing is worse than to be present and allow someone to mollify you. One of my acquantances told me that when he worked in the American embassy in Warsaw he learned the language quite well. Poles often treated him as "their man" and told and informed on others, demanded awards. "It would have been better not to speak Polish. The imposed language barrier would give me protection. I'd be unavailable and would gain in admiration and respect."

28th September, Warsaw

Meetings in the apartment on Kmicica Street. Some friends, when they come, say: "Here we are!" Others say: "Here you are, we can meet at last!"

So many times I want to say: I know, don't explain it, I've seen it...So many times I listen how others react to my words. And so often I want to comment: of course it's the same story. Truth is always an old story.

And one more thing. We talk of our lives, and try to make it in an easy, funny way. But if you allow someone to get in your life, it is not to make fun, is it?

1st October, Łódź

Dinner with Mom, supper with Krzysio and Ania. We have delicious mushrooms, collected by Krzysio early mornings on Saturdays and Sundays. Małgosia talks of the fish in the aquarium in her room. The leader is always the biggest fish, and it keeps order in the group. Małgosia would like to study zoology and work in a zoo, treating animals. I tell her of the zoo in San Diego. Pawełek is interested in wrestling.

"When will Uncle Norman learn Polish, so we can talk to him?," they ask.

"And when will you start learning English?" I ask. "Michał and Łukasz can already talk to Norman."

"Soon, when our German is better, so that we don't mix them up," they reply seriously.

Norman says that the children of Krzysio and Henio are well-mannered and easily likeable. They make a much better impression than many American children who are insolent, unruly and disobedient...spoiled.

2nd October, Łódź

We go to Father's grave, all three of us. Mom washes the tombstone with water from a bucket, then wipes it dry with the cloths she's brought, because she says it's time, and she does it regularly. Doesn't let us help. Norman is amazed that the cemetery is full of people, widows with watering cans, who greet each other and stop to talk.

"Maybe those women care for their husbands now more than when they lived?" he attempts a joke.

When we visited the grave of Krysia Radgowska in Bródno last year, on return he told his friends that cemeteries in Poland were like parks and that people liked to walk there. He was particularly delighted with the flying partridges. Seeing Mom bustling about, washing the grave and refusing help, he tells me later: "It's like it's her grave, her caring for her husband."

He finally understands why we put a carved marker on Father's grave. In America, no one erects tombstones, they just place small headstones or flat plaques on the ground. In winter, when it snows, it's impossible to find the right one. A tradition in Poland is to place a stone (often marble) be it modest or particularly decorative. Tomek's design of my father's grave marker is very beautiful, and Henio took care of having it made properly. I try to tell Norman of how we celebrate the 1st of November, All Saints' Day, a holiday when everyone visits the graves of their relatives, and families meet.

"It's almost like Thanksgiving," he says, surprising me with the comment. "But in America you don't visit the graves of your relatives."

Delicious dinner with Henio and Marysia. We celebrate Michał's name's day. In the evening we are invited by Father Bishop Kulik for tomorrow's ceremony in the cathedral, commerating his anniversary.

19th October, Dallas, Texas

Today Tomek took the flight to Cairo.

I sleep badly...faces...faces of my friends in Poland, faces of people who are part of my life, those who were important, good, unpleasant, cruel even...

21st November, Dallas, Texas

I baked the turkey, the cranberry sauce I've already bought. Thanksgiving will be in a few days. Families gather to have dinner together, starting with a prayer of thanks. I have my own prayer, too. ...Thank you, Lord, for life, for health, for your blessings, for Tomek, my parents, family, Norman, family home, for people who loved me, people who liked me, who helped me, who didn't hurt me, for lack of wars and disasters around me, for the animals around me, for nature, for the sun, forest, oceans, places I've seen, places I've lived, where I felt good, where I could focus, for good thoughts, for not nurturing resentment, for not having bitterness overtake me, for forgetting pain, for not dwelling on the bad, for the chance to love, for all moments and all days...Count your blessing—one by one.

30th November, Dallas, Texas

I'm reading Miłosz's *Rok Myśliwego (A Year of the Hunter)* again. I seem to find new things in it from each reading. He writes that if someone sets himself a goal in life and takes it seriously, he should apply a rule of strict hierarchy, which consists in rejecting everything that is below the highest requirements and standards set for himself. Miłosz writes that such a hierarchy implies a certain inhumanity, because you have to reject the whole sphere of what we call noble sentiments, social rebellion, patriotism etc. The rejections are difficult, because we live among people and are under their power, sharing their emotions, desires and anxieties with them. Thus an enormous pressure of the community. "You have one life, do something with it," writes the Nobel laureate.

Tomek calls from Cairo in the evening.

23rd December

We're flying to Philadelphia. We'd like to spend Christmas at home in Delaware. Norman has days off between Christmas and New Year. Many companies give such time off to their employees. When Christmas Eve came in Poland, life on the streets died and disappeared, streets were empty, stores were closed. Christmas trees glistened with lights in the houses windows. The streets were usually cold and dark, but warmth emanated from the homes. In the States, many weeks before, preparations for Christmas start, stores are decorated, Christmas carols and winter songs are heard, bells ring, often a Salvation Army Santa stands before the store in that weeks-long shopping splurge, his duty soliciting donations. But right after the Christmas day, everything ends! In Poland, everything starts at that time. The tree is decorated right before Christmas, lights are lighted only on Christmas Eve, and then celebration includes the following days.

30th December, Wilmington, Delaware

Like each year, I make a list of the things that happened to me this year. It's always long and detailed, with major and minor things. And separately a list for the next year, things I will pray for. I like that ritual of the end of one and beginning of another year that I've been practicing for so long. I hang calendars on the walls: in the kitchen, over my desk, over Norman's, over Tomek's. I remember Mother's calendars. She hangs them in the kitchen, over the fridge. Traditionally she hangs one with each week given on a separate page. She divides the year into weeks and plans her work. The difference between calendars in Poland and here is that in Polish calendars, Sundays and holidays are marked in color. Here, all days are black like the others. Those calendars without holidays look sad to me. I tell Norman of it, and he says he remembers that once holidays used to be marked differently. And that he doesn't understand when and why this was abandoned...I also miss the noted name's days from Polish calendars. Each year, I carefully note down the few names of people close to me, but I have no contacts with others, so I can't say, for instance, that the child of my friends was born on some patron saint's day.

1st January, Wilmington, Delaware

In the morning I cry some for Tomek, Norman explains, logical and clear. I make New Year's dinner. According to some traditions, one should have pork "for luck." I go through my clipping I brought from Poland. I find an article by Ania Brzozowska published in *Kobieta i Życie* (*Woman and Life*), where she quotes my list of gratefulness, following the example of Marcus Aurelius:

To Mom—for the spirit of piety and a certain charitableness; to Father— for the love of books and knowing the value of human integrity; to my brothers—for the sense of security, because I can always count on them; to my son—for making me develop my own tenderness and sense of responsibility; to Wańkowicz—for interest in the world and a sense of the significance of work; Kąkolewski wrote a dedication for me: "It's not important where you live, but how you live"; to Professor Tatarkiewicz—for the admiration of order; to Michał and Krystyna Radgowski—for a sensible confidence in action; to Janusz Dukszta—for the elegant world on the other side of the ocean; to Ryszard Kapuściński—for diplomatic skills of gathering many friends around me...etc.

I could expand that list after the years that have passed since I talked to Ania. That's a good sign.

10th January, Dallas, Texas

A letter from Szymon Kobyliński, among others. He persuades me to "develop egocentrism," saying that it helps in writing. His drawing: a bear with a pulled-up, seemingly hurt paw, wrapped in the American flag, with a cunning look. The drawing was printed by *Nowy Dziennik*, we made copies and sent it to many people. You don't have to know Polish. It evokes much reaction everywhere.

Another letter from Mariusz Marasek, Dad's young friend, active in politics. He was a Member of Parliament in the Polish Sejm of the 1st term, and Vice-President of the Sejm Defense Committee. He shocked me with the news about *ordynat*[6] Jan Zamoyski, whom Father valued so highly. He writes that death spared Father a great disappointment.

The system of moral judgment in our culture is more severe than the system for intellectual assessment. It resembles the rules of chess, where the worst moments decide, one bad move erases all achievements. Intellectual achievements are defined by the best moments, not by errors. When we form an opinion on the achievements of a scholar or a writer, we take into account mainly their most outstanding works. But when forming opinions of a person's character, we take into consideration not their noble actions, but the foul acts. The bad obscures the good.

20th February 1994, Acapulco, Mexico

Such a view of water, a whole windowful, like I had in Bournemouth, England, in Rio de Janeiro, in Honolulu...We go for lunch at the Princess Hotel, around us flowers bloom. We go to the Old Town. A Mexican in a restaurant says we are *gringos*, and I reply I am from Poland. "Polonia?" he ponders. "Oh!...Papa! Europa!"

I wonder how it is that when I'm home, I force myself to drink three cups of water. When I'm on vacation and a bottle of water costs a dollar and a half, I'm like a sponge.

We spend some time with Canadians from Burlington, Ontario. They are of French origin, and complain a lot about Canada's "socialism," how it tempts people to try various frauds.

They tell us two jokes:

"Who would like to live to be 95?"

"Someone who is 94."

And the other:

"Who dislikes jokes about 82-year-olds?"

"Those who are 81."

A small band plays during supper. Such beautiful songs: *Guadalajara, La Paloma, El Rancho Grande, CuCuRu Cuck'oo, La Cucaracha...*

16th March, Dallas, Texas

Out for lunch with Norman, as usual once a week. I'm reading a book by Stanley Marcus (brother of Neiman, owner of one of the most elegant and expensive shops of Texas), *Quest for the Best*. The author analyzes things of the highest quality that can be bought: the best fabrics, delicacies, beers, shoes, watches, hotels, etc. He writes among others about the world's most delicate and most expensive wool. I have always believed that cashmere is best, but now I learn that it's Indian *shals. Shahtoosh* (literally: king's clothing) is for the women in India, what a mink fur is for us. The fabric comes from the hair on the necks of Alpine ibexes in Kashmir. In spring, the animals climb trees to eat their leaves, and leave some of their hair on the short trees. The locals collect that wool and hand-weave it. A meter of the fabric costs fifteen hundred dollars in the States.

I'm reading the correspondence of Flaubert and George Sand (*Knopf 1933, translated from French into English by Barbara Bray*). I remember a comment by Flaubert's mother: "Your mania for appraising sentences has dried your heart out." Flaubert believed that statement to be exceptionally refined, and I am pondering on it for a long time.

5th April, Dallas, Texas

I received a copy of *Polityka (No. 12, 1994)* from Poland, with Tomek's text about studying in America. It starts: "I have been highly disconcerted when during one of the first lectures a colleague patted a sixty-year-old professor on the back and asked: «How are you, Earl?» The elderly man replied: «I'm fine. Have you had an opportunity to work on your assignment, Ken?» Over the next two months I was gradually changing my notion of the relations between students and teaching staff...(...)"

15th April, Dallas, Texas

Yesterday at 11.30 p.m. (in Poland 6.30a.m.) I called Mom. My birthday. She was moved and so sweet. After Norman and Tomek left, I found a hidden packet, inside a small card *For Mom*. And sunglasses from Gucci. When Tomek returned from work and I thanked him, he said: "I have something else for you." He took a new box from his pocket: "For Mom, with thanks." Inside a box with a Waterman—a French gilded fountain pen of a brown marbled pattern. He also gave me decorative notepaper with matching envelopes. My child showered me with presents and gave me beautiful wishes. From Norman, I received a small Calvin Klein handbag. We all went for dinner to Pappadeaux. Tomek told me of his stay in Egypt. About recognizing a disabled girl selling flowers from a photo in National Geographic. He bought all her flowers for ten dollars and gave to his friend from South Africa. A nice gesture. He said nothing more...

24th April

I return to Dallas with Tomek's epée. They let me through at the airport, people accosted me with nice comments. "You must lend it to me some time," I told Tomek on return. "Everyone took interest in me."

29th April, Dallas, Texas

Lunch with Lee Wilson. She told me about calling to London to the exclusive Harrods store to order a new portion of her favourite tea, and how they couldn't understand her Southern accent. When the order came, Drew, her husband, was surprised on seeing the price: a hundred dollars. He challenged the cost, deciding it was based on the tea being sent in elegant packaging and in beautiful tin boxes. It was heavier and cost more. Lee is very irritated with that and decides to buy tea in Dallas. "It was such an unpleasant experience," she says, "that I don't want that London tea anymore..."

Women like her live in large houses, always smile and are ladylike. Lee used to live in a large house (she took me there), but once her children became independent, she sold the house and lives in an elegant apartment. But she's not sure yet if she will remain there. She started to value the sense of safety provided by your own house with full security. Lee is feminine, educated, and doesn't resemble the "emancipated women," of whom so much is being written and discussed.

I remember that it was Grace from Toronto who made me realize the issue of women in the American continent. I always heard that American women (and Canadian as well) were emancipated and knew what they wanted.

We were returning from Parry Sound, with Piotr, Grace's son, at the wheel. Grace's mother was also there, Piotruś's[7] fiancée, Lauri and me.

Piotruś asked if we wanted some ice cream. We all gladly agreed. Lauri said no, she preferred chips. Piotruś stopped the car and brought a portion of ice cream for everyone, for her as well.

"I didn't want ice cream, I wanted chips."

"They had no chips..."

"But I don't want ice cream."

Piotruś ate the remaining ice cream himself. He took a turn from the highway into some side road and stopped at various places, asking for chips in the shops. Oddly enough, none were to be found anywhere. The situation started to annoy me.

"We are all wasting time because he's looking for chips...She should say that it's all right and wait to return to Toronto, Piotruś will buy her some when there is just the two of them," I said to Grace in Polish, knowing Lauri didn't speak it.

"We, Poles, give up quickly. American women, if they want something, they want it," said Grace.

Later I told Norman of the whole situation, and he disagreed with her.

"It depends on the American," he said, "if we're talking about the spoiled ones, or the normal, pleasant women. A nice woman wouldn't drag a group of people along, including an eighty-year-old grandmother, in search of a pack of chips..."

A women's magazine *New Women* published statements of European men on how they saw American women. The following comments I remembered:

"I like their lack of anxiety, their confidence."

"American women have high expectations. For instance, that a man will give them happiness. In other cultures, particularly oriental ones, it's a woman's role to give happiness to the man. I'd prefer everyone to take care of their own happiness, a woman of hers, and a man of his."

"American women judge men all the time, and the relationship with them. If he is a good lover, if he earns enough."

Here's a joke I heard. What is the difference between heaven and hell? Heaven: American salary, Chinese cook and Japanese wife. Hell: Chinese salary, Japanese cook and American wife.

30th April, Dallas, Texas

I talked to my architect friend, Marek Jaroszewicz: "When you go to Beijing, you see slant-eyed, differently dressed people. You assume that they have a different culture, customs, habits. When you come to America, you see people looking "like us," wearing similar clothes, and you assume they are similar. However, the difference is as big as between Europe and China, or between America and China. And few people who come to America realize that. They all try to find similarities and keep on making comparisons, but that's a wrong approach. Americans are as different as Chinese in comparison to Europeans, they are completely different people.

What great feat it is to be able to value your present, without great concerns about the future or dwelling upon the past.

18th May, Dallas, Texas

We have tea, Lee and I, and discuss an odd topic: can you burn all your bridges?

When I was very young, I thought that my past didn't matter. I thought that all the things I hadn't done, or words said in anger, would remain unnoticed. I believed myself to be a good person who could forget, who made mistakes, but who wasn't bad and didn't hurt anyone. I was mainly busy with my own matters. I thought that time flowed and covered all things forever, so they lost their significance, stopped existing. What counted was the present and the nearest future. I behaved as I wished, paying no attention to what others would think or say. It was my life and I was important. Life was not the highest value, it was rather a vehicle that carried me.

I laughed or shrugged my shoulders on hearing Father say that it all made up my life, influenced it, created it. I thought life was still before me, still to come, and nothing was entered into the books forever. I was young, I had a long life ahead of me, and for some indefinite time I believed I could make mistakes and endlessly examine new possibilities.

One day I woke up and realised I had forty years behind me. I now look at myself and know that I am not a young girl anymore; I am no longer a young woman, despite all efforts to care for myself. Now that I am a middle aged woman, I look back with no regrets. Our real age is important, despite our great stories of an eternally young disposition or eternally young appearance.

I could easily comment on my life and its events: "Well, everything I've done, all exciting events were worth it, because I've had an interesting life..."

Yes and no. I have lost much in my past. Each decision of today is conditioned by the past. Our future is a result of our past. There are no sudden changes, we don't wake up in the morning as a different, new person who will learn to talk or act differently. Everyone knows us as we are: how we act, how we behave, how we treat others. They don't see us as we think we are, or as we wish to be.

I have an adult son and wouldn't want him to do any stupid things in his life. I'd like to tell him: "This will have impact on your life..." Everything we do and say, remains in the memory of the people we've met.

The history of our lives. This is what our children, new acquaintances, new friends ask us about. You cannot change it.

Endnotes
(by Agnieszka Maria Gernand)

1. FAMILY

1. Obóz Wielkiej Polski, founded 4th December 1926 and headed by Roman Dmowski, was a far-right nationalist political organization aiming to unite Polish right-wing organizations and oppose Józef Piłsudski's Sanacja regime.

2. Stronnictwo Narodowe, a Polish political party formed in 1928, gathered together most of the political forces of Poland's right-wing political camp and was one of the main opponents of the Sanacja regime.

3. Roman Dmowski (1864–1939) was a Polish politician and statesman. He saw the successful and aggressive Germanization of Polish territories by the German Empire as the major threat to Poland and therefore advocated a degree of accommodation with Poland's other partitioning power, Russia. He was one of the principal figures who were instrumental in the postwar restoration of Poland's independence.

4. A follower of Józef Piłsudski, leader of the interwar Second Polish Republic.

5. Wielkie Księstwo Poznańskie (1815–1848)—part of the Kingdom of Prussia, created from territories annexed by Prussia after the Partitions of Poland.

6. Przekrój (Cross Section) (1945–now)—a social and cultural weekly.

7. The Katyn massacre, also known as the Katyn Forest massacre was a mass execution of Polish officers and intelligentsia carried out by the NKVD, the Soviet secret police, in April and May 1940, in the Katyn Forest in Russia, the Kalinin and Kharkiv prisons and elsewhere. The number of victims is estimated at about 22,000. The mass graves in the Katyn Forest were discovered by the Germans in 1943. In November 2010, the Russian Parliament (*Duma*) approved a declaration blaming Stalin and other Soviet officials for having personally ordered the massacre, but it still refuses to classify this action as a war crime or an act of genocide. About 1/3 of surviving Russian documents concerning the massacre have never been declassified.

8. Melchior Wańkowicz (1892–1974) was a Polish writer and journalist. More details can be found in the author's other books, most recently *Melchior Wańkowicz: Poland's Master of the Written Word*.

9. The Prussian Homage or Tribute was the formal investment of the duke of the Polish fief of Ducal Prussia. On April 10, 1525, in Kraków, the then Polish capital, Albert of Prussia resigned his position as Grand Master of the Teutonic Knights to receive the title "Duke of Prussia" from the King of Poland. The scene was depicted by a famous Polish painter, Jan Matejko.

10. Tadeusz Reytan (or: Rejtan) (1742–1780) was a Polish nobleman, and member of the Polish Sejm. Reytan is remembered for a dramatic gesture he made in September 1773, as a deputy of the Partition Sejm, trying to prevent the legalization of the first partition of Poland, a scene that has been immortalized as a symbol of patriotism in a famous painting by Jan Matejko and other art works. Despite his efforts, the partition of Poland was legalized soon afterwards.

11. The Polish–Soviet War (February 1919–March 1921) was an armed conflict between Soviet Russia and Soviet Ukraine on one side, and the Second Polish Republic and the Ukrainian People's Republic on the other, over much of today's Ukraine and—at times—Poland's independence. Lenin saw Poland as the bridge the Red Army had to cross to assist other communist movements and bring about other European revolutions.

12. Henryk Sienkiewicz (1846–1916) was one of the most popular Polish writers of the turn of the 19th and 20th centuries, and Nobel Prize-winning novelist; Andrzej Kmicic and Aleksandra (called Oleńka) Billewicz were the main protagonists of his book *The Deluge (Potop)*.

13. Here and further in the letters, all names are used in diminutive forms of endearment.

14. One of the oldest fashion houses in Poland, opened 1958 and still running.

15. Orig. *podpiwek*, a drink made of fermented years and malt, quite like beer, but with very small alcohol content (1–2%). It is quite popular in many Slavic countries.

16. Renowned Polish classical music journalist.

17. The State Folk Group of Song and Dance *Mazowsze* and the Polish National Song and Dance Ensemble *Śląsk*, Poland's largest, best known and most prestigious folk song and dance ensembles.

18. Popular Polish patriotic songs. The titles often come from the first lines of the lyrics.

19. Radio Free Europe is a broadcaster founded by the U.S.Congress that provides "news, information, and analysis" to countries in Eastern Europe, Central Asia, and the Middle East" where the free flow of information is either banned by government authorities or not fully developed" [see: Wikipedia].

20. Actually: Feliks Konarski (1907–1991), a Polish poet, songwriter, and cabaret performer.

2. CHURCH

1. Traditionally, Corpus Christi processions in Poland include small girls dressed in folk costumes or in white who scatter flower petals on the streets before the priest carrying the monstrance with the Eucharyst.

2. Currently: John Paul II Catholic University of Lublin (KUL).

3. A Host-like kind of wafer traditionally shared by Poles on Christmas Eve.

4. Pasterka, the traditional midnight Mass on Christmas Eve.

5. Franciszek Karpiński (1741–1825) was the leading sentimental Polish poet of the Age of Enlightenment. One of his most famous works is the Christmas hymn *Bóg się rodzi, moc truchleje (God is Born, Power Trembles)*, considered one of the most beautiful Polish carols

6. Also available in English as *Infant holy, Infant lowly*, in a translation by Edith M.G.Reed.

7. As is often said in Polish carols, particularly folk ones.

8. Duke Mieszko I (ca. 940–992) was the first historical ruler of Poland. On marrying the Czech princess Dobrawa (or: Dąbrówka), he was baptised in 966, the baptism meaning conversion of the nation to Christianity and symbolically marking the beginning of the Polish state.

9. One of the hymns within the Lenten Lamentations (literary: bitter sorrow)—*Gorzkie Żale*—is a Catholic devotion containing many hymns that developed out of Poland in the 18th century.

10. Traditionally, on *Good Saturday* Polish Catholics visit symbolic graves of Christ in churches, with the Host placed over the grave, and guards (usually members of uniformed services) standing honorary watch.

11. *Śmigus-Dyngus* (or: *Wet Monday*) is the name for Easter Monday in Poland. Once, country boys would pour water on girls on that day, and strike them about the legs with long thin twigs or switches (signifying fertility, and indirectly, attractiveness of a girl). The custom remains in most rural and urban areas in a modified form, with everyone sprinkling everyone with water.

12. The Constitution of May 3, 1791, the second oldest codified national constitution after the U.S. Constitution, and the oldest in Europe. The document remained in force for only 18 months and 3 weeks, due to hostile political and military responses from Poland's powerful neighbors. By 1795, the Second and the Third Partitions of Poland ended the existence of the sovereign Polish state for over a century.

13. The Partitions of Poland (or more precisely Partitions of the Polish–Lithuanian Commonwealth) were a series of three partitions (1772, 1793, 1795) by the Russian Empire, the Kingdom of Prussia and Habsburg Austria that ultimately ended the existence of the Polish–Lithuanian Commonwealth. Poland remained politically non-existent, and under rule of the three partitioning states, for 123 years (until 1918).

14. Based on translation by Robert Strybel, Polish Art Center.

15. Hanka Ordonówna (1902–1950)—born Maria Anna Pietruszyńska, married name (countess) Tyszkiewicz –also known as *Ordonka*, was a famous Polish singer, song writer, dancer and actress.

16. Girls would float flower wreaths—symbols of their virginity—on rivers to tell how soon/whether they would find a husband. Young men might try and capture the flowing wreaths, if interested in a girl.

17. On 1st September 1939, Nazi Germany attacked Poland. On 17th September 1939, Poland was attacked from the East by Soviet Russia.

3. GARDEN

1. In 1944, the Communist authorities officially removed the crown from Poland's coat of arms. It was re-established only after the fall of Communism in 1989. Thus, in times of the Polish People's Republic, a crowned eagle was an illegal, "reactionary" version of the coat of arms.

2. Polish for "cinema."

5. SCHOOL

1. Stanisław Moniuszko (1819–1872)—a Polish composer, conductor and teacher, "father of Polish national opera".

2. Bolesław Prus (1847–1912), born Aleksander Głowacki, was a Polish journalist and writer of novels and short stories (among them *Anielka*).

3. Popular tourist destinations. Zakopane—a town in the Tatra mountains. *Morskie Oko* (literally: *Eye of the Sea*)—the largest and fourth deepest lake in the Tatra Mountains. Gubałówka—a mountain above Zakopane. *Kasprowy Wierch* (in Polish) or *Kasprov Vrch* (in Slovak)—a mountain in the Western Tatras.

4. Jan Brzechwa, born Jan Wiktor Lesman (1898–1966) was a Polish poet and author, known mostly for his contribution to children's literature. Maria Konopnicka née Wasiłowska (1842–1910) was a Polish poet, novelist, writer for children and youth, a translator, journalist and critic, as well as an activist for women's rights and Polish independence. She was one of the most important Polish positivist poets.

5. In Slavic folklore, *Baba Yaga* is a well-known witch-like figure, usually—though not always—portayed as a villain.

6. Kornel Makuszyński (1884–1953) was a Polish writer of children's and youth literature, known for his distinctive humorous and rich language.

7. By Wiktor Teofil Gomulicki (1848–1919), a Polish poet, novelist and essayist.

8. Actually: *Ze wspomnień samowara* (*From the Recollection of Samowar*) by Benedykt Hertz (1872-1952), Polish writer, satyrist and journalist.

9. Winnetou and Old Surehand are the main protagonists of a series of adventure novels set in the American Old West written by Karl May (1842–1912), a popular German writer.

10. Protagonists of *The Trilogy*: *Ogniem i Mieczem* (*With Fire and Sword*)—Jan Skrzetuski; *Potop* (*The Deluge*)—Andrzej Kmicic, and *Pan Wołodyjowski* (*Sir Michael*)—Michał Wołodyjowski.

11. H. Sienkiewicz, *The Teutonic Knights*, New York: Hippocrene Books 2000, p. 10. Translated by Bernard W.A. Massey, edited and revised by Mirosław Lipiński.

12. In 1960s, Aleksander Ford made a film based on Sienkiewicz's *The Teutonic Knights.*

13. A young knight, the main protagonist of the novel and the film.

14. Maria Rodziewiczówna (1863–1944) was a Polish writer, among the most famous of the interwar years.

15. A novel by Kornel Makuszyński, considered one of classic Polish novels for young adults. The "Satan" from the title refers to the main protagonist, a "devilishly clever" high-school pupil.

16. *Ekran (Screen)*—Polish weekly concerning flm and television. *Film*—Polish biweekly, later monthly, devoted to the cinema.

17. Weeklies (*Tygodnik Powszechny*—*Common Weekly, Polityka*—*Politics,Forum, Panorama Północy*—*Panorama of the North, Panorama Śląska*—*Silesian Panorama,WTK*—*Wrocław Catholic Weekly*) and monthlies *Mówią wieki*—*Centuries Speak, Poznaj świat*—*Know the World, Panorama Polska*—*Polish Panorama*) concerning social, geographical or historical issues.

18. *Śluby panieńskie, czyli Magnetyzm serca* and *Zemsta*—comedies by Aleksander Fredro (1793–1876), a Polish poet, playwright and author. *Dziady*—a poetic drama by the Polish poet and dramatist Adam Mickiewicz (1798–1855). It is considered one of the great works of European Romanticism. *Dom otwarty*—a comedy by Michał Bałucki (1837–1901), a Polish playwright and poet. All plays belong to the canon of Polish literature.

19. Aleksander Kamiński (1903–1978) was a Polish writer, historian, author of *Polish Cub Scout* and *Brownie* method, and wartime resistance leader. *Kamienie na szaniec* (lit. *Stones for the Rampart*, also translated as *Stones on the Barricade*) describes the small acts of sabotage carried out by the Polish underground scout movement, the *Grey Ranks*, of whom Kamiński was one of the instructors and leaders. After the war the book entered the canon of Polish literature and remains recommended reading for Polish students in High school.

20. Protagonists of *Kamienie na Szaniec*, while also real *Gray Ranks* members. *Zośka* and *Alek* were the original pseudonyms. *Szare Szeregi* was a codename for the underground para-military Polish Scouting Association active during World War II.

21. Polish-Soviet war (1919–1921).

22. A series of books on civilisation: *Rodowody Cywilizacji (Civilisation origins)*, issued since 1958 by *Państwowy Instytut Wydawniczy (PIW)*.

23. Paweł Jasienica was the pen name of Leon Lech Beynar (1909–1970), a Polish historian, journalist and soldier. He is best known for his 1960s (and still popular) books on Polish history before World War I.

24. Zbigniew Herbert (1924–1998)—Polish poet,essayist,playwright and moralist, member of the Polish resistance movement during WII.

25. Czesław Miłosz (1911–2004) –Polish poet, writer, translator and diplomat of Lithuanian origin, US citizen since 1970. In 1978 he was awarded the Neustadt International Prize for Literature, and in 1980 the Nobel Prize in Literature.

26. Some of the best known authors in the canon of Polish literature: Władysław Reymont (1867–1925). In 1924 he was awarded the Nobel Prize for Literature); Stefan Żeromski (1864–1925); Bolesław Prus (born Aleksander Głowacki, 1847–1912); Eliza Orzeszkowa (1841–1910).

27. Tadeusz Boy-Żeleński (1874–1941)—Polish stage writer, poet, critic, and translator of over 100 French literary classics into Polish, issued 1915–1935 under the collective name *Biblioteka Boya (Boy's Library)*.

28. Ignacy Chrzanowski (1866–1940)—Polish historian of literature.

29. The Polish 1968 political crisis—major student and intellectual protest action against the government of the People's Republic of Poland. It was followed by a wave of repressions.

30. Communist police forces.

31. Czerwone Gitary—one of the most popular rock bands in the history of Polish popular music, sometimes called the "Polish Beatles." The song *Matura* (literally: school-leaving exam) remains for many years now one of their most popular hits.

32. Czesław Niemen (1939–2004), born Czesław Wydrzycki, was one of the most original Polish singer-songwriters and rock balladeers of the last quarter-century.

6. UNIVERSITY—MARRIAGE—
BIRTH OF THOMAS

1. Symbol of maidenhood.

2. Władysław Stanisław Reymont (1867– 1925)—Polish novelist and the 1924 laureate of the Nobel Prize in Literature, whose best known work is the four-part novel *Chłopi (The Peasants)*. (The four parts are for the four seasons in the life of the peasants—*Autumn, Winter, Spring,* and *Summer.*) The novel gives a complete, suggestive and authentic picture of country life. The action is set in a real village of Lipce.

3. In June 1976, a series of protests and demonstrations took place in Poland, after Prime Minister Piotr Jaroszewicz revealed the plan for a sudden increase in the prices of many basic goods, particularly food. The largest violent demonstrations and looting took place in Płock, Warsaw, and particularly Radom. In the Ursus factory there was a workers' strike.

4. *Komitet Obrony Robotników*—the first major anti-communist civic group (and a successful one) in Eastern Europe and in Poland aiming to give aid to prisoners and their families after the protests in 1976 and government crackdown.

7. MELCHIOR WAŃKOWICZ

1. I wrote about it in my book *Melchior Wańkowicz Poland's Master of the written Word,* Lexington Books, 2013.

2. 1799-1842, a painter, family to Melchior Wańkowicz, and friend to the great poet Adam Mickiewicz.

3. *Mickiewicz on the Rock of Judah.*

4. Famous Polish confectionery company, founded 1851.

5. *Państwowy Instytut Wydawniczy—State Publishing Institute,* a Polish publishing house founded in Warsaw in 1946. PIW specializes in literature, history, philosophy and social sciences.

6. When Prof. Julian Krzyzanowski died, the eminent specialist in literature Prof. Janina Kulczycka-Saloni became the guidance counselor of my thesis.

7. *Nowe Książki (New Books)*—widely available journal of new publications in Polish, published by the National Library of Poland.

8. Warmia, Masuria and Powiśle plebiscite (1920)—a plebiscite for self-determination of the regions *Warmia, Masuria and Powiśle,* which had been in parts of East Prussia and West Prussia, conducted by German authorities. According to several Polish sources, the German side engaged in mass persecution of Polish activists, their Masurian supporters, going as far as manhunts and murder to influence the vote.

9. *Instytut Badań Spraw Narodowościowych* (1921–1939)— association for researching the situation of national minorities in interwar Poland.

10. *Polski Związek Zachodni* (originally *Związek Obrony Kresów Zachodnich—Association for Defending the Western Border Areas*)—Polish patriotic organisation established in 1921. It was engaged in cooperation with authorities within Polish-German issues, defence of Polish national rights, fight against separatism in Western border areas of Poland, as well as cultural events, education and economy.

11. *Rój or: Roy*—a publishing company of which Wańkowicz was co-owner, started in the 1920s.

12. Szymon Kobyliński (1927–2002)—Polish graphic artist, caricaturist, satirist, historian, stage and film set designer, one of precursors of Polish comics.

13. Wańkowicz worked for a time in the advertising business, coining a highly popular slogan for the advertisement of sugar—*cukier krzepi (sugar strengthens)*.

14. *Szpilki (Pins)* (1935–1994; suspended during 1939–1945)—illustrated leftist satirical paper. It ridiculed first Piłsudski's Sanation movement, and after WWII opponents of the Communist system.

15. *Zeszyty Prasoznawcze*—a quarterly of the Press Studies Centre of the Jagiellonian University, the oldest Polish journal concerned with mass media and public communication and their various aspects.

16. *Polish Society of Authors and Composers (Związek Autorów i Kompozytorów Scenicznych, ZAIKS)*—Polish organization representing artists and composers.

17. Formerly territory of the eastern provinces of Poland, today in western Ukraine, western Belarus, eastern Lithuania, with such major cities as Lviv, or Vilnius. The territory was included within the *Polish Lithuanian Commonwealth* and *Second Polish Republic* until World War II.

18. Currently in the Minsk Province of Belarus.

19. Major Henryk Dobrzański (1897–1940)—Polish soldier, sportsman and partisan, the first guerrilla commander of WWII in Europe. The pseudonym *Hubal* came from his family coat of arms.

20. *Łazienki Park (Royal Baths Park)*—the largest park in Warsaw (76 hectares), designed in the 17th century in the baroque style, owned by the last King of Poland, Stanisław August Poniatowski. It takes its name from a bathing pavilion that was located there.

21. Pl. *Uniwersytet Latający* (1885–1905, revived between 1977 and 1981)—underground educational enterprise that operated in the People's Republic of Poland to counteract the Party's control and censorship of education. Participants of that second flying university encountered much abuse and harassment from the authorities.

8. HOUSE ON STUDENCKA STREET

1. Translations by Katarzyna Ciechanowicz-Gajewska.

2. *Główny Urząd Kontroli Prasy, Publikacji i Widowisk (Main Office for Control of the Press, Publications, and Public Performances)*—Polish state censorship body functioning in 1946-1990.

3. Mr/Ms used with the first name is a usual half-formal address formula in Polish.

4. Jan Kiepura (1902–1966)—acclaimed Polish singer and actor of international fame (contracts with Convert Garden in London, Opéra Comique in Paris, National Opera in Berlin; his film career included work in Germany and in Hollywood). On October 31, 1936, Kiepura married the Hungarian-born lyric soprano Marta Eggerth. The two often sang together in operettas, in concerts, on records, and in films until his death.

5. Marta Eggerth (1912–2013)—Hungarian singer and actress from the *Silver Age of Operetta*. Many famous operetta composers (e.g. F. Lehár, O. Strauss, P. Abraham) composed works especially for her. She also made more than 40 films in five languages: Hungarian, English, German, French and Italian. She and Jan Kiepura were known as Europe's *Liebespaar (Love Pair)*, much beloved by the public.

6. It was likely because the book describes 17th-century Polish-Ukrainian conflict.

7. A neoclassical palace in Warsaw, seat of the Polish Academy of Sciences.

8. Actually: Szanse powstania listopadowego. *Rozważania historyczne (The Chances of the November Uprising. Historical Reflection)*; November Uprising (1830–31)—armed rebellion in partitioned Poland against the Russian Empire.

9. Jerzy Popiełuszko (1947–1984)—Roman Catholic priest from Poland, associated with the Solidarity movement. In his sermons (often broadcast by *Radio Free Europe*) he openly criticized the system and motivated people to protest. He was murdered by agents of the Polish communist Security Service, which caused an uproar throughout Poland. He was beatified in 2010.

9. THE WRITER'S ILLNESS

1. Full name: *Płomyk. Tygodnik ilustrowany dla dzieci i młodzieży (Flame. Illustrated Weekly for children and teenagers)* (1917–1991)—Polish children and teen magazine.

2. The Battle of Westerplatte was the first clash between Polish and German forces during World War II (and the first battle of the war in Europe). Repeated attacks by 3500 German soldiers were repelled by 180 Polish soldiers for seven days, stalling further German attacks along the coast.

10. BURIAL OF WAŃKOWICZ

1. *Główny Urząd Kontroli Prasy, Publikacji i Widowisk (Main Office for Control of the Press, Publications, and Public Performances)*.

2. Polish lands incorporated in the USSR after 1944.

3. *The Ossolineum* or the *National Ossoliński Institute*—non-profit foundation located in Wrocław, Poland, founded in 1817, the second biggest in the country and one of the most important national cultural institutions.

4. Stanisław Dygat (1914–1978)—writer, husband to Kalina Jędrusik (1930–1991), a famous singer and actress.

5. The Polish 1968 political crisis.

6. *Państwowy Instytut Wydawniczy*

7. Ryszard Kapuściński (1932–2007)—reporter, journalist, traveller, photographer, poet and writer; one of the top Polish writers most frequently translated into foreign languages.

8. *Postal Liaison*, a Polish periodical, started in the interwar period (1932–1950).

9. General Wojciech Jaruzelski (1923–2014)—the last communist leader of Poland (1981–1989): Prime Minister (1981–1985) and head of state (1985–1990). He was also the last commander-in-chief of the Polish People's Army. He resigned from power after the Polish *Round Table Agreement* in 1989 that led to democratic elections in Poland.

10. Dim. of Barbara.

12. ENGLAND AGAIN

1. Helena Modrzejewska (known as *Helena Modjeska* in the US) (1840–1909)—a renowned actress who specialized in Shakespearean and tragic roles. At first the reigning diva of the Polish national theater, in 1876 she immigrated to the United States, and achieved great success there as well. In 1883 she obtained American citizenship. In the 1880s and 1890s she had a reputation of the leading female interpreter of Shakespeare on the American stage.

2. Władysław Tatarkiewicz (1886–1980)—a famous Polish philosopher, historian of philosophy, historian of art, esthetician, and ethicist.

3. *Stowarzyszenie Polskich Artystów Teatru i Filmu (Association of Polish Theatre and Film Artists)*.

13. APARTMENT ON KMICICA STREET

1. Edward Gierek (1913–2001) -First Secretary of the Polish communist Party (1970–1980). He promised economic reform and instituted a program to modernize industry and increase the availability of consumer goods, doing so mostly through foreign loans. Thanks to that, the standard of living increased markedly in the Poland of the 1970s. However, the unsustainable foreign loans were used unwisely, leading directly to an economic crisis in the 1980s.

14. FIRST BOOK: *NEAR WAŃKOWICZ*

1. Aleksander Bardini (1913–1995)—Polish-Jewish theatre and opera director, actor, notable professor at the State Theatre School in Warsaw.

2. Zygmunt Kałużyński (1918–2004)—Polish lawyer, film critic, promoter of cinema,erudite, a TV personality. His opinion were often controversial.

3. *Polish Roman Catholic* weekly magazine, focusing on social and cultural issues, established 1945.

4. *Polski Związek Kulturalno-Oświatowy (PZKO)* represents the Polish minority in the Czech Republic. It is the largest Polish organization with largest membership in the Czech Republic.

5. After Cieszyn Silesia was divided between Poland and Czechoslovakia in 1920, Zaolzie was the part of the region which was in Czechoslovakia. A continuing conflict over the region finally led to its annexation by Poland in October 1938. After the war, Zaolzie returned to Czechoslovakia. [translator's note]

6. Polish and Czech endearment for mama, respectively.

16. RADZIEJOWICE —
PROFESSOR WŁADYSŁAW TATARKIEWICZ

1. Krystyna Zachwatowicz-Wajda (born 1930)—a Polish stage and film set designer, costume designer and actress. She is the wife of film director Andrzej Wajda. Andrzej Wajda (born 1926)—a famous Polish film director, recipient of an honorary Oscar for his contribution to world cinema.

2. Antoni Słonomski (1895–1976)—Polish poet, journalist, playwright and prose writer.

3. Artur Sandauer (1913–1989)—Polish literary critic and translator.

4. People's Tribune, one of the two opinion-forming dailies in Communist Poland

5. Orig. *O szczęściu.*

6. lit. *Stones for the Rampart,* also translated as *Stones on the Barricade.*

17. THOMAS' SCHOOL

1. In Poland, Fat Tuesday, the equivalent of Mardi Gras, is the last Thursday before Lent.

18. NIEBORÓW

1. Stanisław Lorentz (1899–1991)—Polish scholar of museology and history of art.

2. The Radziwiłł family—a noble family of Lithuanian origin, highly prominent for centuries in the *Grand Duchy* of Lithuania, later in the *Polish-Lithuanian Commonwealth* and the *Kingdom of Prussia.*

19. ZAKOPANE

1. Wojciech Młynarski (born 1941)—a well known, prolific Polish singer, songwriter and translator, author of many highly successful songs.

2. *Kabaret Olgi Lipińskiej* (1974–1984, 1990–2005)—a long series of TV shows directed by theatre director and satirical artist Olga Lipińska, featuring renowned artists, using literary texts, often based on absurd, surreal humour and involving satirical criticism of social and political issues.

3. *Rozmowy z Katem* (*The Conversations with an Executioner*)—a series of interviews with a fellow inmate of a notorious Security Office prison, the Nazi war criminal Jürgen Stroop, who was responsible for the destruction of the Warsaw Ghetto after the uprising of 1943. Moczarski himself was imprisoned by communist forces for being a soldier of the Polish Home Army. *Zdążyć przed Panem Bogiem* (first published in English as *Shielding the Flame* and later as *To Outwit God*)—based on an interview with one of the ghetto insurrectionists, the work focuses on the days of the liquidation of the Warsaw Ghetto by the Nazis.

4. *Baśka and Barbara* [Baśka is a diminutive form of Barbara], *Passage through the Red Sea, Crystal Ball, Gentle Eye of the Blue, Hiding Places.*

20. ROMAN RODZIEWICZ

1. The Mermaid is part of Warsaw's coat of arms.

2. Constitution Day in Poland.

3. The American Edition: Aleksandra Ziolkowska-Boehm: *Polish Hero Roman Rodziewicz. Fate of a Hubal Soldier in Auschwitz, Buchenwald, and Postwar England.* Lexington Books, 2013.

21. CANADA

1. *The Women's Auxiliary Service* (WAS) (Polish: *Pomocnicza Służba Kobiet (PSK), Pestki*) was a unit of Polish Armed Forces during II World War established in 1941 by initiative of Lt. Gen.Władysław Anders, while creating Polish Armed Forces in the East.(see: Wikipedia).

2. Stefan Wyszyński (1901–1981)—Polish prelate, Primate of Poland, often called Primate of the Millennium. A spiritual leader of the Polish nation, in opposition to the communist

government, and viewed as a national hero, he was imprisoned for three years by the communists for his beliefs and support for the resistance.

3. Bulat Okudzhava (1924–1997)—Russian poet, writer, musician, novelist, and singer-songwriter of Georgian-Armenian origin. His chanson-like songs with wise, generally-themed lyrics are still popular in Poland.

4. Stanisław Kania (born 1927)—former Polish communist political leader.

5. Anka Kowalska (1932–2008)—Polish poet, writer and activist in the anti-communist resistance movement.

6. Jacek Jan Kuroń (1934–2004)—one of the democratic leaders of opposition in the People's Republic of Poland, a prominent Polish social and political figure.

7. Reference No. IPN BU 0247/575.

8. Jan Kiliński (1760–1819)—one of the commanders of the Kościuszko Uprising against Russia and Prussia, which were occupying Poland, led by Tadeusz Kościuszko in 1794.

22. RETURN TO POLAND

1. *Zmotoryzowane Odwody Milicji Obywatelskiej (Motorized Reserves of the Citizens' Militia)*—paramilitary/police formations in communist Poland. Officially created to fight dangerous criminals, provide security during mass events and help in crises, they became known instead for their brutal (sometimes lethal) actions in riot control and quelling civil rights protests.

2. *Patriotyczny Ruch Odrodzenia Narodowego (PRON*; 1982–1989)—Polish political pro-communist organization, created after the martial law in Poland.

3. J. Kofta, W. Młynarski, J. Przeździecki—well-known Polish writers, songwriters and poets; C. Mondral—athlete, war-time underground courier; St. Brejdygant—actor and director.

4. Marek Edelman (1919 or 1922–2009)—Jewish-Polish political and social activist, cardiologist, the last leader of the Warsaw Ghetto Uprising to pass away.

5. October 1956, March 1968—a political thaw and a political crisis in communist Poland, respectively. *Letter 34* (1964) was a letter protesting the actions of censorship, signed by 34 writers. It was followed by repressions against the signatories.

6. Polishchuks or Poleshuks—people who populated the swamps of Polesie, in the south-western part of the Eastern-European Lowland, with a dialect close to Ukrainian, Belarusian and Polish. Currently in Belarus and Ukraine, the area is partly included in the Chernobyl Exclusion Zone.

7. Zbigniew Bujak (born 1954)—chairman of the Warsaw Solidarity branch. Arrested in 1984 after evading the security forces for over three years, he was the last Solidarity leader to be captured.

8. Mieczysław Rakowski (1926–2008) –Polish communist politician, historian and journalist, second-to-last communist Prime Minister of Poland (1988–89), last First Secretary of the Party (1989–90).

23. VISITING THE UNITED STATES

1. *Cichociemni* (also translated as *Dark and Silent*)—elite paratroops for special operations of the Polish Army in exile, created in Great Britain during World War II to operate in occupied Poland. After careful selection and training, the soldiers were dropped over Poland or other European countries to contact and aid the opposition movement in various ways.

2. Stanisław Barańczak (1946-2014) Polish poet, literary critic, scholar, editor and lecturer. The most prominent translator in recent years of English poetry into Polish (e.g. Shakespeare) and of Polish poetry into English, he received the PEN Translation Prize with Clare Cavanagh in 1996.

3. See: *Open Wounds A Native American Heritage* by A.Z.-B., published By Nemsi Books, 2009.

4. *Klub Inteligencji Katolickiej (Club of Catholic Intellectuals)*—Polish organization grouping Catholic intellectuals, founded in 1956, which later evolved into a mild Catholic-center opposition group in communist Poland.

5. Film directed by Ryszard Ber in 1986, based on the Polish psychological novel (and screenplay) written by Maria Kuncewiczowa, which is considered a classic amongst the inter-war period of Polish literature.

6. *Home Army (Armia Krajowa; AK)*—the main Polish resistance movement in World War II. Due to its allegiance to the (non-communist) Polish Government in Exile, the Soviet Union saw the Home Army as an obstacle to a Soviet takeover of Poland. After the war, most *Home Army* soldiers were captured by communist security services, interrogated and imprisoned on various charges such as "fascism." Many were sent to Soviet forced labour camps, executed, or just disappeared.

7. *The January Uprising* (1863–1865)—an uprising in the former *Polish-Lithuanian Commonwealth* (present-day Poland, Lithuania, Belarus, Latvia, parts of Ukraine, and western Russia) against the Russian Empire. The collapse of the uprising was followed by harsh reprisals.

8. *Orlęta Lwowskie (Lviv Eaglets)*—Polish teenagers who defended the city of the then Polish Lviv during the Polish-Ukrainian War (1918–1919). Since Lviv didn't have units of Polish regular army stationed in it, and most adult men were either in the army or were POWs, the volunteer units defending the city consisted mainly of teenagers, students, labourers and a small number of veterans. Over 1/3 of the fighters were below 25, the youngest being 9 years old. After the conflict, the Lwów Eaglets were interred at the Cemetery of the Defenders of Lwów, part of the Lychakiv Cemetery. After the territory was annexed by the Soviet Union after WWII, the graves were destroyed in 1971, and the Cemetery desecrated. It was officially reopened only in 2005.

9. *Ostra Brama*—a city-gate of Vilnius, the capital of Lithuania, whose chapel contains an icon of *The Blessed Virgin Mary, Mother of Mercy*, an object of veneration for both Roman Catholic and Orthodox inhabitants and pilgrims, who believe it to have miraculous powers.

10. *Centralny Okręg Przemysłowy, COP (The Central Industrial District)*—one of the biggest economic projects in interwar Poland, aiming to create a heavy industrial center in the middle of the country, as far as possible from any borders, strengthen the Polish economy and reduce unemployment. The plan was interrupted by the outbreak of WWII, but the project helped vastly expand Polish industry. *The Central Industrial District* was rebuilt and expanded after the war.

11. No. 303 *("Kościuszko") Polish Fighter Squadron*—the highest scoring squadron of the 16 Polish squadrons in RAF during WWII (Battle of Britain), with a distinguished combat record. See: *A Question of Honor. The Kosciuszko Squadron: Forgotten Heroes of World War II* by Lynne Olson and Stanley Cloud, New York, Knopf, 2003.

12. Actually, such meetings take place before Christmas, and include sharing the Christmas wafer like during Christmas Eve.

13. The proms in Polish high school—*studniówki*—are traditionally organised a hundred days before the final exams, and even named for that (*hundred days—sto dni*).

24. NORMAN

1. See: Aleksandra Ziolkowska-Boehm: *Ingrid Bergman and Her American Relatives*, Hamilton Books, 2013.

2. Granted since 1989 by the *Pilsudski Institute in New York* for outstanding works on Polish history.

3. Jerzy Urban (born 1933)—Polish journalist, commentator, writer and politician. From August 1981 to April 1989, a government spokesperson. Currently editor-in-chief of the weekly *Nie*, an anti-clerical tabloid-like newspaper.

4. Two valleys and a mountain in the Tatras.

5. *Halka*—an opera by Polish composer Stanisław Moniuszko, part of the canon of Polish national operas.

6. *The Ignacy Domeyko Polish Library (Biblioteca Polaca Ignacio Domeyko)*—the biggest Polish library in South America. Founded in 1960 in Buenos Aires, Argentina, named after a Polish geologist and mineralogist. Andrzej Munk (1921–1961)—a famous Polish film director, screen writer and documentalist. Witold Gombrowicz (1904–1969)—Polish novelist and dramatist. His works are characterised by deep psychological analysis, a certain sense of paradox and absurd, anti-nationalist flavour. Considered one of the foremost figures of Polish literature. Zugmunt Grocholski—oil, pastel, watercolor, tempera painter. Author of frescos and icons.

25. NOTES AND THOUGHTS

1. Jeden, dwa, trzy, cztery, pięć, sześć—One, two, three, four, five, six.

2. Phonetically: "st-oow s poh-vyh-wah-nyh-mee noh-gah-mee", "khszonshtch bzhmee f tszchee-nie".

3. Reference to a poem by Cyprian Kamil Norwid, and the Polish custom of picking up bread which fell to the ground.

4. By Ryszard Kapuściński.

5. On 1st September 1939, the German battleship Schleswig-Holstein attacked Polish coast outposts, which marks the outbreak of World War II.

6. Principal heir of a fee tail.

7. Diminutive for Piotr.

Index

About the Author

Aleksandra Ziolkowska-Boehm, PhD (Warsaw University), has been the recipient of several awards, including a grant from the Ontario Ministry of Culture, a literature fellowship by the Delaware Division of the Arts, a Fulbright scholarship at Warsaw University, and a Fulbright award from the Institute of International Education.

Among her books are historical biographies, autobiographical stories, a current outlook of Native Americans, and about her beloved feline Suzy. She is the author of many books published in her native Poland, Canada, and also in the United States, including *Open Wounds—a Native American Heritage; On the Road with Suzy: From Cat to Companion; Kaia, Heroine of the 1944 Warsaw Rising; The Polish Experience through World War II A Better Day Has Not Come; Melchior Wańkowicz: Poland's Master of the Written Word; Polish Hero Roman Rodziewicz Fate of a Hubal Soldier in Auschwitz, Buchenwald, and Postwar England; Ingrid Bergman and Her American Relatives.*